APPLIED INTELLIGENCE

Typical texts develop students' knowledge while only minimally developing the general skills they will need for success in school and in life. The goal of our text is to assist students in acquiring the most important skills for facing the diverse challenges life presents. The book contains an overview of theories of intelligence, but itself is based in large part on a theory according to which individuals need creative skills to generate new ideas and a vision for the future, analytical skills to make sure that the vision is a good one, and practical skills to execute the ideas and to persuade other people of their value. The book considers key skills in problem solving, logical reasoning, analysis of arguments, knowledge acquisition, creative and practical thinking, automatizing information processing, and avoiding life traps that derail even the most intelligent among us.

Robert J. Sternberg is Dean of the School of Arts and Sciences and Professor of Psychology at Tufts University. Before he went to Tufts, he was IBM Professor of Psychology and Education, Professor of Management in the School of Management, and Director of the Center for the Psychology of Abilities, Competencies, and Expertise at Yale University. This Sternberg was the 2003 President of the American Psychological Association and was the 2007–2008 President of the Eastern Psychological Association.

James C. Kaufman is an Associate Professor of Psychology at the California State University at San Bernardino, where he directs the Learning Research Institute. The author/editor of 14 books, he is the founding co-editor of *Psychology of Aesthetics, Creativity, and the Arts* and the associate editor of *Journal of Creative Behavior.*

Elena L. Grigorenko is Associate Professor of Child Studies and Psychology at Yale and Adjunct Professor of Psychology at Columbia University and Moscow State University (Russia). Dr. Grigorenko has published more than 200 peer-reviewed articles, book chapters, and books.

APPLIED INTELLIGENCE

ROBERT J. STERNBERG

Dean of the School of Arts and Sciences, Tufts University

JAMES C. KAUFMAN

California State University, San Bernardino

ELENA L. GRIGORENKO

Yale University

CAMBRIDGE
UNIVERSITY PRESS

CAMBRIDGE UNIVERSITY PRESS
Cambridge, New York, Melbourne, Madrid, Cape Town, Singapore, São Paulo, Delhi

Cambridge University Press
32 Avenue of the Americas, New York, NY 10013-2473, USA

www.cambridge.org
Information on this title: www.cambridge.org/9780521884280

First published 2008

Printed in the United States of America.

A catalog record for this publication is available from the British Library.

Library of Congress Cataloging in Publication Data

Sternberg, Robert J.
Applied intelligence / Robert J. Sternberg, James C. Kaufman, Elena L. Grigorenko.
  p.   cm.
Includes bibliographical references (p.) and index.
ISBN 978-0-521-88428-0 (hardcover) – ISBN 978-0-521-71121-0 (pbk.)
1. Intellect.   2. Intellect–Problems, exercises, etc.   3. Learning, Psychology of.
I. Kaufman, James C.   II. Grigorenko, Elena.   III. Title.
BF431.S7376   2008
153.4–dc22   2007034888

To Seth and Sara

— RJS & ELG

For Allison,
For everything,
For always.

— JCK

CONTENTS

PREFACE

Can people make themselves smarter? Research in psychology suggests that they can – that the brain functions in much the way muscles do. The more you exercise it, the better it functions. Moreover, the better you understand it, the more you are in a position to make optimal use of it.

This book seeks simultaneously to accomplish two goals. It teaches students about the mind and how it functions, and at the same time, it helps them improve that functioning.

The book is written primarily for college students but can also be used by advanced high school students working at a college level. It is relevant in any course on thinking, reasoning, problem solving, decision making, critical thinking, creative thinking, or study skills that seeks simultaneously to help students understand better how they think and to improve their thinking skills. The book is appropriate either as a main text or a supplementary one.

A numer of features make this book unusual, if not unique, among programs for developing intellectual skills. First, the program is based on a contemporary psychological theory (the theory of successful intelligence) that has extensive data to support it (going back 35 years). Second, the book conceptualizes intelligence in a broad way; the range of cognitive skills addressed is much greater than in the typical program of this kind. Third, the book is written to motivate students as well as to teach them. Many practical examples are included, and the examples are drawn from many fields of endeavor. Fourth, the problems range from very abstract and test-like to very concrete and practical. This range is necessary to ensure that students transfer their learning from one task and situation to the next. For this transfer to occur, a program must teach for transfer – which the present program does. It is unlike many other programs that rely solely on test-like problems to enhance students' intellectual skills. Fifth, the book contains an entire chapter on emotional and motivational blocks to the use of intelligence. It does not matter how intelligent people are if they are unable to use their intelligence. This last chapter is intended to help students make full use of their developing intellectual skills.

The book comprises 14 chapters. The first two chapters are introductory. Chapter 1 presents alternative views of intelligence. Chapter 2 then presents the view that motivates this book, the theory of successful intelligence.

Chapter 3 presents metacognition and tools for improving one's metacognitive skills. Chapter 4 deals with advanced steps that can be taken to help one improve one's problem solving. Chapters 5–7 deal with the execution of problem solving. Chapter 5 concentrates on analogical and serial thinking, Chapter 6 on classificational and matrix-based thinking. Chapter 7 deals with logical thinking, and Chapter 8 with the kinds of inferential fallacies that can disrupt both formal and informal logical thinking.

Chapter 9 moves on to learning and knowledge acquisition. It discusses how we can improve our learning, particularly of new words and concepts. Chapter 10 teaches students how better to cope with novelty, and Chapter 11 deals with the umbrella set of skills and attitudes for coping with novelty, namely, creativity. Chapter 12 deals with how we can better automize thinking and other skills as they become routine. Chapter 13 deals with practical intelligence and common sense, and Chapter 14 with why people who are smart often fail despite their high intelligence. The book concludes with a complete set of references and an index.

The three of us have enjoyed working on this book, and we hope that it will be both fun and challenging to read. Many of the topics that we cover are areas that we also study. We would love to inspire you to think about these ideas – and, perhaps, to continue in the tradition of studying how people think, what intelligence is, and why people succeed.

Many people have contributed to making this book possible. The book is a successor to an earlier book, *Intelligence Applied*, written by the senior author and published in 1986. That book was supported by the Venezuelan Ministry for the Development of Intelligence. Luis Alberto Machado and Jose Dominguez Ortega were instrumental in making the earlier book happen, as were El Dividendo Voluntario para la Comunidad, Margarita Rodriguez-Lansberg, and Francisco Rivera. People who have contributed in various ways over the years to the development of the training materials here also include Barbara Conway, Janet Davidson, Louis Forster, Michael Gardner, Ann Kirkland, Robin Lampert, Diana Marr, Elizabeth Neuse, Susan Nolen-Hoeksema, Janet Powell, Craig Smith, Larry Soriano, Rebecca Treiman, and Richard Wagner.

This book was supported in part by CASL – IES grant R305H030281, NSF ROLE grant REC 440171, and NSF REESE grant REC 0633952. Cheri Stahl, Robyn Rissman, and Roja Dilmore-Rios have provided editorial assistance. Alan S. Kaufman has provided a variety of insights and suggestions. Arian Castillo and Daniel Gascon have helped greatly with graphic design. Candace Andrews, Melanie Bromley, Sarah Burgess, Mariah Bussey, Lauren DeCremier, Kristiana Powers, and Terrence Robertson have all provided helpful comments. James Kaufman would like to thank his wife Allison, who also supported development of the book. We are grateful to Eric Schwartz of Cambridge University Press for contracting this book and to Ken Karpinski of Aptara for his great help in bringing the book into print in a readable and elegant format.

RJS
JCK
ELG
September 2007

Views of Intelligence

What is intelligence? There have been countless studies and books on this topic, but we're going to focus on a primary distinction between traditional conceptions and newer conceptions. One new conception of intelligence is the theory of successful intelligence, in which being intelligent is more than just being book-smart; it is knowing how to apply it – hence our title, *Applied Intelligence*. We view intelligence as encompassing many diverse concepts, including critical thinking, being able to know how much you know (metacognition), common sense, practical intelligence, creativity, and logic. We believe that an intelligent person is someone who can tell (or who knows how to check) if a forwarded e-mail is truth or an urban legend; someone who can recognize propaganda versus more convincing arguments; someone who usually has a good idea of how much he or she knows about something; someone who can adapt to new situations; and someone who can learn new things.

Before we discuss the theory of successful intelligence, we're going to attempt to briefly summarize more than one hundred years of research about intelligence and IQ testing. This chapter, therefore, will present a brief overview of the way psychologists and others have conceived of intelligence. For more details, see Sternberg (1990, 1994, 2000, 2004b; Sternberg, Lautrey, & Lubart, 2003; Cianciolo & Sternberg, 2004).

THE DEFINITIONAL APPROACH TO INTELLIGENCE

One way to seek to understand intelligence is simply to define it. We then use the definition as a basis for theorizing about intelligence, testing intelligence, and training intelligence. The nice feature of this approach is that it is simple: We need simply to find out what intelligence is, and then proceed from there. The obvious shortcoming of the approach is that it is not always persuasive. It is one thing to define intelligence; it is another thing to get people to accept the definition. Indeed, a ten-year-old child may create a terrific definition of "a fair allowance," but have more trouble convincing her father to accept it!

We might think that just as a rose is a rose, a definition is a definition. This proposition turns out to be not quite true. In fact, two principal kinds of definitions of intelligence have been proposed-the operational definition and the "real" definition.

Operational Definition

An *operational definition* attempts to define something in terms of the way it is measured. This type of definition is often counterintuitive. If we ask you to define "love," you might be more likely to look through poems than reference books. Indeed, one of the authors of this book frequently uses this as a classroom exercise. Even after explaining what an operational definition is, people resist – the immediate responses still tend to be "a feeling you have for someone else" or "how much you care about someone." But an operational definition is more specific and more exact. Eventually, someone in the class will say something like, "How many times a day you think about a person," or "How many sacrifices would you make for somebody." But it's still usually a sticking point for a small (but vocal) percentage of the class.

Thus, an operational definition might define intelligence as whatever it is that intelligence tests measure. We might think that no serious scientist would propose such a circular definition, or that if one did, no one would take it seriously. But precisely this definition of intelligence-as being whatever it is that intelligence tests measure-was proposed by a famous Harvard psychologist, E. G. Boring (1923). Moreover, Boring did not propose this definition as something merely suitable for scientific use. To the contrary, he suggested it in a popular magazine, the *New Republic*, as part of a public debate.

Many scientists and educators have proceeded in their research and testing as though Boring was right, and intelligence is nothing more and nothing less than what intelligence tests measure. Arthur Jensen (1969), a well-known advocate of the importance of heredity in intelligence, accepted this definition as a basis for his attempted demonstration in the *Harvard Educational Review* that group differences in intelligence can be understood as having a hereditary basis, and that as a result there is little hope for attempts to develop people's intelligence. One kind of group difference that Jensen and other scientists have particularly studied is intelligence differences across ethnicity. There are powerful implications for just how much we rely on a purely operational definition. Once the instruments we use are given the power to determine how we think about a construct, we get into dangerous territory.

Other scientists have been less obvious and forthcoming in admitting their acceptance of the operational definition but have proceeded to use it nevertheless. For example, when new tests of intelligence are proposed, their validity (that is, the extent to which they measure what they are supposed to measure) is usually assessed by comparing scores on the new test to scores on older and more widely accepted tests. Thus, the older tests serve as the operational standard for the newer ones. To the extent that the new tests actually do measure anything new or different, they will then be less related to the old tests. As a result, any new tests that are truly new may be viewed as less valid than these older tests. Even experimental psychologists, who attempt to study intelligence in the laboratory and to go beyond existing IQ-based notions of intelligence, often validate their theories and new instruments against existing tests. Thus, they also become trapped into accepting the operational definition of intelligence. They may not be happy about doing so, but they do it nevertheless.

The operational definition of intelligence has two basic, interrelated problems. The first is that it represents circular reasoning. What is circular reasoning? It's when you assume your conclusion as a given fact. For example, Lauren might say that *Star Wars* is the greatest movie ever made. When someone asks her why, she says, "It just is." This response is an example of circular reasoning. If, by contrast, she says, "The special effects were revolutionary and the story is exciting," she has provided reasons for her conclusion. We will discuss circular reasoning in more detail later on in the book.

Intelligence tests were originally devised in order to measure intelligence, not to define it. The designers of the tests based them on their own conceptions of intelligence and hoped that eventually the definition of intelligence would become clearer. They never intended for these tests actually to define intelligence. On the contrary, some test developers believed that the tests could only make sense if they were based on some prior definition of intelligence. Those who argue that intelligence is simply what intelligence tests measure are going against the philosophies of most of the people who actually develop the tests.

The second problem with the operational definition of intelligence is that it seems to block further progress in understanding the nature of intelligence. If old, established tests are used as the primary or sole criterion against which new tests and conceptions of intelligence are to be assessed, then the new tests and conceptions will be viewed as valid only to the extent that they correspond to the old ones. There is no allowance for the possibility that the new tests or conceptions may actually be better than the older ones. The result is that we become locked into existing conceptions and measurements, regardless of whether they are any good or not. Existing tests of intelligence certainly may serve as one criterion against which to evaluate new tests and theories. It would be a pity, however, if they were to serve as the only criterion. Imagine if television programmers designed new shows based only on the shows that worked in the past. We would only have clones of successful programs (and, indeed, many people argue this is true!). Certainly, there is a reason why we use successful examples for constructing future products; the same ingredients that initially made *Law & Order* a success were later used to similar effect in shows like *CSI*, just as classic shows like *I Love Lucy* and *MASH* built on earlier shows. But when past work is too heavily relied on, you end up with shows that no one watches or remembers.

If past tests were the only consideration for developing future tests, we would lose the chance of ever learning more about the nature of human intelligence.

"Real" Definition

According to the philosopher Robinson (1950), a "*real*" *definition* is one that seeks to tell us the true nature of the thing being defined. Such a definition goes beyond measurement and seeks to understand the underlying nature of intelligence. Perhaps the most common way of trying to find out just what intelligence is has been to ask experts in the field of intelligence to define it.

The most well-known example of this approach was the result of a large meeting of experts published in 1921 in the *Journal of Educational Psychology*. Fourteen experts gave their views on the nature of intelligence, with definitions involving activities such as the ability to carry on abstract thinking, the ability to learn to adjust oneself to the environment, the ability to adapt oneself adequately to relatively new situations in life, the capacity for knowledge, the amount of knowledge possessed, and the capacity to learn or to profit from experience. From one point of view, an examination of the full set of definitions seems to lead to the conclusion that there were as many definitions of intelligence as there were experts asked to define it. From another point of view, however, at least two themes seem to run through several of the definitions: learning from experience and adapting to the environment. A view of intelligence accepted by many of these experts would seem to be one of intelligence as general adaptability to new problems and situations in life.

There have been more recent definitions of intelligence that have been accepted by at least some people in the field. For example, George Ferguson (1956) defined intelligence in terms of a person's ability to transfer his or her learning and accumulated experience from one situation to another (Barnett & Ceci, 2005). According to this definition, then, it is not just what we know that counts. It is also our ability to use this information in new kinds of situations that we confront in our lives. This concept, often called "transfer," is indeed a crucial component to success in the real world. If you learn something, can you apply it to many different areas? If you take information in this book and apply it to your daily life, you've successfully "transferred" the knowledge into another area. Let us imagine, for example, that you are having a debate about local politics with your roommate; she supports one local candidate for mayor, Roberto Diaz, over another, Rafaela Contini. You ask her why she supports Diaz, and your roommate says, "Diaz is simply better than Contini, and that is why I am going to vote for him." You have read this book, however, and you remember back a few pages to the example about circular reasoning. You tell your roommate, "You're giving me a circular reasoning argument that I read about in my book for class." Your roommate will then be thoroughly defeated and will do the dishes, while *you* have demonstrated an excellent instance of knowledge *transfer*. Because definitions can be so subjective, we might think that there is simply no basis for judging one definition as either better or worse than another definition. This is not the case, however. For example, we saw that the operational definition of intelligence is a particularly unproductive one. Sir Cyril Burt's definition of intelligence is also an unproductive one. Burt (1940) defined intelligence as innate general cognitive ability. Some psychologists, such as Jensen, seem to accept a view of intelligence that is quite close to this one, but the definition seems problematical for at least two reasons. First, it assumes that intelligence is innate, or, in others words, inherited and present from birth (i.e., passed through genes). Although intelligence probably is at least partly heritable, the degree of just how heritable is a complex and multilayered question. Assuming that intelligence is solely innate removes the role of the environment out of the definition. These are mighty important factors to disqualify automatically. Think about a class that you took that you enjoyed that was on a subject matter that didn't interest you. Maybe you enjoyed the professor, or maybe you had three good friends in the class with you. The context in which you studied the subject influenced your enthusiasm for the material. Burt seems to assume what really ought to be proved.

Second, the definition also assumes that intelligence is exclusively cognitive (in other words, only related to what people know or think). Although intelligence certainly draws on a wide array of cognitive abilities (such as what you know or how you think), it seems at least possible that it also may involve other kinds of abilities, such as motivation. Imagine all of the possible things that might impact our intelligence – such as our parents, our education, and so on. Once again, Burt seems to assume what really ought to be proved.

In sum, then, the "real" definition of intelligence can have some value if we look for common ideas among various experts' definitions. When we do this, the abilities to learn from experience and to adapt to the environment seem to be essential ingredients of intelligence. However, we must be careful in accepting these definitions without questioning them. First, we have seen that a definition may make too many assumptions without demonstrating issues scientifically. Second, experts obviously disagree among themselves as to the definition of intelligence, and there is no guarantee that any of their definitions are correct. Thus, "real" definitions of intelligence need to be interpreted with due caution.

THEORIES OF INTELLIGENCE

Just as there are different kinds of definitions, there are also different kinds of theories of intelligence. The theory that forms the basis of this book draws at least a little on each kind. Thus, it may be helpful to give a brief review of these theories.

Learning Theory

Although we would think that there must be a close relationship between learning and intelligence, psychologists studying learning have not been among the most active contributors to the field of intelligence. Usually, they have studied learning in its own right without touching on the topic of its relation to intelligence. Learning theorists are an exception to this generalization.

In the learning theorist's view, then, all behavior – no matter how complex or "intelligent" – is seen as of a single type and our "intelligence" is seen as simply a function of the number and strength of stimulus-response connections we have formed and, perhaps, the rate at which we can form new ones.

Learning theorists have tended to emphasize intelligence as being flexible and teachable. This emphasis contrasts to some of the more extreme supporters of intelligence tests, who have sometimes (although by no means always) been associated with points of view emphasizing the importance of heredity. Perhaps the most optimistic statement of what learning theory can do to mold a person's intellect and other skills was provided by John Watson (1930), who said, in one of the most well-known quotations of all psychology:

> Give me a dozen healthy infants, well-formed, and my own specified world to bring them up in and I'll guarantee to take any one at random and train him to become any type of specialist I might select-doctor, lawyer, artist, merchant-chief

and, yes, even beggar-man and thief-regardless of his talents, penchants, tendencies, abilities, vocations, and race of his ancestors.

The main contributions of the learning-theory approach to intelligence seem to have been, first, its focus on the importance of learning in intelligence, and second, its optimism regarding the possibility of human intelligence being modified and improved. Thus, whether or not learning theorists were literally correct in what they said regarding the nature of intelligence, they appear to have been correct in the spirit of what they had to say. We agree with them wholeheartedly that intelligence is a characteristic that can be increased and improved on, and that will be a main theme throughout this book.

Biological Models: Intelligence as a Physiological Phenomenon

Biological approaches seek to understand intelligence by directly studying the brain and its functioning, rather than by studying behavior (Jcrison, 2000; Newman & Just, 2005; Vernon, Wickett, Bazana, & Stelmack, 2000). Early studies seeking to find a biological base of intelligence and other cognitive processes were a resounding failure, despite great efforts (Lashley, 1950). As tools for studying the brain have become more sophisticated, however, we are beginning to see the possibility of finding physiological indications of intelligence. Some researchers (e.g., Matarazzo, 1992) believe that we will have clinically useful psychophysiological measures of intelligence very soon, although tests that can be used in a wider variety of situations will be much longer in coming. In other words, it may be possible in the future to use psychophysiological measurements to assess individuals for characteristics such as mental retardation. For now, some of the current studies offer some appealing possibilities.

Electrophysiological Evidence
Research has found that complex patterns of electrical activity in the brain, which are prompted by specific stimuli, correlate with scores on IQ tests (Caryl, 1994; Jensen, 2005). Also, several studies suggest that the speed of conduction of neural impulses may correlate with intelligence as measured by IQ tests (e.g., Deary, 2000a; Deary, 2000b), although the evidence is mixed. Some investigators (e.g., Jensen, 1997; P. A. Vernon & Mori, 1992) suggest that this research supports a view that intelligence is based on neural efficiency.

Metabolic Evidence
Additional support for neural efficiency as a measure of intelligence can be found by using a different approach to studies of the brain: studies of how the brain metabolizes glucose, a simple sugar required for brain activity, during mental activities. (This process is revealed in PET – Positron Emission Tomography.) Richard Haier and his colleagues (Haier, Siegel, Tang, Abel, Buchsbaum, 1992) argued that higher intelligence correlates with reduced levels of glucose metabolism during problem-solving tasks – that is, "smarter" brains consume less sugar (meaning that they expend less effort) than do less smart brains doing the same task. Luckily, this process does not mean that people who eat less candy are smarter!

Furthermore, Haier and colleagues found that cerebral efficiency increases as a result of learning in a relatively complex task involving visuospatial manipulations (such as in the computer game Tetris, which is a marvelous argument to use if someone ever accuses you of spending too much time playing videogames). As a result of practice, smarter people show not only lower cerebral glucose metabolism overall but also more specifically localized metabolism of glucose. In most areas of their brains, smarter persons show less glucose metabolism, but in selected areas of their brains (thought to be important to the task at hand), they show higher levels of glucose metabolism. Thus, more intelligent people may have learned how to use their brains more efficiently.

Although Haier was one of the first scientists who looked for the "brain signatures" underlying intelligence using modern techniques of neuroimaging, many researchers also have done so within the last decade. In a summary of the recent work on the neurobiology of intelligence that reviewed both PET ("Positron Emission Tomography") and functional Magnetic-Resonance Imaging (fMRI, a form of magnetic resonance imaging of the brain that registers blood flow to functioning areas of the brain), Jeremy Gray and Paul Thompson (2004) stated that intelligent behaviors are supported by the lateral prefrontal cortex, and possibly other areas (e.g., such as the anterior cingulate cortex). Although there is little certainty in "where" in the brain intelligence is located, there is no doubt in the fact that differences in brain structure and brain activity correlate with performance on tests of intelligence. Thus, intelligence is biologically grounded in the brain, at least to some degree.

Psychometric Theory

Psychometric approaches to intelligence are those linked to the psychological measurement of intelligence. Like other approaches, the psychometric approach also looks at individual differences among people. Psychometric researchers use complex statistical techniques such as factor analysis to discover common patterns of individual differences across tests. These patterns are then hypothesized to derive from underlying sources of individual differences, namely, mental abilities.

As a simple example of such a factor analysis, consider five tests of mental abilities: vocabulary, mathematical computation, general information, reading comprehension, and mathematical problem solving. Factor analysis would compute the degree of relationship (*correlation*) between each possible pair of the five tests. These correlations are expressed on a scale from –1 to 1, where –1 means a perfect inverse relationship between scores on two tests, 0 means no relationship between scores on two tests, and 1 means a perfect positive relationship between scores on the two tests. For example, we would expect people's ability to do addition and subtraction problems to have a high positive relation. By contrast, we would expect people's ability to do addition and to run quickly to have very little correlation. What factor analysis does is to cluster together those tests that tend to be more highly correlated. For example, factor analysis would probably group the vocabulary, general information, and reading comprehension tests in one cluster, and the mathematical computation and mathematical problem-solving tests in another. Thus, observable performance on the five tests would be reduced to performance on two hypothesized underlying factors of mental ability, namely, verbal ability and quantitative ability (i.e., mathematical and analytical ability). The idea in factor analysis, then, is to simplify a pattern of scores on a set of tests.

Factor analysis can be used for anything. If you are a baseball fan, imagine entering data about a player's stolen bases, singles, doubles, triples, home runs, and grounding-into-double plays (GIDP). You might guess that stolen bases, singles, triples, and fewer GIDP might be grouped together in a "speed" factor, and doubles and home runs might be grouped together in a "power" factor. Or imagine listing all of your favorite movies. Preferences for the comedies might be grouped together into one factor, action movies into another factor, and horror movies into a third factor.

Psychometric theory and research seem to have evolved along three interrelated but distinguishable lines. These traditions, which convey rather different impressions of what intelligence is, can be traced back to Sir Francis Galton, Alfred Binet, and Charles Spearman. We will spend a little more time on this theory than on some of the other theories because of the influence the psychometric tradition has had on intelligence testing.

The Tradition of Sir Francis Galton

The publication of Charles Darwin's *Origin of Species* (1859) had a profound impact on many lines of scientific endeavor, among them the investigation of human intelligence. Darwin's book suggested that the capabilities of humans were in some sense continuous with those of lower animals and, hence, could be understood through scientific investigation of the kind that had been conducted on animals. There was also the intriguing possibility that in intelligence, as in physical characteristics, the development of intelligence in humans over the life span might in some way resemble the development of intelligence from lower to higher species.

Darwin's cousin, Sir Francis Galton, was probably the first to explore the implications of Darwin's book for the study of intelligence. Galton was an interesting person who dabbled in many different areas (Gillham, 2001). He explored Africa with Dr. Livingstone. He invented both fingerprinting and a whistle (to call for his dog during their walks). He was an ardent meteorologist who discovered the "anticyclone" and created an early weather map. He was obsessed with numbers and measuring things – he once counted how many pretty women he saw in each city he visited (London finished first, a suspicious finding as he was himself a Londoner). Galton took his passion for measuring things and applied it to the field of intelligence.

Galton (1883) proposed two general qualities that distinguished the more gifted from the less gifted. The first was energy or the capacity for labor. The second was sensitivity to physical stimuli:

> The discriminative facility of idiots is curiously low; they hardly distinguish between heat and cold, and their sense of pain is so obtuse that some of the more idiotic seem hardly to know what it is. In their dull lives, such pain as can be excited in them may literally be accepted with a welcome surprise.

For seven years, between 1884 and 1890, Galton maintained an "anthropometric" laboratory at the South Kensington Museum in London where, for a small fee, visitors could have themselves measured on a variety of psychophysical tests, such as weight discrimination and pitch sensitivity.

James McKeen Cattell brought many of Galton's ideas from England to the United States. As head of the psychology laboratory at Columbia University, Cattell was in a good position to publicize the psychophysical approach to the theory and measurement of intelligence. Cattell (1890) proposed a series of fifty psychophysical tests, such as dynamometer pressure (greatest possible squeeze of the hand), rate of arm movement over a distance of fifty centimeters, and the distance on the skin by which two points need to be separated for them to be felt separately. Underlying each was the assumption that physical tests measure mental ability. For example, Cattell claimed, "The greatest squeeze of the hand may be thought by many to be a purely physiological quantity. It is, however, impossible to separate bodily from mental energy."

The *coup de grace* for the Galtonian tradition – at least in its earliest forms – was administered by one of Cattell's own students. Clark Wissler (1901) investigated twenty-one psychophysical tests. His line of approach was correlational, the idea being to show that the various tests are fairly highly correlated and, thus, define some common entity (intelligence) that underlies all of them. Wissler's results were disappointing, however. He found the tests generally to be unrelated, and he concluded that his results "would lead us to doubt the existence of such a thing as general ability."

There is a great deal of irony in Galton's downfall. First and foremost, Galton himself pioneered the correlational statistics used by Wissler. Second, Wissler's study would have never been accepted today – he had very few participants, and they were all students at Columbia. All students would presumably have at least a certain level of intelligence, so the correlations would undoubtedly have been lowered because of this restriction of range.

However, even with Galton's work on intelligence less widely accepted today than at some times in the past, psychologists did not give up hope of finding a construct of general intelligence (Sternberg & Grigorenko, 2002). An alternative approach was already leading to greater success.

The Tradition of Alfred Binet

In 1904, the French Minister of Public Instruction formed a commission to study or create tests that would ensure that mentally defective children received an adequate education. The commission decided that no child suspected of retardation should be placed in a special class for the retarded without first being given an examination "from which it could be certified that because of the state of its intelligence, he was unable to profit, in an average measure, from the instruction given in ordinary schools." Alfred Binet, in collaboration with his colleague, Theodore Simon, devised tests to meet this placement need. Thus, whereas Galton's theory and research grew out of pure scientific concerns, Binet's grew out of practical educational concerns.

At the time, definitions for various degrees of subnormal intelligence lacked both precision and standardization, and personality and intellectual deficits were seen as being of the same type. Binet and Simon (1916/1973) noted a case of one institutionalized child who seemed to be a victim of this state of confusion: "One child, called imbecile in the first certificate, is marked idiot in the second, feebleminded in the third, and degenerate in the fourth." However much people may complain about being "labeled" by IQ tests today, they should be thankful they do not have to deal with these types of labels! Can you imagine being a psychologist and having to tell a worried parent, "I'm afraid your son is simply an idiot"?

Binet and Simon's conception of intelligence and of how to measure it differed substantially from that of Galton and Cattell, whose tests they considered a waste of time. To Binet and Simon, the core of intelligence was good judgment. Binet cited the example of Helen Keller as someone of known extraordinary intelligence whose scores on psychophysical tests would be notably inferior but who could be expected to perform at a very high level on tests of judgment.

According to Binet and Simon, intelligent thought is composed of three distinct elements: direction, adaptation, and criticism. *Direction* consists of knowing what has to be done and how to do it. When we need to add two numbers, for example, we give ourselves a series of instructions on how to proceed, and these instructions form the direction of thought. *Adaptation* refers to the selection and monitoring of our strategy during the course of performance. In solving a problem, we often have many paths to solutions, some of which will lead to better solutions and others to worse. Adaptive people tend to select better strategies, and they monitor their progress along the way to make sure that the strategy is leading where they want to be going. *Criticism* (or *control*) is our ability to criticize our own thoughts and actions – to know not only when we are doing well, but to be able to recognize when we are doing poorly, and to change our behavior in such a way as to improve our performance.

Because of his emphasis on test development, Binet has often been accused of being atheoretical (in other words, not being driven by theories) in his approach to intelligence. This discussion of Binet's views should make it clear that nothing could be further from the case. To the contrary, he and Simon conceived of intelligence in ways that were theoretically sophisticated and that resembled in content much of the most recent thinking regarding cognitive processing (Hunt, 2005). Whatever the distinction between Galton's thinking and Binet's, it was not (as some would have it) that Galton was theoretically motivated and Binet was not. If anything, Binet had a better developed theory of the nature of intelligence. Instead, these scientists differed in the way they selected items for the tests with which they proposed to measure intelligence. Galton's test items were chosen to measure psychophysical abilities, but Galton did not attempt to validate his items. Binet's test items were more cognitive in nature, in that they measured the kinds of reasoning and judgmental abilities that Binet considered to constitute intelligence (see Lohman, 2005). He also chose his items, however, to differentiate between performance of children of different ages or mental capacities as well as to correlate at a reasonably high level.

Most of Binet's measures were verbal (for example, "Use the words *Paris, gutter, and fortune* in a sentence"), and this format was retained when Lewis Terman brought his tests to America. Terman was a professor at Stanford, and called his English version of the test the "Stanford-Binet." Intelligence tests stayed primarily verbal until World War I, when a group of psychologists developed several clever non-verbal tests of mental ability. The goal was to be able to measure the intelligence of people who were illiterate, poorly literate, or who spoke English as a foreign language. It may seem obvious now why you might want to not only use verbal abilities as a construct, but it was new and different then. The time that it might take to administer one nonverbal problem (such as a matrix problem, in which you had to form an analogy between two sets of pictures) could be used to administer twenty different vocabulary items. But there were new problems during World War I. Most pressingly, verbal tests could not accurately measure the mental ability of the growing number of immigrants who spoke little or no English.

A modern version of the Stanford-Binet is still used today. In its fifth edition, the *Stanford-Binet Intelligence Scales* (SB5, Roid, 2003) constitute an individually administered intelligence test used to assess the cognitive abilities of individuals from age two to adult. The latest edition is divided into Verbal and Nonverbal scales, and provides measurement of five separate aspects of intelligence such as Knowledge, Visual-Spatial Reasoning, and Working Memory. Typical tasks include pointing out absurd mistakes in a picture; remembering the last word from a series of questions; being able to create different designs from a form board; and a variation of the classic "shell game," in which a ball in placed under a cup, the cup is moved back-and-forth among other cups, and the person must then pick the cup holding the ball (Roid & Barram, 2004).

Although Binet was the first to invent an intelligence test that resembles modern tests, his test is not the most popular test. That distinction belongs to David Wechsler, one of the psychologists who helped out during World War I. Wechsler's (1997, 2003) intelligence tests for both children and adults are by far the most commonly used IQ tests (Flanagan & Kaufman, 2004). The Wechsler scales are based on Wechsler's notion of intelligence as "the overall capacity of an individual to understand and cope with the world around him" (Wechsler, 1958). Wechsler conceived of intelligence as a global entity in which no one particular ability is of crucial or overwhelming importance. First and foremost, however, Wechsler cared about the person, and believed that intelligence tests were most meaningful if they were interpreted in the context of the individual's personality. He developed his tests primarily to facilitate the clinical assessment of children, adolescents, and adults (Kaufman, 2000).

The Wechsler Intelligence Scales, starting with the Wechsler-Bellevue in 1939, have traditionally been divided into two sections, a Verbal Scale and a Performance (or nonverbal) Scale. They have typically yielded separate standard scores (known as Intelligence Quotients, or IQs) for each part, as well as a global score for the two parts combined.

The most recent version of the Wechsler scales – the Wechsler Intelligence Scale for Children: Fourth Edition (WISC-IV; Wechsler, 2003) – has retained the global IQ, but has abandoned the separate Verbal and Performance IQs in favor of scores in four separate aspects of mental ability: Verbal Comprehension, Perceptual Reasoning, Working Memory, and Processing Speed. Like the Stanford-Binet, Wechsler's tests must be individually administered and consist only of those items appropriate to the age and ability of the subjects being tested. Examinees begin with items easier than those appropriate for their age and end with items difficult enough to result in repeated failure of solution. Also like the most recent edition of the Stanford-Binet (SB5), the WISC-IV has deemphasized global IQs in favor of an array of separate cognitive abilities.

The Verbal parts of the Wechsler tests, past and present, include subtests such as Information, which requires the demonstration of knowledge about the world; Similarities, which requires an indication of how two different objects are alike; and Comprehension, which requires the demonstration of common-sense understanding of social situations. Arithmetic, which requires the solution of arithmetic word problems, has traditionally been included on Wechsler's verbal scales. More recently, however, Arithmetic and tests of short-term memory are included on a separate Working Memory scale.

The Performance part of the test includes subtests such as Picture Completion, which requires recognition of a missing part in a picture of an object; Picture Arrangement, which requires rearrangement of a scrambled set of pictures into an order that tells a coherent story from beginning to end; and Block Design, which requires individuals to reproduce a picture of a design, constructed from a set of red, white, and half-red/half-white blocks, by actually building the design with physical blocks. Digit Symbol (called Coding on Wechsler's children's scales) requires the rapid copying of abstract symbols that are paired with numbers. Although this highly speeded subtest traditionally has been associated with Wechsler's Performance Scale in the past, it is included on the Processing Speed scale in more recent editions of Wechsler's tests.

In sum, the tradition of Alfred Binet involves testing higher-order cognitive skills in order to assess a person's intelligence. Binet and Wechsler were extremely broad in their conceptualizations of intelligence, and their notions are quite compatible with the conception of intelligence that motivates this book. Unfortunately, the tests are somewhat narrower than the conceptions of intelligence that generated them, so that the scores derived from the tests reflect not so much the originators' conceptions of intelligence as a set of higher-order cognitive skills that are used in a variety of academic, and to some extent, other tasks.

Whereas Binet and Wechsler were concerned with theories behind intelligent behavior, their tests were decidedly built on either practical (Binet) or clinical (Wechsler) considerations, and that practical-clinical framework guided test development for seventy-five years. However, new intelligence tests developed during the past twenty years (including the fifth edition of the Stanford-Binet) have been built from theories of intelligence. Even the newest Wechsler test, the WISC-IV, has clear-cut ties to theory (Flanagan & Kaufman, 2004). Indeed, it would be hard for a new or revised test *not* based even loosely on any theory to be competitive.

The Tradition of Charles Spearman

According to Charles Spearman (1927), originator of the factorial tradition, there are two kinds of factors in human intelligence: a general factor, which pervades all intellectual performances; and a set of specific factors, each of which is relevant to just one particular task. Spearman's belief that a single factor of intelligence was responsible for whatever was common in intellectual performance across tasks constituted what he believed to be a law of the "universal unity of the intellective function." This view is still widely held (Brand, 1996; Jensen, 1998, 2006).

What was the actual psychological mechanism that gave rise to such a unity of intellective function-to what Spearman referred to as the g (general) factor? Spearman considered a number of possible explanations, such as attention, will, plasticity of the nervous system, and the state of the blood, but he finally settled on an explanation in terms of mental energy. According to Spearman, the concept of mental energy originated with Aristotle, who defined energy as any actual manifestation of change. For Spearman, the energy was only a latent potential for such change. Thus, for Spearman but not for Aristotle, energy could be an entirely mental construct.

Subsequent Psychometric Theories

Louis Thurstone (1938) proposed a theory that tentatively identified seven primary mental abilities, which were identified through factor analysis. The mental abilities were verbal comprehension, quantitative ability, memory, perceptual speed, space, verbal fluency, and inductive reasoning. These primary mental abilities were later used as a basis for the formulation of the Primary Mental Abilities Tests. As it happened, scores on factors representing the primary mental abilities are almost always correlated with each other. If the scores on these factors are themselves factor analyzed (in much the same way that task or test scores would be), a higher-order general factor emerges from the analysis. Before his death, Thurstone found himself with little choice but to concede the existence of a general factor. Not surprisingly, he believed this general factor to be of little importance. Similarly, Spearman was eventually forced to concede the existence of group factors such as those identified by Thurstone. But Spearman believed that these group factors were of little importance.

J. P. Guilford proposed an extension of Thurstone's theory that incorporates Thurstone's factors while adding many others. He split the primary mental abilities and added new ones, so that the total number of factors is increased from 7 to 120. Guilford (1967) wrote that every mental task requires three elements: an operation, a content, and a product. Guilford pictured the relation among these three elements as that of a cube, with each of the elements-operations, contents, and products-representing a dimension of the cube. There are five kinds of operations: cognition, memory, divergent production, convergent production, and evaluation. There are six kinds of products: units, classes, relations, systems, transformations, and implications. Finally, there are four kinds of contents: figural, symbolic, semantic, and behavioral. Because the subcategories are independently defined, they can be multiplied, yielding 120 ($5 \times 6 \times 4$) different mental abilities. Each of these 120 abilities is represented by Guilford as a small cube embedded in the larger cube. Guilford and his associates devised tests measuring many of these abilities. Cognition of figural relations, for example, is measured by tests such as figural analogies. Memory for semantic relations is measured by presenting subjects with series of relations, such as "Gold is more valuable than iron," and then testing the subjects' retention of these relations using a multiple-choice test.

Theorists of intelligence such as Philip Vernon have proposed hierarchical models of mental ability. Vernon (1971) proposed a hierarchy with general intelligence at the top, verbal-educational and practical-mechanical abilities at the second level, and more specific abilities at lower levels. A more detailed hierarchical model, based on a reanalysis of many data sets from factor-analytic studies, has been proposed by John Carroll (1993). At the top of the hierarchy is general ability; in the middle of the hierarchy are various broad abilities (including learning and memory processes and the effortless production of many ideas). At the bottom of the hierarchy are many narrow, specific abilities such as spelling ability and reasoning speed.

Another similar theory is the Cattell-Horn theory of intelligence (Horn & Cattell, 1966), often referred to as Gf-Gc theory. The Cattell-Horn theory initially proposed two types of intelligence, crystallized (Gc) and fluid (Gf). Gc is what a person knows and has learned, while Gf is how a person handles a new and different situation (i.e., problem solving). Horn expanded the theory to include more dimensions (known as Broad Abilities), such as visualization (Gv), short-term memory (Gsm), long-term retrieval (Glr), and processing speed (Gs) (Horn, 1985; Horn & Hofer, 1992; Horn & Noll, 1997). In recent years, Carroll's hierarchical theory and the Horn-Cattell Gf-Gc theory have been merged into the Cattell-Horn-Carroll or CHC theory (Flanagan, McGrew, & Ortiz, 2000; Flanagan & Ortiz, 2002). The CHC theory has been particularly influential in the development of recent IQ tests, most notably the fifth edition of the Stanford-Binet (Roid, 2003), the Kaufman Assessment Battery for Children – Second Edition (KABC-II; Kaufman & Kaufman, 2004), and the Woodcock-Johnson – Third Edition (WJ-III; Woodcock, McGrew, & Mather, 2001).

The CHC model incorporates both the concept of a general intelligence (all of the different aspects of intelligence are considered to be related to a common "*g*," although this aspect is not often emphasized; see Flanagan & Ortiz, 2002) and the concept of many different aspects of intelligence. Largely because of the influence of CHC theory, all current IQ tests (including the SB5 and WISC-IV) have shifted the historical focus from a small number of part scores to a contemporary emphasis on anywhere from four to seven cognitive abilities. The debate about which is "better," one intelligence versus many aspects of intelligence, still goes on (for a review, see Sternberg & Grigorenko, 2002).

What seems to be missing from most factorial theories of intelligence is any clear notion of the processes involved in intelligence. Jean Piaget's theory sought to specify such processes, as did cognitive theories of intelligence, which will be considered in a later section.

Piaget's Theory

Jean Piaget, a Swiss psychologist, first entered the field of intellectual development when, working in Binet's laboratory, he became intrigued with children's wrong answers to Binet's intelligence test items. To understand intelligence, Piaget reasoned, the investigation must be twofold. First, as was done by Binet, we must look at a person's performance. But also, and here is where Piaget began to part company with Binet, we must consider why the person performs as he or she does, taking account of the cognitive structure underlying the individual's actions. Through his repeated observation of children's performance and particularly of their errors in reasoning, Piaget concluded that there are coherent logical structures underlying children's thought but that these structures are different from those underlying adult thought. In the six decades that followed, Piaget focused his research on defining these cognitive structures at different stages of development and how these structures might evolve from one stage to the next.

Piaget believed that there were two interrelated aspects of intelligence: its function and its structure. A biologist by training, he saw the function of intelligence to be the same as other biological activities – adaptation. According to Piaget (1972), adaptation includes assimilating the environment to one's own structures (whether physiological or cognitive) and accommodating one's mental structures (again either physiological or cognitive) to include new aspects of the environment. According to Piaget, "A certain continuity exists . . . between intelligence and the purely biological process of morphogenesis and adaptation to the environment."

In Piaget's theory, the function of intelligence-adaptation provides continuity with lower biological acts: Piaget believed intelligence to be a system of operations for translating thinking into action.

Piaget rejected the sharp separation proposed by some between intelligent acts, on the one hand, and habits or reflexes, on the other. Instead, he preferred to speak of a continuum in which "behavior becomes more intelligent as the pathways between the subject and the object on which it acts cease to be simple and become progressively more complex."

Piaget further proposed that the internal organizational structure of intelligence and the way intelligence is manifested differ with age. It is obvious that an adult does not deal with the world in the same way as an infant. Indeed, most infants would have skipped this paragraph already: They could not have read it!

The infant typically acts on its environment via sensorimotor structures and as a result is limited to the apparent physical world. The adult, by contrast, is capable of abstract thinking and is thus free to explore the world of possibility. Guided by his interest in the philosophy of knowledge and his observation of children's behavior, Piaget divided the intellectual development of the individual into distinct stages. As the child progresses from one stage to the next, the cognitive structures of the preceding stage are reorganized and extended, through the child's own adaptive actions, to form the underlying structures of the next stage.

Piaget's description of the child's intellectual development depends on three core assumptions about the nature of this developmental process. First, four factors interact to bring about the development of the child. Three of these factors are the ones usually proposed: maturation, experience of the physical environment, and the influence of the social environment. To these three factors, however, Piaget added a fourth, which coordinates and guides the other three: equilibration, that is, the child's own self-regulatory processes. Thus, Piaget's theory centers on the idea that children are active participants in the construction of their own intelligence.

Piaget's second assumption is that this intellectual development results in the appearance of developmental stages that follow an invariable sequential order. Each succeeding stage includes and extends the accomplishments of the preceding stage. Third, although the rate of development may vary across children, Piaget considered the stages themselves and their sequence to be universal.

In sum, Piaget's theory argued for is a single path of intellectual development that all people follow, regardless of how quickly they develop. Notice that Piaget, unlike psychometric theorists, did not rely on individual differences in forming his theory.

Cognitive-Processing Theories

Cognitive-processing conceptions of intelligence seek to understand the ways in which people mentally represent and process information (Pretz & Sternberg, 2005). Cognitive-processing researchers use computer simulations and mathematical models to find patterns of data that suggest strategies of cognitive processing (Sternberg & Pretz, 2005).

Cognitive research has often used the computer program as a metaphor for understanding how humans process information. The major distinguishing feature of the approach, however, is not its reliance on computer concepts, but, rather, its concern with how information is processed during the performance of various kinds of tasks.

Perhaps surprisingly, one psychologist interested in information processing was Charles Spearman, who (as we mentioned) was one of the founders of psychometrics. Spearman might also have been one of the most influential figures in popularizing the cognitive tradition, had the time been right. The time apparently was not right, however. Whereas Spearman's 1904 psychometric theory and methodology were eagerly adopted by workers in the laboratory and in the field, Spearman's later cognitive theories were not. One reason why they were not well accepted may have been that there was not adequate equipment; people in the 1920s could not surf the Internet or run computer programs. Spearman (1923) proposed three principles of cognition (which he might as easily have called *processes* of cognition) that he described using an example of someone solving an analogy. The first principle, apprehension of experience, states that "any lived experience tends to evoke immediately a knowing of its characters and experiencer." In an analogy, such as LAWYER is to CLIENT as DOCTOR is to _____, apprehension of experience would correspond to the encoding of each analogy term, in which the problem solver perceives each word and understands its meaning.

The second principle, eduction of relations, states "the mentally presenting of two or more characters (simple or complex) tends to evoke immediately a knowing relation between them." In the sample analogy, eduction of relations would correspond to understanding the relation between LAWYER and CLIENT (a lawyer provides professional services to a client). The third principle, eduction of correlates, states "the presenting of any character together with any relation tends to evoke immediately a knowing of the correlative character." In the sample analogy, eduction of correlates would correspond to the application of the rule previously inferred to generate an acceptable completion to the analogy: PATIENT.

Almost forty years later, two works appeared that revived the cognitive approach. One was by Newell, Shaw, and Simon (1958), the other by Miller, Galanter, and Pribram (1960). The goal of both programs of research was, as Miller and his colleagues put it, "to discover whether the cybernetic [computer-based] ideas have any relevance to psychology." Both groups concluded that they did have relevance and, moreover, that the computer could be a highly useful tool in developing psychological theories. Miller and his collaborators sought to understand human behavior in terms of "plans," that is, "any hierarchical process in the argument that can control the order in which a sequence of operations is to be performed." Critical for the cognitive approach was the authors' view that "a plan is, for an organism, essentially the same as a program for a computer." The authors acknowledged that this relationship was not proven, however: The reduction of plans to nothing but programs is still a scientific hypothesis and is still in need of further validation. For the present, therefore, it should be less confusing if we regard a computer program that simulates certain features of an organism's behavior as a theory about the organismic plan that generated the behavior.

The computer simulation method allowed cognitive psychologists to test theories of human information processing by comparing predictions generated by computer simulation to actual data collected from human subjects. In computer simulations, the researcher attempts to get the computer to mimic the cognitive processes that would be used by humans, if they were solving the problem at hand. If you have ever played any video game in which you play (or battle) against the computer, then you have experienced these types of simulations. The computer's artificial intelligence tries to create an opponent that is talented enough to challenge you. Playing a game like Rise of Nations or Warcraft simply would not be fun if the opposing soldiers did not try to fight you back! Indeed, many computer games may look good and have interesting concepts – but if they are too easy or too hard, they will not be a success.

Whereas many psychometric theorists of intelligence have agreed that the factor is the fundamental unit of intellectual behavior, many cognitive theorists have agreed that the information-processing component, as it is sometimes called, is the fundamental unit. Cognitive theorists assume that all behavior of the human information-processing system is the result of combinations of elementary processes, although they have disagreed as to exactly which processes are most important to understanding intelligence. Consider just a few of the theories that have been proposed about how information processing is related to intelligence, and also consider how they have been tested.

A primary difference among cognitive theorists is in the level of cognitive functioning they emphasize in attempting to understand intelligence. At one extreme are those who have proposed to understand intelligence in terms of sheer speed of information processing, and who have used very simple tasks to measure pure speed uncontaminated by other variables. At the other extreme are those who have studied very complex forms of problem solving and are less interested in speediness.

Pure Speed

People who believe that individual differences in intelligence can be traced back to sheer speed of information processing have tended to use simple reaction time and related tasks (Neubauer & Fink, 2005). In a simple *reaction-time* paradigm, the individual is required simply to make a single response as quickly as possible following the presentation of a stimulus. For example, we might tell you to press the space bar on your keyboard whenever a picture of a frog showed up. Then we might show you a penguin, a fish, a frog, a giraffe, a frog, and an aardvark. Your reaction time would be measured by how quickly you hit the space bar after the frog was shown each time.

This paradigm has been widely used since the days of Galton as a measure of intelligence. Despite such early support, the levels of correlation obtained between measures of simple reaction time and various standard measures of intelligence have been weak. There seems to be much more to intelligence than pure speed.

Inspection Time

Ian Deary and Laura Stough (1996; for review, see also Deary, 2000a) have proposed that a very low-level psychophysical measure, inspection time, may provide us with insights into the fundamental nature of intelligence (see also Deary, 2000b). The basic idea is that individual differences in intelligence may come from differences in how we process very simple stimulus information. In the inspection-time task, a person looks at two vertical lines of different lengths, and simply has to say which line is longer. Inspection time is the amount of time someone needs, on average, in order to correctly discriminate which of two lines is longer (such as 0.4 seconds). Investigators have found that more intelligent individuals can take less time to pick the longer line. The actual measurement of inspection time is not by reaction time, but by presenting the pair of lines for different amounts of time, with the score taken from the time it takes for someone to earn a certain percentage score of correct comparisons.

Choice Speed

A slight complication of the above view is that intelligence derives not from simple speed of processing, but rather from speed in making choices or decisions to simple stimuli. In a typical *choice reaction-time* paradigm, the individual is presented with one of two or more possible stimuli, each requiring a different response. The individual has to choose the correct response as rapidly as possible following stimulus presentation. Correlations with psychometric measures of intelligence have been higher than those obtained for simple reaction time, but they are still relatively weak.

An interesting finding in the research of Jensen (2006) and others is that the correlation between choice reaction time and IQ tends to increase with the number of stimulus-response choices involved in the task. In other words, the more choices a person has to make (and, therefore, the more complex the task), the more the test scores correlate with measured intelligence.

Speed of Access

Individual differences in intelligence are believed to be related to neural efficiency and speed of information processing (Grabner, Neubauer, & Stern, 2006; Neubauer & Fink, 2005). In 1978, Earl Hunt proposed that individual differences in verbal intelligence may be understandable largely in terms of differences in *speed of access* to verbal information stored in long-term memory. According to Hunt, the more quickly people can access information, the better they can use their time with presented information, hence, the better they can perform on a variety of verbal tasks. Hunt, Lunneborg and Lewis (1975) initiated a paradigm for testing this theory that makes use of a letter-comparison task previously used by two psychologists, Posner and Mitchell (1967), in some of their research.

In this paradigm, subjects are presented with pairs of letters – such as AA, Aa, or Ab – that may be the same or different either physically or in name. For example, AA are the same both physically and in name; Aa are the same in name only; and Ab are the same neither in name nor in physical appearance. No pair of letters, of course, could be the same physically but not the same in name. The task is to indicate as rapidly as possible whether the two pairs are a match.

In one condition, people respond to whether the pairs are a *physical* match; in another, the same subjects respond to whether the letters are a *name* match. What is measured is each person's average name-match time minus physical-match time. This measure is considered to be an index of the time it takes a person to access verbal information in long-term memory. The physical-match time represents a person's sheer speed of responding; it takes little mental effort to see if two things look alike. Subtracting this time from the name-match time creates a relatively pure measure of access time. For example, someone may consistently take 0.1 second to respond to whether two pairs are a physical match, and 0.9 seconds to respond to whether the two pairs are a name match. We could then calculate that the person spent 0.8 seconds on accessing the information. In contrast to those who study simple reaction time and focus on sheer speed of responding, Hunt and his colleagues do what they can to subtract out this element.

The letter-comparison task is consistently correlated with verbal IQ at weak to moderate levels. So although it does appear to be related at some level to intellectual performance at some level, it is at best only one part of what standard psychometric intelligence tests measure.

Working Memory

Recent work suggests that a critical component of intelligence may be working memory. Indeed, some investigators have argued that intelligence may be little more than working memory (Kyllonen, 2002; Kyllonen & Christal, 1990). In one study, participants read sets of passages and, after they had read the passages, try to remember the last word of each passage (Daneman & Carpenter, 1983). Recall was highly correlated with verbal ability. In another study, participants perform a variety of working-memory tasks. In one task, for example, the participants saw a set of simple arithmetic problems, each of which was followed by a word or a digit (Engle, 1994; Engle,

Carullo, & Collins, 1992; Hambrick & Engle, 2005). The participants saw sets of two to six such problems and solved each one. After solving the problems in the set, they tried to recall the words that followed the problems. The number of words recalled was highly correlated with measured intelligence. Thus, it appears that the ability to store and manipulate information in working memory may be an important aspect of intelligence. It is probably not all there is to intelligence, however.

Components of Reasoning and Problem Solving

A number of investigators have emphasized the kinds of higher-order processing involved in reasoning and problem solving in their attempts to understand intelligence, among them Robert Glaser, James Pellegrino, Herbert Simon, and Robert Sternberg (see Cianciolo & Sternberg, 2004; Lohman, 2000). Following in the tradition of Spearman's three principles of cognition, these investigators have sought to understand individual differences in intelligence in terms of information processing in tasks such as analogies, series completions, and syllogisms. Some investigators seek to understand intelligence in terms of information processes, or *components*, by discovering the processes people use in problem solving from the moment they first see a problem to the time they respond. Consider, for example, the widely studied analogy item, such as CHICKEN is to EGG as DOG is to ____. In a typical theory of analogical reasoning, completing this item is broken down into component processes such as *inferring* the relation between the first two terms of the analogy (a CHICKEN produces an EGG) and *applying* this inferred relation to the second half of the analogy (a DOG produces...a PUPPY). The basic idea is that someone's skill in solving these problems derives from the ability to execute these processes. Moreover, the processes involved in analogy solution have been shown to be quite general across many different kinds of problems. The components of information processing are of interest because they are not task-specific. If these components only worked in solving analogies, they would be of much less interest.

Investigators seeking to understand intelligence in terms of executive processes study the ways in which people plan, monitor, and evaluate their performance in reasoning and problem solving. The idea in this approach is not just to look at what individuals do in solving problems but also to look also at why and how they decide to do what they actually do.

Investigators using reasoning and problem-solving items have generally obtained higher correlations between scores on their tasks and psychometrically measured IQ scores than investigators who use some of the other approaches discussed above. Typically, correlations have been moderate to high.

Cultural and Contextual Models

We have seen how psychometric, computational, and biological psychologists view intelligence as something basically residing inside the head. In contrast, contextualist theorists talk about a psychological phenomenon (e.g., intelligence) largely in terms of the context in which someone is observed and suggest that the phenomenon cannot be understood – let alone measured – outside the real-world context of the individual (Serpell, 2000; Sternberg, 2004a, 2004b, 2007a; Sternberg & Grigorenko, 2004; Suzuki & Valencia, 1997). These theorists study how intelligence relates to the external world. In fact, they view intelligence as so inextricably linked to culture that they believe intelligence to be something that a culture creates (Sternberg, 2004a). The purpose of this creation is to define the nature of adaptive performance and to account for why some people perform better than others on the tasks that the culture happens to value (see Suzuki & Valencia, 1997).

Multiple Intelligences

Howard Gardner (1983, 1993, 1999, 2006) does not view intelligence as just a single, unitary construct. However, instead of speaking of the many different abilities that together make up intelligence, as have some other theorists, Gardner has proposed a theory of multiple intelligences, in which eight distinct intelligences function some-what independently of one another, but may interact to produce intelligent behavior: linguistic, logical-mathematical, spatial, musical, bodily-kinesthetic, interpersonal (dealing with other people), intrapersonal (dealing with oneself), and naturalist. Gard-ner (1999, 2006) has also speculated on the possible existence of existential and spir-itual intelligences. Each intelligence is a separate system of functioning, although these systems can interact to produce what we see as intelligent performance.

For example, a playwright might rely heavily on linguistic intelligence but might use logical-mathematical intelligence in plotting story lines or checking through their stories for inconsistencies. Indeed, one of the authors of this book once wrote a play in which a character says that he hates the fact that the college class he is attending at the moment takes place at night; two pages later, another character comments at how beautiful the sun in the sky is. It was quite embarrassing when someone (who likely had higher logical-mathematical intelligence) pointed out the inconsistency! Measuring these intelligences separately might give schools and individuals a profile of a range of skills that is broader than would be obtained, say, from just measuring verbal and mathematical abilities. This profile could then be used to facilitate educational and career decisions.

In order to identify these particular intelligences, Gardner has used converging operations, gathering evidence from multiple sources and types of data. The base of evidence used by Gardner includes (but is not limited to) the distinctive effects of localized brain damage on specific kinds of intelligences, distinctive patterns of devel-opment in each kind of intelligence across the life span, evidence from exceptional individuals (from both ends of the spectrum), and evolutionary history.

Gardner's view of the mind is modular. Modularity theorists believe that different abilities – such as Gardner's intelligences – can be isolated as coming from distinct parts of the brain. Thus, a major task of existing and future research on intelligence would be to isolate the portions of the brain responsible for each of the intelligences. Gardner has speculated as to at least some of these relevant portions, but hard evidence for the existence of the separate intelligences (or any measures that could be used in any type of practical way) has yet to be produced.

Instrumental Enrichment

Another approach to intelligence is to focus on whether and how it can be trained and improved. Instrumental Enrichment (IE), Reuven Feuerstein's well-known training program (1980), was originally designed for children with mental retardation, but it has since been recognized by Feuerstein and others as valuable for a wide variety of students. Based on Feuerstein's theory of intelligence, the IE program is intended to improve the cognitive functioning related to the input, elaboration, and output of information. The idea is that mediation of experience by parents and other care-givers can enhance intellectual functioning (Mintzker, Feuerstein, & Feuerstein, 2006). Feuerstein has compiled a long list of cognitive deficiencies he believes his program can help to correct. Among them are (a) unplanned, impulsive, and unsystematic exploratory behavior; (b) lacking the ability to consider two sources of information at once, so that the child deals with data in a scattered way rather than grouping and organizing facts; and (c) not being able to experience the existence of an actual problem and subsequently define it. Feuerstein's IE program is designed to correct these deficiencies and, at the same time, to increase the student's motivation and feelings of self-worth.

What are some of the characteristics of the Feuerstein program? Instrumental Enrichment does not attempt to teach either specific items of information or abstract thinking through a well-defined, structured knowledge base. To the contrary, it is as content-free as possible. Its materials or "instruments" each emphasize a particular cognitive function and its relationships to various cognitive deficiencies. Feuerstein sees the student's performance on the materials as a means to an end, rather than as an end in itself. Emphasis in analyzing IE performance is on processes rather than on products, so that the student's errors are viewed as a means of insight into how the student solves problems.

The IE program consists of thirteen different types of exercises, which are repeated in cycles throughout the program. Although the problems are abstract and "unworldly," instructors are required to bridge the gap between them and the real world as much as possible. The following samples of the kinds of materials in the program convey a sense of the types of activities in which students engage:

1. *Orientation of dots.* The student is presented with a variety of two-dimensional arrays of dots and is asked to identify and outline, within each array, a set of geometric figures, such as squares, triangles, diamonds, and stars.
2. *Numerical progressions.* In one kind of numerical progression problem, the student is given the first number in a sequence and a rule by which the sequence can be continued, for example, +3, –1. The student then has to generate the continuation of the sequence.

We not only can but we should teach intelligence. Programs are now available that do an excellent, if incomplete, job of improving intellectual skills, but the vast majority of students are not now being exposed to these programs. Indeed, the heavy content of traditional curricula barely allows room for such training. For this reason many scholars believe the time has come to supplement standard curricula with training in intellectual skills. Intelligence should still be tested, but we believe there also should be an emphasis on developing and nurturing intelligence.

Summing Up

To sum up, the various theoretical approaches seem, on the surface, to be quite different. Biological approaches seek to understand intelligence by linking it to specific brain regions or patterns of their activation. Psychometric researchers seek to understand the structure of the mental abilities that constitute intelligence. Piaget sought to understand the stages in the development of intelligence. Cognitive researchers seek to understand the processes of intelligence. Multiple intelligences theory proposes eight distinct intelligences. Instrumental Enrichment seeks to nurture and improve intellectual abilities.

When we look at them in this way, we see that the approaches are not wholly mutually incompatible – they do not so much give different answers to the same questions as they give different answers to different questions. For example, the psychometric researchers emphasize structural models, whereas the cognitive researchers emphasize process models. In fact, the two kinds of models are complementary to each other. The factors of intelligence can be understood in terms of processes that enter into them. So, for example, if one has a factor of verbal ability, it is legitimate to ask what processes are responsible for individual differences in verbal ability. Or we might ask if certain processes tend to go together in intelligent performance in human beings. Factor analysis addresses this question. It conveniently organizes the processes of human intelligence into constellations of higher-order mental abilities. We need to understand intelligence from all these points of view. Which approach an investigator decides to take will be a function of the investigator's theoretical and methodological predispositions, as well as of the particular questions about intelligence that are of the most interest.

The theory presented in this book draws on all these approaches, and others, as well, although it is probably most heavily influenced by the cognitive approach. However, it is not enough just to look at cognitive processing. To understand intelligence fully, we also need to understand how these cognitive processes operate in everyday life. In many respects, the theory of intelligence in this book is more comprehensive than most of the theories discussed in this chapter. As you learn about the theory, you will see how it operates as you solve intellectual games and puzzles that illustrate various aspects of the theory and that may help you to sharpen your thinking skills.

2

The Theory of Successful Human Intelligence

The theory of successful human intelligence presented in this book provides a broader basis for understanding intelligence than do many (and perhaps most) of the theories considered in Chapter 1. The theory consists of three parts (and, therefore, is also called the "triarchic theory"). The first part considers intelligence as what goes on inside of someone – an internal world, so to speak. These "internal" abilities (or "mental mechanisms") can lead to more intelligent or less intelligent behavior (Sternberg, 1997; Sternberg, 1999b; Sternberg, 2003; Sternberg, 2006). There are three kinds of mental processes that are important in planning what things to do, learning how to do the things, and actually doing them.

The second part of the theory examines a person's experience in handling a task or dealing with a situation. There are certain points in the performance of a task in which a person's intelligence has a critical role. In particular, this part of the theory emphasizes dealing with novelty and how mental processing in intelligence sometimes can be made automatic.

The third part of the theory relates intelligence to the external world of the individual, and specifies three kinds of acts – environmental adaptation, environmental selection, and environmental shaping – that characterize intelligent behavior in the everyday world. This part of the theory emphasizes the role of the environment in determining what constitutes intelligent behavior in a given setting.

The first part of the theory, which specifies the mental mechanisms of intelligent behavior, is universal. Individuals may differ in what mental mechanisms they apply to a given task or situation. However, the potential set of mental mechanisms underlying intelligence is claimed to be the same across all individuals, social classes, and cultural groups. For example, people in every culture have to first identify what problems they need to solve (defining problems), and then develop strategies to solve these problems. The fact that some cultures may be defining problems related to farming and others may be defining problems related to selling merchandise online does not matter (Sternberg, 2004a; Sternberg, 2004b).

The portion of the theory dealing with relative novelty (how new something is to you) and automatization of information processing (how quickly you can begin to do something without thinking about it, such as brushing your teeth). Part of being intelligent is figuring out how to cope with relatively new tasks and situations. An example is learning to drive a stick-shift car when you already know how to drive an automatic, or the first time you went to a party where you did not know anyone there. Similarly, people in all cultures have to learn to automatize some of their behavior. For example, what first is relatively novel – driving a stick shift – may soon become automatic as one drives the stick shift without even consciously thinking about it. In other words, driving something other than an automatic may *become* automatic!

This part of the theory is universal in the relationship between relative novelty and how quickly these new-to-you activities can be automatized. It is also relative, however, in that the things that are new and different will change across cultures, groups, and societies. In other words, a task that is quite familiar to urban Americans might be quite unfamiliar to rural Africans, or vice versa (Sternberg, 2004a; Sternberg, 2004b). An average urban American might be able to find a beanie baby on eBay, make a bid, and then pay for the toy with PayPal – and consider this task ordinary and everyday. At the same time, a rural African might know how effectively and effortlessly to hunt various kinds of game that an urban American would have no clue about how to catch.

The third part of the theory is concerned with adaptation to existing environments (changing yourself to fit into the environment), shaping of existing environments into new environments (changing the environment to fit yourself), and selection of new environments (finding a new environment after an old one is a bad fit to your needs, desires, and skills). For example, let's say that you have decided to major in psychology. But you then discover that your psychology department is different then you expected and not as interesting to you as you hoped. You would need to adjust to this new reality – that is, get used to the fact that the department emphasizes things that you find boring. You could then adapt to this existing environment. Next, you might try to shape the environment – maybe you might try to see if you could take courses in related departments (such as Sociology) to fulfill courses for your major. Finally, you could select a new environment – change your major or switch universities.

This part of the theory, like the second part, is also both universal and particular. It is universal with respect to the importance of environmental adaptation, selection, and shaping to survival. It is relative with respect to which behaviors constitute environmental adaptation, selection, and shaping. For example, what is adaptive in one country might not be particularly adaptive in another – and might be grossly maladaptive in a third. Talking about one's political opinions freely, for example, might lead to rewards in one country and to death in another. The definitions of appropriate behavior can very widely from one environment to another.

In short, then, parts of the theory of successful intelligence are culturally universal, and parts are culturally relative. When people ask whether intelligence is the same thing from one culture to another or even from one individual to another, they are asking too simplistic a question. The most complex but appropriate question is, "What aspects of intelligence are universal and what aspects of intelligence are relative with respect to individuals and groups?" This theory addresses and attempts to answer this question.

COMPONENTS OF INTELLIGENCE

The first part of the theory of successful intelligence specifies the internal mental mechanisms that are responsible for intelligent behavior. These mental mechanisms are referred to as information-processing components. *A component* is a mental process. It may translate a sensory input (i.e., something you see or hear) into a mental representation (an image or thought in your mind). It also may transform one mental representation into another, such as when you go from one thought to another. Finally, a component may translate a mental representation into a motor output. For example, you may have the thought that you want to go and eat a mango. Then you can take that thought and physically stand up and walk to the refrigerator (where, most likely, you will be disappointed and not find a mango) (Sternberg, 1977).

Components perform three basic kinds of functions: *Metacomponents* are higher-order processes used in planning, monitoring, and evaluating performance of a task. *Performance components* are processes used in actually doing the task. *Knowledge-acquisition components* are processes used in learning new things (Sternberg, 1985). For example, metacomponents might be used to decide on a topic for a term paper. Performance components might be used to do the actual writing. And knowledge-acquisition components might be used to learn the information about which one will write. It is essential to understand the nature of these components, because they form the mental bases for the other parts of the theory. As mentioned earlier, these are components for dealing with novel kinds of tasks and situations, automatizing performance, and adapting to, shaping, and selecting environments.

Metacomponents

The *metacomponents* are "executive" processes, in that they essentially tell the other kinds of components what to do. They also receive feedback from the other kinds of components as to how things are going in problem solving or task performance. They are responsible for figuring out how to do a particular task or set of tasks, and then for making sure that the task or tasks are done correctly.

The theory of successful intelligence strongly emphasizes the role of metacomponents in intelligence. Consider an example of why these components are so important.

The assumption that "smart is fast" permeates North American society. Interestingly, this assumption is by no means universal. For example, it is not prevalent in most parts of South America. When North Americans call someone as "quick," it's a compliment – they are describing someone as having an attribute that they consider to be associated with an intelligent person. The pervasiveness of this assumption can be seen in a recent study of people's conceptions of intelligence, in which Americans were asked to list behaviors characteristic of intelligent persons (Sternberg et al., 1981). Answers such as "learns rapidly" "acts quickly," "talks quickly," and "makes judgments quickly," were common. It is not only the average person who believes that speed is so important to intelligence: As we discussed in the first chapter, several prominent scholars base their theories of intelligence in part on individual differences in the speed with which people process information.

The assumption that more intelligent people think and act more quickly also underlies the overwhelming majority of intelligence tests. It is rare to find a group test of intelligence that is not timed, or a timed test that virtually everyone can finish at a comfortable rate of problem solving. This assumption is a gross overgeneralization, however: It is true for some people and for some mental operations, but not for all people or all mental operations. What is critical is not speed per se, but speed selection – knowing when to perform at what rate, and being able to think and act rapidly or slowly depending on the task or situational demands.

Let's say, for example, that you and your spouse are writing thank you notes after a wedding. Some thank you notes may be to people whom neither of you know very well (such as your parents' friends). Other notes may be to people you are very close to and who may have given you generous and heartfelt gifts. Someone who just acts quickly would speed through all of the thank you notes. Someone who acts slowly may write long and detailed thank yous on every card. Someone who excels at speed selection, however, will able to spend the appropriate amount of time – longer and more thoughtful messages for those whom you are close to (or who gave you a really expensive gift!) Thus, it is resource allocation, a metacomponential function, which is central to general intelligence (Sternberg, 1984; Sternberg, 1985).

Converging kinds of evidence support this view – that resource allocation rather than simply speed is critical to intelligence. Some of this evidence comes from our everyday experiences in the world. We all know people who take their time in doing things, but do them extremely well. And it is common knowledge that snap judgments are sometimes poor judgments. Indeed, in the Sternberg et al. (1981) study on people's conceptions of intelligence, "does not make snap judgments" was listed as an important attribute of intelligent performance. Moreover, there are theoretical reasons for believing that to be quick is not always to he smart. In a classic but little-known book on the nature of intelligence, Louis Thurstone (1924) proposed that a critical element of intelligent performance is the ability to withhold rapid, instinctive responses, and to substitute for them more rational, well-thought-out responses. According to this view, the instinctive responses a person makes to problems are often not the best ones for solving those problems. Indeed, anyone who has ever had a boss or professor who was unpleasant or incompetent can attest to this phenomenon. If you relied on your instinctive response (such as, "Wow, you're an incredibly big jerk, aren't you? I wonder how you've avoided getting fired!"), you would not last long. The ability to inhibit acting upon these responses and to consider better responses is critical for high-quality task performance.

A number of findings from psychological research by many investigators undermine the validity of the view that to be smart is always to be fast. First, it is well known that, in general, a *reflective* rather than an *impulsive* cognitive style in problem solving is associated with more intelligent problem-solving performance. Jumping into problems without adequate reflection is likely to lead to false starts and erroneous conclusions. Indeed, more intelligent people tend to spend relatively more time than less intelligent people on global (higher-order) planning and relatively less time on local (lower-order) planning (Sternberg, 1981). In contrast, less intelligent people emphasize local rather than global planning. In other words, the more intelligent people spent more time before beginning a task, deciding what to do. They were then less likely to pursue dead ends or get lost in their problem solving. The less intelligent people started tasks without fully thinking them through, and thus had to keep planning and replanning as they made their way through the tasks. They kept turning down blind alleys. If you play either computer- or card-based games of skill or strategy, you have probably already learned this concept. As inherently appealing as it may be to rush in and start playing, better gamers know to read the manual and develop a plan of attack.

The point is that what matters for effectiveness in intelligent task performance often is not total time spent, but rather, how the time is distributed across the various kinds of planning. Although for the problems we used (complex forms of analogies), quicker problem solving was associated, on average, with higher intelligence, looking simply at total time masked the inverse relation in the amounts of time spent on the two kinds of planning.

Yet timed tests (such as the SATs or the GREs) often force a person to solve problems impulsively. The emphasis on speediness is sometimes argued to play a role in gender differences on the SATs and GREs. In mathematics, males tend to use an impulsive style and females tend to use a reflective style. As a result, males are rewarded by the timed format and outscore females, despite females typically performing better in math classes (see Gallagher & Kaufman, 2005, for a review of this literature). It is often claimed that the strict timing of such tests merely mirrors the requirements of highly pressured and productive societies. But most of us seem to encounter few significant problems in work or personal life that demand only the five to fifty seconds allowed on a typical problem on a standardized test. Of course, some people, such as air traffic controllers, must make consequential split-second decisions as an integral part of their everyday lives. But such people seem to be the exception rather than the rule.

In addition, although greater intelligence is associated with more rapid execution of most performance components, problem encoding – understanding exactly what a problem says – is a notable exception to this trend (Sternberg & Rifkin, 1979). The more intelligent person tends to spend relatively more time encoding the terms of a problem, presumably in order to facilitate subsequent operations on these encodings. For example, it is typical of a good medical doctor to spend much time talking to the patient and asking him or her to go through various tests and evaluations. Only when a lot of information on the patient is available, that is, the doctor has encoded as full a picture of the patient's condition as possible, will the doctor engage other mental operations while performing his cycle of decision making and establishing a diagnosis.

Encoding happens not only in professional, but also everyday life. When one of us arrived in his first job, he arranged the books on his shelf in what was pretty much a random order. Whenever anyone wanted to borrow a book or when the author needed one, he had to look through many of the titles before he finally happened on the one he was looking for. Finally, he got fed up with this disorganization and decided to alphabetize the books by title. In effect, he was devoting additional time to encoding the titles of the books in a way that would make them more easily retrievable when he or other people needed them. Then, when he needs a book, he could find it much more rapidly because of the additional time he spent in encoding the book titles. Of course, lending libraries operate on a similar principle.

Obviously, it would be foolish to argue that speed is never important. For example, in driving a car, slow reflexes or thinking can result in an accident that otherwise might have been averted. Indeed, speed is essential in many situations. But most of the important tasks people face in their lives don't require problem solving or decision making at split-second speed. Instead, they require intelligent allocations of time. Ideally, intelligence and achievement tests would stress allocation of time rather than sheer speed in solving various kinds of problems. We believe that the metacomponent of resource allocation is a critical one in intelligence.

Other kinds of metacomponents can matter too. One such metacomponent is the monitoring of one's behavior. In teaching, we tell students that the single easiest and least time-consuming step they can take to improve their grades on papers is to proofread their papers after they write them. Proofreading can catch not only typographical errors but also errors of logic or even of fact. This simple step can make the difference between a student's receiving a pleasing grade and an unsatisfactory grade.

This metacomponent comes in handy during exams and tests. At least one of us regularly finds that most students lose anywhere from five to thirty points on each exam by not reading the directions and thereby carefully monitoring their own test performance. Not answering all of the questions asked, only giving two instead of the requested three examples, and other basic mistakes could be caught by a careful read-through of the exam.

It was only in the 1990s that intelligence tests first started to measure planning abilities. Newer tests such as the Das-Naglieri Cognitive Assessment System (Naglieri & Das, 1997; see also Das, Naglieri, & Kirby, 1994) and the Kaufman Assessment Battery for Children – Second Edition (Kaufman & Kaufman, 2004) include planning in their intelligence assessments.

Performance Components

Performance components are used in the execution of various strategies for solving problems. Whereas metacomponents decide what to do, performance components actually do it. The performance components are probably the ones that are best measured by existing tests of intelligence and academic skills.

The number of performance components that people might use in dealing with anything that might ever face them is without doubt extremely large. If our goal were to identify them all, we could probably fill the rest of this book doing exactly that (thankfully, we won't). Fortunately, certain performance components are more important than others. For example, studies of mental test and academic performance have shown that one set of components – those of inductive reasoning, such as inferring and applying relations – are quite general across many of the items typically found in intelligence tests.

Inferring relations is involved when you try to figure out how two words or concepts are related to each other, such as the concepts of *intelligence* and *achievement*. It is not altogether different from playing "Six Degrees of Kevin Bacon" – the game in which one tries to link someone in film or television to the popular actor Kevin Bacon. Applying relations is involved when you figure out the best way to use knowledge you have inferred for other purposes. For example, you may get a poor grade on a test or assignment in a class. But if your performance on other tests and assignments is good or excellent, a professor will be able to look at the pattern of your performance and, perhaps, decide that your poor grade does not mean that you are bad at psychology. If your pattern of performance is strong overall, then this particular failed assignment might not make much difference in your grade.

A handful of performance components accounts for performance on many of the tasks found on intelligence tests and in many forms of academic achievement. Thus, if you wish to improve your score on IQ or achievement tests, you don't have to identify and improve large numbers of components. You can concentrate on just a few of them, as we will discuss later in this book.

It is important to realize that people can use different performance components to solve a given problem. Let's say that someone who always gets lost asks you for very good directions to your house. When you approach this task, you may use your visual-spatial abilities to draw a detailed map. You may use your verbal abilities to write out clear and concise directions. Maybe you use both sets of abilities and give directions and draw a map (as in the Internet search engine MapQuest). The point is that you might succeed at this task using different combinations of performance components. If one only evaluates the outcome (e.g., were the directions satisfactory?), virtually nothing is revealed about the kinds of mental processes you used to solve the problem.

Separation of the performance components used in solving problems is critically important for diagnosis and remediation of problem-solving performance. Consider a specific example: suppose that people are given a test requiring reasoning by analogy. A typical problem on such a test might be VENEZUELA: SPANISH:: BRAZIL: (a. ENGLISH, b. PORTUGUESE, c. FRENCH, d. GERMAN). In a typical testing situation, people would solve many analogies such as this one, and the measure of their reasoning ability would be their total number correct on the test. There is a problem with the logic of scoring the analogies test in this way, however. Consider a person (let's call her Maria) who is a very competent reasoner but who has a reading disability. In other words, Maria has no trouble reasoning about relations, but has considerable trouble in encoding the terms of the problem on which she must reason. People with a reading disability such as Maria may have great difficulty in obtaining a high score on an analogies test, especially if it is timed, merely because they read the terms slowly and with great difficulty. But the low score does not reflect difficulties in reasoning but, rather, difficulties in encoding the terms of the analogical reasoning problem. Other people might get problems wrong simply because they lack knowledge, such as of what the principal languages of Venezuela and Brazil are. (Do you know?) In other words, merely providing a total score on a test can camouflage rather than clarify a person's strengths and weaknesses. It is for this reason that it is useful to break scores down into their underlying performance and other components.

Knowledge-Acquisition Components

Knowledge-acquisition components are processes used in learning. It has long been known that the ability to learn is an essential part of intelligence, although performance on trivial kinds of learning tasks, such as memorizing nonsense syllables, is not particularly related to intelligence. It is meaningful rather than trivial learning that is important to intellectual ability.

Intelligence often is measured on the basis of past achievement. A test of intelligence, in other words, is often what would have been a test of achievement for the child a few years earlier. What is an intelligence test for children of a given age would be an achievement test for children a few years younger. In some test items, like vocabulary, the achievement orientation is obvious. In others, it is disguised, as, for example, in verbal analogies. Note that the reasoning in the verbal analogy used as an example earlier requires substantial knowledge. The person solving it has to know in advance that most people in Venezuela speak Spanish and that most people in Brazil speak Portuguese. But virtually all tests commonly used for the assessment of intelligence place heavy achievement demands on the people tested.

An emphasis on knowledge reflects some views of differences in expert-versus-beginner performance that stress the role of knowledge. For example, William Chase and Herbert Simon (1973) found that a major distinction between expert and beginning chess players was not in the processes they used to play chess, but rather, in the knowledge they brought to chess playing. Similar results have emerged in studies of expert-versus-nonexpert solvers of physics problems (e.g., Chi, Glaser, & Rees, 1982). Indeed, there can be no doubt that differences in knowledge are critical to differences in performance between more and less skilled individuals in a variety of domains. In some domains, the differences in knowledge are obvious. Think about comparing the top particle physicists in the world to people selected at random on a test of knowledge of particle physics! But this difference exists even in domains that are not as obvious, such as creative writing. Surely the critical question for a theorist of intelligence to ask is how these differences in knowledge came to be (e.g., Ericsson, 1996; Ericsson & Smith, 1991; Grabner, Stern, & Neubauer, 2007; Sternberg, 2003).

Certainly, just sheer differences in amounts of experience are not perfectly correlated with levels of expertise. Many people play the piano for many years, but do not become concert-level pianists; chess buffs do not all become grand masters, no matter how often they play. Simply reading a lot does not guarantee a high vocabulary. And the odds are quite good that no matter how much you practice baseball, you will never be as good as the worst player in the major leagues. What seems to be critical is not sheer amount of experience, but rather, what one has been able to learn from that experience (Sternberg et al., 2000).

According to our view, then, both knowledge and the ability to acquire knowledge are important to intelligence, but individual differences in knowledge-acquisition components have priority over individual differences in knowledge. To understand what makes people better at certain things, we must understand first how current individual differences in knowledge evolve from individual differences in the acquisition of that knowledge.

Consider, for example, vocabulary. It is well known that vocabulary is one of the best predictors, if not the single best predictor of overall IQ score (Jensen, 1998, 2006). Yet vocabulary tests are clearly achievement tests. Can the underlying ability tapped by vocabulary tests be measured without giving people what is essentially an achievement test?

There is reason to believe that vocabulary is such a good predictor of intelligence because it indirectly measures people's ability to acquire information in context. Most vocabulary is learned in an everyday context rather than through direct instruction. New words are usually seen for the first time in textbooks, novels, newspapers, lectures, and the like. Smarter people are better able to use the surrounding contexts to figure out the words' meanings. Recently, some enterprising folks have written books that take advantage of this principle by making it even more explicit. Several mystery thrillers and novels (one of the first was *Tooth and Nail: A Novel Approach to the New SAT*; Elster & Elliot, 1994) have been written to help high school students learn SAT vocabulary words. The books work (at least to an extent) as a typical detective story – except that they weave in SAT words in boldface (and define them in the margins).

As the years go by, people who are better at extracting definitions from these contexts acquire the larger vocabularies. Because so much learning, including vocabulary learning, is contextually determined, people's ability to use context to add to their knowledge base is an important skill in intelligent behavior (Sternberg, 1987; Sternberg & Powell, 1983). Later in this book, you will receive instruction in how to better use context to increase your vocabulary. To conclude, an important aspect of intelligence is the set of mental components that are used in learning how to solve problems, in deciding what strategies to use in solving these problems, and in actually solving the problems (Sternberg, 1997, 2006). The first part of the theory of successful intelligence specifies in some detail what these components are. But these components alone are not enough to completely account for intelligence. To understand why, suppose you are at a restaurant and are trying to decide what to order for lunch. Such a decision requires complex componential processing. You need to decide among different possible meals, balancing what you would like with what you can afford – you may love prime rib, but the $24 price tag may stretch your wallet a bit. You also may need to make decisions regarding each of several parts of a given meal. Maybe the meatloaf sounds terrific, but it only comes with mashed potatoes and carrots, and you want to have coleslaw and squash. Deciding on and ordering a meal can be full of information-processing components. Yet individual differences in people's abilities to decide on and order meals are not particularly indicative of individual differences in their levels of intelligence. A theory that specified only such components would seem to be missing something in terms of specifying just what intelligence is. Let us turn now to a consideration of other aspects of intelligence.

Experience and Intelligence

According to the theory of successful intelligence, there are two facets of a person's experience with tasks or situations that are particularly critical to intelligent behavior. These facets are the ability to deal with novel kinds of tasks and situational demands, and the ability to automatize information processing.

Ability to Deal with Novelty

The idea that intelligence involves the ability to deal with novelty is itself far from novel, having been proposed by a number of scientists, such as John Carroll (1993), Raymond Cattell (1971), John Horn (1979, 1994), Kjell Raaheim (1974), and Richard Snow (1979; see also Cronbach & the Stanford Aptitudes Project, 2001), among others. One of us proposed that intelligence involves not merely the ability to learn and reason with new concepts but the ability to learn and reason with new *kinds* of concepts (Sternberg, 1981; Sternberg, 1982; Sternberg, 2003). Intelligence is not only the ability to learn or think in a familiar context or situation but also the ability to learn and think within new contexts and situations, which can then be brought to bear upon already existing knowledge.

It is important to note that task novelty is not the only determinant of its value in measuring this aspect of the theory. An appropriate task should be new and different, but not totally outside a person's past experience. If the task is too novel, then the person will not have any past experience to bring to bear on it, and as a result, the task will simply be outside the person's range of comprehension. Calculus, for example, would he a highly novel field of endeavor for most five-year-olds. But the calculus tasks would be so far outside their range of experience that such tasks would be worthless for the assessment of their intelligence.

Novelty can be a function of the situation as well the task itself. The idea is that people's intelligence is best shown not in run-of-the-mill situations that are encountered every day, but, rather, in extraordinary situations that challenge people's ability to cope with the environment to which they must adapt; think Superman instead of Clark Kent. If, for example, we were to look at Frodo (from *Lord of the Rings*) in his pre-ring, boring hobbit life, then we would not get the true picture of his abilities. Indeed, we all know people who perform well in a familiar setting but who fall apart when presented with similar or even identical tasks in an unfamiliar context. A person who performs well in his or her everyday environment might find it difficult to perform the same tasks if under intense pressure to get them done. Indeed, Fiedler and Link (1994) have reported that intelligence as conventionally defined relates positively with people's leadership effectiveness under conditions of low stress, but *negatively* to their leadership effectiveness under conditions of high stress. In general, some people can perform well only in situations that are highly favorable to their getting their work done. When the environment is less supportive, the quality of their performance is greatly reduced. It is for this reason that performance in one stage of life is often not accurately predictive of performance in another stage of life.

For example, we have found that the performance of students during the time they are in college is only moderately predictive of how well they will do when they graduate and get jobs. In college, as at home, they were in a highly supportive and nurturing environment. But when they get jobs, they often confront harsh, unfamiliar environments, in which they receive much less support than they received in college. As a result, only some of the students who succeeded in college are able to succeed at high levels in their jobs. In sum, then, the ability to deal with novel tasks and situations is an important aspect of intelligence.

The ability to deal with novelty is illustrated particularly well by the processes of *insight*. Insight, which is often characterized by an "aha!" moment in which the solution suddenly hits you, can occur in a wide variety of situations. There are many puzzle books filled with insight problems, which are also sometimes called "lateral thinking problems." For example, imagine that a man orders a cup of coffee. He puts in cream and sugar, takes a sip, and then notices a large dead fly in the cup. He complains to the waiter, who quickly apologizes and takes the cup away. A moment later, the waiter returns with a new cup of coffee. The man takes a sip and begins yelling at the waiter that this cup is simply his old cup of coffee with the fly removed. Why would he think this? (See below for the answer.)[1] For more puzzles like this, see Sloane (1992), among many others.

According to a theory formulated by Janet Davidson and Sternberg (1984; see also Davidson, 1995; Sternberg, 1985), insights are of three kinds: selective encoding, selective combination, and selective comparison.

Selective encoding involves distinguishing irrelevant from relevant information. We are all presented every day with much more information than we can possibly handle. An important task confronting each of us is to select the information that is important for our purposes, and to filter out the information that is not important. Selective encoding is the process by which this filtering is done. Consider, for example, a particularly significant example of selective encoding in science, the unusual means by which Sir Alexander Fleming discovered penicillin. Fleming was performing an experiment that involved growing (or "culturing") bacteria in a petri dish – a little glass or plastic dish that contains a gelatin in which bacteria grow easily. Unfortunately, from some points of view, the culture was spoiled: A mold grew within the culture and killed the bacteria. A lesser scientist would have bemoaned the failure of the experiment and promised to do a better job next time. Fleming, however, noticed that the mold had killed the bacteria, a discovery that provided the basis for his discovery of the important antibiotic, penicillin.

Selective encoding can happen in day-to-day problem solving as well. Consider the following question: A rooster is sitting on the roof of a house. The roof is the shape

---

[1] He tasted the cream and sugar that he had added earlier.

of a perfect isosceles triangle, with two sides of equal length, and with a large chimney on the left side. There is a gutter seven inches long on the right side, and a smaller gutter three inches long on the left side. If the rooster lays an egg, what side would it roll down, the left or the right? (See below for the answer.)[2]

Insights of *selective combination* involve taking selectively encoded information and combining it in a novel but productive way. Often, it is not enough just to identify the important information for solving a problem. One also must figure out how to put it together. Consider a famous example of what might be called a selective-combination insight, the formulation of the theory of evolution. The information on which Darwin drew to formulate this theory had been available to him and others for a long time. What had eluded Darwin and his contemporaries was how this information could be combined so as to account for observed changes in species. Darwin finally saw how to combine the available information, and thus was born the theory of natural selection.

Again, selective combination can occur on a day-to-day basis. Imagine getting dressed in the morning. You listen to the weather report and find out that it is going to be a warm and sunny day. You look at your calendar and see that it is St. Patrick's Day. Based on the weather report, you pick out an outfit on a T-shirt and shorts. Keeping in mind that it is St. Patrick's Day and wanting to celebrate the Irish, you select a green T-shirt (you probably don't have green shorts). You have used selective combination to decide what to wear.

Insights of *selective comparison* involve novel relating of new information to old information. Creative analogies involve selective comparison. In important problems, we almost always need to bring old knowledge to bear on the solution of new problems, and to relate new knowledge to old knowledge. Insights of selective comparison are the basis for this relating. A famous example of an insight of selective comparison is Kekulé's discovery of the structure of benzene. Kekulé had been seeking this structure for some time, but without success. One night, he dreamed that he was watching a snake dancing around and around. Finally, the snake bit its tail. When Kekulé arose, he realized that the image of the snake biting its tail formed the geometric shape for the structure of the benzene ring.

To sum up, the ability to deal with novelty is a crucial one in intelligence, and one of several ways to measure it is through the assessment of insightful problem solving. The processes of selective encoding, selective combination, and selective comparison form three of many bases for dealing with relatively novel kinds of tasks and situations.

Ability to Automatize Information Processing

Many tasks requiring complex information processing seem so intricate that it is a wonder we can perform them at all. Consider reading, for example. The number and complexity of operations involved in reading is staggering, and what is more staggering is the rate at which these operations are performed. Being able to do something as

---

[2] Roosters don't lay eggs. This is an example of unneeded information – everything about the roof and house was not used in the solution of the problem.

complex as reading would seem to be possible only because a substantial proportion of the operations required are *automatized* – that is, done without conscious thought – and thus require minimal mental effort. Other kinds of behavior that are automatized in greater or lesser degree are riding a bicycle, driving a car, and signing your name. Think, for example, about brushing your teeth. Are you thinking, "Okay, first I'm going to brush my back molar, I'm brushing my back molar, now back and forth on the side molar, up and down on the front teeth," and so on? Probably not! You are more likely to be thinking about what you have to do that day, planning what you're having for lunch, or wondering if that mole on your chin is getting bigger. You are able to multitask because brushing your teeth has become automatic. However, it is likely that a three-year-old just learning to brush her teeth is indeed thinking through the series of events as such.

Deficiencies in reading have been thought to result in large part because these operations are not automatized properly.

The proposal being made here is that complex tasks can be carried out only because many of the relevant operations have been automatized. Failure to automatize such operations, whether fully or in part, results in a breakdown of information processing and as a result less intelligent task performance. Intellectual operations that can be performed smoothly and automatically by more intelligent individuals are performed only haltingly and under conscious control by less intelligent individuals. In sum, more able people can automatize information processing unusually efficiently and effectively.

Relationship between the Ability to Cope with Relative Novelty and the Ability to Automatize

For many (but probably not all) kinds of tasks, the ability to deal with novelty and to automatize information processing may occur along a continuum based on experience. When people first encounter a task or kind of situation, their ability to deal with relative novelty comes into play. More intelligent people will be able to cope with the novel demands being made on them more rapidly and fully. For example, on their first day in a foreign country, tourists almost always have to make various kinds of adjustments to the demands of an unfamiliar culture. Their intelligence is called on in dealing with these unusual demands. The fewer resources needed to process the novelty of a given task or situation, the more the resources left over to automatize performance. In addition, more efficient automatization leaves additional resources for dealing with novel tasks and situations. In the example of the foreign country, the less attention tourists must devote to handling new kinds of stimulation, the more attention they have left over for dealing with the complexities that confront them. Thus, it is easier for an American who speaks only English to change money in England than in France, because the individual does not have to cope, in England, with a new language as well as with a new currency.

As a result, novelty and automatization trade off with each other. The more efficient the person is at one, the more resources left over for the other. As your experience with a given task or situation increases, the novelty decreases. The task or situation will then become less appropriate as a measure of the ability to cope with relative novelty. However, after some amount of practice with the task or in the situation, automatization skills may come into play, in which case the task will start to become an appropriate measure of automatization skill. For example, e-mail became popular when one of the authors was in college. For the first several months, he learned all the different commands – how to look up e-mail addresses, how to copy someone on an e-mail, and so on. After a while, it wasn't new anymore, and he didn't have to spend five minutes making sure he didn't send an e-mail to his entire address book. The task was no longer a good measure of how well he coped to relative novelty. After another several months, however, it became automatic – the author no longer had to use any significant resources on the basics of sending an e-mail. Now, e-mail use could be used to measure his skill at automatization. Not everything will be automatized after time. For example, this author's mother still spends several minutes sending each e-mail to make sure it isn't deleted instead of mailed.

The experiential view suggests one reason why it is so exceedingly difficult to compare levels of intelligence fairly across members of different sociocultural groups. Even if a given test requires the same components of performance for members of the various groups, it is extremely unlikely to be equivalent in terms of its relative novelty and the degree to which performance has been automatized before the examinees took the test.

Consider, for example, nonverbal reasoning tests, requiring skills such as analogy solution. As originally measured in the Binet and Wechsler scales, differences between members of various sociocultural groups are actually greater on these tests than they are on the verbal tests that the nonverbal tests were designed to replace (see Sternberg, 1985).

But traditional nonverbal tests are still commonly used in both research and practice. And, contrary to the claims that have often been made for them, the tests are *not* culture-fair, and they are certainly not culture-free. Individuals who have been brought up in a test-taking culture are likely to have had much more experience with these kinds of items than are individuals not brought up in such a culture. No test is culture-fair. For example, a test of selecting natural herbal medicines to fight off parasitic illnesses might measure intelligence in rural Kenya, but it would not measure intelligence in the United States (Sternberg, Nokes, Geissler, Prince, Okatcha, Bundy, & Grigorenko, 2001): The knowledge is important for adaptation in the rural Kenyan environment but not in the United States.

As a result, the test items will be less novel and more automatized for members of test-taking cultures than of other cultures. Even if the processes used to get a solution are the same, the degrees of novelty and automatization will be different. Hence, the tests will not be measuring the same thing across populations. As useful as the tests may be for within-group comparisons, between-group comparisons may be deceptive and unfair. A fair comparison between groups would require comparable degrees of novelty and automatization of test items as well as comparable processes and strategies.

In sum, a task is particularly related to intelligence when it draws on coping with novelty and automatization of performance. It is not enough merely to specify a set of processes involved in intelligence. Consider, again, selecting lunch from a menu at a restaurant. Such a selection process involves a wide variety of components of various kinds. For example, we need to decide what meal to eat, whether or not to have dessert, and if we are to have dessert, whether we should order less of a main course or skip the appetizer, and so on. Yet even though the task of deciding on a meal may be full of components of cognition, it does not seem to be a particularly good index of individual differences in intelligence. People who are very good at making the best meal choices are not necessarily smarter than people who can't make up their mind. The reason is that this task involves neither novelty nor the development of automatization. It is a task that is just not very interesting from the standpoint of individual differences in intelligence.

THE CONTEXT OF INTELLIGENCE

The theory of successful intelligence defines intelligence in context as *mental activity used toward the adaptation to, shaping of, and selection of real-world environments relevant to one's life* (Sternberg, 1985; Sternberg, 1999; Sternberg, 2006). Consider just what this definition means.

Intelligence is defined in terms of mental activity underlying behavior in real-world environments that are *relevant* to one's life (Sternberg, 2004a). We could not legitimately assess the intelligence of an African Pygmy by placing a Pygmy in a North American culture and using North American tests, unless it were relevant to test the Pygmy for survival in a North American culture and we wished to assess the Pygmy's intelligence in *this culture* (as, for example, if the Pygmy happened to live in such a culture and had to adapt to it). Similarly, a North American's intelligence cannot legitimately be assessed in terms of his or her adaptation to Pygmy society unless adaptation to that society were relevant to the person's life. Moreover, intelligence is *purposive*. It is directed toward goals, however vague or subconscious these goals may be.

Adaptation

Intelligence involves *adaptation* to one's environment. Indeed, definitions of intelligence have traditionally viewed intelligence in terms of adaptation to the environment, but intelligence tests usually do not measure or account for adaptive skills. Consider some examples.

Seymour Sarason, a famous psychologist once described his first job experience (Sarason, personal communication, 1975). His job was to administer a standardized intelligence test to students at an institution for learners with special educational needs. In those days, the students were essentially confined. When Sarason arrived on the scene, he found himself with nothing to do. A number of students had just planned and successfully executed an escape from the school. Eventually, they were rounded up and brought back to Sarason for testing. Sarason gave them the Porteus

Mazes Test, an intelligence test that was, decades ago, deemed appropriate for slow learners. To his surprise and dismay, most of the students were not able to solve even the first problem correctly. It became obvious to him, as perhaps it does to you now, that whatever it is the test measures, it was not the mental skills involved in the successful planning (although only partially successful implementation) of the escape. Clearly, some kind of intelligence or ability not measured by the test was involved in the planning of the break.

Another relevant example comes from Robert Edgerton's (1967) book *The Cloak of Competence*. In this book, Edgerton describes the lives of retarded persons released from institutional settings. In particular, he describes some of the adaptive strategies such people use to make their lives easier. For example, one strategy used by a man who could not tell time was to wear a watch that did not work. In the street he would then look at his watch, pretend to notice that it did not tell the correct time, and then say to a stranger something like, "Excuse me, but I notice my watch isn't working. Could you tell me the correct time?" Again, the ingenuity involved in the broken-watch maneuver implies some form of intelligence. At the same time, we could not call such a man highly intelligent, if only because his inability to tell time is a fact that must be considered in its own right.

Adaptive requirements can differ widely from one culture to another (Sternberg, 2003; Sternberg, 2004a; Sternberg, 2004b; Sternberg & Grigorenko, 2004). For example, we found in one study that rural Kenyans emphasize social-competence skills much more than do North American in their conceptions of intelligence (Grigorenko et al., 2001). Even in the United States, certain cultures, such as Latinos, tend to emphasize social-competence skills more than do other cultures, such as Anglos (Okagaki & Sternberg, 1993).

In a similar vein, North Americans often show off how intelligent they are, whereas Taiwanese Chinese appear to distinguish more between situations that call for one to parade one's intelligence and situations that call for one to conceal it (Yang & Sternberg, 1997). One tactic that con men often use is appearing to be dumb and seeming as though they are easy to fool. People don't realize that the con man is actually quite bright until they have lost their money.

Attempts to impose American concepts of intelligence on a new culture can result in a disaster. Consider, for example, a salient difference between U.S. and Venezuelan cultures. In the United States, time is of the essence, and speed is considered an extremely important part of everyday life. Meetings, college classes, and appointments typically start on time. Although lateness is tolerated in some settings, such as parties, the normal expectation is for people to be prompt. Indeed, at one of the meetings at which one of us recounted the following anecdote, the moderator of the meeting attempted to start the meeting early – a full five minutes before it was scheduled to begin!

Venezuelans and members of many other cultures (including a number of those found in South America and Africa) do not place the same premium on time, nor do they even seem to have the same notions about it. This fact was illustrated to one of us quite dramatically when he went to a meeting on the nature of intelligence held in Venezuela. The meeting was scheduled to begin at 8:00 A.M. on the first day. The author was miffed, as he had arrived tired and had no great desire to wake up for an 8:00 meeting. Nevertheless, he arrived there on time, as did four other people – the only North Americans attending the meeting. Only the North Americans seemed to have even considered the possibility that the meeting would start on time. In fact, it did not start until around 9:30, a full hour and a half after it had been scheduled to begin. This tardiness in starting meetings, as well as in other aspects of everyday life, is common throughout Venezuela as well as other cultures. To be on time for meetings or appointments in these cultures can actually be a sign of poor adaptation, in that most likely there are other things one would rather do than sit around and wait for the meeting to begin. To North Americans, perhaps, this widespread lateness would seem to be maladaptive or even unintelligent. However, in Venezuela, it is quite adaptive and the only sensible way to behave there. In fact, the author asked a Venezuelan about this matter, and she readily admitted that Venezuelans tend to be late. However, she also noted that once they start, Venezuelans are fully ready to engage in the task at hand and are less likely than North Americans to take time out for coffee breaks or idle conversation. And indeed, in the United States, one often finds that even if meetings do start on time, there is a substantial lag until people are really geared up for the meeting, and the starting time is often followed rather soon by coffee or other breaks. What is adaptive may vary from one culture to another.

Differences in what is considered adaptive behavior in various cultures can be seen in the domain of intelligence testing as well as in everyday life. A particularly noteworthy instance of this fact derives from an anecdote told by Joe Glick. Glick and his colleagues (Cole et al., 1971) were studying the cognitive performance of members of the Kpelle tribe in Liberia. One of the tasks they used was a sorting task, in which the participants were given cards with either words or pictures on them and asked to sort the items in a sensible way.

According to U.S. standards, the intelligent and more developmentally advanced way of sorting is by taxonomic category. In other words, if you're given cards that show pictures of an apple, banana, bear, bicycle, car, dog, goat, grape, motorcycle, and strawberry, the intelligent way of sorting is considered to be in terms of categories (fruits, animals, and vehicles). Indeed, in Piaget's theory as well, use of taxonomic categorization is considered more advanced than use of other kinds of categorization, such as functional categorization – using the item's function as the main principle (i.e., things to eat, things to sit on, etc.).

The same principle applies to defining words. So, for example, on the Stanford-Binet and the Wechsler Intelligence Tests, more credit is given for higher order, taxonomic definitions than is given for functional definitions. If asked to define *car*, the participant is given more credit for the definition "a vehicle for transportation" than for a definition such as "uses gas" or "rides along streets."

When Glick asked the Kpelle to sort, he found that the adults uniformly preferred a functional sorting to a taxonomic one. A less able investigator (and many do just this) would have stopped there and simply concluded that the Kpelle are less intelligent than Americans. Indeed, it is a common finding in cross-cultural research that members of other cultures perform less well on standard kinds of intelligence tests than do members of U.S. culture or European cultures. But Glick did not stop there. Rather, he persisted in trying to get the Kpelle to sort taxonomically. At first, he was unsuccessful. Finally, in desperation, he asked them to sort the way stupid people would. At this point, the Kpelle had no difficulty at all in sorting taxonomically. The point is that their conception of what constituted an intelligent basis for this sorting differed from the standard U.S. one. What was adaptive in their culture and what is adaptive in most of Europe and the Americas were quite different. Thus, the standard test was not measuring adaptation relative to Kpelle norms, but relative to U.S. norms.

Environmental Selection

As we have seen, adaptation is an important part of intelligent behavior as it occurs in context. However, contextually appropriate intelligence does not stop with adaptation. There may be instances in which, in a sense, it is actually maladaptive to be adaptive. For example, our values may not correspond to the values of the environment we are in – perhaps a business where the values are too cutthroat for our taste, or perhaps a larger setting, such as a country. For example, it would be hard to argue that adaptation was the most intelligent course of action for people living in Nazi Germany. Similarly, you may someday find that your interests are not well represented by your environment. Maybe you have an utterly boring job that offers you no challenge, or perhaps the students you are friends with in college do things that go against your moral values (such as drugs or excessively listening to bad 80's music). In such a case, it is not necessarily intelligent to adapt to the demands of that particular job or these particular friends. The point is that there are instances in which the more contextually intelligent thing to do may be to *de*select the environment you are in and to *re*select a different environment, a process that can be referred to as *environmental selection*. Such a process may involve leaving one job for another, one spouse for another, or one country for another.

Knowing when to quit is every bit as important as knowing when to persist. For example, in science, researchers inevitably encounter any number of dead ends that are unfruitful for further research. Scientists can waste years of their careers attempting to follow up on these dead ends. This is a no-win strategy. The intelligent scientist, as well as the intelligent person in any other field of endeavor, has to know when to quit as well as when to start. How many of you have kept attempting to ask out or be in a relationship with someone who clearly was not interested? How much time was wasted before you "got the hint"?

Consider how environmental selection can operate in the career choices of individuals, and particularly of seemingly gifted individuals. A rather poignant set of real-world examples is provided by Ruth Feldman (1982) in *Whatever Happened to the Quiz Kids?* The Quiz Kids – on both radio and, later, television – were selected for a number of intellectual and personal traits. All or almost all of them had exceptionally high IQs, typically well over 140 [and in some cases in excess of 200]. Yet Feldman's book shows how much less distinguished the Quiz Kids' later lives have been than their earlier lives – in many cases, even by their own standards. There are undoubtedly many possible reasons for these less-than-impressive later careers, including so-called regression effects, by which extreme performance earlier on tends to be followed by less extreme performance later on. An example of this change occurs when most students who got very high grades on a midterm will score a little lower on the next test, whereas those who received very poor grades will likely do a little better.

But what is striking in biography after biography is that the Quiz Kids who were most successful were those who found what they were good at and were interested in, and then pursued these things relentlessly (see also Amabile, 1996; Sternberg & Lubart, 1995a). The less successful ones had difficulty finding any one thing that interested them, and several floundered while trying to find a niche for themselves.

Environmental Shaping

Intelligence also involves mental activity in *shaping* the environment, a tactic we use when our attempts to adapt to a given environment fail, or when it is impractical, inadmissible, or premature to select a new environment. For example, we may be committed by religious beliefs to the permanence of marriage, and therefore see divorce as an unrealistic alternative. In such a case, we may attempt to reshape our environment so as to improve the fit between us and the environment. The marital partner may attempt to restructure the marriage; the employee may try to convince the boss to see or do things differently; the citizen may try to change the government, through either violent or nonviolent means. In each case, however, they attempt to change the environment so as to improve their fit to the environment, rather than merely trying to adapt to what is already there.

What this means is that there may be no one set of behaviors that is "intelligent" for everyone, in that people can adjust to their environments in different ways. Whereas the components of intelligent behavior are very likely universal, the way they can be used to construct environmentally appropriate behavior is likely to vary – not only across groups, but even across individuals. What does seem to be common among people who master their environments is the ability to capitalize on their strengths and to compensate for their weaknesses. Successful people are able not only to adapt well to their environments but also to actually modify the environments they are in so as to make the best fit between their environment and their adaptive skills.

What is it, for example, that distinguishes the "stars" in any field from the rest of the also-rans? Of course, this question is broad enough to be the topic of a book, and many books have in fact been written on the topic. But for our present purpose, the distinguishing characteristics we should note are (a) at least one very well-developed skill, and (b) an extraordinary ability to capitalize on that skill or skills in one's work. For example, if you were to generate a short list of stars in your own environment (e.g., the best student in the class, the best employee at work), the chances are that they do not share any single ability, as traditionally defined. Rather, each has a talent or set of talents that they make the most of in their work or at school. At the same time, they (c) recognize their weaknesses and (d) minimize the significance of skills in which they are poor, either by delegating tasks requiring those skills to others or by structuring their tasks in such a way that those skills are not required.

Our own list of stars, for example, includes a person with extraordinary spatial visualization skills, a person with a talent for coming up with the counterintuitive but true, and a person who has an extraordinary sense of where events are leading. These three particular persons (and others on our list) share little in terms of what sets them apart, aside from at least one extraordinary talent on which they capitalize fully in their work. Although they are also highly intelligent in the traditional sense, so are many others who never reach the height of accomplishment.

SUCCESSFUL INTELLIGENCE AND INTELLIGENCE TESTS

Where does this theory leave us with regard to existing intelligence tests? No existing test measures all or even most of the skills that have been discussed in this chapter. Indeed, to the extent that intelligence follows the theory that we have proposed, there is no one, wholly appropriate test. Whereas it might be possible to construct tests of componential skills that would apply to quite broad ranges of individuals, tests of skills measuring contextual fit would almost certainly apply to fewer people. Recent IQ tests have made great strides over the last two decades in treating intelligence as a more complex, multifaceted concept. Although they are based on alternative theories, the overriding desire to measure intelligence by tapping into a wide range of abilities and skills is, we believe, at least a step in the right direction.

The ideal instrument for assessing intelligence would probably be one that combines measurements of different kinds that together take into account the considerations above. No one measure or combination of measures would yield a definitive IQ, because any one instrument can work for only some people some of the time. Moreover, it is unclear that any single index can do justice to the variety of skills that constitute the basis for the theory of successful intelligence. A single index would be more likely to mask than to reveal a person's levels and patterns of abilities, and would likely be variable across people within and between sociocultural groups.

It may occur to you to wonder whether, given the seeming fallibility of the IQ test, we should simply stop using tests altogether? The answer depends on what is meant by "using tests." The historical way of using tests – getting one set number to serve as an IQ, and then allowing that number to determine a person's possible future – should be stopped, we believe. There has been a long and dangerous tradition of IQ tests being used for unintended purposes and intentionally or unintentionally favoring different groups based on the narrow definition of intelligence being considered.

But intelligence tests are being used in many different ways today. It is important to distinguish the historical and traditional uses for intelligence tests from some of the newer uses today. To most current practitioners, intelligence tests are more often thought of as cognitive-ability tests because the emphasis has shifted from a focus on global scores (one or more IQs) to scores on anywhere from four to seven cognitive abilities. The current emphasis of test developers and practitioners is to identify and understand children's and adults' strengths and weaknesses in diverse aspects of cognitive ability, *not* to determine where they stand on some measure of "g" (a generalized intelligence).

David Wechsler's system (see Chapter 1) was always organized by the *content* of the tasks (i.e., verbal or nonverbal). Today's tests are organized by the *processes* and *abilities* that the separate scales measure. And that shift from content to process defines the recent versions of Wechsler's scales as well as the newer breed of tests that have sprung up in the past two decades. With the emphasis on profiles of scores on reliable measures of separate abilities, instead of on a small number of global IQs, practitioners are looking to translate test scores to meaningful interventions, not simply to identify the person's level of functioning. These shifts from content to process and from passive classification to action affect how tests are used at all ages and all levels of ability. Appropriate use of cognitive tests for learning-disabilities assessment, for example, requires examiners to identify the person's processing deficits along with cognitive strengths, and to translate those strengths to educational intervention.

Similarly, IQ tests of today are used to identify how to develop the best teaching strategies for preschool children identified as "high risk"; to identify strong and weak areas of functioning in adults diagnosed with Alzheimer's or other types of dementia, to permit caregivers to capitalize on the strengths while helping them compensate for their weaknesses; to relate cognitive profiles of those with known or suspected neurological impairment to specific areas of the brain that might have been damaged, and to plan rehabilitation accordingly; and, in general, to use the results of a multi-scale test of general cognitive ability – whether the WISC-IV, WAIS-III, Stanford Binet 5, WJ-III, KABC-II, or CAS – in a way to that helps answer the reasons for referral in a dynamic, active, insightful way.

Why are single IQ scores still used at all? There is a dangerous allure to exact numbers. An IQ score of 119, an SAT score of 580, a mental-abilities score in the seventy-fourth percentile – these all sound very precise. Indeed, people tend to value accurate-sounding information highly, almost without regard to its validity. But the appearance of precision is not a substitute for validity. Indeed, a test may be precise in its measurements without distinguishing the more from the less intelligent. If we decide to measure your intelligence by counting how many body piercings you have, we will get a very exact measure. That doesn't make it a good measure of intelligence.

When one of us worked one summer at the Psychological Corporation, distributor of the Miller Analogies Test (a widely used test for graduate admissions and financial aid decisions), we heard what we considered then, and still consider, an amazing story: A teachers' college in Mississippi required a score of twenty-five on the Miller test for admission. The use of this cutoff was questionable, to say the least, in that twenty-five represents a chance score on this test. A promising student was admitted to the college despite a sub-twenty-five Miller score, and went through the program with distinction. When it came time for the student to receive a diploma, she was informed that the diploma would be withheld until she could take the test and receive a score of at least twenty-five. Consider the logic here: A test is designed to be a predictor of future success. The future success is the criteria – what the test is trying to help predict.

And yet here, the predictor had somehow come to surpass the criteria in importance! The test had become an end rather than a means.

One of us told this pathetic story to a large meeting of teachers of the gifted, showing them how bad things could be. Afterward, a teacher came up to the author and told him an essentially identical story (except for a higher cutoff score) as it pertained to her own quite reputable university.

That this kind of thinking is not limited to isolated cases is shown by the fact that we have encountered personally, and heard about countless times, similar experiences at many different universities. Consider, for example, the cases of applicants to graduate (and often, undergraduate) programs with stellar credentials except for marginal test scores. In our experience, these applicants receive a "full and open discussion" of their credentials, and then they are rejected. Often, admissions decision makers know in their heart, right from the beginning of the discussion, that the decision will be negative. As a result, the discussion seems more to help reduce their feelings of guilt at going with test scores than anything else. These negative decisions are particularly frustrating when the applicants have shown excellent competence at the criterion task (in our profession, psychological research) and yet are rejected on the basis of test scores that are at best highly, imperfect predictors of performance.

When this happens, the means becomes the end. People stop using the test as a guide, a predictor, or a useful tool – they use it as a standard and end goal. Then the test has become more important than the performance it is supposed to predict. When criterion information is unavailable or scarce, test scores can serve a very useful function. People who might otherwise be denied admission to programs on the basis of inadequate evidence may be admitted because their test scores show them capable of high-level performance. Indeed, the original purpose of the SATs was to fight against the "old boys" network that was common in the top schools, in which money and family history were the most important admission qualifications.

But when criterion information is already available, such achievement or intelligence tests may be unneeded, or even hurtful. The criterion information in these cases should receive the lion's share of attention in making decisions about future performance. It is worth pointing out that in most cases, the test is not the thing at fault. Few IQ or educational test developers would argue that their test should be considered more important than real-life information (such as success in psychological research). It is the often ill-informed administrators and policy makers who misuse the tests. A hammer can be a marvelous tool and can help build houses – or it can be used to hit someone on the head and kill them. If someone misuses the hammer, it's not always the hammer's fault.

We have developed a test (Sternberg & the Rainbow Project Collaborators, 2006) that assesses the three aspects of intelligence in high school seniors and college students. We found that, when it is used as a supplement to the SAT, it doubles prediction of freshman grades and substantially reduces ethnic-group differences among groups. The original version of this test is administered as a timed, high-stakes test, but we also have a version that can be administered through essays on a take-home basis (Sternberg, 2007b). The point is that it is possible to measure analytical, creative, and practical abilities in a way that enhances prediction of success and that decreases differences across groups.

SUMMING UP

To sum up, this chapter has briefly outlined a theory of successful intelligence. The theory comprises three "subtheories": a componential subtheory, which relates intelligence to the internal world of the individual; an experiential subtheory, which relates intelligence to both the external and the internal worlds of the individual; and a contextual subtheory, which relates intelligence to the external world of the individual. The componential subtheory specifies the mental mechanisms responsible for planning, carrying out, and evaluating intelligent behavior. The experiential subtheory expands on this definition by focusing on those important behaviors that involves either adjustment to relative novelty, automatization of information processing, or both. The contextual subtheory defines intelligent behavior as involving purposeful adaptation to, selection of, and shaping of real-world environments relevant to one's life.

An important issue concerns the combination rule for the abilities specified by the three subtheories. How does the intelligence of a person who is average in the abilities specified by all three subtheories compare to the intelligence of a person who is gifted in some abilities but low in others? Or what can be said of the intelligence of a person whose environmental opportunities are so restricted that he or she is unable to adapt to, shape, or select the environment, such as a child growing up with abusive parents? There seems little point in specifying any combination rule at all, in that no single formula for intelligence is likely to be very useful. Different people may be more or less intelligent through different patterns of abilities. In the first case above, the two individuals are quite different in their patterns of abilities, and an overall index will hide this fact.

In the second case, it may not be possible to obtain any meaningful measurement at all from the person's functioning in his or her environment. Consider, as further examples, the comparison between (a) a person who is very adept at componential functioning and thus likely to score well on standard intelligence and achievement tests, but who is lacking in insight, or more generally, in the ability to cope well with novel kinds of tasks or situations versus (b) a person who is very insightful but not particularly adept at testlike componential operations. The first person might come across to people as smart but not terribly creative, the second as creative but not terribly smart. Although it might well be possible to obtain some average score on componential abilities and abilities to deal with novel tasks and situations, such a composite would obscure the critical differences between the two individuals. Or consider a person who is both componentially adept and insightful, but who at the same time makes little effort to fit into the environment in which he or she lives. An intelligence test that overly punished this person for poor adaptive skills and as a result gave a low overall score would not be very meaningful.

The point to be made, then, is that intelligence is not a single thing: It comprises a very wide array of cognitive and other skills. Our goal in theory, research, and measurement ought to be to define what these skills are and to learn how best to assess and possibly to train them, not to figure out how to combine them into a single number that sheds no light on these complexities.

In the next section of this book, you will encounter a variety of exercises for increasing your intellectual skills along the lines suggested by all three subtheories of the theory of successful intelligence. The exercises in this book cover the broad range of cognitive and other skills specified by this theory. We hope you learn from them!

3

Metacognition: Thinking with Metacomponents

A colleague of ours was about to take a trip to California. He had his plane reservation all set. In order to get to the airport in New York City, he would take a limousine from New Haven, Connecticut. The colleague woke up late; concerned that he would miss the limousine and therefore the plane, he rushed to get ready to leave. Because the limousine makes stops along the way to the airport, and as a result takes a while to reach the airport, it was necessary to get to the limousine terminal well before the plane departed. He packed quickly, realizing that he was probably forgetting some of the things he would need for the trip. But he had no time to reflect on what he would and would not need. After he had packed, he jumped into his car and rushed over to the limousine terminal. Because he was traveling during the morning rush hour, his progress in driving to the limousine terminal was slow. To make things worse, he seemed to hit every red light, and there was construction on one of the roads, slowing down traffic. He arrived at the limousine terminal just as the limousine was pulling out. The colleague was extremely agitated that he had missed the limousine, but saw nothing he could do. The next limousine would not leave for another hour, and it would arrive at the airport too late for him to make the airplane. He waited for that limousine anyway, even though he did miss his plane and had to take the next one out.

This anecdote provides an almost classic example of poor planning, which in this instance led to a failure to accomplish a goal. Had it not been for a string of poor planning decisions, the colleague easily could have made his plane. First, he could have packed the night before his departure, so that he would not have to spend his time in the morning rushing to get his things together. Second, he could have set an alarm clock or been more careful to wake up on time so that he would not have been rushed and risked missing his limousine. Third, he could have planned out a route to the limousine terminal that would minimize the number of traffic lights and the amount of traffic, and would avoid road construction. Fourth, when he missed his limousine, he could have considered other possibilities than merely waiting for the next limousine. For example, he might have driven rapidly to the next limousine stop and picked up the limousine there. Or he could have driven to the airport and parked there. Although this would have added some minor expense to the cost of the trip, he could have made his plane. Finally, he could have checked into the possibility of a commuter flight from New Haven to the New York airport. There was, in fact, such a flight that he could have taken that would have gotten him to the airport on time.

This anecdote illustrates the importance of planning and decision making in everyday intelligence. Good planning and decision making, as well as accurate evaluation of one's actions, can lead to a variety of positive and satisfying outcomes. Poor planning and decision making, or the failure adequately to evaluate one's course of action, can lead to dissatisfaction and a string of negative outcomes. What is sometimes referred to as "executive information processing" proves to be an important part of everyone's intelligence.

As you will remember from Chapter 2, *metacomponents* are the metacognitive or executive processes used in planning, monitoring, and evaluating problem solving and performance. Metacomponents are an essential ingredient of intelligence, and any effort to improve our intelligence must necessarily involve metacomponential skills. What are these skills? This chapter presents some of the most important ones.

DEFINING THE NATURE OF A PROBLEM

Consider the anecdote above about our colleague missing his plane. He could have made his plane had he redefined the problem facing him. From beginning to end, he defined his problem as one of reaching the limousine terminal in time for him to take a limousine to the airport. Had he redefined the problem as one of finding a way – any way – to reach the airport so that he could make his plane, he might have considered transportation alternatives other than the limousine. But by considering only the limousine, he lost the opportunity to arrive on time.

Another even more commonplace example of the dangers of inadequate definition of the nature of the problem derives from Shirley Heath's account of life in "Roadville," a town in the Piedmont Carolinas of the United States. Heath (1983) describes how the residents of the town often find themselves, like many others, without sufficient money to make ends meet. When they find themselves with inadequate funds, they view their problem as one of finding more money in order to pay their bills. Often they will look for second and even third jobs in order to obtain the needed funds. Curiously, they seem not to consider the possibility of reducing their spending, and thereby decreasing their need for funds. Thus, they define their problem as one of insufficient funds rather than as one of overspending. By redefining their problem, they could achieve their goal of making ends meet, without overtaxing themselves.

The unhappy consequences of a poor definition of a problem can be seen in the political arena as well as in private life. In 1972, a group of men broke into the Democratic National Committee headquarters at the Watergate complex in Washington, DC. To this day, it is not known exactly why the break-in took place. When members of the Nixon administration started receiving details regarding the break-in, they viewed their problem as one of containing and covering up the situation as much as possible. As more and more information about the break-in leaked out, the members of the Nixon political team made increasingly useless efforts to prevent disclosure of unpleasant and embarrassing facts. Eventually, the cover-up became considerably more of a problem than even the break-in had been. By defining their problem as one of covering up the break-in rather than as one of providing full disclosure in a minimally harmful way, the campaign committee seriously reduced tile credibility of the Nixon administration and Nixon eventually found himself obliged to resign. More recently, both the Clinton and Bush (Jr.) administrations have apparently covered up some of the errors they made, largely unsuccessfully, although of course we do not know what may have been covered up successfully

The effects of inadequate definition of problems can be seen strikingly in some psychological investigations. For example, one of the authors (Sternberg & Rifkin, 1979), asked children in grades 2, 4, and 6, as well as college students, to solve pictorial analogies. In these analogy problems, items were presented in the form A is to B as C is to D_1, or D_2, where D_1, and D_2 are two alternative answer options. We were interested in how many analogies children at the different grade levels could solve correctly.

We encountered an unwelcome surprise when we attempted to score the test booklets of some of the second graders. Rather than circling either the first or the second of the two answer options, as the instructions had indicated they should, some of these children had circled either the first term or the second term (A or B) of the analogy. At first, this strategy seemed to make no sense at all, and we had no idea why these children had circled one of the first two terms rather than one of the answer options. We soon found out. The children in the experiment were elementary school students at a Jewish day school. At this school, instruction was typically in English in the morning and in Hebrew in the afternoon. As a result, the children were accustomed to reading in a left-to-right fashion in the morning, and in a right-to-left fashion in the afternoon. What some of these children had done was to inappropriately transfer their right-to-left reading behavior to the analogy problem, which, in fact, had been administered during the afternoon. In other words, they had defined the problem in a way that was appropriate to their usual afternoon activity – reading Hebrew – but in a way that was inappropriate for the analogy-solving activity.

IMPROVING YOUR DEFINITION OF THE NATURE OF A PROBLEM

You can do several things to improve the ways in which you define problems. When you are confronted with a problem that you are having difficulty solving, consider the following strategies that may help you to redefine the problem in a better way:

1. *Reread or reconsider the question.* In certain kinds of problems, such as mathematical word problems, you will be given some background information and then asked a question that requires you to use this background information in order to reach a solution to the problem. If you misread the question, you will often find it impossible to solve the problem. Even if a solution is reached, it is to a different

Some of the classic problems in psychology are difficult because people tend to misdefine their nature. These problems highlight the importance of correctly defining a problem to intelligent performance. Consider three such problems.

THE NINE-DOT PROBLEM

Figure 3–1 contains nine dots arrayed three by three. The "nine-dot problem" is simply stated:

> Your task is to connect all nine dots with a set of line segments. You must never lift your pencil off the page, and you must not use more than four lines. See if you can connect the nine dots with a series of line segments without ever taking your pencil off the page. After you have tried the problem, only then look at the solution (Figure 3–6) at the end of the chapter. Do not read on until you have tried the problem.

Figure 3–1. The Nine Dot Problem

As you can now see, the nine-dot problem can be solved. However, people find it extremely difficult to arrive at the solution, and most never do, no matter how hard they try. An examination of the solution reveals why. Most people assume that the lines must he kept within the confines of the square formed by the nine dots. They do not allow their solution to extend beyond the boundaries of the dots, even though there is nothing in the problem that even suggests this constraint. Nevertheless, most people assume that it exists. Perhaps years of being told not to color outside the lines have made most people unwilling to make that leap.

The problem cannot be solved with four lines restricted to the interior of the figure. In other words, by placing an unnecessary and unwarranted constraint on themselves, people make the problem unsolvable. This problem provides a classic example of how defining a problem in a poor way can reduce, and in this case eliminate, the chances of finding a solution to the problem. Unfortunately, people do this all the time, as the nine-dot problem shows. Of course, simply knowing that you can go outside the borders does not solve the nine-dot problem; to the contrary, it still remains a challenge. The point is, though, that until you accept the possibility of going outside the borders, the problem cannot be solved. The lesson for you to learn is that you should not place constraints on your solution that are neither inherent in nor implied by the problem.

THE MONK PROBLEM

A monk wishes to pursue study and contemplation in a retreat at the top of a mountain. The monk starts climbing the mountain at 7:00 A.M. and arrives at the top of the mountain at 5:00 P.M. of the same day. During the course of his ascent, he travels at variable speeds, and takes a break for lunch. He spends the evening in study and contemplation. The next day, the monk starts his descent at 7:00 A.M. again, along the same route. Normally his descent would be faster than his ascent, but because he is tired and afraid of tripping and hurting himself, he descends the mountain slowly, not arriving at the bottom until 5:00 P.M. of the day after he started his ascent. Figure 3–2 shows the monk's route. The question is this: Must there be a point on the mountain that the monk passes at exactly the same time of day on the two successive days of his ascent and descent? If so, provide a plausible demonstration that this is the case. If not, show why this need not necessarily be the case. Do not read on until you have finished your attempt to solve the monk problem. Only then check the solution (Figure 3–7) at the end of the chapter.

Figure 3–2. The Monk Problem

In fact, it is necessarily the case that the monk must pass through exactly the same point (or altitude) on the mountain at corresponding times on the days of his ascent and descent. The solution shows why this must be the case. The problem becomes much easier to conceptualize if rather than imagining the same monk climbing the mountain one day and going down the mountain the next, you imagine two different monks, one ascending and the other descending the mountain on the same day. You may assume the monks start and finish at the same time, although this assumption is not necessary for solution of the problem. Note that in this redefinition of the problem, the monk's descent on the second day is reconceptualized as a different monk's descent on the same day as the first monk's ascent. This reconceptualization does not charge the nature of or solution to the problem, but only makes it easier to see what that solution is.

Note how, if there were two monks, their paths of ascent and descent would necessarily cross each other. The point at which the two lines of ascent and descent cross each other is the point at which the original monk's paths of ascent descent must "cross each other" at the same time of day. In terms of the reconceptualization of the problem, it is at this point that the two monks meet. Obviously, their meeting must be in a given place at a given time. The redefinition of the problem simply makes it easier to see how it must be the case that at some point the original monk will be at a given point at a given time of day on the two consecutive days.

Unlike the nine-dots problem, the monk problem is solvable in its original form. The argument that the monk's paths of ascent and descent must reach a given point at a given time on the two consecutive days can be made without the suggested reconceptualization of the problem. However, redefining the problem in the way suggested makes the problem much easier to solve. This problem provides an example of how redefining a problem can make the solution easier. The redefinition highlights the critical feature of the solution to the problem.

THE HAT RACK PROBLEM

The hat rack problem is a construction problem in which a person is required to build a structure sufficiently stable to support a man's hat and overcoat using only two sticks (one, $1'' \times 2'' \times 60''$, the other, $1'' \times 2'' \times 43''$) and a $2''$ C-clamp. The opening of the clamp is wide enough so that both sticks can be inserted and held together securely when the clamp is tightened. The room is $12'3'' \times 13'5''$. The ceiling is 8' high, but two beams jut down from the ceiling about 1', dividing the room into thirds.

Study Figure 3–3 and try to solve this problem before reading on or checking the solution (Figure 3–8) at the end of the chapter.

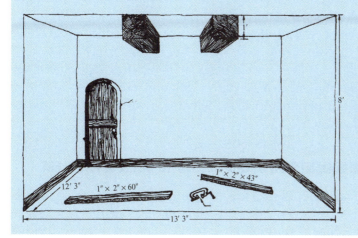

Figure 3–3. The Hat Rack Problem

The solution shows that the hat rack can be constructed by wedging together the two poles against the floor and the ceiling by means of the C-clamp. The C-clamp is used as a hook on which to hang the hat and coat. Most people have a great deal of trouble solving this problem. There are many different reasons for this, some of which will not be considered until later. But a major reason for this difficulty is that people focus on the materials found in the room and never think of the possibility of using the floor and the ceiling as part of their solution. By failing to consider this possibility, they eliminate their chance of solving the problem. Notice that there is nothing in the problem that precludes use of the floor and the ceiling. Once again, we see how people artificially restrict the range of possibilities for their problem solutions. They place constraints into their solution that are neither contained in nor even implied by the problem. By redefining the problem to allow use of the floor and ceiling, people can readily solve the hat rack problem.

People have great difficulty solving all three of these problems. One might think that the difficulty is due to the perversity of psychologists in thinking of difficult problems for people to solve. However, there are many problems in our everyday lives that we fail to solve or solve in an inefficient way because of our inadequate definition of the nature of the problem.

problem altogether. It is therefore important to make sure that the problem you are attempting to solve is in fact the problem that is being posed. In other words, it is important to make sure that the question being answered is the same as the question being asked.

2. *Simplify your goals.* Sometimes, you may set certain goals for yourself or others that prove difficult to meet. You may then try harder (or make others try harder) in an attempt to reach the goals. Sometimes this strategy works, and the problem can therefore be solved. At other times, however, the strategy fails: You find yourself simply unable to meet the goals, or you find that others cannot reach the goals you have set for them. In such instances, consider whether you can simplify the goals to make them attainable. Often, you can substitute an attainable goal with little or no loss in terms of the ultimate outcome. Sometimes, arriving at a lesser goal can make you aware of ways in which the more difficult goal can be reached.

3. *Redefine your goals.* Sometimes, instead of setting an easier goal for yourself, you need only to change the goal to make it more appropriate for what you wish to accomplish. In such instances, you need to define the problem in a way that leads toward this redefined goal.

SELECTING THE COMPONENTS OR STEPS NEEDED TO SOLVE A PROBLEM

Anyone who has ever bought a house or rented an apartment knows the great difficulty people often confront in deciding which house to buy or which apartment to rent. At first, it may seem like a simple matter of finding our dream house or dream apartment.

Unfortunately, we rarely find the house or apartment of our dreams. Even if we were able to find such a house or apartment, the chances are that its price would put it beyond our reach. As a result, we have to start making compromises and trade-offs in an attempt to decide which of several options is the best one. For example, one of us lived for three years in an apartment with a kitchen so small that you had to first open the refrigerator before you could open the silverware drawer. But it was cheap!

Typically, none of the houses or apartments will seem quite right. They will vary in quality on many dimensions, and what these dimensions are will probably not even be clear at first. Unless we find some systematic way of deciding among the options, we may be overwhelmed by the difficulty involved in choosing the best place in which to live. How would you go about solving the problem of choosing the best house or apartment?

What can at first seem like an unsolvable problem can become solvable if you decide on a set of criteria for evaluating places to live, and a set of weights for evaluating the criteria. For example, you might first decide which features are important to you in selecting a house or apartment. Such features might include the overall size of the place, its location, its price, how close it is to your school or place of work, its condition, the amount of closet space, and so on. The important thing is that the list contains each everything that is important to you in making your decision. Another person might produce a different list, of course.

Once you have decided on the set of criteria, you need to decide on a set of weights to assign to each of those criteria. These weights indicate how important each of the criteria is in making the final decision. For example, you might decide to use a 5-point scale, where 1 represents a low weight and 5 a high weight. On this scale, you might decide, for instance, that size of the place is very important (5), whereas condition of the place is not so important (2), because you can always improve it. With these criteria for making a decision and these weights to use in assessing the criteria, you have gone a long way toward arriving at a solution to the problem. Still other steps remain to be taken, and these will be considered later in this chapter.

Let's move to another example. Let's say that you decide to get a new pet. Picking which pet to get is a significant decision that can affect your life for many years to come. First you might establish the criteria that are important to you. Maybe you live in an apartment and do not have room for a dog (or horse or hippo). Maybe you are struggling financially and cannot afford an expensive pet like a hyacinth macaw (a pricey parrot). Maybe you are gone many hours during the day and need a self-sufficient pet. Once you have defined and weighed your criteria, you can go through each possible choice and see how it fairs. A fish might score high on self-sufficiency and price, but low on affection (have you ever tried to kiss a fish? Wait; don't answer that question out loud). A dog might score high on being friendly, serving as protection, and giving lots of doggie kisses, but poorly on price and time commitment. A pet rock might score quite high on price and protection (a rock makes a good weapon), but low on a snuggle-factor. It is not enough simply to identify a problem that needs to be solved (such as "I need to figure out what pet to get"); you need to also be able to establish a plan for selecting the best pet for you and your current situation.

The importance of choosing an appropriate set of steps for problem solution can be seen in the international as well as in the personal domain. For example, the problem of how to mutually reduce weapons and arms across nations is largely (although not exclusively) a matter of finding a set of appropriate steps for accomplishing the reduction. The greatest difficulty arms negotiators seem to face is finding a set of steps for reduction that is mutually agreeable to all parties. If only such steps could be found, the negotiators would be a long way toward solving their problem.

Sometimes, people are unable to solve problems because they do not have the means to do so. A striking example of this can be seen in the attempts by children of different ages to solve analogies. It has often been found that very young children have great difficulty with analogy problems. The great epistemologist Jean Piaget (1972) even suggested that children are virtually unable to solve analogies before around the age of eleven or twelve. Why do young children have so much difficulty in solving analogies? Research by a number of investigators indicates that young children are unable to conceive of second-order relations-that is, relations between relations. Consider, for example, the analogy used in Chapter 1, LAWYER is to CLIENT as DOCTOR is to (a) MEDICINE, (b) PATIENT. A number of steps are needed to solve this analogy. But the single step that seems to present an insurmountable problem for young children is that of "mapping" the higher-order relations between LAWYER and CLIENT on the one hand, and DOCTOR and PATIENT on the other. Notice that the essence of analogy is the relationship between these two relations. In both cases, a professional provides services to an individual. Thus, although the lower-order relations are not the same (one involves legal services and the other medical services), there is a higher-order relation between the two kinds of services. Children under about age eleven are unable to see this higher-order relation. In effect, the step of "mapping" seems to be unavailable to them.

Examples can be found in many areas, however. Consider a popular puzzle: You are walking down the street in the summer and you see a carrot, a scarf, and pieces of coal on someone's front lawn. What's a reasonable explanation to how they got there? If you have never lived through snow-filled winters, you might not be able to get the correct answer (a melted snowman). The needed problem-solving tools might be physical – if we ask you to wash our cars (and if you meet us, we might) but don't give you any soap, towels, rags, or water, it might be difficult to accomplish this task successfully.

It is important in these and other cases to distinguish between the notions of *availability* and *accessibility* of problem-solving components. Sometimes, people simply lack the mental or physical means to solve a problem. At other times, however, the components to the solution may be available, but relatively inaccessible. In other words, an individual may be able to perform a certain step, but does not realize its applicability.

Consider, for example, how you would go about memorizing the following list of words: BOOK, TABLE, CHAIR, NEWSPAPER, SOFA, MAGAZINE, NOVEL, DESK, POEM, BED,

PAMPHLET. People usually use two basic strategies in memorizing such a list. In the first strategy, called "rehearsal," they simply repeat the words to themselves over and over again in the order given – "Book, table, chair, newspaper, sofa, magazine, novel, desk, poem, bed, pamphlet, book, table, chair ..."

The second strategy is called "category clustering." In this particular list, the words tend to fall into two general categories: pieces of furniture and things to read. A list is usually more easily remembered if the words are mentally clustered by content categories. Rehearsal and category clustering both improve long-term recall of lists of words, and these two strategies are *available* to almost everyone. However, Earl Butterfield and John Belmont (1977) have found that mentally retarded individuals do not tend to use these strategies spontaneously. If they are explicitly told to use them, then, in fact, they will. In other words, their problem is not one of strategy availability; rather, it is one of strategy accessibility. The strategies simply are not *accessible* to these individuals. They have to be reminded again and again of the applicability of rehearsal and clustering to the recall task.

Improving Your Selection of Task Components

There are several things you can keep in mind that will help you choose the steps or components needed to solve the problem.

1. *Choose steps that are the right size for solving the problem, that is, steps that are neither too small nor too large.* One of the biggest difficulties people face in solving problems is that of choosing steps that are the wrong size. If the steps are too large, people simply find themselves unable to solve the problem. In effect, they have bitten off more than they can chew. But choosing steps that are too small can result in extremely long problem-solving processes and the frustration that goes with them. You will usually want to solve a problem in as little time as possible, and choosing very small steps can thwart your attainment of this goal.

2. *Make the first step an easy one.* People often find that the hardest step to take in solving a problem or in accomplishing a task is the first one. They have difficulty getting started. This difficulty may come from their inability to see how to start the problem, or it may result from their difficulty in getting the momentum to start problem solving or task performance. For example, graduate students have a notoriously hard time getting their Ph.D. dissertations started. They tend to find smaller, less important tasks to fill their time, and to put off starting the more important but seemingly infinitely larger task. At a more mundane level, people often put off the more difficult chores they have to do around the house, doing the easier ones first. For example, every adult has more than once encountered the task of cleaning out his or her closets, but cleaning it seems like a Herculean task. In such situations, people often manage to find other chores to do around the house for weeks on end, putting off the inevitable cleaning of the closet that they know most needs to be done. By making the first step an easy one to get the task started, people can often acquire the momentum they need to complete the task. Whenever one of us has a paper to write, the first thing he does is to write out the title page, complete with the list of authors, and insert the

EXERCISE 3.2

1. Suppose you have been admitted to three different colleges. Your selection of college will determine a great deal about what the next four years of your life will be like. List some of the steps you would take in order to help you decide among colleges and choose the best one.

2. You are in a foreign country where you don't speak the language. You have a bad headache and serious stomach problems. You realize you need a doctor. What steps might you take (a) to communicate to an inhabitant of the country that you need a doctor and (b) to communicate to the inhabitant what your symptoms are?

3. One of the most serious issues facing the world today is preparing for another possible terrorist attack. A major problem is that the steps to preventing terrorist attacks are unclear; there is no established guide that can be used. What steps can you think of that might reduce the chance of another terrorist attack?

appropriate headers and footers. The paper becomes more "real," both physically and metaphorically. Plus, it's pretty easy to do.

3. *Consider alternative steps to the solution before choosing any one set of steps.* In his famous book *Administrative Behavior*, Nobel Prize–winner Herbert Simon (1957) described a strategy frequently used by people in solving problems. In this strategy, called "satisficing," people choose the first minimally acceptable course of action (i.e., something "good enough"), rather than considering all the available options and only then settling on the optimal course of action. Clearly a poor strategy, "satisficing" is an easy strategy to avoid. Before settling on a suboptimal set of steps for solution just because it happened to be the first one you thought of, consider other alternatives. Why do people do it? Because it's easier. If you're home and hungry, you may quickly go through the possible options in your mind. Once you hit something that sounds edible, you'll probably stop and go get it. For little decisions (macaroni and cheese vs. peanut butter and jelly), it's not terribly important. For bigger decisions, it's not the best thing to do.

SELECTING A STRATEGY FOR ORDERING COMPONENTS OF PROBLEM SOLVING

When solving a problem of any kind, it is not enough to simply select the information-processing components that will best, or even satisfactorily, solve the problem. You must combine these components into a workable strategy for problem solution.

First, you must decide in what order to execute the components or steps. For example, in solving a mathematical word problem, it is not enough to know that solution of the problem requires multiplication, subtraction, and division. You must know the order in which these steps need to be performed, as the order of step execution usually affects the solution to the problem. Indeed, one well-known test for understanding mathematical concepts, the Stanford Achievement Test, asks for the operations that need to be performed for each mathematics problem and the order in which they should be performed. Consider a very simple example:

Joe gave a storekeeper $1.00 for two apples. The apples cost 35¢ apiece. How much change should Joe receive?

This problem can be solved by a multiplication and a subtraction. But in what *order* are these operations executed? If the operations are not done in proper order [$1.00 − (2 × 35¢)], then the problem will be solved incorrectly. The multiplication must be done first.

Improving Your Selection of a Strategy

There are some steps you can take in order to improve your selection of a strategy in problem solving. Some of these steps are listed here.

1. *Be sure you consider the full problem.* Problem solvers often make errors because they believe they have solved the problem before they have actually finished. Their answer to the problem is thus only an answer to a smaller part of the full problem. Test item writers are aware of this tendency, and often create distracters (wrong answers) that seem reasonable because they are solutions to these smaller parts of the problems. The problem solver solves part of the problem, sees the solution he or she has reached as one of the answer options, and quickly selects it. Unfortunately, the solver did not complete all of the steps necessary to solve the full problem. Research on problem solving has shown that these partial solutions are one of the main sources of error in problem solving. For example, Sternberg's research has shown that in solving analogies, younger children tend to score worse than older children in large part because they did not consider all of the available possible answers of the problem. Moreover, adults who make errors on analogy problems frequently do so because they have not considered the terms of the problems fully enough. So make sure that you consider the full problem before offering or choosing a solution.

2. *Don't immediately assume the "obvious."* In *Silence of the Lambs*, FBI agent Jack Crawford warns Clarice Starling not to assume anything. Such advice can apply to both hunting down a Hannibal Lecter–type serial killer or to more routine problem solving. Indeed, another frequent source of error in problem solving occurs when the problem solver assumes the "obvious" but the obvious turns out to be wrong. Such assumptions can take various forms. For example, sometimes a problem appears to be a certain type of familiar problem, whereas in fact it is not this type of familiar problem at all. Other times, the problem solver simply makes assumptions that are unjustified. We saw, for example, in the nine-dot problem how the assumption that one must stay within the borders of the nine dots makes the problem impossible to solve. Other assumptions can relate specifically to the issue of ordering the steps of a problem. For example, solvers often assume that they should work forward in solving a problem. However, it is often easier to work backward – that is, to

EXERCISE 3.3

SEARCHING THE FIELD

Consider the following problem, which is a type of problem found on standardized achievement tests.

Figure 3–4 shows an irregularly shaped field. Somewhere in that field is a valuable gold coin. Your problem is to set up a strategy of search so that by systematically walking through the field, you will find that gold coin. Draw lines with your pencil the systematic search strategy you might use that would guarantee your finding the gold coin.

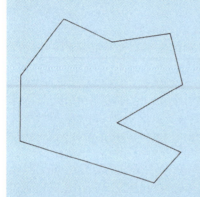

Figure 3–4. Searching the Field Problem

The critical element for solution of this problem is to have a search strategy that is ordered and systematic. Randomly roaming around the field or random trying to look at different parts are unlikely to yield the gold coin. A variant of this problem is found in everyday life when one misplaces something in the home. For example, one of us frequently loses his glasses and then has to search his house for them. Anyone who has searched for the car keys in his or her house knows the importance of setting up a systematic, ordered strategy for search. Random wandering around the house or apartment can lead to multiple looks in a given place where one has already looked, and no looks in other places that may very well have keys. Anyone who has been through this experience can remember with embarrassment looking several times in one spot and not finding the missing keys, but then failing to look in another spot where they are.

start with a solution, and then attempt to generate the premises of the problem. Backward problem solving often works particularly well in logical and mathematical proofs. Similarly, people often assume that they should start with the premises and work directly toward the conclusion. But sometimes problems that are unmanageable when solved as wholes become easier when broken down into a series of smaller problems. The problem solver formulates a series of different, smaller goals. Rather than trying to reach the final goal directly, he or she tries to reach each of the sequence of these goals. Accomplishment of each of these goals then leads to solution of the whole problem.

For example, one of the authors used to have a very messy house. When his wife entered the picture, she decided that the house had to be cleaned. Yet, looking at this problem as having only the central goal of a clean house would have been too frustrating – it might have felt easier to get a new house (or for her to find a new husband). Instead, she made a list of smaller goals and saw each one through. A first step was doing some basic organization of books, then CDs, and then DVDs. The next smaller goal was getting rid of much of the junk that one of us had accumulated over several years of bachelorhood – ugly furniture, and so on. She continued working on different smaller goals over several months until the larger goal was reached, and a (somewhat) clean house became a reality. If she had tried to directly seek the final goal, she easily might have gotten overwhelmed and never finished.

3. *Make sure your sequencing of steps follows a natural or logical order toward the goal you wish to reach*. Often, problem solvers choose a sequence of steps for working out a problem, and then attempt to order the steps in a way that will reach the ultimate goal of solution. Before actually carrying out the steps, make sure that the order you have selected is the most natural or most logical one for the given problem, and that none of the steps assumes information that, given your ordering, will not be attained until later. Consider, for example, the case of a friend who needed a bookcase for his office. We decided to go looking together at the local stores. It was not until we had gotten to the first store and seen the selection available that the friend realized he had failed to measure the space into which the bookcase was to fit. He had been all ready to select among different styles of bookcases before addressing the earlier (and essential!) question of the size of bookcase that he could fit into the available space.

Permutation Problems

A related problem in which setting up a systematic order of steps is crucial is the "permutation problem" used by Piaget and others as a measure of formal-operational (advanced) reasoning. This kind of reasoning is usually identified with children who are at least twelve or so years of age and with adults, although the large majority of these children and adults seem not to be fully formal in their reasoning. Thus, your ability to solve this particular problem may give you an indication of just how capable you are in formal reasoning. If you do not initially solve the problem through formal reasoning, then you will be able to do it in a few minutes. This shows how easy it can be to improve your intellectual skills!

Here are four letters: A, B, C, D. Provide a listing of all the possible permutations (orders) in which these four letters can be written. (For example, A, B, C, D is one permutation and D, C, B, A is another.)

This problem can be either quite easy or quite difficult, depending on the strategy used to solve it. If you simply attempt to solve it in an unsystematic fashion, the chances of your listing all of the possible permutations are probably quite slim. However, if you set up a systematic strategy, ordering your listing of the permutations in a systematic way, you will easily be able to list them all. In fact, when this item is used as a measure of formal operations, the important thing the examiner looks for is not so much the number of permutations listed as the strategy that is used to generate these permutations. In other words, the ordering of steps is the critical feature that the examiner looks for in scoring performance on this problem.

In order to get to the solution, the first thing you need to know is the number of possible permutations. This knowledge will let you check to make sure that you have listed them all. There is a simple formula for computing the number of possible permutations. This formula makes use of the idea of a factorial, which is represented as an exclamation point (!) after the number for which the factorial is being sought. In this case, because there are four letters for which we are seeking all possible permutations, the expression is 4!. The value of 4! is equal to the number of possible permutations. This expression is solved by taking the number after which the exclamation point appears and then multiplying it by each of the natural numbers that is less than that number down to 1. In this case, one would multiply $4 \times 3 \times 2 \times 1$, attaining a product of 24, the number of possible permutations.

Now that we know there are 24 possible permutations, we have to list them. A systematic way of obtaining the entire list is to hold one letter constant and to vary subsequent letters systematically, repeating the procedure for each letter. For the present example, this strategy would yield:

1.	A	B	C	D
2.	A	B	D	C
3.	A	C	B	D
4.	A	C	D	B
5.	A	D	B	C
6.	A	D	C	B

Note how the first letter, A, is held constant in each of these six permutations and variation is done from the right end moving toward the left. In other words, first the last two letters, C and D, are interchanged with each other, and only then is the third-to-last place interchanged. As a result, there are six permutations with the letter A appearing first, and two permutations each with B, C, and D, in the second position. Because there are 24 possible permutations, we know that we must be one-quarter of the way through the entire list. As all of these permutations have had A in their first position, we know we must be on the right track, because now we need to generate six permutations with each of B, C, and D in the first position.

The rest of the list of permutations is:

7.	B	A	C	D
8.	B	A	D	C
9.	B	C	A	D
10.	B	C	D	A
11.	B	D	A	C
12.	B	D	C	A
13.	C	A	B	D
14.	C	A	D	B
15.	C	B	A	D
16.	C	B	D	A
17.	C	D	A	B
18.	C	D	B	A
19.	D	A	B	C
20.	D	A	C	B
21.	D	B	A	C
22.	D	B	C	A
23.	D	C	A	B
24.	D	C	B	A

Here are two more permutation problems you can try on your own: (1) H, N, Q, T, and (2) 3, 5, 6, 9. See if you can list all possible permutations of these sets of letters and numbers.

Missionaries and Cannibals Problem

One of the most famous problems requiring careful ordering of steps is the so-called Missionaries and Cannibals problem, which has been in the problem-solving folklore for many years and also has been studied extensively by psychologists. Try to solve the problem, which goes like this:

> Three missionaries and three cannibals are on a riverbank. The missionaries and cannibals need to cross over to the other side of the river. They have for this purpose a small rowboat that will hold just two people. There is one problem, however. If the number of cannibals on either riverbank exceeds the number of missionaries, the cannibals will eat the missionaries. How can all six get across to the other side of the river in a way that guarantees that they all arrive there alive and uneaten?

You will find the solution to the Missionaries and Cannibals problem at the end of the chapter (see Figure 3–9). The solution contains several noteworthy features. First, the problem can he solved in a minimum of eleven steps, including the first and the last steps. Second, the solution is essentially linear in nature. At all but two steps along the solution path, the only error that can be made is to go directly backward in the solution. In other words, there are only two possible moves, the last one to have been made and the next one that can be made. At two steps, there are two possible forward-moving responses, but both of these lead toward the correct answer. Thus, again, the only error possible is returning to a previous state in the solution of the problem. A secondary problem is making an illegal move – that is, a move that is not permitted according to the terms of the problem. An example of an illegal move would be one that resulted in more than two individuals in the boat. You might wonder, given the essentially linear nature of the solution path, why or how people have trouble solving this kind of problem at all. The biggest problems they seem to have, according to those who have studied the problem, are (a) inadvertently moving backward, (b) making illegal moves, and (c) not realizing the nature of the next legal move.

If you are now ready for a somewhat more difficult challenge in terms of ordering the steps of the Missionaries and Cannibals problem, then try the Missionaries and Cannibals problem again, except with five missionaries and five cannibals. Again, your task is to get all of the missionaries and cannibals from one bank of the river to the other and no more than three individuals are allowed in the boat at any one time. Moreover, once again, you must never allow it to happen that there are more cannibals than missionaries on either bank or in the boat, for, as before, the cannibals would eat the missionaries.

This problem is quite a bit more difficult than the earlier version because the solution is no longer linear. Try the problem before checking the solution (Figure 3–10) at the end of the chapter. As you can see from the figure, many more moves are legal, but some lead to dead ends.

Herbert Simon and Stephen Reed (1976) did research in order to find out the strategies people actually use in solving the Missionaries and Cannibals problem when there are five missionaries and five cannibals to be transported across the river. Their research has indicated that people seeking to solve this problem use either of two strategies or a combination of these two strategies. The first strategy, a *balance* strategy, results in the problem solver selecting the move that balances the number of missionaries with the number of cannibals on each side of the river. This strategy makes sense because the problem solver is seeking to avoid a situation where the number of cannibals is greater than the number of missionaries on either side of the river. The second strategy, a *means-ends* strategy, selects moves that maximize the number of persons across the river (odd-numbered moves) and minimize the number of persons on the initial side of the river (even numbered moves). At some steps along the paths to solution, these two strategies yield the same move. At other steps, they do not. Both strategies assume that problem solvers will make only legal moves and that they will test for previous moves so as not to go back to an earlier state of problem solving. Interestingly, a pure means-ends strategy will result in the problem being solved in eleven moves, whereas a pure balance strategy will result in the problem never being solved at all! Instead, a pure balance strategy will result in the problem solver getting stuck in an "infinite loop." Simon and Reed hypothesized, and their results confirmed, that what problem solvers tend to do is to start off problem solving with a balance strategy, and later shift to a means-ends strategy. Problem solvers differ in the exact point during problem solving at which they switch from one strategy to the other.

Water-jug Problem

A related kind of problem, which also requires a carefully ordered sequence of steps, is the water-jug problem. The water-jug problem was featured in a slightly different form in *Die Hard 3*; try solving it here – without a ticking bomb to worry about!

> A mother sends her boy to the river in order to measure out three quarts of water. The mother gives her son a seven-quart bucket and a four-quart bucket. How can the son measure out exactly three quarts of water using nothing but these two buckets and not guessing as to the amount of water that he brings home? Try to solve this problem before reading on.

This is a simple example of a water-jug problem. To solve the problem, the son merely needs to fill the seven-quart bucket and pour the water into the four-quart bucket. He is now left with three quarts of water in the seven-quart bucket.

Consider now a slightly harder water-jug problem:

> A circus owner sends one of his clowns to bring back from a nearby river seven gallons of water to give to the elephants. He gives the clown a five-gallon bucket and a three-gallon bucket and tells him to bring back exactly seven gallons of water. How can the clown measure out exactly seven gallons of water using nothing but these two buckets and not guessing at the amount?

This problem is a bit more difficult. First, the clown needs to fill the five-gallon bucket. Next, he must pour the water into the three-gallon bucket. Having done this, he throws the three gallons back into the river. He now takes the two gallons left in the five-gallon bucket and pours them into the three-gallon bucket. By filling the five-gallon bucket again, he will now have five gallons in that bucket and two gallons in the other bucket, for a total of seven gallons.

Of course, there are "water-jug" problems that do not make use of either jugs or water. Such problems, which are identical in form to the water-jug problem but which make use of different entities in the problem statements, are called "problem isomorphs." Although they are parallel in form to the original problems, research by John Hayes and Herbert Simon (1976), among others, has shown that problem isomorphs are sometimes easier and some times harder than the original problem. In other words, changing the content of a problem can change its difficulty, even if the form of the problem remains unchanged. So consider a problem isomorph for the water-jug problem:

> A cook needs one gram of salt to season a special meal he is cooking. When he opens the drawer to get a measuring spoon, he finds out that he has only an eleven-gram measuring spoon and a four-gram measuring spoon. How can the cook measure out exactly one gram of salt using nothing but these two spoons without guessing at the amount?

What the cook needs to do is to fill the four-gram measuring spoon first and pour the salt into the eleven-gram measuring spoon. Then, he needs to repeat this procedure two more times. The third time, he will be able to pour only three of the four grams into the eleven-gram spoon. He will be left with one gram of salt on the four-gram spoon. Now consider a similar problem:

> With a five-minute hourglass and a nine-minute hourglass, what is the quickest way to time a thirteen-minute steak?

One strategy for solving this problem is to start both hourglasses and the steak together. After the five-minute hourglass runs out, turn it over. When the nine-minute hourglass runs out, turn over the five-minute hourglass. It will run for four minutes, yielding a total time of thirteen minutes.

The type of problem characterized in this section can be made somewhat more difficult by including three rather than two water jugs, hourglasses, or whatever. Consider, for example, this problem:

> You have three jugs – A, B, and C. Jug A has a capacity of eight quarts, Jug B has a capacity of five quarts, and Jug C has a capacity of three quarts. Initially Jug A is full, but the two smaller jugs are empty. How can you divide the contents of the largest jug evenly between the largest and middle-sized jugs-that is, between jugs A and B?

This problem is quite a bit harder than the problem that has preceded it. See if you can solve it, and then check the solution (Figure 3–11) at the end of the chapter. As shown in the figure, you pour three quarts from Jug A into jug C, and then pour Jug C into Jug B. Pour three more quarts from Jug A into Jug C. Now pour two quarts from Jug C into Jug B, filling Jug B (five quarts). One quart is left in Jug C. Empty Jug B into Jug A; then pour the one quart from Jug C into Jug B. Fill Jug C again from Jug A. Finally, empty Jug C into Jug B.

The Tower of Hanoi and its Variations

One of the most famous problems in the problem-solving literature is the Tower of Hanoi problem. In this problem, the solver is presented with three sticks and a set of discs mounted on the first of those sticks. The discs are of unequal sizes, and they are mounted so that the largest one is on the bottom, the next largest one is immediately above that, and so on until the top of the pile, which contains the smallest disc. The number of discs varies from one version of the problem to another. The idea is to transfer all of the discs from the first stick to the third stick, using the middle stick for intermediate steps of problem solving. In transferring the discs, the solver is never allowed to place a larger disc on top of a smaller disc. A picture of a typical Tower of Hanoi puzzle is shown in Figure 3–5.

Because this book does not come with a set of discs and sticks, it is necessary to use isomorphs to the Tower of Hanoi problem in order to give you a chance to solve problems of this type. Consider the following isomorph, studied by John Hayes and Herbert Simon (1976):

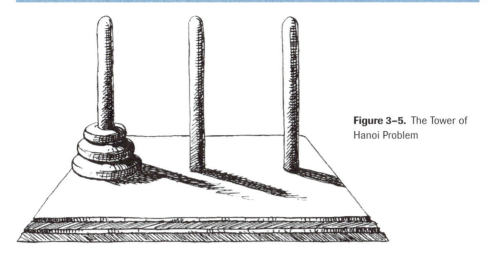

Figure 3–5. The Tower of Hanoi Problem

Three five-handed extraterrestrial monsters were holding three crystal globes. Because of the quantum-mechanical peculiarities of their neighborhood, both monsters and globes come in exactly three sizes with no others permitted: small, medium, and large. The medium-sized monster was holding the small globe; the small monster was holding the large globe; and the large monster was holding the medium-sized globe. Since this situation offended their keenly developed sense of symmetry, they proceeded to transfer globes from one monster to another so that each monster would have a globe proportionate to his own size. Monster etiquette complicated the solution of the problem because it requires: (a) that only one globe be transferred at a time; (b) that if a monster is holding two globes, only the larger of the two may be transferred; and (c) that a globe may not be transferred to a monster who is holding a larger globe. By what sequence of transfers could the monsters have solved this problem?

Try to solve the problem before checking the solution (Figure 3–12) at the end of the chapter.

In this section, we have seen different instances in which the metacomponent of deciding on an order for performance components may be exercised. As you have seen, a wide variety of problems require careful ordering of steps to solution. In each of the kinds of problems in this section, the hardest part of the problem is not actually coming up with the steps, but deciding on the order in which the steps should be taken. Other kinds of problems, of course, are more or less difficult for other reasons.

We started this chapter with an example of a friend who missed his plane because of his poor planning and inefficient decision making. We stated that in order to improve one's planning and decision making, one needs to pay attention to the following components ("-ings") of the problem-solving cycle: (1) defining the nature of the problem; (2) selecting the steps needed to solve a problem; and (3) selecting a strategy for ordering components of problem solving. In the next chapter, we will discuss the final three ways to improve planning and decision making; (4) selecting a mental representation for information; (5) allocating resources; and (6) monitoring the solution.

Finally, here are the solutions:

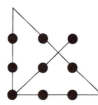

Figure 3–6. Solution to the Nine Dot Problem

Figure 3–7. Solution to the Monk Problem

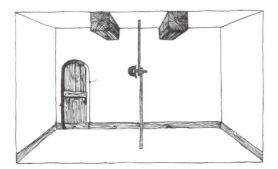

Figure 3–8. Solution to the Hat Rack Problem

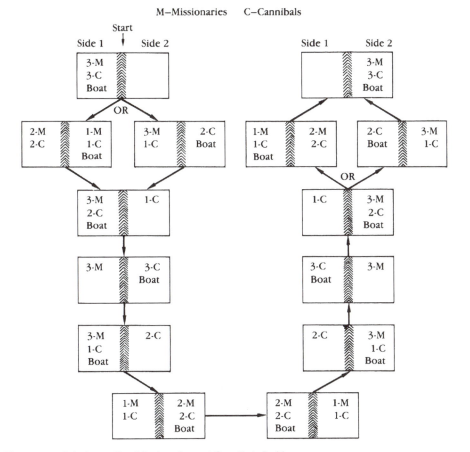

Figure 3–9. Solution to First Missionaries and Cannibals Problem

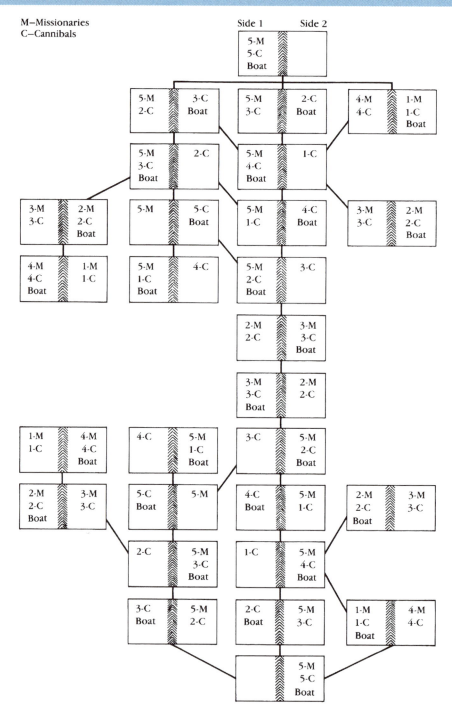

Figure 3–10. Solution to Second Missionaries and Cannibals Problem

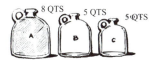

1.    2.

3.    4.

Figure 3–11. Solution to the Water Jug Problem

5.    6.

7.    8.

Figure 3–12. Solution to the Extraterrestrial Monsters Problem

1.	M	L	S		3.	M	L	S		5.	M	L	S
	s	m	l			–	l & m	s			m	–	l & s
2.	M	L	S		4.	M	L	S		6.	M	L	S
	s	l & m	–			–	m	l & s			m	l	s

4

Advanced Problem-Solving Steps

We will now discuss the final three components that can improve planning and decision making.

SELECTING A MENTAL REPRESENTATION FOR INFORMATION

An important part of many kinds of problem solving is the way that information is represented mentally. Such a mental representation might be in the form of a picture, a list of ideas, an algebraic equation, or yet some other format. Problems that could be solved easily using one form of mental representation are often solved only with difficulty or not at all using another. Sometimes, you will need to supplement your mental representation with an external representation of information. So, for example, in solving a mathematics problem, you may find it helpful to draw a diagram or to set up a series of equations that represent the terms of the problem. Such diagrams can then help your problem solving, especially the way in which you proceed to represent information about the problem in your head. Psychologists studying mental representations have learned some interesting things about them.

Examples

One psychologist studying mental representations, Patricia Linville (1982), looked at the relation between the way in which we represent information about other people and our stereotypes about and prejudices toward these people. One of her most interesting findings is that simple mental representations tend to lead toward extreme judgments about people, whether favorable or unfavorable. The converse also holds: Extreme judgments tend to imply simple representations about people. For example, she has found that prejudices toward members of certain groups tend to be accompanied by simple mental representations about the members of those groups. This finding makes sense, because almost inevitably, a complex representation simply will not support the prejudice. This finding gives credence to the view that one of the best ways to fight prejudice is through fighting ignorance – the more we know about the members of any group, the less likely it is that we will be prejudiced toward them. Indeed, think of the first person you ever got to know from a group that was different from your own (i.e., a different ethnicity, religion, or sexual orientation). Just knowing someone from that group makes it less likely that you will feel negatively about that group.

Linville also discovered a connection between simplicity of mental representations about unfavorable events and depression following those events. People who become depressed after a particular event, such as the loss of a love, tend to view that event in very simple terms. As the complexity of their view increases, their tendency to be depressed about the event decreases. This finding gives credence to Aaron Beck's notion (1976; Beck, Rush, Shaw, & Emery, 1979) that depression is at least partly cognitive in nature, and that a way to fight depression is to teach people to reason realistically and logically about the event or events leading to the depressive state. It is much easier after breaking up with someone to lie on your bed in your underwear, eating chips and ice cream and watching bad television, and thinking, "Why did she leave? Bad that she left. Miss her. All alone." It's harder (but healthier) to try to take a broader perspective.

Another instance in which proper representation can help problem solving is in major decisions we face in our lives, such as the decision of whether to buy a car, whether to undergo surgery, what college to attend, and so on. In trying to make such decisions, we often find ourselves overwhelmed by the available information, and at a loss to know just what to do with it. Because the extent of the information exceeds the capacities of our working memories to hold it all at one time, we can deal only with limited aspects of the decision at one time. We sometimes find ourselves going over the same information again and again, but not really making progress in evaluating all of the useful information available.

It is of interest to note here that studies of children's encoding strategies and working-memory capacities, such as ones by Micheline Chi (1978), have tended to suggest that younger children differ from older ones not in the number of "slots" in their working memory, but, rather, in the amount of information they can pack into each of these slots because of their greater efficiency of encoding presented information. In other words, when people mature, they develop not in their raw capacity to memorize as much information as possible, but in their capacity to encode information efficiently.

A quick example of better efficiency in encoding information can be seen with remembering phone numbers. People can usually remember between five and nine numbers in their head at once. You might reasonably ask how anyone can remember an entire phone number. Including area codes, a phone number is ten digits. If someone has an extension number, it might be fourteen! The answer is found in chunking – you can look at "909" and instead of remembering it as "9," "0," and "9," you'll remember it as one number, "909" (which happens to be the area code for San Bernardino).

In other studies, it has been found that people of the same age often will solve cognitive problems differently, depending on their particular pattern of abilities (Mayer,

2000). An important theme running throughout this book is that intelligent people (who are usually effective problem solvers) tend to be people who capitalize on their strengths and compensate for their weaknesses in solving problems. Thus, it is important for you to know what your strengths and weaknesses are. This is true in nearly all areas – if you are in a class that allows your final presentation to be either a written paper or an oral report, it makes sense to pick the method in which you excel. If you are a poor public speaker, it would not be to your advantage to pick the oral report.

In the realm of mental representation of information, some people tend to be better at representing information spatially, or in the form of mental images; other people tend to be better at representing the same information linguistically, or in words.

Consider, for example, the so-called sentence-picture comparison problem. In this fairly simple problem, solvers are asked to compare the contents of a sentence to the contents of a picture, and then to say whether or not they match. For example, they might be presented with the sentence, "Star is below plus," and then with the picture +*. In this particular case, the content of the sentence and the picture do not match, so the answer is "no." Another example of the problem is "Star is not below plus," +*. In this somewhat harder example, the correct answer is "yes." Colin MacLeod, Earl Hunt, and Nancy Mathews (1978) studied people's strategies for solving this kind of sentence picture comparison problem. In their article they reported that people use either of two primary strategies for solving these problems. One strategy involves representing information from the sentence verbally. The solver takes the sentence and summarizes its content in the form of a propositional string, such as [star above plus]. In the other strategy, the solver represents information from the sentence spatially. In this strategy, the solver converts the verbal information into an image, and then compares this image to the picture that is presented. MacLeod and his colleagues found that whether people represented information linguistically or spatially was in part a function of their respective ability levels in these two domains. People who were "more verbal" were more likely to represent information linguistically. People who were "more spatial" were more likely to represent information spatially. They were adopting the mental representation that most suited their own patterns of ability.

Unfortunately, people do not always use the mental representation that is most suited to their abilities. In a study of linear syllogistic reasoning[1] (that is, reasoning for problems such as "John is taller than Pete. Pete is taller than Sam. Who is shortest?"), for example, Sternberg and Evelyn Weil found in 1980 that although there exist both linguistic and spatial strategies for solving these problems, as well as a strategy that combines linguistic and spatial elements, people do not tend to select the strategy that is best suited to their strengths. Perhaps because of the greater complexity of these problems relative to the sentence-picture comparison problems, the best strategy is less obvious. Indeed, in these problems, people are usually not initially aware that there are other strategies. Thus, use of better mental representations could help their problem solving.

[1] For more about syllogisms, see chapter 7.

IMPROVING YOUR SELECTION OF A MENTAL REPRESENTATION

There are some steps you can take to help you better mentally represent problems. Here are some of them:

1. *Know your pattern of abilities.* Sometimes, problems can be solved in different ways. For example, the sentence-picture comparison problems described earlier can be solved using either a spatial or a linguistic mental representation. Knowing your pattern of abilities can help you choose which kind of representation is optimal for you. If you are better at spatial tasks than at linguistic tasks, you may well be better off choosing a spatial mental representation. Conversely, if you tend to be better at linguistic tasks, you may be better off selecting a linguistic representation. If you are equally skilled at both kinds of tasks, than you may choose either option, depending on the particular problem, or else choose a mixed strategy that employs both spatial and linguistic elements. The point is that if you know your pattern of abilities, you are in a better position to use the kind of mental representation that you will find most convenient.

Consider a concrete example of how important knowledge of one's pattern of abilities can be. Both Sternberg and Grigorenko have taught several statistics courses that involve fairly complicated kinds of statistical techniques, several of which can be understood geometrically, algebraically, or both, although ultimately the two kinds of representations of information are equivalent. They teach the conceptual bases for the techniques both ways, and find quite a bit of diversity in which route students choose. If a student knows where his or her pattern of abilities lies, it is easier to use this information to help learning these complicated statistical techniques.

2. *Use multiple representations whenever possible.* In problems where multiple representations for information are possible, it often helps to use at least two of these representations. If you know you are better at representing information one way than another, then you can pick one of the representations to be your first choice and the other to be your second choice. The advantage to using multiple representations is that even if they seem to be the same, they may not be. Sometimes, you can see aspects of a problem when representing it one way that are not obvious when you represent the problem another way. Using multiple forms of representation may help you recognize more aspects of the nature of the problem. For example, drawing a diagram often helps you solve a problem algebraically, even though the diagram is strictly geometric.

Sometimes the problem is not one of multiple *forms* of representation but of multiple representations of a given form. Consider the problem of mutual arms reduction or elimination. One of the major difficulties in achieving any progress at all toward this goal has been the inability or unwillingness of major world powers to see things from each other's point of view. When each side tries to solve the problem from its own point of view, the attempt invariably fails, because solution of the problem is dependent on mutual steps toward reduction, which in turn are dependent on mutual understanding. In international relations, in general, problems are often difficult to solve because of the inability or unwillingness of one side to see the other side's point of view.

EXERCISE 4.1

1. Pete is faster than Bill. Sam is slower than Bill. Who is slowest?

This rather simple problem is a straightforward illustration of how a spatial representation for information–whether mental or external–can help in your solution of a problem. The easiest way to solve this problem is simply to construct a vertical linear array (similar to a list) and to place the individuals along this array, as in Figure 4–1.

Figure 4–1. Example of a Vertical Linear Array

2. Bill is faster than Tom. Pete is faster than Sam. Pete is slower than Tom. Bill is slower than Mike. Sam is faster than Jack. Who is fastest?

Again, the easiest way to solve this problem is through the use of a linear array. In this case, however, you need to have six people on the array rather than just three. In this problem, the relation between individuals is one of speed rather than height. It is probably still easiest to represent the individuals in terms of a vertical linear array with the "fastest" pole at the top of the array and the "slowest" pole at the bottom of the array. However, you also may choose to use a horizontal linear array, placing either "faster"; or "slower" at the left or right sides of the array, respectively. One correct solution is shown in Figure 4–2.

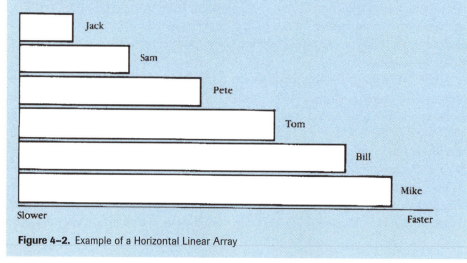

Figure 4–2. Example of a Horizontal Linear Array

3. Glen is older than Pete but not as old as Cal. Cal is older than both Pete and Nate. Nate is younger than Pete but older than Ted. Who is youngest?

This problem is similar to the others, except that each sentence contains two relations between individuals rather than just one. Again, however, the problem can be solved via a simple linear ordering, as in Figure 4–3.

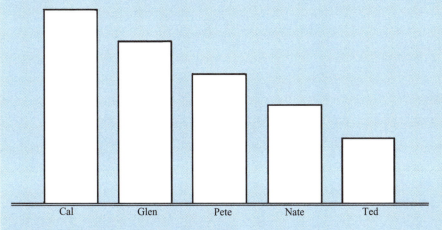

Figure 4–3. Example of a Simple Linear Ordering

4. Three men – Henry, Louis, and Pete – differ in their levels of wealth. The last names of these three men are Toliver, Gray, and Masters, but not necessarily in that order. Louis is not as wealthy as Henry. Pete is wealthier than Louis but not as wealthy as Henry. Toliver is wealthier than Gray. Masters is not as wealthy as Gray. What is the full name of the least wealthy individual?

This problem requires two spatial arrays, one of which relates the first names to each other, the other the last names. The problem can then be solved by correctly linking up the corresponding first and last names. The solution appears in Figure 4–4.

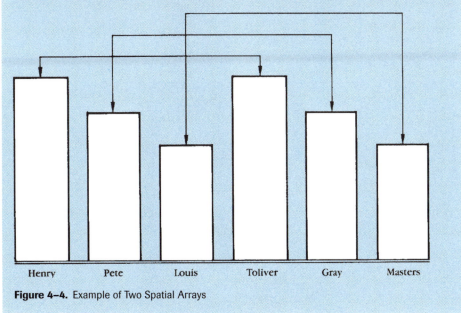

Figure 4–4. Example of Two Spatial Arrays

5. Three boys – Tom, José, and Harry – have among them thirteen marbles and twice as many baseball cards. Tom has four more baseball cards than marbles. José's two marbles are four fewer than Tom's, and José has twice as many baseball cards as he has marbles. Harry has two more baseball cards than does Tom. How many marbles does Harry have?

The easiest way to solve this problem is through the construction of a table listing Tom, José, and Harry as three rows down and marbles and baseball cards as two columns across. As you are given information, you should place it in the table. As this problem is a bit more difficult than the ones that have preceded it, Figure 4–5 goes through each of the steps.

Figure 4–5. Answer Using a Table (Question 5)

	MARBLES	BASEBALL CARDS
Tom	(2 + 4) = 6	(6 [# marbles] + 4) = 10
José	2	(2 [# marbles] x 2) = 4
Harry	(13 – [6 + 2]) = 5	(10 + 2) = 12

6. Maria, Frank, and Sue are interested in cooking. Among them they own a total of sixteen cookbooks. Of Maria's four books, half are French but none are Italian. Frank owns the same number of books as Maria, but owns only half as many French cookbooks as does Maria, and the same number of Italian cookbooks as does Maria. Sue owns only one Chinese cookbook, but the same number of Italian cookbooks as Maria owns Chinese cookbooks. How many French cookbooks does Sue own?

This problem, like the preceding one, is best solved by setting up a table. The table might have the names arrayed as rows down the left side of the table and the kinds of cookbooks as columns arrayed across the top. Again, you must enter the information in the problem in order to figure out the solution. Figure 4–6 shows the complete table and the correct answer.

Figure 4–6. Answer Using a Table (Question 6)

	French	Italian	Chinese
Maria	2	0	2
Frank	1	0	3
Sue	(16 – 11) = 5	2	1

7. Three women – Joan, Patty, and Sandy – have among them three children – Sam, Louise, and Dave. Sam likes to play with Patty's son. Sandy occasionally baby-sits for Joan's children. Who is Louise's mother?

This problem is solved by creating a table listing Joan, Patty, and Sandy in three rows and Sam, Louise, and Dave in three columns. The full solution appears in Figure 4–7.

Figure 4–7. Answer Using a Table (Question 7)

	Sam	Louise	Dave
Joan	×	×	
Patty			×
Sandy			

8. One day last week, Carlos went to the doctor, ate lunch at a restaurant, played basketball, and went to the movies in the evening. On Wednesday, they only show a matinee, but they do show evening movies all the other days except Thursday. The doctor does not have office hours on Friday or Saturday, and the restaurant is closed on Monday. On Sundays, Carlos has a habit of always cooking his own meals. On what day of the week did Carlos go to the doctor, eat lunch at the restaurant, play basketball, and go to the movies?

This problem, like the ones preceding it, is most easily solved by making a table. You may either array the four activities as four separate rows and the seven days of the week as seven separate columns, or you may simply choose to cross out days of the week as they are eliminated. The last procedure is the easiest, and probably the more efficient one. The solution appears in Figure 4–8.

Figure 4–8. Answer Using a Table (Question 8)

	Su	M	Tu	W	Th	F	Sa
Doctor						×	×
Restaurant	×	×					
Golf							
Movies				×	×		

9. Janet, Barbara, and Elaine are a housewife, lawyer, and physicist, although not necessarily in that order. Janet lives next door to the housewife. Barbara is the physicist's best friend. Elaine once wanted to be a lawyer but decided against it. Janet has seen Barbara within the last two days, but has not seen the physicist. Indicate the respective occupations of Janet, Barbara, and Elaine.

This problem, like the last two, is best worked out by creating a table (are you sensing a pattern yet?). The table might have Janet, Barbara, and Elaine as rows, and housewife, lawyer, and physicist as columns. Figure 4–9 shows the solution.

Figure 4–9. Answer Using a Table (Question 9)

	Lawyer	Housewife	Physicist
Janet	×		
Barbara		×	
Elaine			×

10. A marketing company is doing a survey of a limited number of people who own General Motors cars. In their survey, they phone fifteen hundred people who own Chevys, twelve hundred people who own Buicks, eight hundred people who own Oldsmobiles, fifty people who own both Chevys and Buicks, twenty people who own both Buicks and Oldsmobiles, and thirty people who own both Chevys and Oldsmobiles. What is the total number of people phoned by the marketing company? (Note that the owners of particular types of cars, such as Chevys, may also be owners of second cars. In other words, the figure for the ownership of a single kind of car includes within it the number of individuals owning that kind of car or that plus another kind of car.)

This problem is most easily solved by creating a diagram with overlapping circles representing the numbers of people owning each possible combination of cars, as in Figure 4–10.

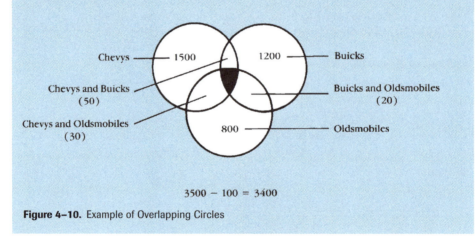

$$3500 - 100 = 3400$$

Figure 4–10. Example of Overlapping Circles

The same is true, of course, in smaller-scale relations, such as marriage. Many married couples have repeated fights and arguments, which may lead to separation or divorce, mostly because they are unable or unwilling to put themselves in each other's shoes. In problems between individuals or groups, satisfactory solutions nearly always depend on each party's being able to represent information in the way that the other party does. Experience has shown that such mutual understanding is not easy to come by.

   3. *Use external representation.* Many complicated problems can become simpler if you do not rely totally on mental representations of the problem. Consider again a

linear syllogism, in which properties of various people or objects are compared. The problem is much simpler to solve if you draw a little diagram representing the relations among people or objects. Suppose, for example, you are told, "Sam is not as tall as Bill. Bill is not as tall as Pete. Who is shortest?" The solution is much easier to come by if you list the three individuals in a vertical linear ordering expressing their relative heights. The point, then, is to use external representations of information whenever possible in order to reduce your "cognitive load" – that is, how much mental effort you have to spend.

ALLOCATING YOUR RESOURCES

Perhaps no metacomponent is more important to successful problem solving, and even successful living in general, than the metacomponent involved in resource allocation. People are constantly making decisions about resource allocation that have significant and even profound effects on their lives.

Examples

Consider the plight of a typical college freshman who has been used to a routine that she established in high school. But this routine no longer applies. Not only is the student likely to have more work than she has ever encountered before, but she is often faced by a dazzling number of possibilities for extracurricular involvement, participation in sports, participation in dramatic activities, going to movies, dating classmates, working on the college newspaper, and so on. There just doesn't seem to be enough time to do everything she would like to do. For this reason, new college students usually need to rearrange their schedules and their styles of living. At least one of us remembers quite well the thrill of being away from home, and how it was quite difficult to be convinced that reading "The Iliad" was more important than doing various bad things. The way in which students allocate their time can have a substantial effect on their success in college, no matter how "success" is defined. For instance, many first-year students who run into academic trouble do so because they did not budget enough time for academic work.

Now consider the student who is taking a scholastic aptitude test. Such tests usually do not allot sufficient time for the student to solve every problem carefully and to his complete satisfaction. As a result, he finds himself having to allocate his time in a way that will get him the highest score. Students who are "test smart" learn certain strategies for budgeting their time effectively: skipping over difficult items and coming back to them later, saving very time-consuming problems for later, and not spending too much time on a problem in which initial attempts do not immediately reach a solution. By efficiently allocating their time during a test, they can perform much better. Notice that although such a test is not designed to measure the metacomponent of resource allocation directly, the use of a time limit means that it is likely to measure this metacomponent indirectly.

Resource allocation continues to be important beyond the student years. A difficult decision many adults face is that of how to allocate their time among their family, friends, and work. Many of us find that although the demands upon our time are different from those that we faced in our student days, they are nonetheless equally or even more pressing. A poignant ballad by the late folksinger Harry Chapin, "The Cat's in the Cradle," highlights this dilemma. As a boy grew up, his father never found much time to spend with him. In later years, when the father wanted to spend time with his now-adult son, the son had become too busy. The father realizes that his son has grown up to become just like him. The son is unable (or willing) to spend with him the time that the father had been unable to spend with his son when they were both younger.

Earl Hunt and Marcy Lansman (1982) and others studied resource allocation within the context of a dual-task paradigm. Participants in their experiments were asked to solve a difficult primary task (such as a matrix reasoning test) at the same time that they were asked to solve a secondary, usually simpler, task (such as a basic reaction-time task). The idea is that while the participants are solving the primary task, a visual or auditory signal may appear, and the participants must press a button as quickly as possible. Thus, although they allocate most of their mental-processing resources to the difficult primary task, they nevertheless have to allocate at least some of their processing resources to the simpler secondary task. Hunt and Lansman (1982) found that smarter people are better able to allocate resources and to divide their attention between the two tasks effectively.

Barbara Hayes-Roth and her colleagues also studied allocation of resources in planning for a number of years. They were particularly interested in what makes a person a good planner. Consider, for example, the problem of performing a number of errands on a single trip. Often you have only limited time to perform the errands, and the order in which you do them needs to reflect both the importance of each errand and the locations of the places in which the errands can be performed. Indeed, think of your last run of errands. Maybe you had to get ice cream, fill your car with gas, get a haircut, and buy a present for your niece.

Hayes-Roth studied how individuals go about handling this type of planning situation. With Sarah Goldin (1980), she found several interesting results. First, as mentioned in Chapter 2, good planners tend to spend relatively more time on higher-level planning (or metaplanning) than do poorer planners, especially taking into account the importance of each errand and how far away you have to go for each errand. Second, good planners show more attentional flexibility than do poor planners. Third, good planners make more use of knowledge about the outside world (for example, when stores open and close) in their planning than do poor planners.

Improving Your Allocation of Resources

As the above examples imply, there are a number of steps you can take to improve your allocation of mental and physical resources. Here are some of those steps:

1. *Be willing to spend relatively large amounts of time on high-level planning.* Both Sternberg's results and those of Goldin and Hayes-Roth (1981) show the importance of a person's willingness to spend large amounts of time on high-level planning. Notice

the use of the term *willingness* here. Many people who could be better planners aren't because they are simply unwilling to spend the time it takes to be a good planner. They impulsively jump into tasks before they are ready to perform them, with the result that they do not perform the tasks as effectively and efficiently as they otherwise might have. As a result, they often have to go back and make up for the time they should have spent on planning. Thus, when you are confronted with a new problem, it is important for you to spend the time needed to plan a strategy that will maximize performance on the task.

2. *Make full use of your prior knowledge in planning and allocating your resources.* Although people differ greatly in the amount of knowledge that they bring to a task, they differ at least as greatly in the extent to which they use whatever knowledge they have to help approach that task. Your allocation of resources will be much more effective if you use all of the information you have available in order to plan and allocate time effectively. For example, in planning a strategy for doing errands, mentally visualizing the various paths you may have to traverse in order to do the errands constitutes a sensible and effective use of prior knowledge. If you have in your mind even a vague image of the geographical layout of the paths you have to travel, then use it in planning your errands or tasks.

3. *Be flexible and willing to change your plans and allocations of resources.* As we all know, even the best-laid plans can go astray. It is therefore important that you keep in mind the possibility of plans going awry, and maintain flexibility in your plans. If a given strategy or allocation of resources does not succeed, then you must be ready to change to another plan or set other priorities for resource allocation. For example, one of the most damaging strategies in taking a test is that of spending too long on a given problem. Occasionally, you may find that a problem you had thought you could solve in a reasonable amount of time is taking much longer than you had anticipated. Just as you have to know when and how to start a problem, you also have to know when and how to stop. Sometimes the best decision is just to give up and to move on. Similarly, in other kinds of situations, you may follow a path that turns out to be a dead end. For example, you may choose a topic for a term paper and later find that there is little reference material on this topic, or that the ideas for the term paper just aren't coming to mind. Persevering in that choice of topic may result in a frustrating experience and a poor grade on the paper. The point is that it is just as important for you to know when to change your allocation of resources as it is to know how to allocate them initially.

4. *Be on the lookout for new kinds of resources.* People often come to take for granted the resources they have available for accomplishing a given task and close their eyes to the possibility that new resources will improve their performance of the task. For many years, for example, one of us used to write his papers directly on a typewriter. He would write each page and then revise it as many times as needed until he got the page just the way he wanted it. The result was a fairly polished first draft, but also a lot of wasted paper, as he would do each page over and over again in an attempt to make it approach final form. When personal computers entered the scene, he was reluctant to switch over from his typewriter; he had become so used to a particular

style of writing that he could not imagine that any other style would suit him better. After repeated urgings from his colleagues, he eventually decided to try, writing with a word processing program on a microcomputer. To his surprise, he found that the speed with which he could write a paper increased at least twofold. The reason was that all the changes he needed to make on a given page could be made without starting the whole page over from scratch. Formerly, if he wanted to insert a new sentence in the middle of a page, he had to retype the whole page. Under the new system, he could simply insert the sentence and go on. We all have our own examples of blindness to new possibilities for resources that could improve our performance. Try your best to be open to new possibilities as they arise.

5. *Utilize mnemonics to better store resources.* What are mnemonics? A mnemonic is any type of memory trick that you can use to help you remember something. Sometimes it can be an ordered string of visual images – also known as the method of loci. In this method, think of a place very familiar to you, such as your house. Place items you need to remember at various points in the house. So let's say that you are trying to remember a shopping list. You might place the marshmallows in your main hall, the roast beef on your couch, the guava juice in your fireplace, the frozen pizzas on the dinner table, and so on. When you are actually in the grocery store, you can mentally walk through your house and find everything on your list.

Other techniques are more word-based. One of the most common mnemonics is to make up a song, and turn whatever you are trying to remember into song lyrics. In fact, if you hum out loud the melody of "Twinkle, Twinkle, Little Star" (or "Baa Baa Black Sheep"), you will also be humming one of the first mnemonics you may have heard – the Alphabet Song (A-B-C-D-E-F-G, H-I-J-K, L-M-N-O, P, and so on). Rhymes are sometimes used – for example, "I before e except after c" to remember how to spell words like thief ("i" before "e") or believe ("i" before "e") or conceit (it's after "c," so it's "ei"). Another common one is "Thirty days hath September/April, June, and November" to remember which months only have thirty days.

Sometimes, you can take a long list of terms and use the first letter of each of the words to remember the list. You can form a whole word sometimes, such as HOMES to remember all of the great lakes (Huron, Ontario, Michigan, Erie, and Superior, although the one of us who is writing this admits to using Google to look up the actual names). Sometimes, you can take the initials and use them to form other words, spelling out a funny sentence. So to remember the order of operations in math, many people say, "People Excuse My Dear Aunt Sally" – Parentheses, Exponents, Multiply, Divide, Add, Subtract. To remember the notes of the music staff, you can use both types. One row of notes reads FACE. The row of notes is EGBDF, also known as Every Good Boy Deserves Fudge (or Every Good Boy Does Fine, as one of our less-indulgent grandmothers taught). Two more common mnemonics are "Roy G. Biv" and "My Very Elegant Mother Just Sat Upon Nine Pins." Can you figure out what they stand for?[2]

---

[2] Roy G. Biv represents the colors of the rainbow – Red, orange, yellow, green, blue, indigo, and violet. My Very Elegant Mother Just Sat Upon Nine Pins is the order of the planets – Mars, Venus, Earth, Mercury, Jupiter, Saturn, Uranus, Neptune, and Pluto. No word on how a mysterious tenth planet would affect the mnemonic, or how Pluto's disputed status as a planet would affect it!

EXERCISE 4.2

1. Think of the major categories that you might use to represent the kinds of activities you do during your waking hours. Such categories might include study time, eating time, sleeping time, talking-on-the-phone time, watching-television time, and so on. Estimate the number of hours you spent on each of these types of activities during the past week. Then calculate the percentage of total time spent on each of these activities. Draw a pie (circle) graph representing your allocation of time among these various activities. Each piece of the pie should be proportional to the percentage of time you spent on the activity it represents. Now draw a pie graph representing the way in which you would ideally like to allocate your time among these activities. Compare the two graphs, and consider how you might be able to make your actual distribution of time correspond more closely to your ideal distribution of time.

Use the street grid of San Pedro in Figure 4–11 to help you solve the following two exercises.

2. You are going to France this afternoon. There are some things you need to get in town before you go back home. You have to go to one of the local banks (20 or 86) to buy some travelers' checks. Your finest jacket was eaten by moths so you need to buy a new one to wear on your trip (39 or 59). As you are going on a student exchange program, you want to buy a present at a gift store (100 or 31) for the family you are staying with. This family has a farm with a stable and a swimming pool, so you want to get a bathing suit and riding boots either at the sports supplies store (75) or in one of the department stores (26 or 64). Your mother suggested you buy a French phrase book (48) to help you over the language barrier even though your French is very fluent. You have a book from the library that is due in two days, and you want to return it before you leave (68). Finally, you have to pick up your sister at her swimming lesson (57) and take the subway (34 or 104) home.

It is now 9:30 A.M. You just took a final exam at the university (25), and you need to be home by 1:00 P.M. to finish packing. You have to do your errands by foot. It takes fifteen minutes to cross the town by foot in either direction. You probably won't be able to do everything but do the best you can.

3. This afternoon you will be quite busy. At 5:30 P.M. you have to pick up your husband at the telephone company (8) and go back home together but before that you have lots of chores to do.

Before 4:00 P.M. (closing time), you have to pick up your new car at the car dealer (42). Then, you have to take it to the gas station (2) and park it in a parking lot (23) to do your errands by foot.

You want to go to the health spa (19) to do some exercising for at least one hour. You need a baby-sitter for tomorrow and you know that at the fire station (63) you can get a list of names from a friendly fireman. You want to buy some records at the record store (46). Tomorrow is your son's birthday so you want to buy him a bicycle either in the bicycle shop (93) or in either of the department stores (26 or 64). Because you are changing the curtains in your living room, you need to buy

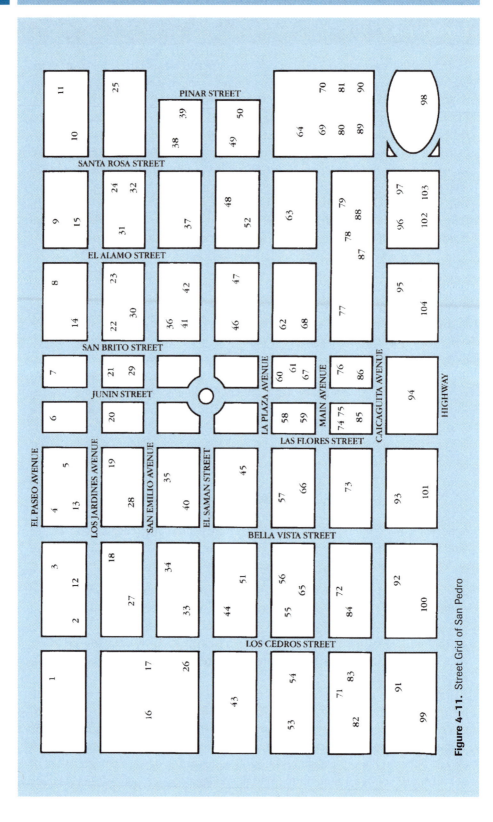

Figure 4–11. Street Grid of San Pedro

some fabric at the fabrics store (66) and get some curtain rods at the hardware store (29 or 82).

It is 2:30 P.M. You are standing at the subway station at El Saman Street (34). You have to do your errands by foot. It takes fifteen minutes to cross the town by foot in either direction. You probably won't be able to do everything but do the best you can.

Now consider how your solutions to exercises 2 and 3 might have changed if you had decided that certain errands were more important than others. In such a case, you would take into account priority as well as location of each errand.

4. A subtest occasionally found on intelligence tests measures a skill called word fluency. In this kind of subtest, you are often asked to think of as many words as you can beginning with a certain letter in a fixed amount of time. For example, you might be asked to produce in four minutes all the words you can that begin with the letter y (yarn, yawn, yell, yip, yodel, yin, yang, yellow, yonder, etc.). People frequently try to solve this kind of problem without any particular strategy, simply writing down whatever words come to mind. However, it is possible to improve one's performance on this kind of task by spending the time in advance to think up a systematic strategy. Think up a systematic strategy for performing this kind of test. Then give yourself four minutes exactly to think of as many words as you can that begin with the letter d. Did your strategy contribute to your effective performance on this task?

5. Another kind of subtest frequently found on achievement tests is the anagram. In anagram problems, you are presented with scrambled words. Your task is to rearrange the letters of each word so as to form an intact word. Usually, the total number of possible rearrangements is staggeringly large. You thus need to formulate strategies that will enable you to look at only a subset of the possible rearrangements. Below are five anagrams. Think first about what kinds of strategies you can use so that you will not have to list all possible rearrangements of the letters. Then use these strategies, plus whatever other new strategies you can think of, to help your solution of the anagrams. The answers are at the bottom of the page, but do not look until you have tried to unscramble the words.

(a) T-N-K-H-G-I
(b) H-U-L-A-G
(c) P-T-T-M-E
(d) E-R-H-O-S[3]

6. Imagine you are in charge of allocating funds for various charities whose goal is to fight different diseases, such as heart disease, cancer, and tuberculosis. These charities both support research on the various diseases and also help those who are suffering from the diseases. You have $500,000. What considerations would you use

---

[3] The answers are (a) *knight*, (b) *laugh*, (c) *tempt*, and (d) *horse* or *shore*.

in deciding how much money to allocate to the various charities? For example, two possibilities are the number of people who suffer from the disease and the mortality rate for the disease. Once you have decided on the considerations you would use in deciding among charities, decide on how much you would weigh each of these considerations in allocating funds.

7. You are the campaign manager for a senatorial candidate, and have $1,000,000 to spend on a political campaign. On what activities should you spend these funds, and how much money should you allocate to each activity? (Some possible examples of activities are fund-raising events, newspaper advertisements, television spots, and the like.)

8. You are a top-level business executive, and have to decide whether to begin mass production of a new product, the "widget." Before mass marketing the widget, you need to decide how well it will sell. The product is designed to reduce household electrical consumption. What kinds of tests might you perform to decide how successful the widget will be before you actually spend money to mass-produce it?

Mnemonics can help you easily store more information in your head than you might normally be able to. Sometimes it is just short term (such as when studying for an exam); other mnemonics can be useful your whole life.

SOLUTION MONITORING

In problem solving, many of the most important decisions are made at the beginning. First you make a decision as to the nature of the problem. Then you decide what processes to use, how to represent information, and so on. You may often make the wrong decisions for any number of reasons. For one thing, you may have misread the terms of the problem; for another, you may have picked a strategy that, although able solve the problem, will solve it only slowly or with great difficulty. It is important for you as a problem solver to realize that your initial decisions are not irrevocable. To the contrary, you should view them as tentative and be prepared to change them as the need arises. It is one thing to make an incorrect decision at the start of problem solving; it is another to continue with that decision, either because you are unaware of how to change it or because you are unwilling to change it.

Examples of Solution Monitoring

Careful monitoring of the solution process might have or should have led to a change in strategy in any number of decisions at any level. For example, the experience of the United States in Vietnam is an instance in which virtually no matter how the situation was monitored, indications were that our involvement did not accomplish whatever it was supposed to accomplish. A number of factors led to continued involvement, such as national pride, the desire to meet a commitment to another government, and so on. However, it became clear to most people in the United States that the reasons for staying were not enough.

A second example of solution monitoring occurs in our everyday interactions with others, and especially interactions involving high stakes, such as job interviews. During such conversations, we are almost continually receiving feedback about the kind of impression we are making. Sometimes this feedback is subtle, such as a downward glance. Sometimes this feedback is obvious, as when people say, "My word, you are the most boring person I've ever met; please go away and never speak to me again."

Some of this feedback may be verbal; the rest of it is nonverbal. Careful monitoring of this feedback and acting on it increases the probability of our attaining the goals set out for that conversation, whatever they may be. Indeed, whole books have been written about how to interpret nonverbal signals during the course of a conversation.

In our own work, we frequently have to give presentations to diverse audiences. Before giving any talk, Sternberg, for example, asks about the composition of the audience, including questions such as the number of people expected, their level of background in psychology, their interests, and their reason for coming to hear him speak. He then attempts to tailor his presentation so as to meet the needs and background of the audience. Occasionally, he makes a misjudgment. However, he tries to recognize this misjudgment early during the talk rather than after the talk is over. When Sternberg becomes aware that a talk is not going over well, he tries to change it as much as possible to suit the audience better. Obviously, there is less he can do in the middle of a talk than before it starts, but it is often not too late to make some changes in the middle that will make at least a modest success out of what otherwise might have been a failure. Thus, as a speaker, Sternberg sees his job as partially one of monitoring audience reaction.

The same monitoring applies to a teaching situation. Talented teachers try to stay aware of whether their students are understanding and are interested in the material presented. If students look confused or bored, good teachers attempt to figure out why. Then they correct their presentation to make it more comprehensible or more interesting. What kinds of cues are useful in determining whether an audience is with the speaker, whether it is an audience of professionals or students? The kinds of things good speakers generally do is to look for eye contact, for absence of whispering or side conversations that are obviously irrelevant, for audience or class questions that show mental engagement with the material, and for facial expressions showing interest in the material.

Solution monitoring is important in many different phases of life. Here are a few more examples. Many of us, at one time or another, seek some kind of therapy, whether physical or psychological. During the course of the therapy, we can observe whether things are improving. If they are not, we ought to consider getting out of therapy, or at least switching therapists. Without doubt, any number of people go to a therapist for years without any noticeable sign of improvement without considering stopping or changing the therapy. One of us recently went in for physical therapy, to have a massage for back pain. After the massage, his back felt better – but his neck hurt for the next week! Proper solution monitoring encouraged him to seek ways of helping his back other than going to that particular therapist.

A second example of the need to monitor is in enrollment in book clubs, CD clubs, and so on. Such clubs often have highly attractive initial offers designed to get people to join. Twelve CDs for the price of one! No obligation to buy! One wonders how the clubs can afford such offers. One of the things they count on is that people's inertia will prevent them from quitting, even if they are dissatisfied with the products of the club. Many clubs will automatically send a book or CD every month unless the club member specifically tells them not to. The strategy here is that most people simply will not bother to return the postcard indicating lack desire for the product. Similarly, the clubs often offer to refund people's money if the purchase is mailed back. Here, they bank on the fact that wrapping up a book or a record and sending it back is enough of an inconvenience to prevent many people from bothering to do it.

A third example of the need for solution monitoring is in choosing stores, such as supermarkets. Many people decide on a supermarket for any of several reasons, and then continue to patronize it over the years. Often, they do not continue to monitor whether the quality of the products at that supermarket is superior to that at other local places, or whether the prices are lower. In other words, once the decision is made to go to a certain store, the decision is not often analyzed enough. The result can be wasting money or being unhappy with what you've purchased.

The need for solution monitoring can be shown in psychological research as well as in everyday experience. One striking example of solution monitoring can be seen in children's reading. Ellen Markman (1979) presented children with reading passages in which there are blatant self-contradictions. So, for example, one piece of information is given early in the passage; later, the exact same bit of information is contradicted. Astonishingly, the children often fail to notice these contradictions. Their monitoring of their reading comprehension is apparently inadequate, with the result that they cannot see the contradiction in the paragraph. Adults can also do the same thing. The point of all these examples is a simple one: The decision-making process in problem solving does not end once the initial decisions have been made and solution of the problem proper has begun. Rather, decision-making must continue throughout the solution of the problem until the solver is completely satisfied with the solution.

IMPROVING YOUR SOLUTION MONITORING

There are several steps you can take to improve your solution monitoring in problem solving. Here are some of these steps:

1. *Be aware of the need for solution monitoring, and act on this need.* The most important step you can take is simply to be aware of the need to monitor your solution strategies, and then to act on this awareness. Many people simply fail to monitor their problem-solving strategies. If they do monitor them, they do nothing with the feedback. The most important step you can take is to be aware of the need to continually check to see whether your strategy or decisions are working. If they are not, you need to act.

2. *Beware of entrapment.* You also need to be aware of what social psychologists call entrapment, or the "justification of effort." Entrapment is a strikingly powerful force in human thought and action. The more that you invest in a decision, the more you are likely to find reasons why this decision is a good one. The higher the investment, the harder it is to walk away from it. Many people will choose to continue with their initial decision or plan – and will continue to do so even when it is unwise. Some people will stick with an original plan even if the amount of time or money needed to make this plan successful would still be higher than an alternate plan. For example, you may have an old car that's falling apart. If you've already spent money on repairing the brakes and fixing the engine and replacing a side mirror, you are more likely to keep spending money – even if this cost of a new repair is actually *more* than your car is worth! This pitfall can also be seen in romance – how many people do you know who stick with their old boyfriend or girlfriend, even though the relationship is going nowhere, just because they've been together for a long time and are unwilling to start something new?

The same problem, of course, confronts business executives every day. When a new product is introduced, an enormous investment often goes into the production and marketing of that product. No matter how adequate the initial marketing tests are, a product initially believed to be successful may fail. A product that was once successful may no longer be selling. One of the toughest decisions that business executives face is when to discontinue or stop promoting a product. Despite their enormous investment in trying to make the product successful, the correct decision is often to withdraw it from the market.

In a similar vein, scientists often have to recognize when they are pursuing a dead end. It can be easy to waste an entire career by being unable or unwilling to recognize the need to move on. Being a good scientist requires not only knowing which problems to pursue and how to pursue them, but also knowing when to give up gracefully and to proceed to something else.

3. *Avoid being impulsive.* Sometimes you will realize that something is wrong and that you need to do something to correct this problem. For example, if you are taking a test and rechecking your answers, you may find one that you start to question. Maybe it's a math test, and you've gotten a different solution. Avoid the tendency immediately to pick the second answer. It is always possible that it is your solution monitoring – not the original answer – that is wrong. Indeed, studies of behavior on multiple-choice tests have shown that what you may have always feared is true. When you erase an original response and put a new one, your first answer is often right and the new answer wrong.

Of course, you should not avoid monitoring solutions altogether. You should recognize, however, that the solution-monitoring process, like the original problem-solving process, is susceptible to error. As a result, you need to take care in how you use the results of the monitoring process. Being careful in solution monitoring has become particularly important because of computers. It is common to find a mistake when you check a paper you have written (or a program you have created). With a computer, you can very easily delete an entire file, assuming it is not usable. You may

EXERCISE 4.3

1. Consider a real-life problem that you have solved in the past month. How might more adequate monitoring of your solution processes improve your solution of the problem?

2. You are in a job interview and concerned that you make the best impression possible. During the interview, you find yourself monitoring both your own behavior and that of the interviewer in order to determine how well the interview is going. What kinds of signs might you look for to get some idea of what the interviewer thinks of you?

3. Marriages often break down because the people involved fail to monitor the quality of their relationship. If they do monitor it, they are not alert to signs of a breakdown. What kinds of signs should one look for that indicate that a marriage is faltering, and what constructive steps might be taken in response to the realization that any of these signs indicates trouble?

4. In Chapter 3, you solved several versions of the Missionaries and Cannibals problem. This is a problem in which solution monitoring can help you solve the problem much faster. What kinds of monitoring should you do in order to improve your performance on this problem?

5. One of the primary purposes of this book is to effect an improvement in its readers' intellectual skills. How could you or your instructor go about monitoring – both formally and informally – whether this goal is being met?

6. One of the most important questions scientists face is whether their research is progressing, and at a larger level, whether their field is progressing. What are some of the signs that a field is progressing, and what are some of the signs that it is stagnant?

regret it later on, if you realize that the deleted material was actually not too bad, or at least partly usable.

4. *Actively seek external feedback.* Often, people are surprised by the lack of feedback they receive for their efforts. For example, people frequently feel that they have very little idea of what their spouse or significant other thinks of them. Junior executives vying for promotion sometimes feel that they don't know either their superiors' opinions of them or what their chances for promotions are. The point of all this is that people are often willing to give feedback, but only if they are asked. In each of these situations, asking for the feedback that may not come spontaneously might quickly compensate for the lack of external information.

5. *Be open to, but evaluative of external feedback.* You may receive external feedback on your problem-solving from many different sources. It may be from your parents, your friends, your professors, or anyone close to you. This external feedback can be helpful to you in your problem-solving monitoring. Others may pick up errors

in problem-solving that you fail to pick up yourself. However, it is important to evaluate external feedback just as carefully as you evaluate your own internal feedback. You need to consider the probable reliability of the source of the feedback and the usefulness of the feedback. All of us have been in situations in which we receive feedback from someone who knows less about the problem than we do. Such feedback is not necessarily worthless, but its source needs to be considered. A professor's advice to take a class that fits your major will probably be more valuable than a Best Buy clerk's advice. But the clerk's advice on a stereo system will probably be more valuable than the professor's. Another possibility is that you will receive accurate feedback, but find that it is not helpful. For example, a suggestion to solve a difficult problem via a computer is not useful if you have no computer available. In sum, be receptive to, but critical of, external feedback. Most importantly, avoid being defensive in receiving such feedback. Defensiveness will hurt your ability to get high-quality problem solutions. First, it will blind you to recognizing the problems in your solutions. Second, it discourages others from even giving feedback. If others realize that you will react defensively, they may be reluctant to comment on your performance. As a result, they may withhold feedback that would have been helpful.

EVERYDAY DECISION MAKING

"What should I do"? Each of us has asked him- or herself this question. We have asked it many times; in fact, it is an unavoidable question. Even if we try never to deal with making decisions, we nevertheless have to do it. And so we do it!

Decision making is potentially about anything and everything. It could be about you and your life:

Should I go to the grocery store now or later?
Should I have lunch at noon or 1 P.M.?
Should I get married?
Should I get a new job?
Should I quit smoking?
Should I climb Mount Kilimanjaro?
Should I see if I could do a handstand?

Or it could be about your family, your community, your country, or the world at large:

Should the United States create more national parks?
Should American public schools be reformed?
Should the space program be given more money to explore distant planets?
Should purchases made on the Internet be taxable?
Should the Israeli government give up its claim to all of Jerusalem?
Should Hollywood make more movies about giraffes?

Anything and everything over which you have the slightest control in your life – whether large or small – boils down to making decisions.

By definition, decisions are possible to make only when there is a choice. When there is a choice, there is a possibility of at least two outcomes. For example, you can decide to *go* or *not to go* out on a date. How do you know which decision is the best one to make?

Understanding Decision Making

In order to make the best decision, one has to understand the situation. One of the most important steps in decision making is to describe the situation in terms of cause and effect. Having a plan in place can help you to make the best decision.

Let's apply what we have discussed about problem solving to the area of everyday decision making.

Defining the Issue

In everyday life, decision making starts with the first component of the problem-solving cycle – the definition of the nature of a problem. This definition is usually described in terms of both its cognitive and emotional implications. Decision making starts by one's having a vague feeling that there is an issue or problem that needs to be resolved. The philosopher Charles Pierce called this sensation a "feeling of doubt." The role of this feeling is to help decision makers begin a crucial part of the decision-making cycle – the *motivation to decide*. A decision maker should *want* to find the best possible decision. In other words, caring matters. You need to be motivated to resolve the feeling of doubt, and to resolve it in the best possible way. If you do not care about making good choices, then you will most likely not find the best possible choice. Moreover, the motivation to decide is better when it is strong – making good decisions involves hard work. Feelings of doubt are usually expressed in statements similar to the following:

> *I'm worried my brother is having relationship problems with his girlfriend.*
> *My boss said he'd promote me to assistant manager after four months, but it's been six months and he hasn't said anything again.*
> *I wonder if I like chemistry enough to take another class in it.*
> *I've been getting stomachaches more often since eating too much junk food.*

A feeling of doubt is only the beginning, however. If you simply stop there, nothing will get done. The best possible outcome is that you may gain some support and agreement of others who share similar feelings of frustration. But what feelings of doubt can do is to trigger a complex process of decision making and provide the motivation to follow through. The next step in the decision-making process is to define the nature of the problem (also called the "issue"). In the next chapter, we define the concept of a *claim* as a statement that argues for a particular characteristic, quality, or property of something or someone.

An *issue* refers to the tension created when there are at least two opposing claims in response to a question. For example, let's suppose someone asks the question, "Should

EXERCISE 4.4

Each statement here could be an issue that could lead to someone making a decision. Analyze each statement and identify the type of issue (factual, value, or moral) expressed.

1. Only 5 percent of students in Dr. Baker's class received an "A," but 65 percent of students in Dr. Wallace's class received an "A."

2. Ryan found out that his best friend has been cheating in the biology class they have together.

3. Juliet looks nicer in the blouse she bought for $20 than in the blouse she bought for $50.

4. Mark spent over $500 on Amazon.com last month.

5. Tomas heard some of his fraternity brothers use words for women that made him feel uncomfortable.

6. Luis found out that the hamburgers he eats for lunch each day have 150 percent of his daily-recommended saturated fat.

7. The players on Doug's high school football team were not as good as the players on his college football team.

8. Shanika liked Bill throughout their first date, until he yelled at a waiter for forgetting their drinks.

9. Roberto likes his history class more than his geometry class.

10. Sara was assigned more than two hundred pages of reading in her chemistry class last week!

11. Marco got an 87 on his midterm, but a 64 on his final exam.

12. Candace hates her new cell phone plan.[4]

universities raise student tuitions?" If one person says *yes* and another person says *no*, there is an issue. Issues are best expressed with the words *should, will, does,* or *is.* They assume that a decision needs to be made to either get rid of the issue or revise the issue and open another. For example, the issue of raising student tuition can be revised with the following question: "Will increased student tuition help the university offer more classes, therefore making it easier for students to get into popular courses?"

Issues can be roughly divided into three categories: *factual, value,* and *moral* issues. *Factual issues* arise in response to claims based on facts (such as that José Canseco hit 462 home runs). For example, the factual issue of which college to choose can emerge in response to factual claims that Tweedle-Dee College offers you more financial aid than Tweedle-Dum College. *Value issues* arise in response to claims about the quality of a person, place, thing, or idea (such as that José Canseco was a

---

[4] Factual claims were 1, 4, 6, 10, and 11; value claims were 3, 7, 9, and 12; moral claims were 2, 5, and 8.

very good baseball player). For example, the value issue of which college to choose can emerge in the context of the value claim that the football team of Tweedle-Dee College is better than the football team of Tweedle-Dum College. Finally, a *moral issue* can emerge in response to claims about morally-charged questions or debates, such as that of whether a baseball player who has confessed to the use of steroids can be an upstanding member of society and a part of his community. Moral issues can emerge when someone tells you that you should go to Tweedle-Dee College because its competitor, Tweedle-Dum College, has been historically opposed to accepting minority and foreign students.

The next stage of decision making is to gather together knowledge about the problem. This process includes: (1) selecting the steps needed to solve a problem; (2) selecting a strategy for ordering these steps; and (3) selecting a mental representation for information. The knowledge-gathering stage of decision making usually takes the most time. This component can also be subdivided into a number of components. Specifically, when doing the groundwork for informed decision-making, people (a) infer causal relationships; (b) formulate a proposition; and (c) generate, evaluate, select, and validate alternatives. We will present the key features of these processes later in this chapter.

Inferring Causal Relationships

In describing the process of inferring causal relationships, we will start by discussing the issues of cause and effect. Understanding causality means being aware of what causes what, of how things work, and why causes and consequences matter. Causal inference is an essential part of our thinking. We constantly interpret the world as comprising causes and effects: The alarm went off, so you woke up; the alarm caused you to wake up. As Doug walked to school, his foot hit a rock and he fell down. The rock caused him to slip. Our cause-and-effect judgments may not necessarily be correct. Melanie may think that her brother is annoyed at her because she borrowed his CDs and didn't return them – but she may be misinterpreting his behavior. Maybe he's upset with Melanie because she told his friends he likes disco music. Or maybe his behavior has nothing to Melanie at all – he's acting grumpy because he got into a fight with his girlfriend, or he has a midterm, or he's hungry.

Indeed, both "average folks" and people who study cognitive psychology can experience great difficulties in establishing causal relationships and determining when one event *really causes* another. One of us was visiting a friend who had a little Chihuahua dog named Hercules. Hercules was cute in a weird kind of way. The author fed him a lot of table scraps – half-eaten French fries, a meatball or two, and so on. The next day, Hercules had a seizure and had to be rushed to the vet. (Thankfully, he was okay.) The vet made it clear to Hercules' owner that the seizure was caused by the dog's asthmatic condition – it was bound to happen. Even though the coauthor was not only aware of causality *but had taught the concept in class*, he still felt responsible. It is natural to assume an event is causal (e.g., feeding a dog table scraps) even when it is not, if the event comes just before the event in question (e.g., the dog's becoming sick).

It is just as natural, in other circumstances, not to see causality. Indeed, one common source of disputes of people in relationships occurs when neither person can see cause and effect in his or her actions. Let's suppose, for example, that Katrina asks Henry to wash the dishes. Maybe he forgets, or maybe he just doesn't want to, and the dishes stay dirty. When, two hours later, Henry asks Katrina for a backrub, he may be surprised when she says no, calls him an idiot, and walks away. Henry may then get angry at Katrina's reaction – not realizing that it was his own behavior that was the immediate cause.

We may associate things together that have nothing to do with each other. Take, for example, the case against water (e.g., Mitchell & Jolley, 2004). Nearly all convicted felons are regular water-drinkers. Most violent crimes are committed within twenty-four hours of touching water in some way. And most people who die at home are near a sink, which can produce water. Obviously, water doesn't *cause* these things. This example is a little silly. But think about some of the arguments made by talk radio hosts and guests, and the assumptions that are made about cause and effect. Some of these examples aren't as funny as bad water – such as arguments that rising crime rates or poverty are especially caused by certain groups of people.

Cause-effect considerations are present through many aspects of our life. We deal with causes and effects when we make our decision to vote for a presidential candidate, when we decide what clothes to wear, or even when we try to understand why Paris Hilton and Donald Trump have stayed popular for so long.

For our discussion, however, it is important to concentrate on two issues: (1) how we establish causal relationships (causes and effects), and (2) why labeling causal relationships is important for decision making.

So, how do people establish causes? First one needs to think about different possible causes. When you think about these potential causes, your mental list will hopefully include the actual cause. Once you have your list, try to eliminate as many causes as possible. The idea is to narrow down your mental list to one (or two) items. If you can do that, then the remaining cause is often a good choice.

Mill's Causes

In the nineteenth century, the English philosopher John Stuart Mill described a number of types of causes and linked them with specific methods of elimination. Of the causes Mill described, we will mention only four.

Type 1. This type of cause is referred to as *a necessary cause*. A necessary cause is a condition that is required to produce an effect. If a particular cause is needed for a particular effect, then this effect will never occur without this cause. For example, HIV is a necessary cause of AIDS. AIDS never occurs without HIV, but someone can be HIV-positive, yet not have AIDS. An effect may have a number of causes, all of which are necessary for the effect to occur. For example, nuclear reactions require the presence of special radioactive chemical elements (e.g., uranium or plutonium) as well as the exposure of these radioactive elements to certain conditions (e.g., high pressure and temperatures).

Type 2. This type of cause is referred to as *a sufficient cause*. A condition is referred to as a sufficient cause of an effect when there are other possible causes but this particular cause nevertheless always has the desired effect. For example, a loud, ringing doorbell is a sufficient cause of a baby waking up. For those of you who may have children or younger siblings, you know quite well how quickly (and grumpily) a baby will wake up when someone rings the doorbell loudly. But there are many, many other ways that a baby can wake up – a dog barking, a car honking, and so on. In a similar way, washing your car with soap and water is a sufficient cause for it to get clean. If you wash your car, it will get clean. But there are other ways a car can get clean – maybe you got lucky and it rained, or you took your car to an automatic car wash.

Type 3. This type of cause is referred to as both *necessary and sufficient*. In other words, these causes always produce a given effect, and the effect is never caused by anything else but these causes. For example, the rotation of Earth around the terrestrial axis is necessary and sufficient for the change between night and day. Without this rotation, no change of daytime will occur. With it, there will always be a night-to-day change (barring the sun extinguishing itself).

Type 4. This type of cause is referred to as *causal dependence of one variable quantity on another*. This is how it works: If a change in one variable always produces a corresponding change in another, then the second variable can be said to be "casually dependent" on the first one (even though "casually dependent" sounds like a self-help book title, we promise it's the real term!). For example, your professor may assign a final paper worth 20 percent of your grade. Let's say that you have a "B" going into the final paper. If you do "A" work on your paper, then your grade will rise correspondingly. If you do "C" work on your paper, then your grade will lower correspondingly. And if you continue to do "B" work on the paper, then your grade will be unchanged. In this example, there are no other factors influencing the rest of your grade – the last 20 percent of your grade is that final paper, and nothing else. In some examples, there can be other factors that also determine the outcome. Let's imagine that you are at a campfire roasting marshmallows. The amount of heat that you feel is a function of your distance from the campfire. The closer to the campfire you are, the hotter you will feel. If you move further away, you will feel less heat. As before, an effect may be causally related to more than one cause. For example, the amount of heat you feel may vary depending on if you are wearing a sweater or a tee shirt.

As we mentioned before, Mill developed taxonomies of both different types of causes and different methods for figuring out if these causes are valid or not. The point here is that we, trying to understand the world around us, would like to understand the nature of various causal relationships (e.g., why Michael likes Leila and not Cathy or Susan or Marie). Mill developed four different critical-thinking techniques and claimed that each of these logical methods of evaluating causal relationships is better suited for a particular type of cause. These methods are: the method of agreement (for Type 1 causes, i.e., necessary causes of an event), the method of difference (for Type 2

EXERCISE 4.5

Classify the kind of causality characteristic of the following statements:

1. Opening the tap will start the water running.

2. Closing the neighborhood water pipeline will result in people not having water in their homes.

3. Not taking care of your garbage will cause your home to smell.

4. Starting the ignition will cause the car's engine to run.

5. Wetting your clothes will make them heavier.

6. Putting a cube of ice in a glass with cola at room temperature will cause the ice to melt.

7. Reading a book about whales will teach you something about whales.

8. Dropping the temperature in the greenhouse during winter will cause the death of many orchids.

Answers

(1) Necessary (but not sufficient: The water will not run if the central supply pipe is closed).

(2) Sufficient (but not necessary: The water will stop running also if the tap is closed).

(3) Sufficient (but not necessary: Your home may smell for other reasons).

(4) Necessary (but not sufficient: The car would not run without gas).

(5) Dependent (The more rain drops there are on the clothes, the heavier they are).

(6) Sufficient.

(7) Sufficient (but not necessary; there are other ways of learning about whales, such as a science program).

(8) Dependent (The lower the temperature, the greater the number of orchids that will die).

causes, i.e., sufficient causes of an event), the method of agreement and difference (for Type 3 causes, i.e., sufficient and necessary causes of an event), and the method of concomitant variation (Type 4, i.e., for quantitative causal relationships). Here, for illustration purposes, we discuss only two methods, the method of agreement and the method of difference.

Method of agreement. The method of agreement is a procedure developed to identify necessary causal conditions (Type 1 causes). Necessary causes, you should remember, are those in which a condition is required to produce an effect. In order to narrow down a list of potential causes, we would (ideally) need to look at every time an effect occurred and list the cause that might have caused this event. We would then have to examine this list and look for which causes appear in every list. Those causes that do appear in every list are likely the true necessary causes. For example, let's suppose that you realize that you tend to have a bad time whenever you go out to parties. This strikes you as odd, because you like people and would think that you would enjoy parties. You could create a list that looked like the followed:

Events	Possible causes
Party at Mark's house	Music too loud
	Not enough chips
	Jerome was there
Party at Janel's house	Rainy night
	Frank was there
	Jerome was there
Party at Joanna's house	TV on too loud
	People left early
	Jerome was there
Party at Dave's house	Tuna melts were too spicy
	Music too loud
	Jerome was thcre
Party at Josh's house	Had sore throat
	People left early
	Frank was there
	Jerome was there

In looking for a solution to this problem, notice that only one of the possible causes was present at all occurrences – at all parties, Jerome was there. Some causes were there more than once; only Jerome's presence was true for all of them. Maybe when you think about the issue more, you realize that Jerome often says bad things about you behind your back. Whenever he's there, you feel self-conscious and wonder what he's saying about you. As a result, you don't have a good time. Perhaps in the future, you will only go to parties where Jerome will not be there.

Method of difference

The method of difference is used when we are looking for sufficient rather than necessary causes (Type 2 causes). In Type 2, a sufficient cause for an effect is a circumstance in which a cause always leads to an effect, but several other possible causes may also lead to that effect. As an illustration, consider the following example. Suppose we are interested in determining a sufficient cause for lighting a candle.

First, we try lighting a candle with a cucumber. We have the candle and a cucumber, and nothing happens – it doesn't light.

Next, we try lighting a candle by rubbing two sticks together on top of the candle. Note that sometimes, you might get a spark by rubbing two sticks together and this procedure may work sometimes. But it doesn't always work (indeed, it doesn't *often* work, unless you're a Boy Scout). In this case, it doesn't work.

Finally, we try lighting a candle by striking a match. This attempt works and the candle is lit. The sufficient cause for lighting a candle in this case would be successfully striking a match. When you successfully strike a working match, you will create a small fire and can light a candle. There are many other ways of lighting a fire, but striking a match is sufficient in all cases.

Formulating a Proposition

The next step in the decision-making cycle is that of formulating a proposition. A proposition is a statement that makes a claim of some kind. The proposition will either be rejected or accepted by the decision maker. The following example illustrates claims that result in the development of a proposition.

1. Claim: Lydia studies for her Geography class for two hours each night, whereas Morton studies only twenty minutes a week (factual).
2. Claim: Mr. Hodge, the Geography teacher, assigns students to work together on group projects based on where their last names fall alphabetically, so that students whose names start with the same letter are likely to be assigned to work together (factual).
3. Claim: This method of assignment is chosen because it is easier for the teacher (value).
4. Claim: Lydia ended up doing 80 percent of the work on their group project, yet both students received the same grade (factual).
5. Claim: Forcing students like Lydia and Morton to work together is unfair (moral).

Proposition: Mr. Hodge should let the students choose their own groups.

Working with Alternatives

A thorough decision maker looks hard for alternative potential decisions. Some alternatives are quickly thought of as possibilities; other alternatives may take careful thought and consideration. For example, alternative decisions to the proposition above might include:

(1) Mr. Hodge should stop assigning group work.
(2) Students in Mr. Hodge's class need to better communicate with him the problems of alphabetical group assignments.
(3) Mr. Hodge should better monitor group participation.
(4) One group assignment could be with fixed groups, and another group assignment could give students the freedom to pick their own groups.
(5) Mr. Hodge could assign groups based on where students sit in the class.
(6) Just as life can be unfair, so can group projects in school. Lydia and other students penalized by the group project process should simply accept this inequality.
(7) Mr. Hodge should give everyone in the class "A"s and let students eat ice cream all day.

Notice that all these alternatives are characterized by different degrees of appeal and rationality. For example, alternative (7) appears to be unrealistic, alternative (6) seems a little harsh, and alternative (1) is pretty extreme.

IMPROVING YOUR EVERYDAY DECISION MAKING

Researchers and philosophers have pointed out a few helpful rules of the decision-making process. Some of the same principles that we discussed under improving solution monitoring are also relevant. In addition, here are a few other ways that you can improve your decision-making process.

(1) *Anybody can make bad decisions.* Always try to make the best decision possible. But be prepared at times to make nonoptimal decisions and then to have to learn to live with them, or later, to reverse them. Often, the way you follow up on a decision is more important than the decision you make. That is, you can make a decision work for you, even if it turns out to have been nonoptimal.

(2) *Enter the process of decision making with a positive state of mind – look for best possible outcomes.* Often, what seems negative in the short run is of little consequence or may even be positive in the long run.

(3) *Consider the worst possible outcome.* If the worst possible outcome is too bad, make a different decision. If you are struggling in a class, one decision could be to cheat. For most people, the worst possible outcome – getting caught and then being humiliated as well as suspended or expelled – would be too negative to make cheating worth contemplating. They may also believe that no matter how much they may want a better grade, their sense of ethics will not allow them to cheat to get that grade.

(4) *There are almost no decisions that influence only the present moment.* When making decisions, think about the future.

(5) *If possible, consider all possible options.* In other words, try to analyze the situation from all possible angles and consider all possible causes and outcomes.

(6) *Avoid overconfidence.* Confidence is, in general, a great thing. There are reasons why there are no children's stories called *The Fuzzy Rabbit Who Thought He Could Fly, But Who Couldn't and Landed Messily in the Field*. But people are often overconfident. People think they're better looking, more likely to get better grades, better drivers, and more likely to make more money than their friends and classmates (Tilson, 2000). You may argue that some people lack self-confidence or expect the worst; certainly not everyone thinks he or she is better looking than other people. Yet even those of us who are the least confident may nonetheless overestimate our competence about certain basic tasks. Here are two examples (adapted from Tilson, 2000). First, is the capital of New Mexico pronounced "Al-buh-quirk-ee" or "Al-bah-kir-key"? How confident are you about your pick? See later in this chapter for the answer.[5] Second, how much does the Statue of Liberty weigh (in pounds)? We're not asking for the exact answer; we're asking you to pick a low weight and high weight. We want you to be 95 percent confident that the

---

[5] It is pronounced "San-ta Fe." How many of you got it right? When one of us teaches this in class, it is rare to have more than two or three people out of sixty know the correct answer.

true weight of the Statue of Liberty falls between the low and the high estimate. Got them? Okay, see below for the answer.[6]

(7) *Be careful of reciprocity.* There are often many different factors that can affect our decision making. Some of them can lead to poor decisions. An example of one of these factors is the need for reciprocity. Reciprocity is that feeling you get when someone has done something nice for you, and you feel compelled to do something nice for him or her. It is a very strong feeling in most people. If someone does us a favor, we feel obligated to return this favor. This, in part, is how the Hare Krishna movement has survived – the Hare Krishnas would give out flowers to people. These people would then feel obligated to give them money, even if the flower was unwanted (Cialdini, 1998). Make sure that when you make a decision, you are doing so for the right reasons. If you feel like you "owe" someone, it is very easy to make an irrational and costly decision. We're not saying that you should never return favors, of course. But be mindful about it.

Be aware of biases in risk assessment. Even the most rational person is susceptible to biases in risk assessment. Many opinions about risk of doing something are not based on fact. Which is more dangerous, flying or driving? Many people are afraid of flying, yet the odds of an accident are much, much worse in a car. Fear of flying got so extreme in the wake of September 11, 2001, that many more people drove cars, and the number of car accidents increased. Gigerenzer (2004) calculated that because of this increase, more people died in car crashes (who wouldn't have otherwise died) than were killed in the four planes that crashed on September 11. In other words, plane travel is so much safer than car travel that people's fear about planes after the attacks cost more lives than were initially lost (on the planes). What makes us more likely to think that something is risky? Some of the factors include increased media coverage and hence increased availability (see the availability heuristic in chapter 8); if something is memorable; things that we cannot control; and things that are artificial and man-made (Sjöberg, 2000). What are the practical implications of some of these things? Well, how many of you went trick or treating as a child and had some candy screened or taken away because your parents were afraid some of the candy might be poisoned? The idea of Halloween candy being risky or dangerous has been made popular by the media – and, indeed, there have been incidents of pins or other sharp objects being inserted into candy. A quick check makes perfect sense. But some of the hysteria about poison being hidden in candy is a little absurd. A review of the last forty-five years of trick-or-treating found only two children poisoned to death – by family members, hoping to blame the deaths on the Halloween candy. Yet because of the media coverage, the "risk" of eating Halloween candy is greatly exaggerated (Mikkelson & Mikkelson, 2002). We started this chapter by continuing to discuss ways of improving planning and decision-making. We discussed (1) selecting a mental

---

[6] The correct answer is that the Statue of Liberty weighs 450,000 pounds. Was this weight between your high and low estimates? If so, great! If not, then why not? If you had no idea, why not simply pick "0 pounds" and "100 million pounds," as there are no limits to the estimates?

representation for information; (2) allocating resources; and (3) monitoring the solution. Then we illustrated each of these components with specific examples and suggested ways of improving these processes. Next, we considered what it takes to be a smart and successful decision-maker. We've discussed the actual processes that go into decision making, the need for understanding cause and effect, and the nature of some common pitfalls. Next, we will analyze the performance components that are used to actually solve problems.

In the following chapter, we will return to the issue of decision making in everyday life.

Cognitive Processing

PERFORMANCE COMPONENTS (I)

Whereas people use metacomponents to plan, monitor, and evaluate their course of action during problem solving, they use *performance components* to do the actual problem solving. We might view metacomponents as the manager at a McDonald's, and performance components as the workers getting the burgers and fries together based on the manager's instructions. Metacomponents and performance components must work together. Metacomponents alone are not enough to solve a problem. They make the decisions about what to do, but do not actually do it. Performance components alone are inadequate for solving problems because they execute a problem-solving strategy, but they do not decide what strategy to use in the first place. Thus, problem solving requires both metacomponents and performance components.

The number of performance components used in problem solving is quite large. The performance components used in solving a problem depend on the type of problem. So, for example, a mathematical problem is likely to require different performance components than a verbal problem. It would be impossible and silly to try to list and describe all of the possible performance components here. Instead, we will concentrate on those performance components that research has shown to be most important in both academic and everyday problem solving.

ENCODING

Encoding is the process by which people understand a problem and access relevant information stored in their long-term memory. A good encoding of a problem can often go a long way toward solving the problem. Conversely, a poor encoding can often guarantee that the problem will not be solved. Consider the verbal analogy WASHINGTON: ONE as LINCOLN : (a) FIVE, (b) FIFTEEN, (c) TWENTY, (d) TWENTY-FIVE. Many people find this analogy challenging not because it uses difficult reasoning or hard vocabulary. Instead, it is because they fail to properly encode the information that will lead to a correct solution. Most frequently, people think of George Washington as the first U.S. president, and so they look for the number corresponding to the

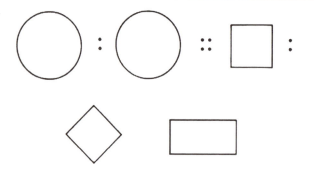

Figure 5–1. Example of a Nonverbal Analogy

original position of Lincoln as president. As it turns out, Lincoln was the sixteenth president. If you've encoded the problem this way, there is no solution that makes sense. The correct solution is FIVE, because Washington's portrait appears on a $1 bill, and Lincoln's portrait appears on a $5 bill. Notice how, in this analogy, you need to be able to encode many possible attributes of Washington and Lincoln to get a correct solution.

Consider another example of how encoding can be important in the solution of a problem, in this case, the nonverbal, or figural, analogy shown in Figure 5–1.

In this analogy, the first two terms appear to be exactly the same; both are simply circles. The third term is a square, and the two options for fourth terms are a diamond and a rectangle. At first glance, neither of these two options appears to be correct or even plausible. After all, we have understandably encoded the first two terms of the analogy as being identical. However, if we now consider the possibility that the second circle represents a forty-five-degree rotation of the first circle, it is possible to reencode the second term as a rotated version of the first term. In this case, the second term would still look like the first term, but it would be a rotated version of it. It is now possible to select the diamond as the correct answer, as it is a forty-five-degree rotated version of the square. The important point to notice in this problem is that an initial encoding is not necessarily the final one. It is sometimes necessary to reencode terms; your first inclination may not always be the most appropriate one for the given problem.

INFERENCE

If we were to select one performance component as most important of all, we might well select *inference* as that component. Inference is the discovery of one or more relations between objects or events. For example, if you hear that a friend is in the hospital, you are likely to infer that the friend is either ill or injured. Nothing in what you heard may have directly stated this. It is possible, for example, that the friend is merely visiting someone in the hospital or has taken a job in the hospital. But unless you have evidence to the contrary, you are quite likely to infer that there is a problem and to become concerned.

KINDS OF INFERENCES

Inferences can be of many different kinds, and there also exist many different classification schemes for analyzing the various kinds of inferences. The classification scheme described here is one that we have used for classifying the kinds of inferences between pairs of words that can be used on the Miller Analogies Test, a high-level test used for graduate selection and placement purposes. Remember that this scheme applies to inferences between pairs of words. Other schemes would be needed for inferences between pairs of pictures or between various kinds of events. Some of the latter kinds of inferences are discussed later in this book.

1. *Similarity*. Relationships are between synonyms or words that are nearly the same in meaning. An example is HAPPY : GLAD. These two words are synonyms. Think of two or three other pairs of words that have a similarity relation between them.
2. *Contrast*. Relationships are between antonyms or words that are nearly the opposite in meaning. An example of a contrast relation is WET : DRY. These two words are antonyms. Think of two or three other contrasts.
3. *Predication*. Terms are related by a verb or verbal relationship. One term describes something about the other term. Some of the possibilities are: A is caused by B; A makes B; A rides on B; A eats B; A is a source of B; A induces B; A studies B; A is made of B; A uses B. An example of a predication relation is AUTOMOBILE : ROAD. An AUTOMOBILE rides on a ROAD. Another example of predication with a rather different kind of relation is DOG : BARKS. A DOG performs the action of BARKING. Think of two or three other examples of predication relations.
4. *Subordination*. Relations are those in which an object A is a type of B. An example of a subordination relation is TROUT : FISH, or PEPSI : SODA. A TROUT is a type of FISH, and PEPSI is a type of SODA. Think of two or three other subordination relations.
5. *Coordination*. The two terms are a single type of thing, that is, they are members of the same category. An example of a coordination relation is LETTUCE : CABBAGE. In this case, both terms are vegetables. Think of two or three other coordination relations.
6. *Superordination*. Relations are those in which A is a category in which B falls. An example of a superordination relation is BIRD : ROBIN. In this case, BIRD is a category into which ROBIN falls. Think of two or three other superordination relations.
7. *Completion*. In this case, each term is part of a complete expression. An example of a completion relation is SAN : JOSE. In this case, the two words form a single unit, giving the names either of a saint or of a city, depending on your point of view and context. Think of two or three other completions.
8. *Part–Whole*. In these relations, A is a part of B. An example of a part–whole relation is DAY : WEEK. In this case, a DAY is a part (one-seventh) of a WEEK. Think of two or three other part-whole relations.

9. *Whole–Part.* In these relations, B is a part of A. An example of a whole–part relation is PIE : SLICE. A PIE is a whole of which a SLICE is a part. Think of two or three other whole–part relations.

10. *Equality.* These relations involve mathematical or logical equivalence. An example is TWO-FIFTHS : FORTY PERCENT. TWO-FIFTHS and FORTY PERCENT are the same thing. Think of two or three other equality relations.

11. *Negation.* Negation relations involve logical or mathematical negations. An example is EQUAL : UNEQUAL. In this case, all relationships between numbers can be covered by these two terms, which are mathematical negations of each other. Another example is TRUE : FALSE. Think of two or three other negation relations.

12. *Word Relations.* These inferences involve grammatical relations between words. An example is EAT : ATE. In this case, ATE is the past tense of EAT. Think of two or three more word-relation inferences.

13. *Nonsemantic Relations.* In these relations, words are related to each other in a way that involves properties other than the semantic properties of the words. An example of such a relation is EAT : MEET. In this case, the words happen to rhyme. Another kind of nonsemantic relation involves the letters in the word, for example, PAT : TAP. In this case, PAT is TAP spelled backward.

These relations may seem quite straightforward and obvious. However, their importance is shown not only in recognizing kinds of inferences, but also in solving more complex kinds of problems that require inferences as part of their solution (for example, analogies). An analogy that may be obscure or difficult can become easier once you recognize the inferential relation on which it is based.

Below is a list of twenty-five pairs of words. Your task is to write next to each pair of words how the two words are related to each other and then to classify the pair of words in terms of the thirteen categories of relations just presented. The answer key appears at the end of the problem set.

Word Pair	Relation	Classification
1. COVER : BOOK	_____	_____
2. BLUE : CHEW	_____	_____
3. AIRPLANE : FLY	_____	_____
4. DAFFODIL : LILAC	_____	_____
5. 3/4 : .75	_____	_____
6. CLUE : HINT	_____	_____
7. LAID : DIAL	_____	_____
8. EARLY : LATE	_____	_____
9. LADDER : RUNG	_____	_____
10. NEGATIVE : NONNEGATIVE	_____	_____
11. BETTER : BEST	_____	_____
12. HUMAN : MAMMAL	_____	_____
13. NEW : ORLEANS	_____	_____

Word Pair	Relation	Classification
14. DOG : BEAGLE	_____	_____
15. CARPENTER : HAMMER	_____	_____
16. X OR Y : NOT X AND NOT Y	_____	_____
17. CIRCLE : SEMICIRCLE	_____	_____
18. PLATE : FREIGHT	_____	_____
19. FURNITURE : CHAIR	_____	_____
20. ENHANCE : IMPROVE	_____	_____
21. STICK : STUCK	_____	_____
22. HEAVENLY : HELLISH	_____	_____
23. FINGER : HAND	_____	_____
24. SQUARE ROOT OF 64 : 2^3	_____	_____
25. MACE : WEAPON	_____	_____

Answers to Inference Pair Problems

Relation	Classification
1. A cover is a part of a book.	Part–Whole
2. *Blue* and *chew* rhyme.	Nonsemantic Relation
3. An airplane flies for its means of locomotion.	Predication
4. A daffodil and a lilac are both kinds of flowers.	Coordination
5. 3/4 and .75 are mathematically equivalent.	Equality
6. *Clue* and *hint* are synonymous.	Similarity
7. *Dial is laid* spelled backward.	Nonsemantic Relation
8. *Early* and *late* are antonyms.	Contrast
9. A ladder is made up in part of rungs.	Whole–Part
10. All real numbers that are not negative are nonnegative.	Negation
11. *Better* is the comparative form, and *best* the superlative form, of *good*.	Word Relation
12. A human is a kind of mammal.	Subordination
13. New Orleans is a city.	Completion
14. A beagle is a kind of dog.	Superordination
15. A carpenter uses a hammer.	Predication
16. The logical negation of X *or Y* is *Not X and Not Y*	Negation
17. A circle can be divided into two semicircles.	Whole–Part
18. *Plate* and *freight* rhyme.	Nonsemantic Relation
19. One kind of furniture is a chair.	Superordination
20. *Enhance* and *improve* are synonyms.	Similarity
21. *Stuck is* the past tense of *stick*.	Word Relation
22. *Heavenly* and *hellish* are antonyms.	Contrast
23. A finger is part of a hand.	Part–Whole
24. The square root of *64* and 2^3 both equal 8.	Equality
25. A mace is a kind of weapon.	Subordination

MAPPING

Mapping is the recognition of a higher-order relation between two lower-order relations. It is related to inference, but is a specifically different cognitive process. Inference is the recognition of a relation between two terms or single items. Mapping compares two different pairs of terms. For example, recognizing the relation between GRAY and ELEPHANT requires an inference. Recognizing the relation between GRAY and ELEPHANT, on the one hand, and BROWN and GRIZZLY BEAR, on the other hand, requires mapping.

Psychological research has shown that performing inferences is easier than performing mappings, on the average. The ability to perform inferences develops earlier in children than the ability to perform mappings. For example, Sternberg and Rifkin (1979) showed that children solving analogies can perform inferences as young as the second grade, or roughly seven years of age. In contrast, children cannot map relations until, at earliest, roughly the fourth grade (or nine years of age). In Jean Piaget's well-known theory of cognitive development (discussed in the first chapter), the ability to map second order relations is a hallmark of entrance into what Piaget calls the "formal operational period," which begins at roughly, eleven or twelve years of age. The ability to infer relations, however, begins much earlier, probably as early as four years of age.

Mapping is essential to solving most kinds of analogies. Indeed, we might argue that mapping forms the essence of an analogy, in that analogical reasoning and problem solving require us to see the second-order relation between two lower-order relations. Consider a sample analogy, such as GRAPES is to WINE as BARLEY is to BEER. The essence of the analogy is the recognition that grapes are used to make wine just as barley is used to make beer.

Following are twenty-five sets of pairs of terms, as would be found in verbal analogies. See if you can figure out the second-order relation that relates the first two terms to the second two terms. In the above example, the relation would have been that the first item (either GRAPES or BARLEY) can be used as a basis for making the second item (either WINE or BEER). Note that the first-order relations must be inferred before the second-order relations can he mapped, and that these first-order relations can be classified according to the relations described earlier in the chapter. Note also that the inferences and mappings required by verbal items can often require both substantial knowledge as well as reasoning ability. Answers appear after the problems.

First Relation	Second Relation	Relation between Relations
1. CHECK : PROBABLE	CASH : CERTAIN	_____
2. IRISH : SETTER	LABRADOR : RETRIEVER	_____
3. MORNINGSTAR : VENUS	EVENING STAR : VENUS	_____
4. SHORTEST : DECEMBER	LONGEST : JUNE	_____
5. VANILLA : BEAN	TEA : LEAF	_____
6. NOON : EVE	12:21 : 10:01	_____
7. STEP : STAIRCASE	RUNG : LADDER	_____

First Relation	Second Relation	Relation between Relations
8. SCARLET : RED	LAVENDER : PURPLE	_____
9. STOP : POTS	STOOL : LOOTS	_____
10. UNICORN : SINGLE	DUET : BICYCLE	_____
11. CLUB : LOWEST	SPADE : HIGHEST	_____
12. VITAMIN C : LEMON	VITAMIN A : LIVER	_____
13. PACIFIC : OCEAN	JUPITER : PLANET	_____
14. ELECT : SELECT	TIE : STY	_____
15. SHIRT : WEAR	BLOODY MARY : DRINK	_____
16. APRIL : 30	FEBRUARY : 28	_____
17. COMPARATIVE : BETTER	SUPERLATIVE : BEST	_____
18. OTHELLO : JEALOUS	HAMLET : REFLECTIVE	_____
19. SKIRMISH : BATTLE	DRIZZLE : RAINFALL	_____
20. GERIATRICS : OLD AGE	PEDIATRICS : CHILDHOOD	_____
21. DOVE : PEACE	HAWK : WAR	_____
22. CAR : ROAD	TRAIN : TRACK	_____
23. EGYPT : PHARAOH	ROMAN EMPIRE : EMPEROR	_____
24. NEW YORKER : USA	MUSCOVITE : RUSSIA	_____
25. ATOM : MOLECULE	CELL : ORGANISM	_____

Answers to Verbal Mapping Problems

1. A check has probable value in a financial transaction (in that it is not certain to clear). Cash has a certain value. Thus, the two first-order relations pertain to the likelihood of value that the first item has in a financial transaction.

2. An Irish Setter and a Labrador Retriever are both kinds of dogs. Thus, both first-order relations specify names of dogs.

3. The morning star is a name for Venus, as is the evening star. Thus, both first-order relations specify names for Venus.

4. The shortest day of the year occurs in December. The longest day of the year occurs in June. Thus, each first-order relation specifies the length of day in a critical month of the year.

5. Vanilla comes from a bean, whereas tea comes from a leaf. Thus, the two first-order relations specify the origin of the first item in each relation.

6. *Noon* and *eve* are both palindromes (that is, what they spell is the same both forward and backward). Similarly, 12:21 and 10:01 are both numerical palindromes. Thus, each first-order relation specifies a palindrome.

7. A step is a part of a staircase, just as a rung is part of a ladder. Thus, each first-order relation is a part–whole relation.

8. Scarlet is a shade of red, whereas lavender is a shade of purple. Thus, each first-order relation specifies the shade one color is of another.

9. "Pots" is "stop" spelled backward. Similarly, "loots" is "stool" spelled backward. Thus, in each pair, the second word is the first word spelled backward.

10. A unicorn and a single both refer to one of something. A duet and a bicycle both refer to two of something. Thus, the two elements in each pair both refer to number.

11. In certain games of cards, such as bridge, the suit of clubs is the lowest, whereas the suit of spades is the highest. Thus, each first-order relation relates a suit to its rank order.

12. A lemon is an excellent source of vitamin C, whereas liver is an excellent source of vitamin A. Thus, each first-order relation relates a vitamin to a particularly good source of that vitamin.

13. The Pacific is an ocean, whereas Jupiter is a planet. Thus, each first-order relation is one of set membership (subordination).

14. "Select" sounds the same as "elect" except for its initial "S" sound. "Sty" sounds the same as "tie" except for its initial "S." Thus, each first-order relation involves placing an "S" sound before the first term of the pair.

15. One wears a shirt whereas one drinks a Bloody Mary. Thus, each first-order relation specifies a predication of the second term to the first.

16. April has 30 days, whereas February has 28. Thus, each first-order relation specifies the number of days in a month.

17. "Better" is the comparative degree of "good," whereas "best" is the superlative degree. Thus, each first-order relation specifies the given degree of the word "good."

18. In the Shakespearean plays named, Othello was noteworthy for his tendency to be jealous, whereas Hamlet was noteworthy for his tendency to be reflective. Thus, each first-order relation specifies a particularly prominent trait of a Shakespearean protagonist.

19. A skirmish is a small battle, whereas a drizzle is a small rainfall. Thus, each first-order relation specifies at the left a scaled-down version of what is stated at the right.

20. Geriatrics is a medical specialty dealing with old age, whereas pediatrics is a medical specialty dealing with childhood. Thus, each first-order relation specifies a medical specialty dealing with a certain age group.

21. A dove is a symbol of peace, whereas a hawk is a symbol of war. Thus, each first-order relation specifies an animal symbol of a given political state.

22. A car travels on a road, whereas a train travels on a track. Thus, each first-order relation specifies a means of transportation.

23. In ancient times, a Pharaoh ruled Egypt whereas an Emperor ruled the Roman Empire. Thus, each first-order relation pertains to the kind of ruler an ancient state had.

24. A New Yorker is from the United States of America – USA (New York City). A Muscovite is from Russia (Moscow). Thus, each first-order relation specifies the country of origin of a person from a particular city.

25. Atoms combine to form a molecule. Cells combine to form an organism. Thus, each first-order relation specifies a part-whole relationship.

APPLICATION

Application involves applying a relation that has been previously inferred. For example, in the simple analogy LAWYER : CLIENT :: DOCTOR : ?, you must first *infer* the relation between LAWYER and CLIENT, *map* this relation to the new domain headed by

DOCTOR, and then *apply* the relation so as to generate the best possible completi
namely, PATIENT. Sometimes, instead of being asked to generate the correct respor
you will be asked to choose the correct response from several answer options.
for example, the sample analogy might have read LAWYER : CLIENT :: DOCTOR :
MEDICINE, (b) NURSE, (c) PATIENT, (d) M.D.

JUSTIFICATION

Justification is necessary when none of the available answer options for a probl
seems to be quite correct. Your task then becomes that of choosing the best, althou
imperfect, answer option. In problems requiring justification, you must use even mc
than the usual degree of good judgment. Consider, for example, the analogy LAWYI
CLIENT :: DOCTOR : (a) MEDICINE, (b) SICK PERSON. In this analogy, the better of the t\
answer options is clearly SICK PERSON. However, this answer option seems to be impe
fect. PATIENT would probably be a better completion to the analogy. In this examp
we had to choose the better of the two answer options. We recognize, however, th
this option, although better, is not necessarily the one that best fits the analogy.

PRACTICE PROBLEMS USING PERFORMANCE COMPONENTS

Analogies

Analogies can be expressed with verbal or figural (geometric) content. In the case
figural analogies, the problem solver's task is the same as in verbal analogies, exce]
that the possible relations are different (you will recall our discussion of verbal rel;
tions under *Inference*). Just as in verbal analogies, you use the same mental process(
of encoding, inference, mapping, application, and justification. Only the stimulus
different. Typically, geometric analogies involve additions, deletions, and transforma
tions of geometric figures, and the problem solver's task is to figure out what thes
additions, deletions, and transformations are.

    Consider, for example, the figural analogy in Figure 5–2a. In this analogy, ther
are three terms initially given and four answer options. Your task is to figure out whic
answer option best completes the analogy. In the first term of the analogy, two set
of two parallel lines intersect at right angles. In the second term of the analogy, tw
single lines intersect at right angles. What has been done to the first figure in orde
to arrive at the second figure? You can probably *infer* that the relation between th
first term and the second term is one of deletion. Two of the perpendicular lines hav
been taken away from the first figure in order to create the second figure. This deletioi
needs to be mapped in relation to the second half of the analogy. The third term o
the analogy also involves a set of parallel lines intersecting at right angles. In this thir(
term, however, there are four sets of parallel lines instead of two. In addition, the\
are more complexly interrelated than in the first term. In order to *apply* the relatior
inferred in the first half of the analogy, you need to delete one from each of the set o
parallel lines. Doing this generates the third of the four answer options, and this is the
correct answer.

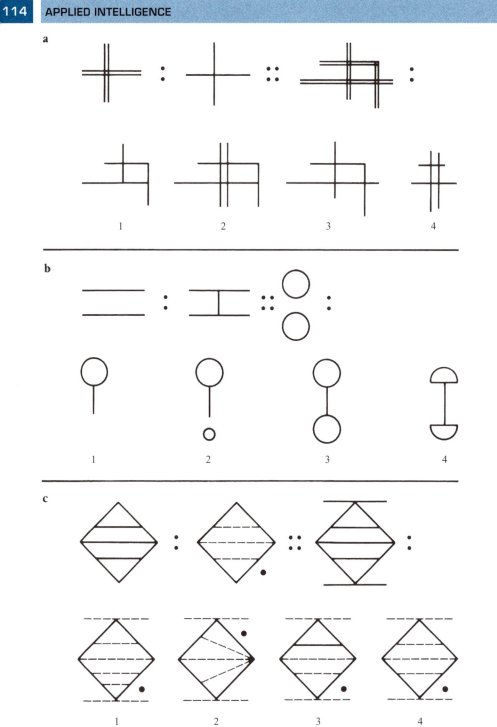

Figure 5–2. Sample Figural Analogies

Now look at the second sample analogy (Figure 5–2b). The first term involves two horizontal parallel lines. The second term seems to have the same two parallel lines, as well as a perpendicular line connecting the two parallel lines extending from the top line to the bottom line. The relation you are likely to *infer* in this analogy is one of addition of a part. That part, of course, is the perpendicular line. So, you will need to *map* the addition relation over to the second half of the analogy. The third term contains two empty circles that are located one above the other. You will now need to *apply*, the relation you inferred above. The best answer option is the one with the two empty circles connected by a line, as in the first half of the analogy.

Now consider a third sample analogy (Figure 5–2c). In this analogy, the first term involves a diamond with three horizontal lines within its borders. The three horizontal lines divide the diamond into four segments. In the second term, the diamond appears again and so do the horizontal lines. But in the second figure, the horizontal lines have become broken rather than solid lines. A relation to be *inferred is* thus one of transformation. The solid lines have been transformed into broken lines. In addition, a dot has been added. This relation now needs to be *mapped* to the second half of the analogy. The third term of the analogy involves the same diamond, except with additional horizontal lines at the top and the bottom of the diamond. *Applying* the relation inferred above, which completion do you find best satisfies the transformation inference? The answer is (4), the only completion that has five broken horizontal lines.

You have thus seen three sample analogies, one involving *deletion* in the relation between the first two terms, one involving *addition* in the relation between the first two terms, and one involving *transformation* (as well as addition) in the relation between the first two terms. Below are forty verbal and thirty more figural analogies for you to solve, all of which involve various combinations of addition, deletion, and transformation in the relations between terms. Answers appear after the problems.

Verbal Analogies

1. SHOE : LEATHER :: TIRE :
   - (a) AUTOMOBILE,
   - (b) ROUND,
   - (c) RUBBER,
   - (d) HOLLOW.

2. SPOUSE : HUSBAND :: SIBLING :
   - (a) FATHER,
   - (b) UNCLE,
   - (c) BROTHER,
   - (d) SON.

3. 480% : 4.8 :: 3.6% :
   - (a) .0036,
   - (b) .036,
   - (c) .36,
   - (d) 3.6.

4. EINSTEIN : RELATIVITY :: DARWIN :

    (a) GRAVITY,
    (b) PLANETARY ORBITS,
    (c) EVOLUTION,
    (d) MAGNETISM.

5. SONATA : COMPOSER :: LITHOGRAPH :

    (a) PHYSICIST,
    (b) ARTIST,
    (c) SCULPTOR,
    (d) AUTHOR.

6. MISDEMEANOR : CRIME :: PECCADILLO :

    (a) STUTTER,
    (b) PRETENSE,
    (c) AMNESIA,
    (d) SIN.

7. STUBBORN : MULE :: STRONG :

    (a) CHAMELEON,
    (b) OX,
    (c) FISH,
    (d) COW.

8. HEAR : DEAFNESS :: SEE :

    (a) EYEBALL,
    (b) EYES,
    (c) GLASSES,
    (d) BLINDNESS.

9. CORPORAL : BEAT :: CAPITAL :

    (a) STUN,
    (b) MAIM,
    (c) KILL,
    (d) SHOCK.

10. WATER : ICE :: RAIN :

    (a) CYCLONE,
    (b) HAIL,
    (c) FIRE,
    (d) DRY ICE.

11. RECIPE : CAKE :: BLUEPRINT :

    (a) SQUARE,
    (b) HOUSE,
    (c) COLOR,
    (d) TREE.

12. LEGISLATOR : LOBBYIST :: JURY :

    (a) LAWYER,
    (b) JUDGE,
    (c) COURT STENOGRAPHER,
    (d) FOREMAN.

13. TRAP : PART :: RAT :

    (a) GOOD-BYE,
    (b) WHOLE,
    (c) BAIT,
    (d) TAR.

14. GOLD : MINE :: PEARL :
    (a) OYSTER,
    (b) CLAM,
    (c) MINE,
    (d) RIVER.

15. AIR : VACUUM :: COLOR :
    (a) ART,
    (b) VIOLET,
    (c) RAINBOW,
    (d) BLACK.

16. OLD : MAID :: TWENTY :
    (a) ONE,
    (b) NINE,
    (c) SIXTY,
    (d) ONE HUNDRED.

17. V : X :: 10 :
    (a) 5,
    (b) 10,
    (c) 15,
    (d) 20.

18. CONE : MEGAPHONE :: TORNADO :
    (a) FUNNEL,
    (b) CLOUD,
    (c) HURRICANE,
    (d) SPHERE.

19. ACTUAL : VIRTUAL :: IN FACT :
    (a) IN CAUSE,
    (b) IN TIME,
    (c) IN TRUTH,
    (d) IN EFFECT.

20. CANINE : DOG :: EQUINE :
    (a) COW,
    (b) GOAT,
    (c) HORSE,
    (d) PIG.

21. COLT : HORSE :: LAMB :
    (a) GOAT,
    (b) SHEEP,
    (c) MULE,
    (d) COW.

22. COWARDLY : SAD :: YELLOW :
    (a) BLUE,
    (b) WHITE,
    (c) GREEN,
    (d) RED.

23. RAINCOAT : RAIN :: FOXHOLE :
    (a) FOXES,
    (b) GUNFIRE,
    (c) DISCOVER,
    (d) EARTHQUAKES.

24. OWL : FOOLISH :: LION :
    (a) FEARFUL,
    (b) LARGE,
    (c) WISE,
    (d) TEMPERAMENTAL.

25. BALD : HAIR :: ALBINO :
    (a) HEIGHT,
    (b) PAIN,
    (c) SIGHT,
    (d) PIGMENT.

26. GREEK : GREEK :: ROMAN :
    (a) INDO-EUROPEAN,
    (b) LATIN,
    (c) MEDITERRANEAN,
    (d) ROMANISH.

27. BUDDHISM : NIRVANA :: CHRISTIANITY :
    (a) JESUS,
    (b) HELL,
    (c) HEAVEN,
    (d) SATAN.

28. REDUCE :INCREASE :: INCREDIBLE :
    (a) BELIEVABLE,
    (b) WRONG,
    (c) FANCIFUL,
    (d) HUMOROUS.

29. PARTICIPLE : WALKING :: INFINITIVE :
    (a) HAVING EATEN,
    (b) TO SLEEP,
    (c) HAS TRIED,
    (d) TO THE STORE.

30. HOUND : BLOOD :: DOG :
    (a) SHEEP,
    (b) PLASMA,
    (c) VULTURE,
    (d) HARASS.

31. HEAVY-FOOTED : PLODDING ::
HEAVY-HANDED :
    (a) UNCOORDINATED,
    (b) HARSH,
    (c) STRONG,
    (d) COORDINATED.

32. LION : EAGLE :: SPHINX :
    (a) PTERODACTYL,
    (b) DODO,
    (c) VULTURE,
    (d) PHOENIX.

33. DISLIKE : HATE :: RESPECT :
    (a) LIMIT,
    (b) PROTECT,
    (c) REVERE,
    (d) ECHO.

34. BEND : PLIABLE :: BREAK :

(a) BRITTLE,

(b) TRANSPARENT,

(c) OPAQUE,

(d) FLEXIBLE.

35. CAN : MAY :: ABILITY :

(a) ACHIEVEMENT,

(b) PERMISSION,

(c) MONTH,

(d) DESIRE.

36. ALCOHOL : LIVER :: CIGARETTES :

(a) KIDNEYS,

(b) LUNGS,

(c) FEET,

(d) SPLEEN.

37. STARES : LOOKS ::: STAIRS

(a) LOOKS,

(b) STRAIGHT,

(c) UP,

(d) STEPS.

38. ROCKET : ROCK :: JACKET :

(a) COAT,

(b) CLOTH,

(c) JACK,

(d) WASP.

39. FAMINE : FOOD :: DROUGHT :

(a) DESERT,

(b) THIRST,

(c) RAIN,

(d) CROPS.

40. LEGISLATOR : MAKES :: POLICEMAN ::

(a) INTERPRETS,

(b) ENFORCES,

(c) BREAKS,

(d) DEMONSTRATES.

Answers to Verbal Analogy Problems

1. (c). A shoe is frequently made of leather. A tire is frequently made of rubber.
2. (c). A husband is a spouse. A brother is a sibling.
3. (b). 480 percent is equal to 4.8. 3.6 percent is equal to .036.
4. (c). Albert Einstein was primarily responsible for relativity theory. Charles Darwin was primarily responsible for the theory of evolution.
5. (b). A sonata is the creation of a composer. A lithograph is the creation of an artist.
6. (d). A misdemeanor is a minor crime. A peccadillo is a minor sin.
7. (a). A mule is supposedly stubborn. An ox is supposedly strong.
8. (d). Deafness involves loss of hearing. Blindness involves loss of seeing.
9. (c). In corporal punishment, a person is beaten. In capital punishment, a person is killed.

10. (b). When water is frozen, it becomes ice. When rain is frozen, it becomes hail.
11. (b). A recipe is used to make a cake. A blueprint is used to make a house.
12. (a). The job of a lobbyist is to persuade a legislator. The job of a lawyer is to persuade a jury.
13. (d). *Part is trap* spelled backward. *Tar* is *rat* spelled backward.
14. (a). Gold is found in mines. Pearls are found in oysters.
15. (d). A vacuum is the absence of air. Black is the absence of color.
16. (a). Old Maid and Twenty-One are both names of card games.
17. (d). V is the Roman numeral 5, and X is the Roman numeral 10. Just as 5 is half of 10, so is 10 half of 20.
18. (a). A cone and a megaphone have roughly the same shape, as do a tornado and a funnel.
19. (d). *Actual* means in fact. *Virtual* means in effect.
20. (c). *Canine* means doglike. *Equine* means horselike.
21. (b). A colt is a young horse. A lamb is a young sheep.
22. (a). A cowardly person is often referred to as "yellow." A person who feels sad is often referred to as "blue."
23. (b). A raincoat provides protection from rain. A foxhole provides protection from gunfire.
24. (a). An owl is reputed to be wise, which is the opposite of foolish. A lion is reputed to be bold, which is the opposite of fearful.
25. (d). A bald person lacks hair. An albino lacks pigment.
26. (b). The ancient Greeks spoke Greek. The ancient Romans spoke Latin.
27. (c). The concept of heaven in Christianity is analogous to that of Nirvana in Buddhism.
28. (a). *Reduce* and *increase* are antonyms, as are *incredible* and *believable*.
29. (b). *Walking* is a participle. To *sleep* is an infinitive.
30. (a). A bloodhound and a sheep dog are both types of dogs.
31. (b). Someone who is heavy-footed is plodding. Someone who is heavy-handed is harsh.
32. (d). A lion and an eagle are both real animals. A sphinx and a phoenix are both mythological animals.
33. (c). To hate someone is to dislike them a great deal. To revere someone is to respect them a great deal.
34. (a). A pliable object will easily bend, whereas a brittle object will easily break.
35. (b). When people can do something, they are able to do it. When people may do something, they have permission to do it.
36. (b). Alcohol can cause specific damage to the liver. Cigarettes can cause specific damage to the lungs.
37. (d). The verb *stares* has the same meaning as *looks*. *Stairs* has the same meaning as *steps*.
38. (c). *Rocket is rock* with an *et* at the end. *Jacket is jack* with an *et* at the end.
39. (c). A famine is caused by a lack of food. A drought is caused by a lack of rain.
40. (b). A legislator makes the laws. A policeman enforces them.

FIGURAL ANALOGY PROBLEMS [FIGURE 5–3]

1.

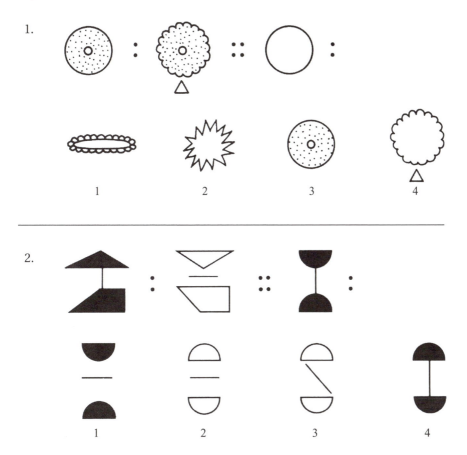

2.

3.

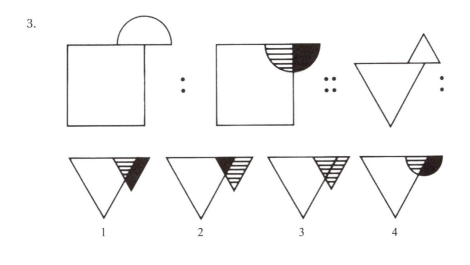

4.

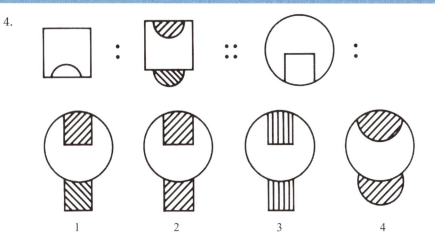

5.

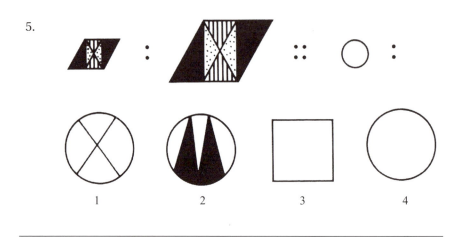

6.

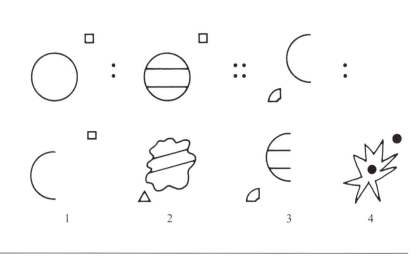

7.

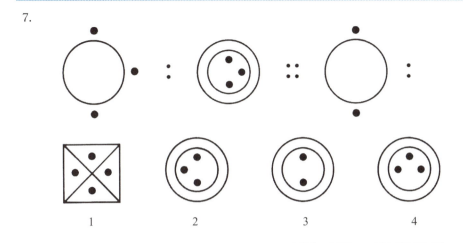

| 1 | 2 | 3 | 4 |

8.

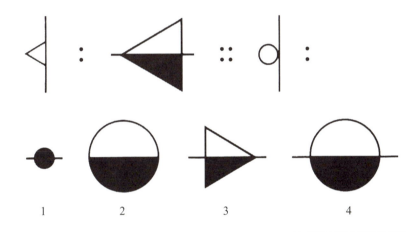

| 1 | 2 | 3 | 4 |

9.

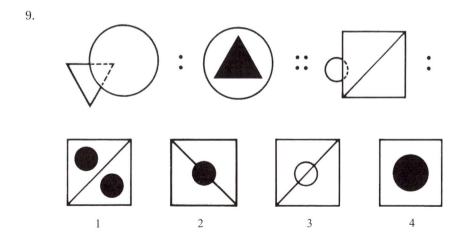

| 1 | 2 | 3 | 4 |

10.

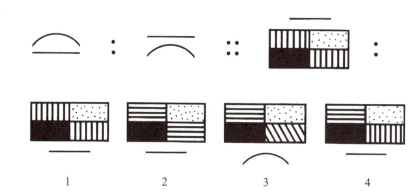

| 1 | 2 | 3 | 4 |

11.

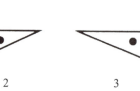

| 1 | 2 | 3 | 4 |

12.

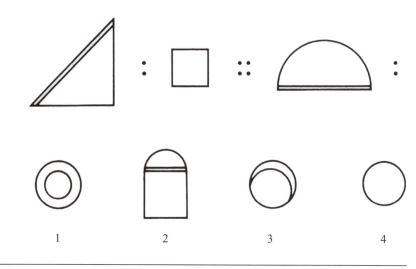

| 1 | 2 | 3 | 4 |

13.

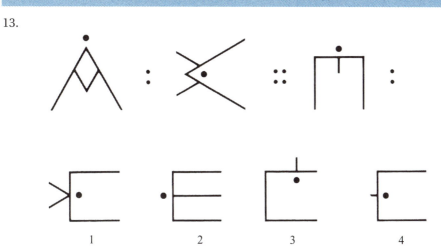

14.

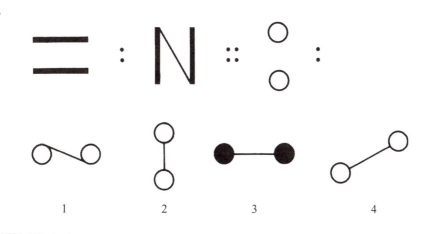

15.

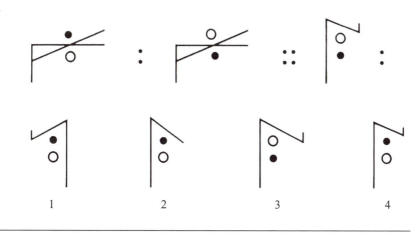

16.

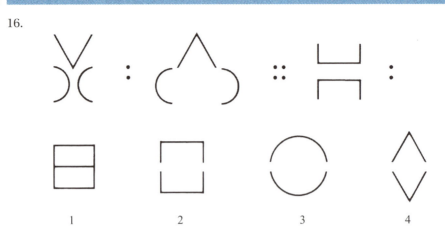

17.

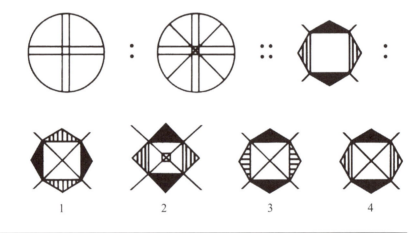

18.

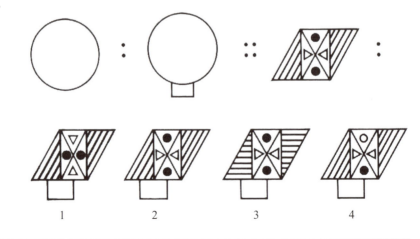

19.

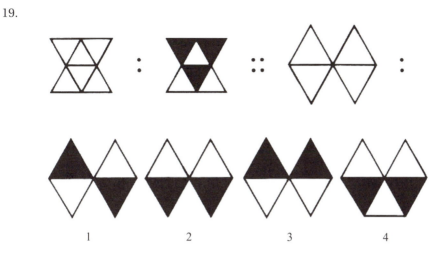

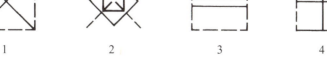

20.

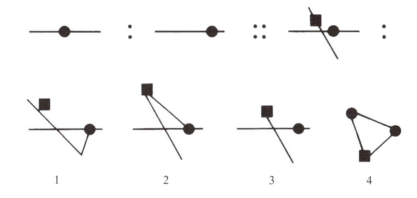

21.

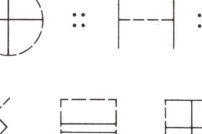

22.

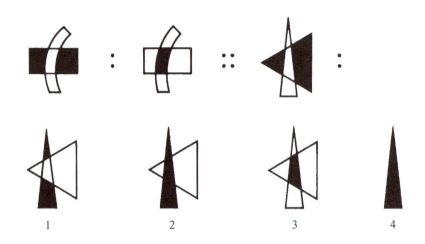

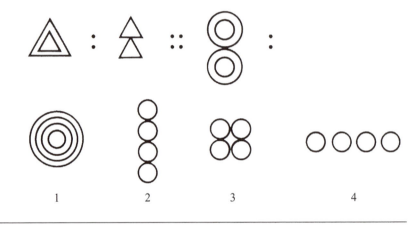

23.

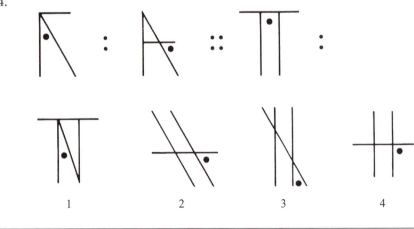

24.

25.

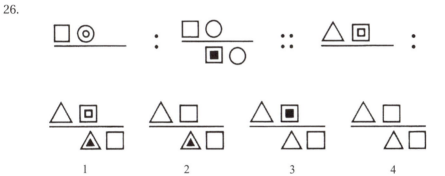

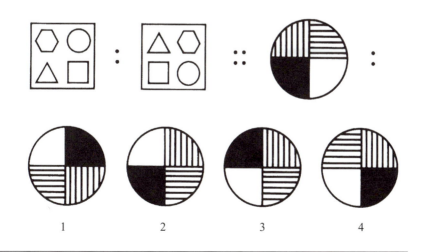

26.

27.

28.

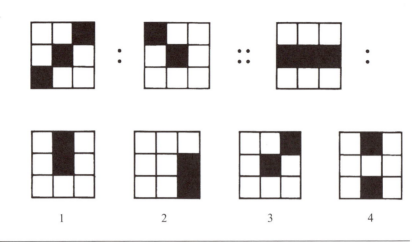

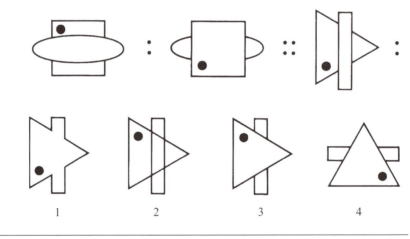

29.

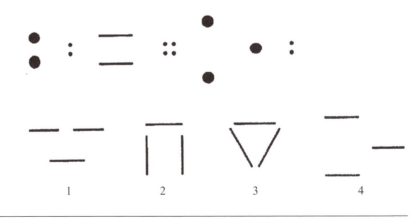

30.

Answers to Figural Analogy Problems (FIGURE 5–3)

1. 4	6. 3	11. 3	16. 2	21. 1	26. 2
2. 2	7. 3	12. 4	17. 4	22. 3	27. 3
3. 1	8. 4	13. 4	18. 2	23. 2	28. 1
4. 1	9. 2	14. 1	19. 2	24. 4	29. 3
5. 4	10. 1	15. 4	20. 3	25. 2	30. 4

SERIES COMPLETIONS

The performance components of inference, mapping, application, and justification apply to other kinds of inductive reasoning problems besides analogies. One of the most common types of problems is the series-completion problem. In these problems, the solver is usually given some terms that form a series, and the task is to complete the series. Consider, for example, this simple series completion problem: 2, 5, 8, _. In this problem, you first must *encode* the terms. Then you must *infer* the relation between each successive pair of numbers – in this case, it is +3. Finally, you *apply* this relation to generate a correct completion, namely, 11. Note that mapping is not needed in this form of series completion, because all the terms are within a single domain. It is possible, however, to create complex series completion problems where mapping is required. Suppose, instead, that the problem had read: 2, 5, 8, 11 : 4, _. In this case, the inferred relation is the same as before, namely, +3. However, before applying this relation, you must *map* it to a new numerical domain, one starting with the number 4. *Applying* the +3 relation thus produces an answer of 7 in this form of the problem.

Series completion problems, like analogies, can involve words or figures. Consider the following series completion problem: LIE, KNEEL, STAND : HIGH, (a) TALL, (b) HIGHER. In this problem, the relation to be *inferred is* one of progressively greater vertical height. This relation needs to be *mapped* to the term HIGH and then applied so as to yield a correct answer. If HIGHER is not thought to be the best answer option, then *justification* is required to recognize this answer option as better than TALL. Note that the performance components used to solve an analogy are being applied to a series of completion problem. The form of the problem is somewhat different from the form of the analogy, but the mental operations are practically identical. The main difference is that instead of having to infer the relation between only two terms, you must infer successive relations between each adjacent pair of three terms. Thus, in the sample, you need to infer first the relation between LIE and KNEEL, and second the relation between KNEEL and STAND.

Here are forty sample verbal series completions that require you to use the performance components of inference, mapping, application, and justification, followed by thirty sample figural series completions. Some of these problems are hard; don't feel bad if you don't get them all! Answers follow the problems.

Verbal Series Completions

1. BABY, TODDLER, CHILD : SEEDLING, (a) LEAF, (b) BRANCH, (c) TREE, (d) BARK.

2. HEAD, NECK, WRIST : BRACELET, (a) ARTIST, (b) SHOULDER, (c) TOE, (d) RING.

3. BURNT, WELL-DONE, MEDIUM : PINK, (a) RED, (b) BLACK, (c) GRAY, (d) WHITE.

4. EYE, JAY, KAY : TEA, (a) LAY, (b) SEA, (c) YOU, (d) COFFEE.

5. CHERRY, ORANGE, GRAPEFRUIT : BASEBALL, (a) NEEDLE, (b) GOLF BALL,
   (c) FOOTBALL, (d) VOLLEYBALL

6. CITY, COUNTY, STATE : PROVINCE, (a) COUNTRY, (b) LORE, (c)TOWN (d) GOVERNMENT.

7. ARID, DRY, DAMP : WET, (a) SOAKING, (b) SPEAKING, (c) MOIST, (d) DESERT.

8. CANTALOUPE, MELON, FRUIT : VEGETABLE, (a) MINERAL, (b) FOOD, (c) LETTUCE,
   (d) LEMON

9. GREAT GRANDFATHER, GRANDFATHER, FATHER : MOTHER, (a) GRANDDAUGHTER,
   (b) DAUGHTER, (c) GRANDMOTHER, (d) CHILD.

10. CONCEPTION, BIRTH, MARRIAGE : 23, (a) 0, (b) 10, (c) -5, (d) 82.

11. ROCKET, JET, HELICOPTER : TORTOISE, (a) CHEETAH, (b) HARE, (c) SNAIL,
    (d) MARSUPIAL.

12. RHODE ISLAND, CONNECTICUT, NEBRASKA : GERMANY, (a) CANADA, (b) ALASKA,
    (c) MONACO, (d) BERLIN.

13. TABLE OF CONTENTS, INTRODUCTION, CONCLUSION : EPILOGUE, (a) INK,
    (b) PROLOGUE, (c) PLOT, (d) INDEX.

14. LOITERING, SMUGGLING, KIDNAPPING : LIFE IMPRISONMENT, (a) MURDER,
    (b) ELECTRIC CHAIR, (c) DETENTION, (d) CRIME.

15. ANIMAL, MAMMAL, DOG : REPTILE, (a) PIG, (b) BIRD, (c) SNAKE, (d) FROG.

16. PLAY, ACT, SCENE : BOOK, (a) CHAPTER, (b) LIBRARY, (c) NOVEL, (d) AUTHOR.

17. ZERO, ONE, TWO : CIRCLE, (a) CUBE, (b) ELLIPSE, (c) SPHERE, (d) ROUND.

18. 4,3,2 : CHESS, (a) BRIDGE, (b) PAWN, (c) SOLITAIRE, (d) GAME.

19. SPRING, SUMMER, FALL : JACKET, (a) DRESS, (b) COAT, (c) WOOL, (d) BOOTS.

20. CONSERVATIVE, MODERATE, LIBERAL : PROGRESSIVE, (a) POLITICAL,
    (b) REACTIONARY, (c) DEMOCRATIC, (d) RADICAL.

21. ANCIENT, MEDIEVAL, RENAISSANCE : CANDLE, (a) LIGHT BULB, (b) ELECTRICITY,
    (c) SUN, (d) TALLOW.

22. EIGHTH, QUARTER, HALF : DOUBLE, (a) TRIPLE, (b) QUADRUPLE, (c) NOTHING,
    (d) FRACTIONAL.

23. TRUNK, SUITCASE, HANDBAG : PITCHER, (a) CUP, (b) WATER, (c) LITER, (d) AQUARIUM.

24. VILLAGE, TOWN, CITY : NEW ORLEANS, (a) REDLANDS, (b) LOS ANGELES, (c) HAMLET,
    (d) OKLAHOMA CITY.

25. ENGAGED, MARRIED, SEPARATED : BIRTH, (a) EARTH, (b) LIFE, (c) CONCEPTION,
    (d) DEATH.

26. MATCH, PENCIL, BROOMSTICK : NEEDLE, (a) WIG, (b) HAYSTACK, (c) SWORD,
    (d) AUTOMOBILE.

27. IMPOSSIBLE, UNLIKELY, POSSIBLE : MAYBE, (a) NEVER, (b) PROBABLY, (c) UNCERTAIN
    (d) UNKNOWN,

28. HEALTHY, SICK, DYING : HOSPITAL, (a) OFFICE, (b) HOSPICE, (c) DUST, (d) OLD AGE
    HOME.

29. ALERT, FATIGUED, DROWSY : YAWN, (a) ASLEEP, (b) LAUGH, (c) SIGH, (d) SNORE.
30. MEASURE, MIX, BAKE : EAT, (a) DIGEST, (b) STOVE, (c) COOL, (d) PAN.
31. ANTARCTICA, SOUTH AMERICA, CENTRAL AMERICA : MIAMI, (a) LOS ANGELES, (b) GUATEMALA, (c) SWEDEN, (d) WASHINGTON, D.C.
32. ONLY CHILD, TWINS, TRIPLETS : TRICYCLE, (a) BICYCLE, (b) CAR, (c) UNICYCLE, (d) ICE SKATES.
33. FRIEND, GIRL FRIEND, FIANCÉE : MISS, (a) MRS., (b) HIT, (c) WIFE, (d) MOTHER.
34. PLOW, PLANT, HARVEST : GRAIN, (a) MOLECULE, (b) FLOUR, (c) SEED, (d) FLOWER.
35. A, E, I, : EYE, (a) SEE, (b) O, (c) OH, (d) EAR.
36. 100%, .75, 1/2 : 3/6, (a) WHOLE, (b) ONE-EIGHTH, (c) .4, (d) 1/4.
37. DESPISE, DISLIKE, LIKE : GOOD, (a) EVIL, (b) LOVE, (c) BETTER, (d) ADMIRE.
38. BACH, BEETHOVEN, GERSHWIN : VAN GOGH, (a) PICASSO, (b) MICHELANGELO, (c) VONNEGUT, (d) MOZART.
39. ALL, MANY, FEW : SEVERAL, (a) EARLY, (b) NONE, (c) ALL, (d) NUMEROUS.
40. EINSTEIN, NEWTON, PYTHAGORAS : CHAUCER, (a) SATAN, (b) HEMINGWAY, (c) GALILEO, (d) HOMER.

Answers to Verbal Series Completion Problems

1. (c). A baby, as it grows older, becomes a toddler and then a child; a seedling becomes a tree.
2. (d). Parts of the body moving down and outward are the head, neck, and wrist; jewelry to be worn on the body, moving outward, are a bracelet and a ring.
3. (a). Successively lesser degrees of cooking meat are burnt, well-done, medium. Red meat is still less cooked than pink meat.
4. (c). These words are pronounced the same as the successive letters of the alphabet, I, J, and K; similarly, tea is pronounced like the letter T and you is pronounced like the successive letter, U.
5. (d). These round fruits are successively larger in size; a volleyball has the same spherical shape as a baseball, but is larger in size.
6. (a). A city, county, and state are units of government of successively greater size; a province and a country are units of government, also of successively greater size.
7. (a). Arid, dry, and damp are degrees of dampness that increase in amounts of moisture; wet and soaking are also increasing degrees of dampness in amounts of moisture.
8. (b). A cantaloupe is a kind of melon and a melon is a kind of fruit; a vegetable is a kind of food.
9. (b). A great grandfather, grandfather, and father are successive generations; a mother and a daughter are also successive generations.
10. (d). Conception, birth, and marriage for people occur at successively later ages; 23 and 82 are successively later ages for people.
11. (c). A rocket, jet, and helicopter are successively slower in their movements; a snail is slower in movement than a tortoise.
12. (a). Rhode Island, Connecticut, and Nebraska are successively larger states; Canada is a larger country than Germany.

13. (d). The table of contents, introduction, and conclusion come successively later in a book; the index comes later than the epilogue.

14. (b). Loitering, smuggling, and kidnapping are successively more serious crimes; life imprisonment and the electric chair are successively more serious punishments.

15. (c). A dog is a type of mammal, which is a type of animal; a snake is a kind of reptile.

16. (a). A play, act, and scene are successively smaller units of drama; a book and a chapter are successively smaller units of prose.

17. (c). Zero, one, and two are successively greater numbers of dimensions; a sphere is a circle expanded into a successively greater number of dimensions (from 2 to 3).

18. (c). 4, 3, and 2 are successively smaller numbers of players; chess and solitaire are played by successively smaller numbers of players (2 and 1).

19. (b). Spring, summer, and fall are successive seasons; a jacket and a coat are worn in successive seasons (often, fall and winter).

20. (d). A conservative, moderate, and liberal are successively further left on the political spectrum; a progressive and a radical are also successively further left.

21. (a). Ancient, medieval, and Renaissance times are successively more modern; a light bulb is a more modern form of lighting than a candle.

22. (b). Eighth, quarter, and half are, successively, twice as large as each other; quadruple is twice as large as double.

23. (a). A trunk, suitcase, and handbag hold successively less content; a cup holds less content than a pitcher.

24. (b). A village, town, and city are successively larger units of urban populations; New Orleans and Los Angeles are successively larger cities.

25. (d). Engaged, married, and separated refer to successive potential events in the course of life; birth and death are also successive events in life.

26. (c). A match, pencil, and broomstick are successively longer straight objects; a sword is a longer straight object than a needle.

27. (b). Impossible, unlikely, and possible refer to increasing probabilities of occurrence; probably represents a higher probability of assent than maybe.

28. (b). Healthy, sick, and dying refer to three successively lesser states of health; a hospital and a hospice refer to locations of persons in successively lesser states of health.

29. (d). Alert, fatigued, and drowsy refer to successively lower states of arousal; a yawn and a snore are oral outputs from successively lower states of arousal (tiredness and sleep).

30. (a). In making a cake, one first measures, then mixes, then bakes. Later on, one first eats and then digests the cake.

31. (d). Antarctica, South America, and Central America are geographic areas successively in the northward direction; Miami and Washington, DC, are geographic areas successively in the northward direction.

32. (b). An only child, twins, and triplets refer to successively increasing numbers of items, in this case, siblings; a tricycle and a car have successively increasing numbers of items, in this case, wheels.

33. (a). Friend, girl friend, and fiancée and refer to successive states in a heterosexual inter-personal relationship; Miss and Mrs. also refer to successive states in a heterosexual interpersonal relationship.

34. (b). In farming, one first plows, then plants, and then harvests; similarly, in milling, one first has grain and then flour.

35. (c). A, E, and I are successive vowels; eye and oh are words sounding the same as the names of successive vowels.

36. (d). 100%, .75, and 1/2 are quantities that successively decrease by 1/4; 3/6 and 1/4 are also quantities that successively decrease by 1/4.

37. (c). Despise, dislike, and like refer to increasingly favorable dispositions toward someone; good and better are also increasingly favorable dispositions.

38. (a). Bach, Beethoven, and Gershwin were successively later composers; Van Gogh and Picasso were successively later artists.

39. (b). All, many, and few refer to successively lesser amounts; several and none also refer to successively lesser amounts.

40. (d). Einstein, Newton, and Pythagoras were successively less recent scientists; Chaucer and Homer were successively less recent authors.

FIGURAL SERIES COMPLETION PROBLEMS [FIGURE 5–4]

1.

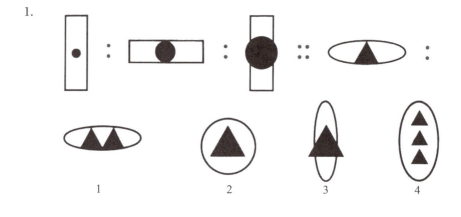

2.

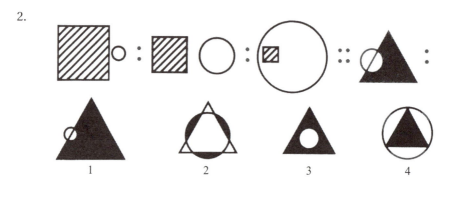

3.

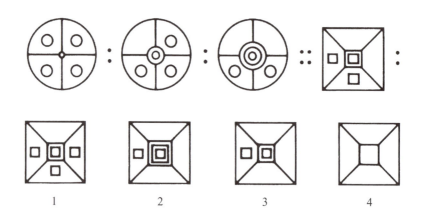

4.

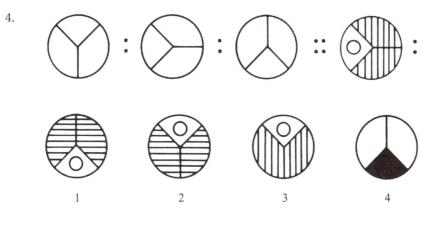

| 1 | 2 | 3 | 4 |

5.

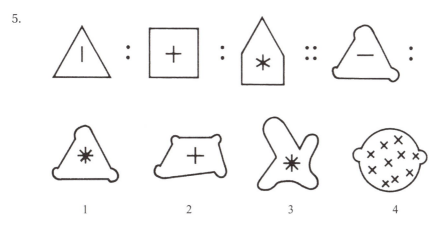

| 1 | 2 | 3 | 4 |

6.

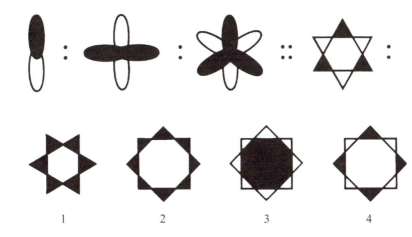

| 1 | 2 | 3 | 4 |

7.

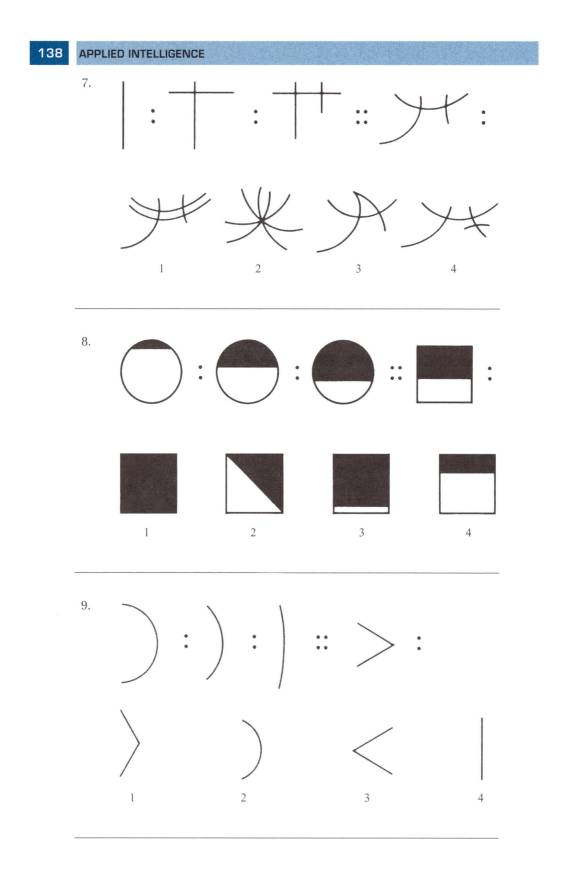

10.

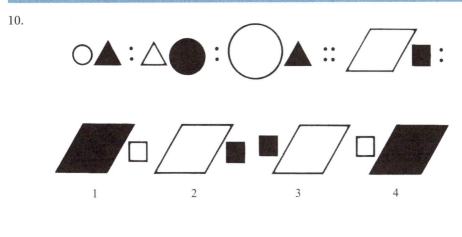

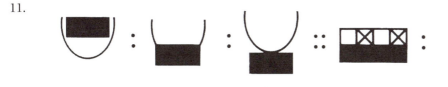

11.

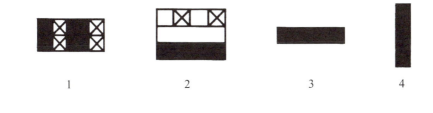

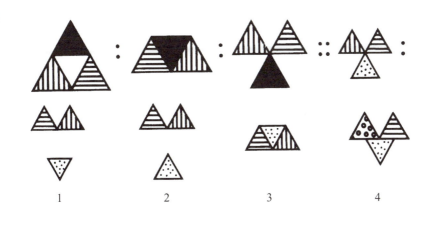

12.

13.

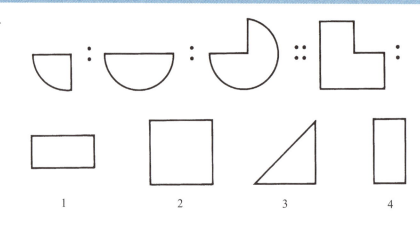

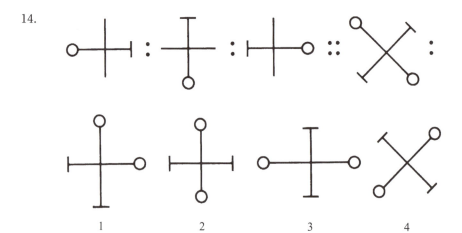

15.

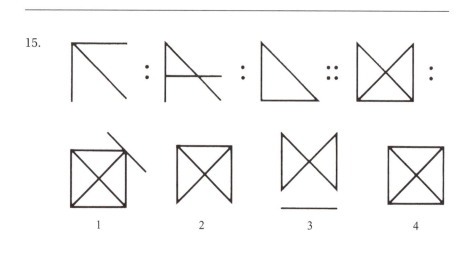

16.

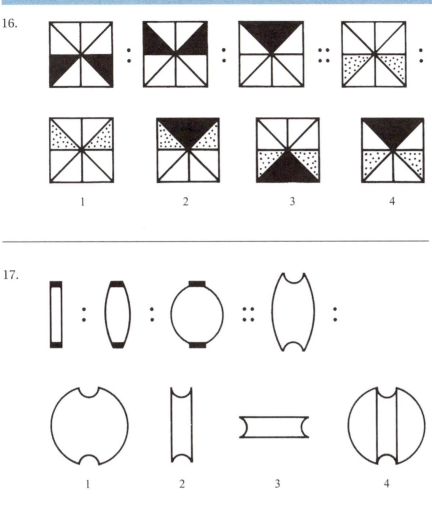

17.

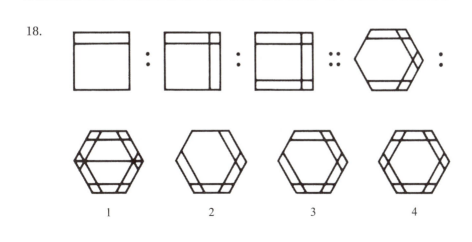

18.

19.

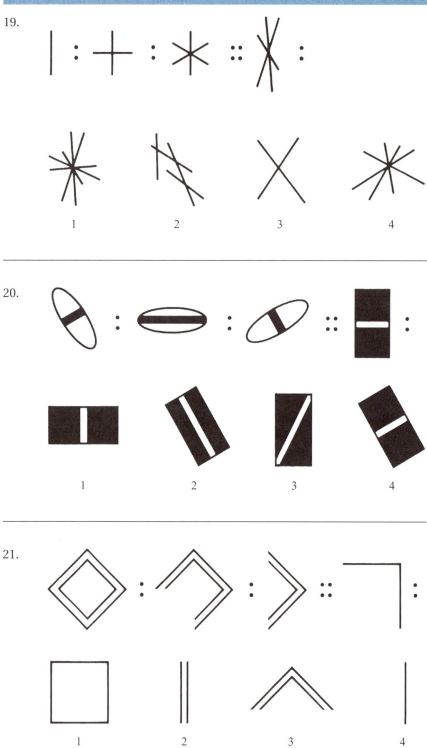

20.

21.

22.

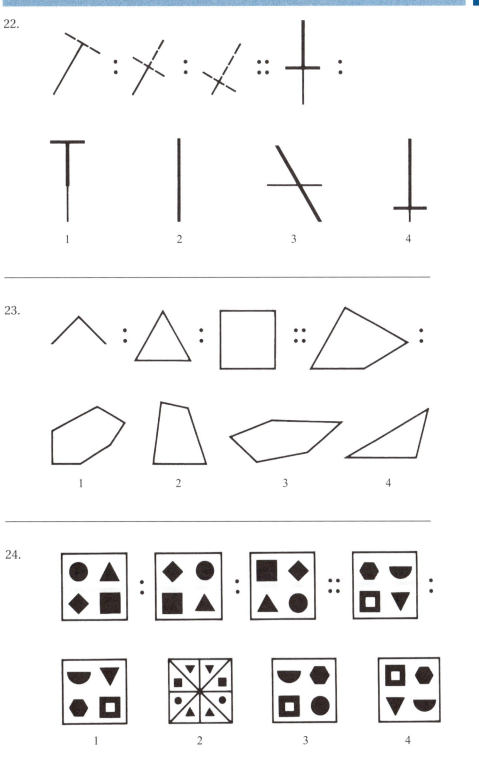

23.

24.

25.

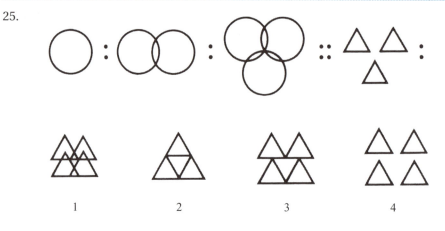

1   2   3   4

26.

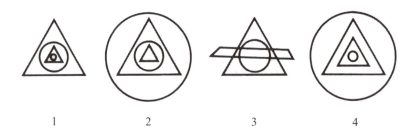

1   2   3   4

27.

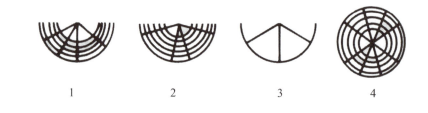

1   2   3   4

28.

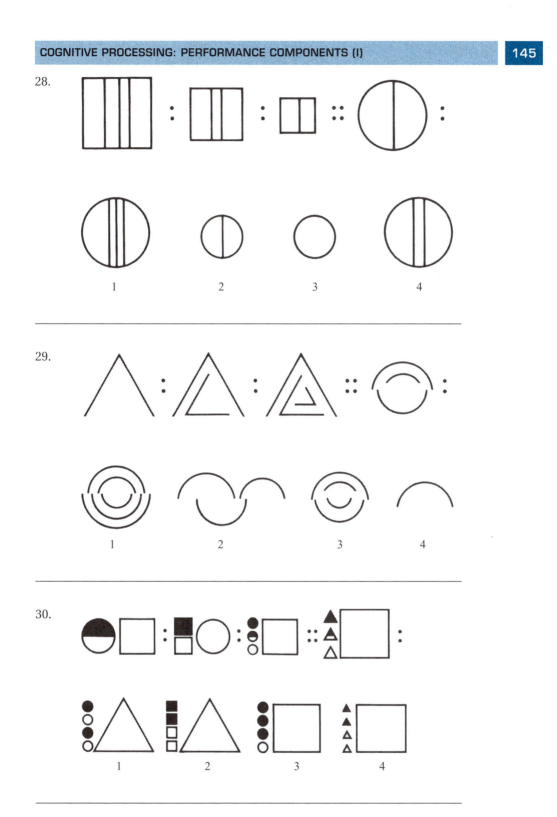

29.

30.

Answers to Figural Series Completion Problems (Figure 5–4)

1. 3	6. 4	11. 2	16. 1	21. 4	26. 2
2. 4	7. 4	12. 1	17. 1	22. 4	27. 1
3. 2	8. 3	13. 2	18. 3	23. 3	28. 3
4. 1	9. 1	14. 4	19. 4	24. 4	29. 3
5. 2	10. 4	15. 3	20. 2	25. 1	30. 2

Cognitive Processing

PERFORMANCE COMPONENTS (II)

CLASSIFICATIONS

Classification problems require essentially the same set of performance components as analogy and series completion problems. Like analogies and series completions, classification problems can come in a variety of forms.

One form consists of a set of terms; one of them does not belong with the others. The task of the solver is to figure out which term does not belong with the others. For example, in the problem PESO, POUND, DOLLAR, CURRENCY, RUPEE, the word CURRENCY does not fit with the others, because it is a superordinate term with respect to the other terms. A peso, a pound, a dollar, and a rupee are all units of currency. Another example is BAKED, ROASTED, DELETED, MASHED, FRENCH FRIED, and BOILED. The word DELETED does not fit, because all of the other terms described ways of cooking a potato. A third example might be FLEW, COUP, THROUGH, BOO, SEW, and RUE. The word "SEW" is the only word in the list that is not pronounced with an "OOH" sound.

Another form of classification problem consists of a set of terms followed by a set of answer options. One example is LION, DOG, GIRAFFE, FOX, (a) FROG, (b) WHALE, (c) TUNA, (d) WASP. Here, the task is to figure out which of the answer options belongs with the original set of terms. The best response to this problem is WHALE. The original terms are all mammals, and a whale is the only mammal of the possible choices.

Another format sometimes used in understanding and solving classification problems is somewhat different. This form consists of a single term, and then four sets of two terms each. The way to solve the problem is to figure out which pair of terms fit the initial single term. So try, for example, SECRET (a) VISIBLE, OBVIOUS; (b) HIDDEN, CONCEALED; (c) SILENT, QUIET (d) LIKELY, PROBABLE. Which pair of words would fit best with secret? The correct answer is (b). Why? The performance components used to solve this are very similar to those used to solve analogies and series completions. They're just applied in a slightly different way. First, you must *encode* the terms. Next, you must *infer* the relation between each of the two terms in each pair. For example, VISIBLE and OBVIOUS both refer to things being easy to see or to understand. HIDDEN and CONCEALED both refer to things being difficult to see or understand. Next, you must *map* the higher-order differences from these relations. You need to map these

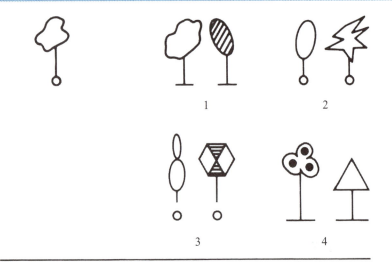

Figure 6–1. A Sample Figural Classification Problems

differences because you will use them as the basis for deciding in which of the four categories the single word belongs. Finally, you need to *apply* what you have learned in order to figure out the correct category. In this case, applying what you have learned leads you to classify SECRET with the second set of terms.

The same performance components apply to figural classification problems. Consider, for example, the classification problem in Figure 6–1. First, you must *encode* the terms of the problem. Next, you must *infer* what is common to each of the pairs of two terms. In this example, what seems to be common is that they have a vertical line extending down from a shape, and an object at the bottom. What distinguishes the four sets of figures? Apparently, it is the set of shapes at the top and the objects at the bottom. The differences must be *mapped*. Now look at the single term. It has a shape with a single region at the top and a circle at the bottom. *Application* reveals that it belongs with the second pair of terms (2). Notice that although the content is different, the performance components used to solve the problem are the same as those used with verbal content.

Following are forty verbal and thirty nonverbal classification problems. Use the performance components of encoding, inference, mapping, and application to solve these problems. In some instances, the single word or picture will not seem to fit particularly well with either the terms at the left or the terms at the right. In these instances, you must use the performance components of *justification* in order to decide which of the four classes of terms provide the best, although not ideal, fit.

FIGURAL CLASSIFICATION PROBLEMS [FIGURE 6–2]

1.

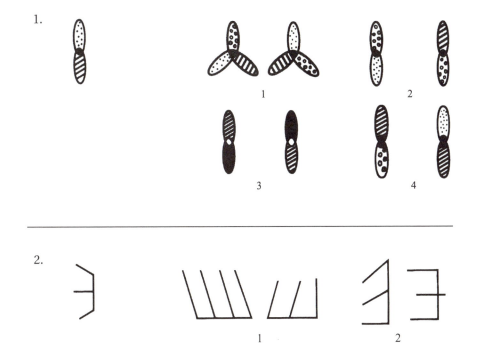

2.

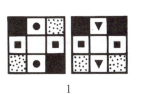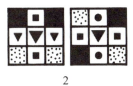

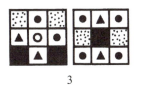

3.

4.

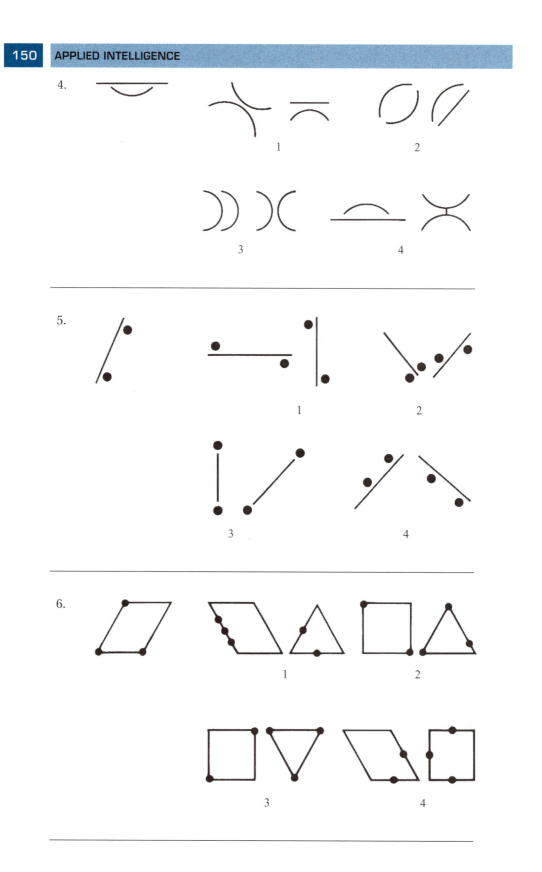

5.

6.

7.

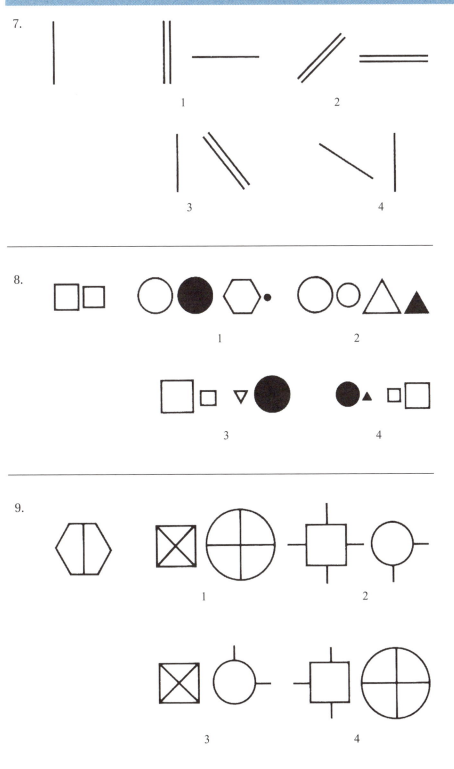

1

2

3

4

8.

1

2

3

4

9.

1

2

3

4

10.

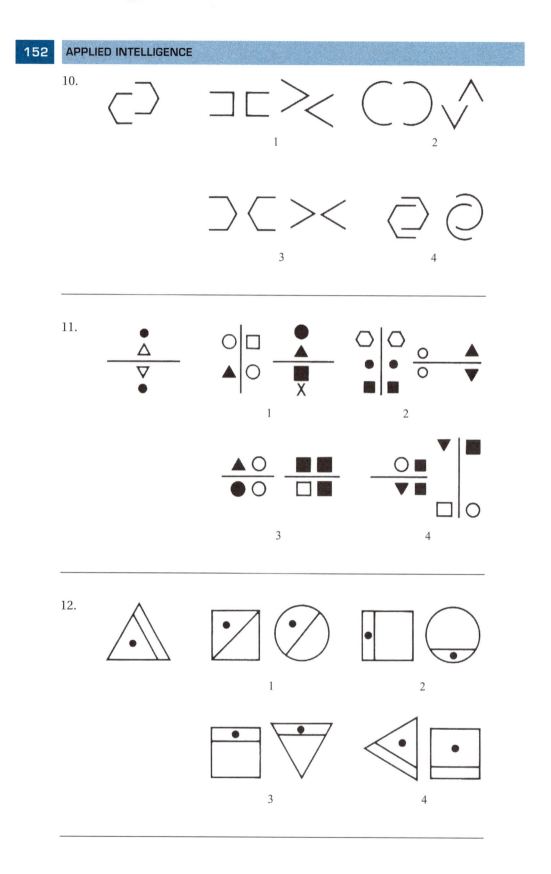

11.

12.

13.

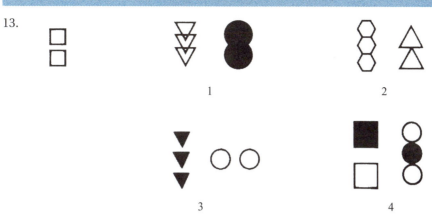

1

2

3

4

14.

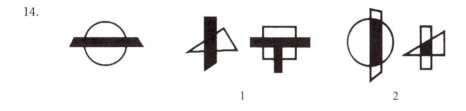

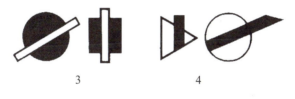

1

2

3

4

15.

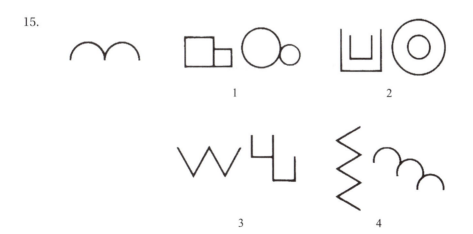

1

2

3

4

16.

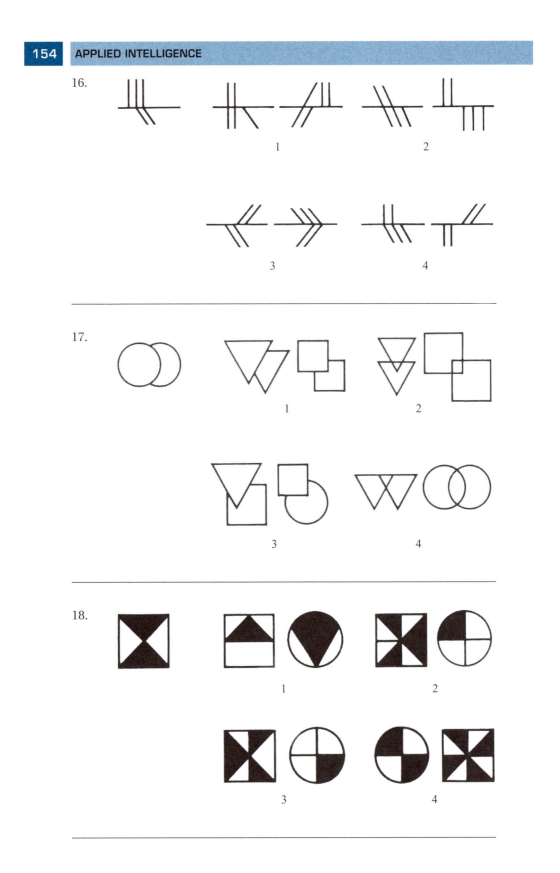

17.

18.

19.

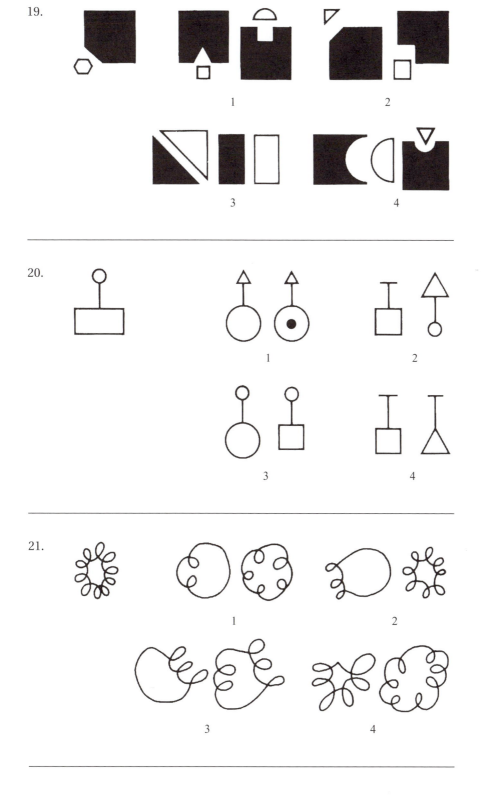

20.

21.

22.

23.

24.

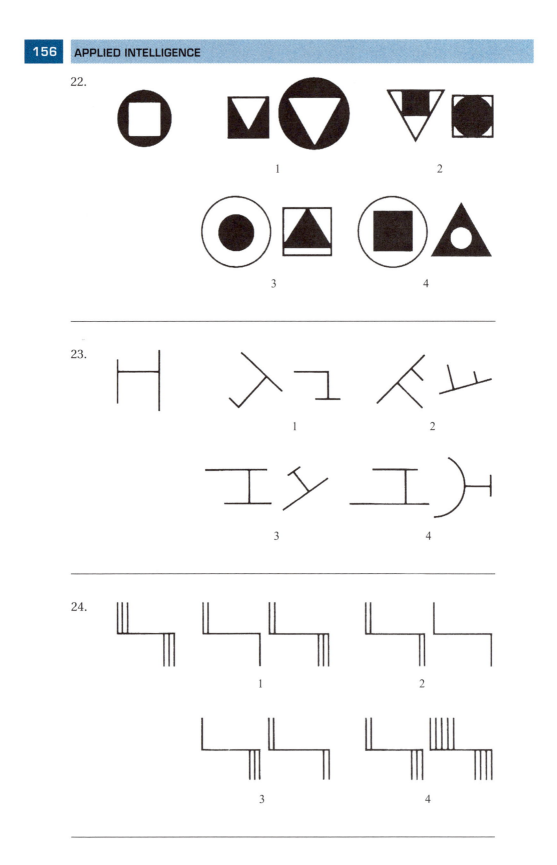

25.

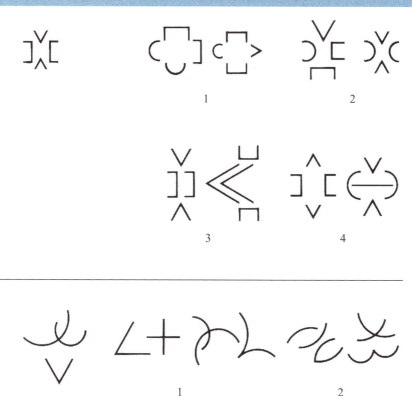

1

2

3

4

26.

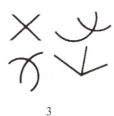

1

2

3

4

27.

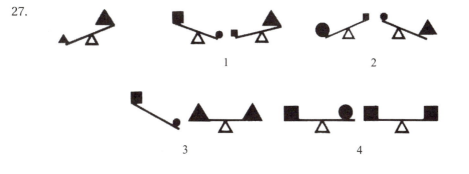

1

2

3

4

28.

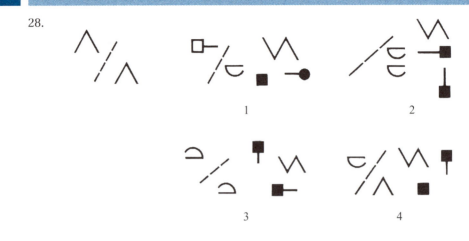

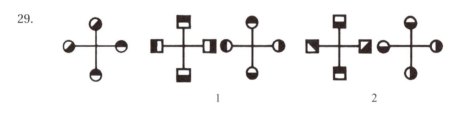

29.

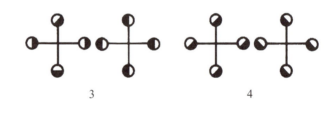

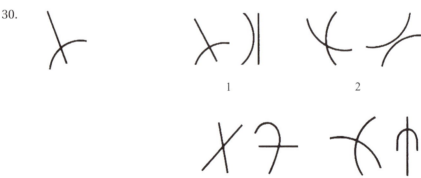

30.

Answers to Figural Classification Problems (Figure 6–2)

1. 2	11. 2	21. 2
2. 3	12. 4	22. 1
3. 1	13. 3	23. 3
4. 2	14. 1	24. 2
5. 4	15. 3	25. 2
6. 3	16. 4	26. 4
7. 4	17. 1	27. 1
8. 4	18. 4	28. 3
9. 1	19. 1	29. 2
10. 2	20. 3	30. 1

VERBAL CLASSIFICATION PROBLEMS

In each of the following problems, a single word is followed by four pairs of words. Your task is to decide with which of the four pairs of words the single word most appropriately belongs, and then to choose this pair as the correct answer. Answers appear after the problems.

1. MAGAZINE (a) LECTURE, SERMON; (b) BOOK, LETTER; (c) AUTHOR, NOVELIST; (d) WORD, SENTENCE.

2. BLACK (a) GRAY, WHITE; (b) YELLOW, PURPLE; (c) COLOR, CHROMATIC; (d) DARK, OPAQUE.

3. PASTE (a) SCISSORS, KNIFE; (b) RULER, STRAIGHT EDGE; (c) PAPER, CARDBOARD; (d) GLUE, TAPE.

4. CORNEA (a) EYEBROW, EYELASH; (b) PUPIL, IRIS; (c) EYE, EAR; (d) VISION, SIGHT.

5. GOLD (a) DIAMOND, RUBY; (b) SAPPHIRE, TURQUOISE; (c) SILVER, PLATINUM; (d) MONEY, CURRENCY.

6. KNEE (a) LEG, ARM; (b) FINGER, TOE; (c) THIGH, FOREARM; (d) ELBOW, HIP.

7. GOOSE (a) CHICKEN, DUCK; (b) HAWK, CANARY; (c) EGG, OFFSPRING; (d) BIRD, OMNIVORE.

8. TRUNK (a) TABLE, COUNTER; (b) ELEPHANT, SUITCASE; (c) CHEST, CABINET; (d) BREATHING, DRINKING.

9. POLE (a) GOLF BALL, MARBLE; (b) PENCIL, ROD; (c) VAULTER, JUMPER; (d) NORTH, SOUTH.

10. APPLE JUICE (a) LEMONADE, ICED TEA; (b) ROOT BEER, GINGER ALE; (c) WINE, BEER; (d) MACINTOSH, GRANNY SMITH.

11. FLOUNDER (a) FROG, TOAD; (b) HESITATE, DELIBERATE ON; (c) GOLDFISH, GUPPIE; (d) TROUT, BASS.

12. GREENLAND (a) FRANCE, GERMANY; (b) ITALY, GREECE; (c) CUBA, ENGLAND; (d) ICELAND, GERMANY.

13. SUN (a) DAFFODIL, LEMON; (b) TOMATO, APPLE; (c) LETTUCE, LIME; (d) NIGHT, LIMOUSINE.

14. LIKELY (a) DEFINITE, CERTAIN; (b) IMPOSSIBLE, UNDOABLE; (c) POSSIBLE, PROBABLE; (d) LIKABLE, FRIENDLY.

15. BILL CLINTON (a) DICK CHENEY, AL GORE; (b) COLIN POWELL, MADELEINE ALBRIGHT; (c) JIMMY CARTER, RONALD REAGAN; (d) TONY BLAIR, MARGARET THATCHER

16. UNCLE (a) GRANDMOTHER, GRANDSON; (b) FATHER, DAUGHTER; (c) AUNT, NEPHEW; (d) MOTHER, SON.

17. SHARK (a) TRUCK, TAXI; (b) FERRY, TUGBOAT; (c) JET, HELICOPTER; (d) SATELLITE, ROCKET SHIP.

18. STREAM (a) LAKE, POND; (b) OCEAN, SEA; (c) RIVER, BROOK; (d) PUDDLE, POOL.

19. CONTRIBUTE (a) DONATE, GIVE; (b) LEASE, SELL; (c) BUY, RENT; (d) INVEST, SPECULATE.

20. ASSAULT (a) THEFT, ARSON; (b) KIDNAPPING, MURDER; (c) PERJURY, CONTEMPT; (d) HANG, ELECTROCUTE.

21. ORANGE (a) PEAR, APPLE; (b) GRAPE, KUMQUAT; (c) CANTALOUPE, HONEYDEW; (d) LEMON, GRAPEFRUIT.

22. FRENCH (a) GERMAN, SWEDISH; (b) RUSSIAN, SERBO-CROATIAN; (c) SPANISH, ITALIAN; (d) LATIN, GREEK.

23. BULL (a) DOE, MARE; (b) CAMEL, HORSE; (c) STALLION, ROOSTER; (d) COW, GOAT.

24. CIRCLE (a) TRIANGLE, SHAPE; (b) SPHERE, PYRAMID; (c) POINT, LINE; (d) ELLIPSE, POLYGON.

25. CABIN (a) MANSION, CASTLE; (b) HUT, BUNGALOW; (c) TENT, WIGWAM; (d) HIVE, NEST.

26. PALMISTRY (a) CHEMISTRY, GEOLOGY; (b) ASTROLOGY, PHRENOLOGY; (c) ALCHEMY, MAGIC; (d) SOCIOLOGY, PSYCHOLOGY.

27. MATTHEW (a) HERMAN, JEFFREY; (b) ABIGAIL, MARGARET; (c) ROBERT, ALEXANDER; (d) MARK, JOHN.

28. ALUMINUM (a) BRASS, PEWTER; (b) URANIUM, RADIUM; (c) LEAD, COPPER; (d) BAUXITE, PYRITE.

29. HAMBURGER (a) CHEESE, BUTTER; (b) MEATBALLS, STEAK; (c) CHICKEN, TURKEY; (d) MUFFINS, BISCUITS.

30. HIS (a) MY, ITS; (b) OUR, THEIR; (c) YOU, HE; (d) US, THEM.

31. WOULD (a) CAN, WILL; (b) MIGHT, COULD; (c) MAY, SHOULD; (d) WON'T, CAN'T.

32. APRIL (a) TUESDAY, SATURDAY; (b) JANUARY, AUGUST; (c) SPRING, SEASON; (d) JUNE, SEPTEMBER.

33. HUMID (a) HOT, COLD; (b) CLIMATE, WEATHER; (c) DRY, DAMP; (d) WINDY, STILL.

34. STONE (a) BRICK, WOOD; (b) FEATHER, PAPER; (c) ROCK, CAVE; (d) SCULPTURE, MOSAIC.

35. PROTON (a) ELECTRON, NEUTRON; (b) ATOM, MOLECULE; (c) POSITRON, NUCLEON; (d) QUARK, CHARM.

36. SAPPHIRE (a) RHINESTONE, COAL; (b) CORAL, AMBER; (c) GOLD,SILVER; (d) EMERALD, RUBY.

37. LOBSTER (a) PEANUT BUTTER, FILET MIGNON; (b) TUNA, CAVIAR; (c) CRAB, MUSSEL; (d) THERMIDOR, LANGOSTINO.

38. COW (a) MAN, KANGAROO; (b) ROBIN, BLUEBIRD; (c) CAT, ELEPHANT; (d) WORM, SNAKE.

39. LINOLEUM (a) CARPET, RUG; (b) FLOOR, CEILING; (c) MUG, CUP; (d) CARBON, VINYL.
40. KING (a) FIREFIGHTER, POLICEMAN; (b) EMPEROR, MONARCH; (c) DUKE, PRINCE; (d) EARL, DUCHESS.

Answers to Verbal Classification Problems

1. (b). A book and a letter, like a magazine, are written forms of communication.
2. (a). Gray and white, like black, are achromatic shadings. (In other words, they have no hue.)
3. (d). Glue and tape, like paste, are used to fasten things together.
4. (b). The pupil and the iris, like the cornea, are parts of the eyeball.
5. (c). Silver and platinum, like gold, are precious metals.
6. (d). The elbow and the hip, like the knee, are joints.
7. (a). A chicken and a duck, like a goose, are forms of poultry.
8. (c). A chest and a cabinet, like a trunk, are storage containers.
9. (b). A pencil and a rod, like a pole, are basically cylindrical in shape.
10. (a). Lemonade and iced tea, like apple juice, are noncarbonated beverages.
11. (d). Trout and bass, like flounder, are kinds of fish.
12. (c). Cuba and England, like Greenland, are islands.
13. (a). A daffodil and a lemon, like the sun, are generally yellow in color.
14. (c). The words *possible* and *probable*, like the word *likely*, are adjectives referring to probability where the probability is neither zero nor one.
15. (c). Jimmy Carter and Ronald Reagan, like Bill Clinton, were presidents of the United States.
16. (c). An aunt, a nephew, and an uncle are indirect relatives (i.e., they are not direct descendants or ancestors).
17. (b). A ferry and a tugboat, like a shark, move in water.
18. (c). A river and a brook, like a stream, are continuously flowing bodies of water.
19. (a). To donate and to give, like to contribute, are ways of handing over resources of one kind or another.
20. (b). Kidnapping and murder, like assault, are crimes specifically against people.
21. (d). A lemon and a grapefruit, like an orange, are citrus fruits.
22. (c). Spanish and Italian, like French, are modern romance languages.
23. (c). A stallion and a rooster, like a bull, are male animals.
24. (d). An ellipse and a polygon, like a circle, are completely enclosed continuous curves.
25. (b). A hut and a bungalow, like a cabin, are modest places to live that are designed to be permanently placed.
26. (b). Astrology and phrenology, like palmistry, are pseudosciences devoted to understanding human beings and their potential futures.
27. (d). Matthew and John, like Paul, are books in the New Testament.
28. (c). Lead and copper, like aluminum, are metals (but not alloys).
29. (b). Steak and meatballs, like hamburger, are usually made from beef.
30. (a). My and its, like his, are singular possessive adjectives.
31. (b). *Might* and *could*, like *would*, are "helping" verbs used to express conditionality.

32. (d). June and September, like April, are months which each have thirty days.
33. (c). Dry and damp, like humid, refer to levels of moisture in the air.
34. (a). Brick and wood, like stone, are solid materials that can be used (for example) to construct a house.
35. (a). An electron and a neutron, like a proton, are basic particles constituting an atom.
36. (d). An emerald and a ruby, like a sapphire, are birthstones.
37. (c). A crab and a mussel, like a lobster, are shellfish.
38. (c). A cat and an elephant, like a cow, are animals that walk on four legs.
39. (a). A carpet and a rug, like linoleum, can be used as surfaces for floors.
40. (b). An emperor and a monarch, like a king, are rulers of a country.

MATRIX PROBLEMS

The matrix problem combines elements of analogy, series completion, and classification problems. In a matrix problem, there are typically nine small squares, or cells, embedded in one large square. In each of the cells is a figural design that is part of several patterns. The patterns go both horizontally across the matrix and vertically down the matrix. Usually, one of the cells of the matrix is blank, most typically, the cell at the lower right. The task of the solver is to figure out what figural design should go in the empty cell in order to finish the various patterns – that is, what figure will complete the horizontal and vertical patterns of which it is a part. Matrix problems are good but difficult tests of general intelligence. Indeed, one of the most famous intelligence tests of all time, the Raven Progressive Matrices, is composed exclusively of matrix problems.

Figure 6–3 contains some sample matrix problems for you to try. The first one is worked out for you. In the first sample problem, only things unique to the two uppermost or leftmost boxes in each column or row are added. Things common to the two boxes are dropped. In column 1, the top and bottom triangles are unique to the two boxes, A and D (they appear in one box, but not in the other). In box G, they are added together. The right triangle is common in both (A and D), so it is dropped from G. In column 2, the left and right triangles are unique to boxes B and E; therefore, they both appear in box H. In column 3, the top and bottom triangles, as well as the left and right triangles, are unique in boxes C and F; therefore, they appear in 1. Does this rule also work in a horizontal direction? Yes. If you take row 1, you will see that the top, left, and right triangles are unique in boxes A and B, so they appear in C. Now try the other rows on your own. In "unique addition," you do not have to add from left to right or from top to bottom; you also can go from right to left and from bottom to top. Do these matrices on your own. Some of them follow the "unique addition" rule; others follow other rules.

Notice that there is a sense in which these problems are two-dimensional series problems. In choosing the correct element for the empty lower-right cell, you need to choose the element that correctly completes each of the horizontal and vertical series simultaneously. Answers to these matrix problems appear after the problems.

SAMPLE MATRIX PROBLEMS [FIGURE 6–3]

Matrices

COLUMNS

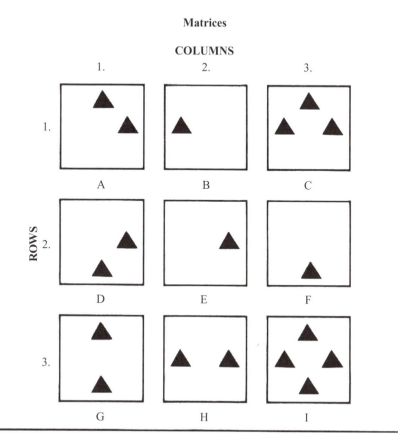

1.

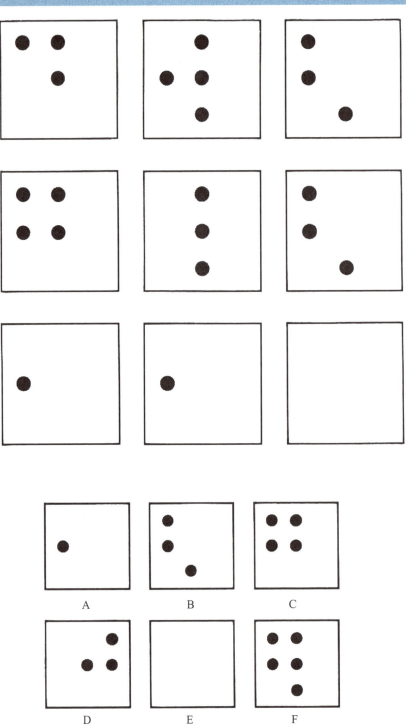

2.

3.

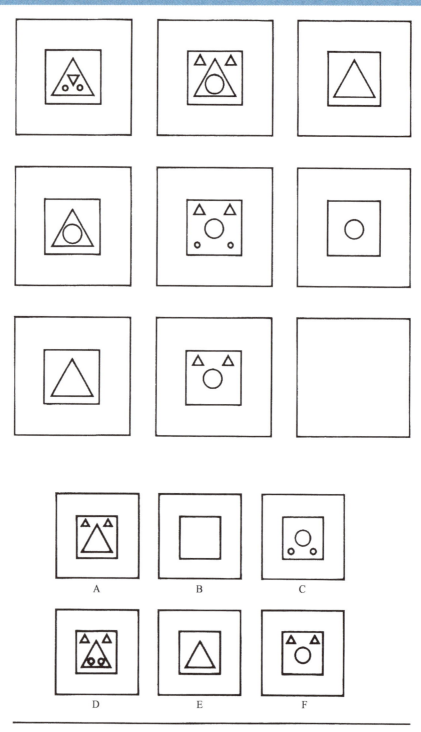

4.

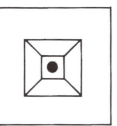 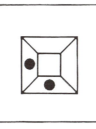 

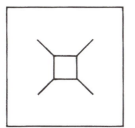 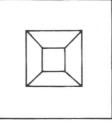 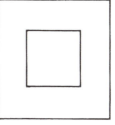

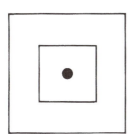 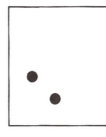 

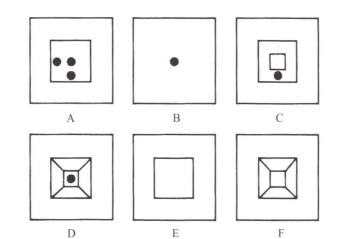

A   B   C

D   E   F

5.

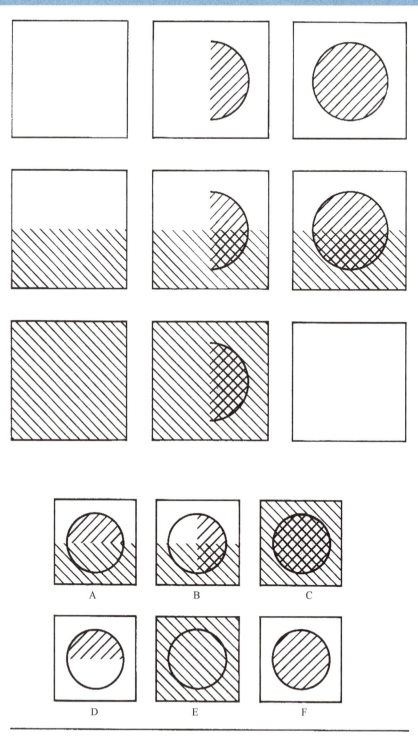

6.

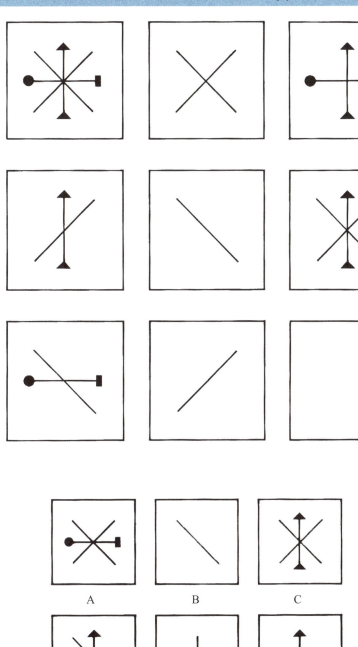

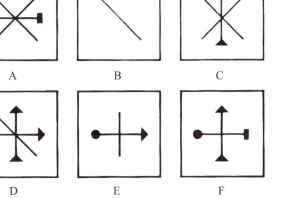

A   B   C

D   E   F

7.

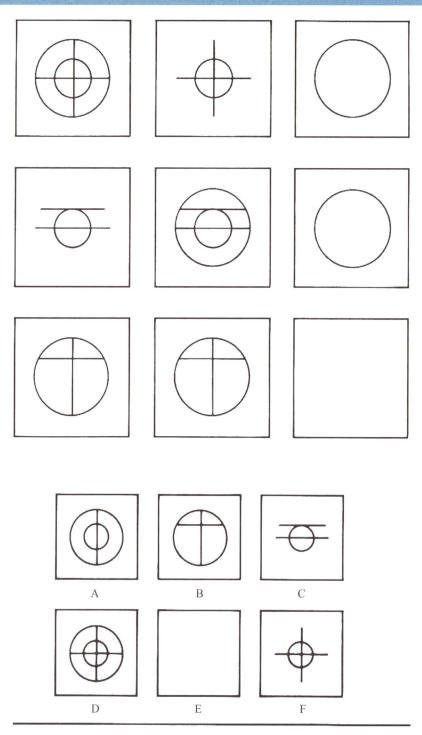

8.

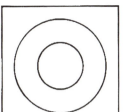
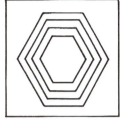
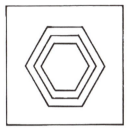
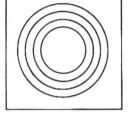

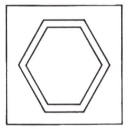

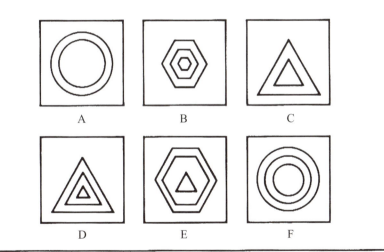

A   B   C

D   E   F

9.

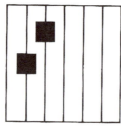 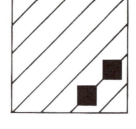 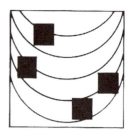

 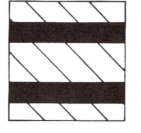 

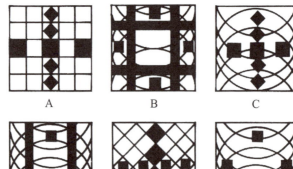

A   B   C

D   E   F

10.

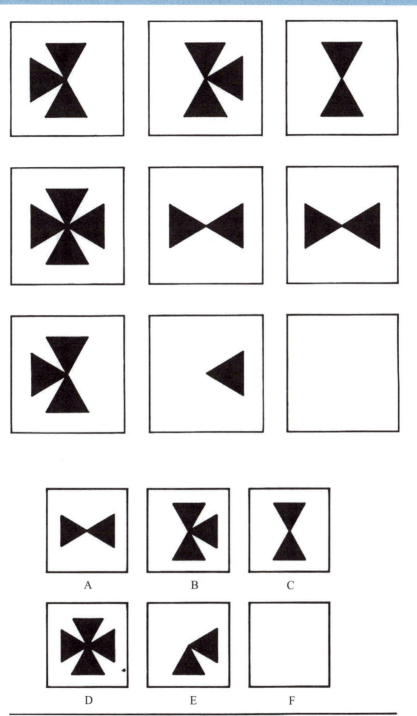

Answers to Matrix Problems (Figure 6–3)

1. E	3. B	5. C	7. E	9. C
2. D	4. A	6. A	8. F	10. F

PRACTICAL REASONING PROBLEMS

The analogy, series completion, classification, and matrix problems described here are among the problem types most frequently found on traditional or older intelligence tests. The reason is that scores on these problems tend to correlate very highly with scores on psychometrically based intelligence tests, achievement tests, and tests of academic performance. However, these kinds of problems are, in a sense, quite obscure. Few people encounter these types of straightforward analogy, series completion, classification, or matrix problems in either everyday life, at school, or at work. Our goal in training intellectual skills is for the skills to generalize beyond esoteric problems to the kinds of reasoning that people need in everyday life. The problems presented in this section give you an opportunity to do exactly this. These problems require you to *encode* information, *infer* relations, and *apply* these relations to new situations. The two kinds of problems presented here are legal and clinical reasoning problems.

Legal Reasoning Problems

In legal reasoning, a lawyer, a judge, or a client has to consider the principles of law and the facts of the case (among other things). One of the most difficult problems the legal reasoner faces is figuring out which principles of law are relevant to the case, and which facts of the case have legal implications. In any one case, there may be thousand of principles of law that seem relevant, and the job of picking the most relevant pieces is quite difficult. The number of facts relating to a given case can be extremely large, but only a small proportion of these facts have legal consequences. A frustration often faced by participants in legal battles is that the facts of the case that are relevant from a legal standpoint are often not those that seem most relevant from a personal standpoint. For example, settlements of lawsuits sometimes hinge on what may appear to be minor technicalities rather than the seemingly more major injustices that the plaintiff may believe that he or she has suffered. In the legal reasoning problems presented here, you are asked to engage in legal reasoning, only in a simplified form.

In each of the cases here, you will be presented with a brief story describing a legal proceeding, followed by some principles of law, some facts extracted from the case, and a choice of two outcomes for the legal proceeding. First, you need to *infer* which principle of law from among those given is most relevant to the particular case. You should indicate which of these principles you have chosen. Second, you need to (selectively) *encode* which fact this principle most directly bears upon. You should again indicate your response. Finally, you need to *apply* the selective principle to the chosen fact in order to decide the outcome of the case. You should again indicate your response, here communicating what you believe to be the correct outcome for this particular case. Although, of course, the reasoning you will be required to do here is a gross simplification of the kind of reasoning lawyers and judges have to do in an actual case, it will give you the flavor of what is required in legal reasoning, and particularly of how the performance components of induction can be applied in a real-world setting.

Below are ten legal reasoning problems. Read each case carefully; then solve the problems on your own, inferring principles, encoding facts, and applying the principles to the facts so as to obtain a legal outcome for the case. In each problem, choose the one principle and the one fact that are critical to solving the case, and then solve it. Use only the information in each problem. Please keep in mind that the principles given below, as well as the facts of the particular cases, are imaginary, even though the kind of reasoning you need to apply is not. Answers are at the end of the problem set.

PROBLEM 1   On May 1, Dillenger Industries sent a letter to Ecolo Engineering offering to buy Ecolo's new antismog device. The letter offered to pay Ecolo $200,000 for the rights to the device. It requested that Ecolo submit its acceptance by letter.

Ecolo's president, Harold Koffer, phoned Dillenger on May 3 and indicated interest in discussing the offer further. After some discussion, he said that he intended to agree to Dillenger's original offer in a letter of confirmation.

On May 8, Koffer sent a letter of acceptance to Dillenger but requested that Dillenger pay $225,000. When Dillenger received the letter (May 10), he phoned Koffer and asked him to wait a few days so that he could raise the extra money. The next day (May 11), Koffer phoned Dillenger and informed him that he had sold the device to General Filters instead. Dillenger brought suit against Ecolo for breach of contract. Will Dillenger win?

PRINCIPLES

1. In order for a contract to be legally enforceable, the services to be performed under the contract must be legal under the law of the place where the contract is to be performed.
2. In order to form a contract, there must be an offer and an acceptance. Acceptance is an expression of assent to the terms of the offer made by the accepter in a manner requested by the person making the offer.

FACTS

1. Dillenger made an offer to Ecolo Industries requesting reply by letter.
2. Koffer indicated interest in the offer.
3. Koffer's letter of acceptance changed the terms of Dillenger's original offer.
4. Koffer sold the device to General Filters instead of to Dillenger.

OUTCOMES

1. Dillenger will win.
2. Dillenger will lose.

PROBLEM 2   Captain Taylor was hired under a contract to command a ship belonging to Mr. Mayer. The ship was to sail from San Francisco to Manila and back. While in Manila, Taylor had a fight with the first mate, and he resigned his command. A new captain was appointed. However, because the radio had been knocked out in a storm, notice of this change was not communicated to Mayer. Taylor helped the new captain on the trip back to San Francisco. The ship arrived safely. No damages had resulted from the change of command. When the ship arrived in San Francisco, Mayer learned the above facts. He paid Taylor for his services as captain up to the time he quit, but he refused to pay him for his services in helping get the vessel home. Taylor sued Mayer to recover wages for his services on the return trip. Will Taylor win?

PRINCIPLES

1. A man is not required to pay for that which he has had no opportunity of rejecting. Under circumstances in which there is no opportunity of rejecting, acquiescence cannot be presumed to arise from silence.
2. If one of two parties to a contract breaks the obligation that the contract imposes and the other party is injured as a result of the break, then the injured party has the right of action for damages.

FACTS

1. Taylor voluntarily resigned his command.
2. Mayer did not learn of Taylor's resignation until the ship arrived home.
3. Taylor helped the new captain on the return trip.
4. The ship arrived safely in San Francisco.

OUTCOMES

1. Taylor will win.
2. Taylor will lose.

PROBLEM 3   Harris Co. was a U.S. department store, and Ross-Jones Co. was an English manufacturing firm. The two firms entered into a written agreement spelling out in detail arrangements for carrying out their business with each other. Under the agreement, the English firm was to accept as binding or reject as not binding orders from Harris Co. promptly following receipt of each order, and was to make deliveries during the following six-month period. The agreement also stated, "This memo is not written as a formal or legal agreement and shall not be subject to legal jurisdiction in the law courts of either the United States or England."

A dispute arose between the parties, and the English firm terminated the agreement without giving reasonable notice. They refused to deliver certain orders then outstanding that they had already accepted. Harris Co. sued Ross-Jones Co. to recover damages from the nondelivery of goods that were to have been delivered during the following six-month period. Will Harris Co. win?

PRINCIPLES

1. A written agreement is not a legally binding contract unless both parties intended to enter into legal obligations and communicated these intentions to each other.
2. Orders accepted under a written agreement become legally binding contracts upon acceptance.

FACTS

1. Harris Co. and Ross-Jones Co. entered into a written agreement.
2. The parties did not intend for the agreement to be a legal contract.
3. Ross-Jones Co. terminated the agreement without giving reasonable notice.
4. Ross-Jones Co. refused to deliver orders that they had accepted as binding according to the written agreement.

OUTCOMES

1. Harris Co. will win.
2. Harris Co. will lose.

PROBLEM 4   Mrs. Brown wanted to buy two vacation houses at a beach resort. She intended to use one for her family and to give the second to her married son and his family.

Mrs. Brown found a suitable house for her own family and signed a written agreement with the owner, Mr. James, to purchase the house. Under the agreement, Mrs. Brown agreed to take title within thirty days, at which time she would pay the balance of the $150,000 price. She paid $20,000 in signing the agreement, leaving a balance of $130,000. She also agreed to sign a full-length contract-of-purchase within ninety days. A copy of the contract with all the essential terms clearly stated therein was attached to the agreement.

Mrs. Brown found another house suitable for her son about one block from the James house. This house was owned by Mrs. Hanks. She signed a agreement that stated that the parties contemplated a sale of the Hanks property to Mrs. Brown "subject to the terms of a contract being arranged." Mrs. Brown paid $100 to Mrs. Hanks for signing the agreement. The parties did not begin to arrange the contract at this meeting.

A few days later, it developed that Mr. James was anxious to complete the sale of his home to Mrs. Brown, but Mrs. Hanks was not willing to sell her property at a reasonable price. Mrs. Brown took legal action against Mrs. Hanks to force her to sell her property in accordance with their agreement. Will Mrs. Brown win?

PRINCIPLES

1. An acceptance of an offer by signing a agreement with an attached copy of the contract containing all the essential terms of the agreement constitutes a complete, enforceable contract.
2. An agreement to try to arrange terms for a contract is merely an expression of willingness to negotiate and is not an enforceable contract.

FACTS

1. Mrs. Brown signed an agreement with Mr. James to purchase his house.
2. The agreement for the James house included a copy of the contract.
3. Mrs. Brown signed an agreement with Mrs. Hanks to purchase her house.
4. The agreement for the Hanks house stated that the parties contemplated a sale of the Hanks property to Mrs. Brown subject to the terms of a contract to be arranged later.

OUTCOMES

1. Mrs. Brown will win.
2. Mrs. Brown will lose.

PROBLEM 5   The manager of ABC Jewelry Co. suspected one of his employees, Miss Jones, of taking a valuable ring from the display case. On the night of June 24, the manager sent one of his friends, who was experienced in the repossession of merchandise, to Miss Jones's apartment. He knocked on the door, and when she opened it he said, "I have been looking for you." In the room the repossessor demanded the ring, but on discovering that the ring Miss Jones was carrying in her pocketbook was not the missing ring, he left. On June 25, the manager called Miss Jones into his office. Behind closed doors, the manager and a private detective charged her with theft and threatened to send her to jail if she did not sign a statement admitting the theft. Miss Jones said she was quitting the firm and asked permission to make a telephone call. The request to use the phone was denied, and she was subjected to continued restraint and high-pressure questioning.

Miss Jones later sued the repossessor and the ABC Jewelry Co. for damages resulting from false imprisonment in her apartment on the night of June 24. Will Miss Jones win?

PRINCIPLES

1. Force and threats used to restrain freedom of action and to keep a person in a place against his or her will constitute false imprisonment, and a person so restrained can recover damages.
2. Although inquiry after stolen property may affect a suspect unpleasantly, as long as the subject's freedom of action is in no way restrained, such inquiry does not constitute false imprisonment.

FACTS

1. On the night of June 24, the repossessor knocked on Miss Jones's door and demanded the ring, saying "I have been looking for you."
2. The repossessor did not restrain Miss Jones in her apartment against her will.
3. On June 25, the manager restrained Miss Jones in his office while questioning her.
4. The manager did not permit Miss Jones to make a phone call.

OUTCOMES

1. Miss Jones will win.
2. Miss Jones will lose.

PROBLEM 6   Mr. Peters owned an apartment building near the county airport. Some airplanes flew over the building at low altitudes, while others flew over at higher altitudes. One day Mr. Peters erected a tall television antenna on top of his building. A low-flying plane owned by Top Flight Airlines hit the antenna with its wingtip, causing some damage to both the plane and the antenna.

Mr. Peters brought suit against Top Flight Airlines for the damage to his property. Will Mr. Peters win?

PRINCIPLES

1. A landowner who in no way contributes to the injury of an uninvited trespasser is not liable to that trespasser.
2. The owner of land has the exclusive right to as much of the space above it as may be actually occupied and used by him and necessarily incident to such occupation and use, and anyone passing through such space without the owner's consent is a trespasser. The owner may recover damages for such trespass.

FACTS

1. Mr. Peters erected a television antenna on top of the apartment building that he owned, and a plane hit the antenna.
2. Airplanes had previously flown in the area occupied by the antenna.
3. The antenna was very tall.
4. The plane was damaged when it hit the antenna.

OUTCOMES

1. Mr. Peters will win.
2. Mr. Peters will lose.

PROBLEM 7   Mr. Yankin agreed to sell Mr. Wheeler "100 eggs for $50." He intended 100 dozen, while Mr. Wheeler intended 100 crates. Later, Mr. Yankin agreed to sell Mr. Wheeler butter at 30 cents per pound, but Mr. Yankin really meant to say 40 cents per pound.

On delivering the 100 dozen eggs, Yankin found that Wheeler expected 100 crates of eggs. Yankin got mad and refused to sell any eggs at all to Wheeler. Wheeler sued Yankin to force him to sell 100 crates of eggs for $50. Will Wheeler win?

PRINCIPLES

1. Parties to an agreement are bound by what each states and not what each means.
2. Mutual mistakes by both parties to an agreement regarding quantity might or would prevent a meeting of the minds, and without a meeting of the minds there is no legally enforceable obligation.

FACTS

1. Yankin and Wheeler agreed on a contract for eggs.
2. Yankin and Wheeler had different interpretations of the quantity of eggs to be sold.

3. Yankin agreed to sell Wheeler butter at a certain price.

4. Yankin meant to sell the butter at a different price.

OUTCOMES

1. Wheeler will win.

2. Wheeler will lose.

PROBLEM 8   Mr. Watson and Mr. Parson went into business together to manufacture vests for large dogs. They signed articles of co-partnership under which each was to receive 50 percent of the profits for the total operations of the partnership. It was further specified that Watson would have primary direction of the warehouse and that Parson would have primary direction of marketing. At the time of making the written agreement, there was some talk about Watson's receiving 60 percent of the profit and Parson 40 percent because Watson had superior experience. Later, Watson sued Parson to secure 60 percent of the profits. Will Watson win?

PRINCIPLES

1. A written instrument cannot be changed by oral evidence because written agreements are more definite than oral ones and the usefulness of written instruments cannot be impaired by such oral contradiction.

2. Oral evidence can be introduced in a trial to explain ambiguities and technical terms so that the written agreement may be enforced as intended by the parties when the agreement was made.

FACTS

1. According to the written agreement, Watson and Parson were each to receive 50 percent of the profits.

2. According to the written agreement, Watson would have primary direction of the warehouse.

3. According to the written agreement, Parson would have primary direction of the marketing.

4. Watson had more experience than Parson.

OUTCOMES

1. Watson will win.

2. Watson will lose.

PROBLEM 9   Johnson bought a valuable oil painting, but had no way to get the painting home at that time. He asked Smith, the art dealer who sold the painting, to leave the painting on the wall of the store. Johnson said that he would pick it up that evening.

Two hours later, Nielson entered Smith's shop and a clerk sold the same painting to Nielson without realizing that Smith had previously sold it to Johnson. Johnson returned that evening and found the painting missing. He sued Nielson to recover the painting. Will Johnson win?

PRINCIPLES

1. If a seller of goods retains possession following the initial sale to one party, and later he or his agent sells the goods to a second party, then the seller shall be liable for damages to the wronged first purchaser.
2. If a buyer temporarily leaves goods he buys in the seller's possession and the seller or his agent resells these goods to an innocent subsequent purchaser, the subsequent purchaser who has possession of the goods has the better claim of title.

FACTS

1. The painting in question was valuable and irreplaceable.
2. Smith sold the painting to Johnson.
3. Johnson had no means of getting the painting home at the time he bought it.
4. Johnson left the painting in Smith's store, and a clerk unknowingly sold it to Nielson.

OUTCOMES

1. Johnson will win.
2. Johnson will lose.

PROBLEM 10   Mr. Schmidt brought some new ballpoint pens to his wealthy friend Mr. Crass, with a pad of "blank" paper on which to test the pens. Unknown to Crass, Schmidt had prepared two negotiable promissory notes on two of the pages of the writing pad in such a way as not to be readily noticeable. Crass told Schmidt he would appreciate a gift of a couple of the pens, and Schmidt asked Crass to try the pens on the pad of "blank" paper to be sure they worked well. Schmidt flipped the pages for Crass to test the pen, but Schmidt was careful to conceal the two pages containing the promissory notes so that Crass could see only the blank bottom portions when he signed his name. Schmidt kept one of the notes for $1000 and sold the other to Mr. Crown, who did not know of the deception. Crown presented the note to Crass, and Crass refused to pay. Crown sued Crass to recover the amount of the note. Will Crown win?

PRINCIPLES

1. A person who acquires a negotiable note in good faith may recover the amount thereof from the maker.
2. A person who has been guilty of fraud and deception in having a maker execute a negotiable note cannot recover on it from the maker.

FACTS

1. Schmidt fraudulently had Crass sign two promissory notes.
2. Schmidt kept one note.

3. Schmidt sold the other note to Crown.
4. Crown did not know of Schmidt's deception when he bought the note.

OUTCOMES

1. Crown will win.
2. Crown will lose.

Answers to Legal Reasoning Problems

Principles	Facts	Outcomes
1. 2	3	2
2. 1	2	2
3. 2	4	1
4. 2	4	2
5. 2	2	2
6. 2	1	1
7. 2	2	2
8. 1	1	2
9. 2	4	2
10. 1	4	1

Clinical Reasoning Problems

People often think of lawyers and doctors as being similar in little other than their professional status and income. However, there are striking similarities in the kinds of reasoning they need to do on the job. Medical diagnosis problems are in many respects similar to legal reasoning problems. The problems presented here will require you to make clinical inferences for a test that is sometimes used in psychiatric diagnosis, the Rorschach Inkblots Test. Although the principles given here, as well as the facts of the particular cases, are imaginary, the kind of reasoning you need to apply is not.

In each hypothetical case, you will receive a file folder for a patient made up of the patient's response to the presentation of an inkblot, and the patient's description of what he or she sees in the inkblot. You also will be presented with some principles of interpretation for the Rorschach test, some facts summarized from the entire protocol, and some alternative diagnoses. Your task will be first to *infer* which principle is most relevant for making a clinical diagnosis in this case, second, to (selectively) *encode* the fact to which this principle most directly applies, and third, to *apply* the principle to the fragment in order to select the correct diagnosis. In reality, of course, a clinician would not make a diagnosis based on the application of a principle of test scoring to a single response. As with the legal reasoning problems, this task represents a gross simplification of the reasoning in which professionals must engage. Nevertheless, it gives you some idea of the kind of reasoning in which clinicians must engage when making their clinical diagnoses. Note that the structure of these problems is parallel to the structure of the legal reasoning problems.

As noted earlier, for all the difference in contents, the inductive reasoning processes required for clinical diagnosis are quite similar to those required for legal reasoning.

Below are ten clinical diagnosis problems. Choose the relevant principle and the relevant fact, and then make your diagnosis. Solutions to the problems appear after the problems. To repeat: *All principles and responses are imaginary.*

PROBLEM 1   "Well I see the whole blot as a big bat. It has two antennae, and it's flapping its wings. I guess it uses its radar to fly around. Oh, now it looks like the bat is turning into something else. Yes, I see two angels, one on each side of the card. They have big wings. And in the middle there's a woman. She has her hands up. There's those little blobs that look like hands at the top. She's raising her hands up to Heaven, you see, because the angels are taking her to Heaven." *Diagnose:* High intelligence or not.

PRINCIPLES
1. Responses in which adjacent areas of the blot are combined in a meaningful way indicate high intelligence.
2. When a subject gives two or more responses that are vague or lacking in detail, low intelligence is indicated.

FACTS
1. The subject gives two responses to the card.
2. The first response is a bat.
3. The second response is two angels and a woman.
4. The angels are carrying the woman to Heaven.

OUTCOMES
1. The subject has high intelligence.
2. The subject does not have high intelligence.

PROBLEM 2   "I see a demon. Oh, there are his eyes (pointing to the triangular white areas). I think he's staring at me. . . . There is his nose (pointing to the pointed black area at the bottom), and his two pointed ears at the sides. . . . That demon looks really mean. He looks ready to strike. His fangs are out. His nose is smelling out the enemy." *Diagnose:* Paranoid or not.

PRINCIPLES
1. When the subject treats the card as having personal content, paranoia is indicated.
2. When the subject sees aggressive movement taking place, paranoia is contraindicated.

FACTS
1. The demon is staring at the subject.
2. The demon has triangular white eyes.

3. The demon is ready to strike.
4. The demon is mean.

OUTCOMES
1. The subject is paranoid.
2. The subject is not paranoid.

PROBLEM 3 "It's a bat. . . . No it's not; it turned into a cockroach. In the middle of the card, there's the cockroach. That cockroach is really dirty, like the ones crawling around my sink at home. Wait, now it became a butterfly. Yes, I know what it is – it is a butterfly. The bat metamorphosed into a butterfly because the cockroach bit him. That cockroach is really mean and dirty." *Diagnose:* Brain damage or not.

PRINCIPLES
1. Shifting responses coupled with inability to recall previous responses indicate brain damage.
2. Illogical use of cause and effect relationships contraindicates brain damage.

FACTS
1. The subject sees three different animals in the card.
2. Each animal is seen to be turning into the next one.
3. The bat changed into a butterfly because the cockroach bit it.
4. The cockroach is dirty.

OUTCOMES
1. The subject has no brain damage.
2. The subject has brain damage.

PROBLEM 4 "It's an angel – looks like he's conducting an orchestra or something. But he doesn't have a head. Those two pincer-like things at the top, those are the hands conducting. And you can see the wings out at the sides. The part in the middle is the body, and down there are his feet." *Diagnose.* High intelligence or not.

PRINCIPLES
1. A response that uses all parts of the blot indicates high intelligence.
2. A response that includes movement over a large area of the blot indicates low intelligence.

FACTS
1. The angel's body is in the middle of the card, its wings are at the sides, and its hands are at the top.
2. The angel is moving its hands.
3. The angel lacks a head.
4. The angel is male.

OUTCOMES

1. The subject has high intelligence.
2. The subject has low intelligence.

PROBLEM 5   "It's two witches with big black cloaks. It must be Halloween. They're dancing around, and their cloaks are blowing in the breeze. It's Halloween night. They each have a rabbit. The rabbits are just sitting there in midair." *Diagnose:* Introverted or not.

PRINCIPLES

1. When both human and animal figures are seen, but only the animals are moving, introversion is indicated.
2. If the subject locates the scene he or she sees in the blot in a specific time or place, introversion is contraindicated.

FACTS

1. The subject sees human and animal figures.
2. The rabbits are floating in the air.
3. The witches are dancing.
4. It is Halloween night.

OUTCOMES

1. The subject is introverted.
2. The subject is not introverted.

PROBLEM 6   "Well, at the top there's the two black clouds. And the pointed thing is a rocket. It seems to be shooting up into the clouds. And in the middle there's a big white hole. There's some black dirt all around the hole." *Diagnose:* Impulsive or not.

PRINCIPLES

1. Use of enclosed white areas indicates lack of impulsiveness.
2. Use of color terms indicates impulsiveness.

FACTS

1. The two blobs at the top are black clouds.
2. The pointed shape near the top is a rocket.
3. The white area in the middle is a hole.
4. The black circular area is dirt.

OUTCOMES

1. The subject is impulsive.
2. The subject is not impulsive.

PROBLEM 7   "It's a fur muff. In the middle is where you put your hands. I think it's made out of lamb's fur . . . it looks white and fluffy. My sister has a muff like that. But what are those two blobs at the top? That might be the ends of her scarf dangling down. She has a pretty scarf that goes with her muff." *Diagnose:* Suicidal tendencies or not.

PRINCIPLES
1. Suicidal tendencies are present if and only if texture and dark colors are used in combination.
2. If the subject uses texture on one side of the blot only, suicidal tendencies are indicated.

FACTS
1. The subject sees the muff.
2. The muff is white and fluffy.
3. The subject's sister owns a similar muff.
4. The muff is made of lamb's fur.

OUTCOMES
1. The subject has suicidal tendencies.
2. The subject does not have suicidal tendencies.

PROBLEM 8   "Hmm. . . . I don't know what this card is supposed to be. Oh yes, in the middle, the pointed thing is a carrot. Actually, it's two carrots next to each other. I can't see anything else. Oh . . . I do see a stomach. Yes, there's a big hole where all the stomach is digesting the carrot." *Diagnose:* Compulsive or not.

PRINCIPLES
1. Hesitation in responding indicates compulsiveness.
2. Anatomical content in the initial sentence indicates compulsiveness.

FACTS
1. The subject first sees two carrots.
2. The subject then sees a stomach.
3. The subject pauses frequently in responding.
4. The subject attempts to integrate the two responses.

OUTCOMES
1. The subject is compulsive.
2. The subject is not compulsive.

PROBLEM 9　"It's some clouds in the sky. They look like storm clouds; they're big black clouds. I see the drops of rain coming down at the bottom. Oh, now I see something else. It's two people facing each other. They seem to be sitting down. It looks like they're playing patty-cake with each other. See, they're holding their hands up." *Diagnose:* Psychopathic or not.

PRINCIPLES

1. If intact human bodies are seen, psychopathy is not present.
2. If humans are perceived as performing actions not usually performed by humans, psychopathy is indicated.

FACTS

1. The subject sees two different things in the blot.
2. The first response is clouds.
3. The second response is two people.
4. The people are playing patty-cake.

OUTCOMES

1. The subject is not psychopathic.
2. The subject is psychopathic.

PROBLEM 10　"It's two magicians facing each other. They have just made a bow tie appear, and it's floating in the air between them. On each side I see two rabbits. The magicians made the rabbits appear just a while ago, and they're floating in the air, too. Now the magicians are leaning toward each other and are pulling open a hat or something. I think something might come out of the hat." *Diagnose:* Schizophrenic or not.

PRINCIPLES

1. If the figures on either side of the blot are in a helping relationship, schizophrenia is not present.
2. If animate beings are seen to be falling, schizophrenia is indicated.

FACTS

1. The magicians are both pulling open a hat.
2. The magicians have produced a bow tie and two rabbits.
3. The bow tie and rabbits are floating in the air.
4. The magicians are facing each other.

OUTCOMES

1. The subject is not schizophrenic.
2. The subject is schizophrenic.

Answers to Clinical Reasoning Problems

Principles	Facts	Outcomes
1. 1	4	1
2. 1	1	1
3. 2	3	1
4. 1	1	1
5. 2	4	2
6. 1	3	2
7. 1	2	2
8. 1	3	1
9. 1	3	1
10. 1	1	1

Logical Reasoning and Analysis of Arguments

PERFORMANCE COMPONENTS (III)

WHAT IS LOGICAL REASONING?

Suppose that four friends – Mike, Zoe, Ira, and Kate – are having a conversation about the death penalty. Zoe says, "I think the death penalty is wrong." Zoe is making a *claim*. A claim is a statement asserting a particular characteristic, quality, or property of something or someone and is subject to dispute. In other words, claims can be supported or undermined and may be false or true. Claims are inferential beliefs derived from other statements.

Claims form the basis of everyday conversations, public dispute, mass media, and scientific debates. But how do we determine whether these claims are true? To return to the example, how would Mike decide whether Zoe's claim, that the death penalty is wrong, is true or false?

Mike could consider the majority opinion on the issue. Often claims are evaluated based on whether there is a *consensus* (or a general agreement) of opinions on the matter. For example, imagine if Mike lived in Texas, the U.S. state with the highest number of executions performed since 1982.[1] Then he might argue that, in his state, legislators have reached a consensus that is the opposite of Zoe's claim. Ira, on the other hand, might sustain Zoe's argument by appealing to *facts* (events that are taken as actual and not likely to change). He might discuss statistics showing that, since the reinstatement of the death penalty in the late 1970s, a number of prisoners who have been retried have been found innocent and released from death row. Kate might support Ira's position by adding that *research evidence* demonstrates that murder rates are higher in those states with the death penalty than in their neighboring non–death penalty states (http://www.deathpenaltyinfo.org).

These facts can be open to alternative interpretations. It may be that there were only very few innocent death-row inmates, all of whom were let go. Or, perhaps, the higher murder rates in death-penalty states are causes rather than effects of having

---

[1] Four hundred people have been executed in Texas since 1982 (http://www.tdcj.state.tx.us/stat/executedoffenders.htm; http://www.deathpenaltyinfo.org/article.php?scid = 8&did = 477.

the death penalty in those states. In other words, the states may have adopted the death penalty because they had so many murders.

If you were to study the reasons why these four friends agreed and disagreed about the death penalty, you would be engaged in *formal logic*. This is a branch of philosophy that is concerned with rules for deriving (logically) valid conclusions. In asserting claims to someone else, you may start an exchange of opinions. As shown in the death penalty example, three types of evidence are commonly introduced: consensus, fact, and research. In formal logic, this exchange of ideas is usually referred to as an *argument*. An argument has a different meaning in this context than it does in everyday life. If you hear that someone say that Dave and Paul had an argument, you might picture them yelling or getting angry at each other. In formal logic terms, an argument does not necessarily have the same negative associations.

The process of supporting an argument with evidence using certain kinds of rules is called *reasoning*. Reasoning originates from evidence (facts, consensuses, or research data), that might result in valid (logical) or invalid (illogical) conclusions. Psychologists often are more concerned with how people process information when they perform tasks requiring reasoning than they are with the particular conclusions people reach. Therefore, psychologists deal with both valid and invalid conclusions. Invalid conclusions are also called *fallacies*.

The two types of reasoning most often referred to are *inductive* and *deductive* reasoning. Inductive reasoning involves drawing general conclusions based on specific information or evidence. When you reason inductively, you gather facts and observations together to form a broad conclusion. You can visualize inductive reasoning as bottom-up thinking – you start at the bottom with all of the different facts, and you move up toward a general principle. For example, suppose you are trying to get in shape and you have just started attending a new gym. As a part of your membership package, you get towel service. When you go to the gym on Monday, an attendant gives you a blue towel. When you go back Tuesday, you once again get a blue towel. Your next trip to the gym falls on Friday and, lo and behold, you are handed a blue towel again! Based on these instances, your induction might be "This gym only has blue towels."

Another example might be if you are considering taking a class with a professor you don't know, Dr. Katz. You ask your friends, and Jean says she took his course last year and got an A. Joe says he took Dr. Katz last semester and got an A. You keep asking people, and Steve, Beth, Robert, and Maya all tell you that they've taken courses with Dr. Katz and received an A. You then log onto a Web site that rates professors, and you see that ten people have posted about Dr. Katz, and they all mention that they received As in his course. You might then come to the conclusion that Dr. Katz gives As to all of his students.

It is important to note, however, that the conclusions that you may initially draw can never be proven. Just because you've only been handed blue towels or you've only heard about Dr. Katz giving out As doesn't mean that either will always be true. Even if you get ten thousand straight blue towels, or hear about ten thousand people who received As, you still cannot say that you have proven your hypothesis. It only takes one non-blue towel or one non-A grade to disprove everything. In some cases, you may find out a specific rule that changes things. For example, you may discover that the gym uses blue towels on every day except Sunday, or that they use blue towels for members of one sex (your own) but towels of a different color for members of the opposite sex. Or you may find out that you have only spoken to economics majors, and Dr. Katz's course is in economics. Non-majors may be more likely to get Bs or Cs.

If inductive reasoning is making general conclusions from specific observations, then deductive reason is thinking in the opposite direction. Deductive reasoning starts with general theories and then makes specific predictions based on these theories. You may visualize deductive reasoning as being top-down thinking – you start with a larger idea and then move down and draw conclusions about specific facts or observations. The starting point of deductive reasoning, therefore, is a statement that is believed to be true. Your conclusion is reached by following a pattern of deductive reasoning and therefore is considered to be logically true. For example, you may start with the theory of gravity – in very simple terms, what goes up must come down. Based on this starting point, what would you say if Aviva asked you, "What would happen if I threw an egg in the air?" Following deductive reasoning, you would think, "All things that go up must come down. If you throw an egg up in the air, and all things thrown in the air must come down, then the egg should come down. Therefore, I should tell Aviva that the egg would fall back down."

To return to our towel example, suppose that you know Mike, the manager of the gym you attend. Mike tells you that he likes blue and bought enough blue towels to replace all the towels in the gym. He now uses only blue towels. Knowing this information, you now can safely deduce that, regardless of whether you come to the gym in the mornings or the evening (or on Monday versus Saturday), you will get a blue towel. The reason is that all towels owed by the gym are blue! In other words, if all towels at the gym are blue, and what you have in your hands is a towel, then what you have in your hands is blue.

Another example might be if on the first day of class, your professor tells you, "All tests will be short answer." Based on this statement, it is reasonable to assume that the midterm will be short answer – and you can adjust how you study accordingly. If your general belief is false, then your deductions may be false. For example, maybe you misheard your professor, and she actually said, "The first test will be short answer." In this circumstance, the final exam may be filled with multiple-choice items. Deductive reasoning only "works" if the initial general theory is correct.

Someone who is very good at using and applying his or her intelligence can use both inductive and deductive reasoning, often together. For example, let's say that Rebecca watches a movie that stars Brad Pitt. She absolutely loves this movie, and thinks that Brad Pitt is wonderful. So she sees another Brad Pitt movie, and another, and then another. She loves them all. Using inductive reasoning, she might conclude that Brad Pitt makes great movies. Rebecca might then use this belief as the basis for deductive reasoning. In other words, once she has this conclusion that Brad Pitt makes wonderful movies, she can make predictions about future Brad Pitt movies (i.e., she will like them). So when the next Brad Pitt movie comes out, Rebecca can deduce that she will enjoy it.

LINEAR SYLLOGISMS

Recall that you can apply reasoning skills by solving problems such as *linear syllogisms*.[2] Linear syllogisms involve comparisons. Most linear syllogisms are conjuncts. Consider the following example:

Mary is slower than Kate but faster than June. Who is fastest?

The problem gives information about how to order the people from fastest to slowest. This order can be expressed as a linear continuum. So, for example, in the problem above,

(a) Mary is slower than Kate.

Therefore, she should be placed lower than Kate:

Kate

Mary

(b) ... but faster than June

so June is placed below Mary:

Kate

Mary

June

Linear syllogisms differ in degree of difficulty. For example, the syllogism

Max is taller than Pete, Pete is taller than Dave. Who is the tallest?

appears to be easier than the linear syllogism

Ian is not as tall as Jim; Jack is not as short as Jim. Who is the tallest?

Linear syllogisms are easier to solve when:

- the same comparative word is used in all of the premises (e.g., *taller, taller,* and *tallest* in the first syllogism and not *tall, short, short,* and *tallest* in the second)
- when there are only positive statements, with no negations (e.g., the second syllogism has the negation *not as tall as,* which makes the syllogism more difficult)
- when terms are in the easier of two directions (e.g., better and smarter) rather than the harder one (e.g., worse, stupider) [Sternberg, 1980].

In addition, linear syllogisms differ in whether or not they are able to be solved (Sternberg, 1981). For example, in the linear syllogism

Len is taller than Bob, Bob is taller than Sam. Who is the tallest?

---

[2] For more examples of syllogisms, see chapter 4.

it is possible to determine the relationship between each possible pair of terms. However, not all linear syllogisms are solvable. For example, the linear syllogism

Len is taller than Bob, Len is taller than Sam. Who is the shortest?

is unanswerable, because we do not have enough information to figure out the answer. Even though we can determine that Len is the tallest, we cannot distinguish the relative heights of Bob and Sam, so we cannot say who is shorter.

THE STRUCTURE OF AN ARGUMENT

As you remember, we are using the term "argument" in a slightly different way than that to which you might be accustomed. An argument, as we are using the word, does not mean a fight or even necessarily a disagreement. We define an *argument* as a series of *premises* (reasons) organized in such a way that they provide support for a conclusion. Every argument has at least one premise and one conclusion.

Premises

In an argument, a premise is a claim or statement that provides support for a conclusion. They are the reasons behind the argument. Premises can be difficult to identify, however. One useful trick is to search for so-called *premise markers* – words that indicate the sentence is a premise. Some of these markers are *for, because (since), assuming (seeing, granted, given) that, if, first (second, etc.), whereas, as demonstrated (indicated, shown), this is true because, for the reason that, in view of the fact that, it is a fact that, one cannot doubt that.*

Here are some examples of premises:

- Assuming that Wally truly intends to make up all of his missed work . . .
- . . . because red wine can actually help reduce your risk of cancer.
- It is a fact that Dr. Mitchell assigns more work than Dr. Bromley.
- . . . as shown by your failure to wake up on time for three straight days.
- This is true because red hair simply looks better in sunlight than blonde hair.

Premises are intended to support, prove, or provide evidence for a conclusion. They can be either facts or opinions – consider, for example:

The Red Sox finally won the World Series in 2004, because they had the determination, spirit, and never-say-die attitude that a winner needs (opinion).

versus

The Red Sox finally won the World Series because David Ortiz and Manny Ramirez hit more than forty homers during the regular season and Curt Schilling went 21–6 with three key postseason wins (facts).

Both of these statements are premises.

For a statement to qualify as a premise, it does not actually need to support the conclusion. Indeed, when the premises do not support the conclusion, the argument may simply be poor or unconvincing. For example, Maryann might say, "I've only had six drinks, and I'm still more sober than Sandy; therefore, I'm going to have another beer." Her premises ("I've only had six drinks" and "I'm still more sober than Sandy") don't necessarily lead to the conclusion that she should have another beer. Yet even if her argument is not particularly convincing, it is still technically an argument.

Conclusions

Conclusions are the end results of the argument and are usually easier to recognize than are premises. Like premises, conclusions have markers that help identify them. Some of these *conclusion markers* are *therefore, hence, thus, so, for this reason, this being so, it follows that, the moral is, which proves that, which means that, from which we can infer that, in conclusion, consequently, accordingly, in summary, as a result,* and *then.*

Here are some examples of conclusions:

- . . . therefore, we need to go out to a restaurant to eat.
- As a result, Hector broke his left hand and wasn't allowed back into the grocery store.
- Accordingly, I offered the salsa to Larissa.
- The moral is never to gamble with a man who can juggle with his elbows.
- In summary, we have spent seventeen hours total on the report.

Thus, the task of distinguishing arguments from nonarguments appears to be easy: One simply looks for one or more premises and a conclusion. This distinction is often not easy to make, however, as verbal arguments are usually incomplete. Sometimes premises are not stated openly and must be inferred; other times, conclusions are not stated openly but must be figured out from context. Consider the following examples:

How can the crime rate be decreasing? More guns are sold every day.

Technically, this example is not an argument, because the first sentence is a question. However, the question is merely rhetorical, suggesting the following argument:

Premise: More guns are sold every day.
Conclusion: The crime rate cannot be decreasing.

Premise and conclusion indicators are the main clues that help us identify arguments and figure out their structure. If you can identify a premise and a conclusion, then you have an argument. There are some other components that can be included in arguments.

Statements

A *statement* in an argument is a phrase or sentence that can be identified as either true or false. All statements (in arguments) are sentences, but not all sentences are statements. Note that a sentence can be a statement whether it is *actually* true or false.

What matters is whether the true/false distinction can be applied to the sentence. The following are examples of sentences that are *not* statements:

Commands: "Go to your room."
Questions: "Does Ann like classical music?"
Exclamations: "Oh, boy!"

In addition, some sentences that seem to be true or false are actually not. For example, "I understand" is inherently neither true nor false. It may simultaneously be uttered by the same person as true in one situation and as false in another. If your father asks you to bring back milk from the grocery store, you may truthfully say, "I understand." If your calculus teacher explains a complicated equation, you may lie and say, "I understand." It can go either way. Similarly, the sentence "She is beautiful" is intrinsically neither true nor false because tastes regarding beauty differ from one person to the next. Indeed, one famous episode of the old television show *The Twilight Zone* shows how beauty is in the eye of the beholder. A woman is undergoing a series of operations to correct an apparent facial deformity. At the end of the episode, the bandages are taken off and she is revealed to be beautiful (by most standards). The doctors and nurses, however, have piglike faces with huge snouts – and think that she is very ugly.

To extend a series of nonstatements, consider the following sentences: "Apples are delicious," "I like roses," "Mountains are far," "Stomach bacteria are good for your health," and "The bear is close." All of these sentences are nonstatements (in arguments) because all of them might be true for some speakers but false for the rest, or else they might be true in one situation and false in another.

Other Components of Arguments

Some arguments proceed in stages. In such cases, a conclusion is drawn from a set of premises. Then, that conclusion, possibly in combination with some other statements, is used as a premise to draw a further conclusion – which, in turn, might become a premise for yet another conclusion. Such stage-based arguments are called *complex arguments*. First-order premises (premises that are not conclusions from previous premises) are called *basic premises* or *assumptions*. Second-order premises (premises that are conclusions from previous premises) are called *nonbasic premises* or *intermediate conclusions*.

For example, consider this argument:

Jeremiah studies the class notes and reads the textbook carefully. Therefore, he will earn a high grade on the final exam. Jeremiah also attends class regularly and participates in discussions. He gave an excellent presentation to the class last week. As a result of all of these things, Jeremiah will receive an A in the class.

Assumptions

Assumptions are statements not supported by any proof or evidence. Assumptions can be either explicit (openly communicated) or implicit (concealed and not openly communicated). Most arguments contain unstated, or implicit, assumptions. For example, consider the following statement:

> The party should take place at Burgers-R-Us, the most popular burger restaurant in town.

This statement has both an explicit and implicit assumption. The explicit assumption is that Burgers-R-Us is the most popular restaurant in town. There's no backing evidence (such as, "More than three hundred people eat there every day!"). Yet there is also an unstated assumption – that a popular burger restaurant is a *good* burger restaurant. If the speaker is recommending you have party at *Burgers-R-Us* and only telling you that it is popular, then there is an implicit assumption that being popular is a good thing and an indicator of quality.

Implicit premises or conclusions should be "read into" an argument only if they are crucial to the argument itself. The rule here is that because we are trying to understand the speaker's line of reasoning, no implicit statement should be inferred unless it is obvious that the speaker would accept the statement. The *principle of charity* holds that the speaker should be given the benefit of the doubt. According to this principle, the person listening to the argument should try to minimize misinterpretation (whether deliberate or accidental) while remaining faithful to the speaker's line of reasoning.

Qualifiers

To confine or constrain a particular conclusion, arguments often contain *qualifiers*. Qualifiers are statements that assert the conditions under which a given conclusion is supported. Consider the following example:

> Experts agree that it is important that all people learn how to bake rhubarb pie. Research studies have shown that people who can bake rhubarb pie live longer and are happier people. For this reason, a national cooking program that shows people how to bake rhubarb pie is needed. However, if people are not taught how to grow rhubarb in their gardens, such knowledge will be in vain.

This argument consists of (1) two premises (experts agree that all people should bake rhubarb pie and research has shown rhubarb-pie bakers live longer and are happier), (2) a conclusion (there should be a national cooking program to teach about rhubarb pie), and (3) a qualifier (people must be also taught how to grow rhubarb in their garden).

Counterarguments

Counterarguments are statements that refute a conclusion of an argument. Often arguments are extended to include counterarguments as well. Consider, for example, the argument presented earlier, with a counterargument added:

> Experts agree that it is important that all people learn how to bake rhubarb pie. Research studies have shown that people who can bake rhubarb pie live longer

and are happier people. For this reason, a national cooking program that shows people how to bake rhubarb pie is needed. However, if people are not taught how to grow rhubarb in their own garden, such knowledge will be in vain. Some experts point to other, different skills that influence general happiness, such as learning how to properly teach a dog to play poker.

Notice that the role of a counterargument is often to make the audience of the argument aware of how to refute particular conclusions. Using a counterargument is a tricky move – if not skillfully presented, the counterargument may be turned against the person making it. However, when used properly, counterarguments can greatly strengthen original arguments.

Conditional Arguments

Conditional arguments take the form "if A, then B." For example,

> *If my dog eats cheese, then she will have an upset stomach.*
> *If Mike studies for the exam, then he will get a good grade.*
> *If Juanita watches television, then she will eat some potato chips.*

There are different types of *if ... then* statements used in conditional arguments. For example, consider the following conditional arguments:

(1) *If today is Saturday, then I have to water my plants.*
  Today is Saturday.
  Therefore, I have to water my plants.
(2) *If your French is good, then you can read* Les Miserables *in French.*
  Your French is good.
  Therefore, you can read Les Miserables *in French.*
(3) *If you eat too much food, you gain weight.*
  You gain weight.
  Therefore, you eat too much food.

The three arguments take the same form, known as *modus ponens*. This mode exists in two forms. The first form looks like the following:

> If *A*, then *B*.
> *A*.
> *Therefore, B.*

This form is called *affirming the antecedent*. Problems (1) and (2) take this form.
  The second form looks like the following:

> If *A*, then *B*.
> *B*.
> *Therefore, A.*

This form is called *affirming the consequent*. Problem (3) takes this form. In general, this form of argument is considered invalid. For example, the conclusion of the following argument is obviously invalid:

If you go to Burger King, then you will eat a hamburger.
You are eating a hamburger.
Therefore, you went to Burger King.

Why is this invalid? There are many other places you could have gotten the hamburger – maybe you went McDonald's, or Carl's Jr., or Wendy's, or In-n-Out, or maybe your mom made you a hamburger.

The arguments below illustrate a different form of the *if . . . then* syllogism – the so-called *modus tollens* (denying mode).

(1) *If Rose saw the letter, then she will be angry.*
      Rose is not angry.
      Therefore, she did not see the letter.
(2) *If Professor Hecht wrote the midterm, then the students will be sad.*
      The students are not sad.
      Therefore, Professor Hecht did not write the midterm.
(3) *If Jessica wins the lottery, then she will buy a new car.*
      Jessica did not win the lottery.
      Therefore, she did not buy a new car.

As you can see, this form also appears in two types:

denying the consequent:

If *A*, then *B*.
It is not the case that *B*.
Therefore, it is not the case that *A*.

This form of argument is deductively valid. Thus, if we say that "If it rains, I will use my umbrella" and "I am not using my umbrella," it is valid to conclude that it is not raining. The reason is that, were it raining, I would be using my umbrella.

The second form of *modus tollens* is *denying the antecedent*:

If *A*, then *B*.
It is not the case that *A*.
Therefore, it is not the case that *B*.

This form of argument is *not* deductively valid. Suppose, again, we say, "If it rains, I will use my umbrella." If we also say "It is not raining," can we conclude that I am not using my umbrella? No, we cannot conclude this, because I may use my umbrella for other purposes. For example, I may use it to protect myself from the sun, or as a prop in an elaborate song-and-dance number.

In the examples given here, the first two are in the form of denying the consequent and the third is in the form of denying the antecedent. Thus, the first two syllogisms are valid and the third is not. In the third example, note that even if Jessica did not win the lottery, she may still have saved enough money to buy a car (or her father may have bought her a car as a graduation present).

The Four-Card Problem

People have trouble recognizing how to use *modus ponens* and *modus tollens* together to verify their thinking. To illustrate this point, consider a kind of problem called the

| A | D | 4 | 7 |

Figure 7–1. The Four Card Selection Task

"four-card selection task" (Johnson-Laird & Wason, 1970). In this task, four cards are lying face up on a table in front of you (see Figure 7–1). Each card is labeled with a letter on one side and a number on the other. The participant's task is to decide if the following rule is true:

> If a card has a vowel on one side, then it has an even number on the other side. You should turn over only the minimum number of cards necessary to determine if this rule is true. Which card or cards do you need to turn over to find out whether the rule is true or false?

The correct answer is "A and 7." However, very few people select this answer. Most people respond "A only" or "A and 4." Let us consider all possible answers.

1. If A does not have an even number on the other side, the rule is false (*modus ponens*). Therefore, it is necessary to turn over "A."
2. If 7 has a vowel on the other side, the rule is false (*modus tollens*). Therefore, it is necessary to turn over "7."
3. D is a consonant; therefore, it does not matter whether its other side has an odd or an even number. The rule says nothing about consonants. If you turn over the D, you would be committing the error of affirming the consequent.
4. 4 is an even number, but the rule does not specify whether an even-number card has a consonant or a vowel on the other side. If you turn over 4, you would be committing the error of denying the antecedent.

One reason why the four-card task is difficult is that it does not appear to have any connection to real life. There will be few situations (presumably) where you actually have to prove or disprove an abstract rule about cards with letters and numbers on them. However, consider an alternate form of the problem, proposed by Griggs and Cox (1982) and paraphrased here:

Pretend that you are a police officer and you walk into a bar. You know that the drinking age in your state is twenty-one. So if anyone under twenty-one is drinking alcohol, you need to write a citation for the bar and arrest the underage drinker. You see four people drinking at the bar. As you walk closer, you see that one person is clearly drinking beer. Another person is clearly drinking soda. The third person is holding her driver's license, which says that she is twenty-seven. The fourth person is holding his driver's license, which says that he is eighteen. You need to decide who to approach (to check either their driver's license or their beverage) and who you don't need to approach. Another way of presenting this problem is:

The problem is much easier to solve now![3]

---

[3] The correct answer is to approach the person drinking the beer and the person who is eighteen years old.

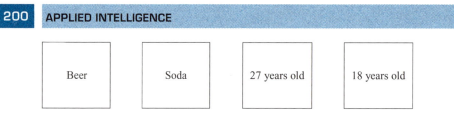

Figure 7–2. The Four Card Selection Task (modified)

ARGUMENT EVALUATION

Both "regular" and conditional arguments differ in their quality. Moreover, different steps of the same argument might even be of different quality. The more complex the argument, the more difficult it can be to evaluate the quality of the argument. Because complex arguments typically include multiple steps, there may be a need to assess all premises separately (reviewing the strength of each of them) and simultaneously (reviewing the links between them). There are different types of relations in an argument between premises and conclusions. Premises can be (a) supportive of conclusions, (b) contradictory to conclusions, and (c) unrelated to conclusions. The type of relation needs to be taken into account in evaluating the argument.

There are a number of techniques that help one to think about and evaluate arguments critically. The most frequently used criteria for evaluating arguments are the

(a)   acceptability and consistency of the premises (i.e., the quality of the evidence);
(b)   probability of the conclusion given the truth of the premises;
(c)   links between premises and conclusions (i.e., the quality of the reasoning itself);
(d)   structure of the argument; and
(e)   strength of counterarguments.

These criteria are dealt with in the following rules of logic: truth of premises, validity, and relevance.

Truth of Premises

No matter how good an argument is, the truth of the conclusion cannot be established if any of the argument's premises is false. The acceptability of premises rests on whether they represent knowledge commonly believed to be true. For example, it is known that penguins live close to the South Pole, whereas polar bears are found at the North Pole. Therefore, the premise *Because polar bears hunt penguins . . .* is not acceptable because it contradicts two pieces of common knowledge.

Another important factor is the variability of the data underlying the premise. Suppose you had three blonde female friends and each of them ended up marrying blonde men. How confident would you be in the generalization "Blonde women tend to marry blonde men?" Even though three out of three instances confirm your conclusion, this is a very small sample. Results vary, and there may be many alternate explanations of your data. You may be amazed by the coincidence and you may see the pathway of inductive reasoning that allows you to arrive at this conclusion. However, the variability of the data suggests that the conclusion is wrong. In fact, if you think for a minute, you yourself may come up with lists of friends, family, and neighbors for whom this conclusion does not hold. By coming up with three instances of blonde women marrying nonblonde men, you can induce that blonde women do not always marry blonde men.

There is no single recipe you can follow to determine how acceptable a premise is. Often when analyzing an argument, the major part of the job is to determine how acceptable/unacceptable the premises are. For example, an analysis of the argument *Because listening to Mozart's music enhances children's cognitive development, every child should listen to Mozart's music on a daily basis* would require a fair amount of research on the part of those of us who are not intimately involved with this research area. How acceptable is the premise that listening to Mozart's music enhances children's cognitive development? To evaluate the acceptability of this argument, one would need to evaluate the research evidence (i.e., how strongly this statement is supported by data), the factual accuracy of the premise (i.e., how accurately the data are reflected in the premise), and the premise's underlying variability (i.e., how variable the data underlying the premises are). One would also need to consider the opinions of experts in the area.

Often it is unknown whether a premise is true or false. When this happens, the argument fails to establish its conclusion *so far as we know*. When we lack sufficient information to judge the quality of the premises, it is useful to suspend judgment until further information is available.

For example, consider the following argument.

All acts of murder are acts of killing.
Therefore, those who kill in self-defense are murderers.

The premise of this argument is acceptable and consistent. It nevertheless fails to establish its conclusion because the premise leaves open the possibility that some kinds of killing are not murder. It is possible that killing done in self-defense is of such a kind. Certainly, the premise does not rule out this possibility. The premise, although true, does not adequately support the conclusion. We need additional criteria beyond truth of premises to evaluate arguments to assess the degree to which a set of premises provides direct evidence for a conclusion.

Validity and Relevance

In inductive reasoning, you should remember, we can never be completely sure of the validity of inductive arguments. We can say, however, that certain things are more or less probable based on a variety of factors, including quality of evidence. If the premises seem unrelated or contradictory to the conclusion, then an argument is likely invalid. Take the following argument, for example:

Ida went to see the newest Johnny Depp movie at the local theater. The seat was very comfortable, and she had not gotten enough sleep the night before.

> She fell asleep during the movie and woke up during the credits. Clearly, she thought, Johnny Depp just isn't a very good actor.

This argument is not valid, because the premises are not supportive of the conclusion. Indeed, they are not relevant to the conclusion at all. The fact that Ida was tired and fell asleep during the movie does not seem to be directly connected to whether Johnny Depp is a good actor. A better conclusion for these premises might be, "Ida realized she should not go to a movie when she is so tired." Sometimes, an argument may be presented in which some premises are relevant and some are not. For example:

> High school and college students around the world have fallen in love with Holden Caulfield, the young hero of J. D. Salinger's *Catcher in the Rye*. Many students identify with his resistance to authority and hatred of being phony. The book was originally published in 1951. J. D. Salinger has not written a novel since then. Clearly, *Catcher in the Rye* is one of the most influential books published this century.

In this paragraph, the first two sentences are relevant to the conclusion, but the sentences about the original publication data and Salinger's subsequent life are not. The year that book was published and Salinger's other works have little obvious relationship to the book's influence.

Sometimes, premises aren't just irrelevant to a conclusion. Some arguments offer premises that seem to specifically contradict the conclusion. When you can identify the premises as contracting the conclusion, you have found an argument that is not valid. Here is an example of premises contradicting a conclusion.

> Buck is a second baseman on the college baseball team. He is always at every game and rooting hard for the team, but he usually does not actually play. When he did play, he struck out three times and made an error. Thus, he should win the Most Valuable Player award.

SUMMING UP

Putting it all together, here is how to analyze an argument:

Step 1: Detect the argument itself. This task, although it may appear simple, is sometimes the most difficult part of the process. Remember: Not every written text or oral discourse contains an argument. Sometimes you need to read many words to detect an argument.

Step 2: When (and if) an argument is identified, the next step is to find and specify its stated and unstated components (premises, conclusions, assumptions, qualifiers, and counterarguments).

Step 3: Evaluate the argument, including:
   (a) the nature of the argument (i.e., whether it is inductive or deductive).

EXERCISE 7.1 PRACTICE IN LOGICAL REASONING

1. Read the arguments below. Come up with counterarguments:

a. Space exploration costs a lot of money. There are many poor people that need money. Thus, space exmplaration should not be allowed.

b. Giving birth causes a lot of pain; therefore childbirth should be prohibited.

c. The chance of winning a lottery is very slim. Thus, nobody should buy lottery tickets.

d. Spending time with friends takes away time from studying in college. Therefore, while studying in college, one should not have friends.

2. Your roommate Jon says: "It is bad for one's health to feel tired all the time. Working on my class assignments makes me tired all the time. Therefore, I should stop working on my class assignments." Think about how you can show that this argument is not true, although the premises might true. Come up with other examples of arguments in which the premises might be true, but the conclusions are not reasonable (e.g., School takes time away form play. Children should spend a lot of time playing. Thus, children not to go to school.)

3. Generate a complex argument. Ask your roommate to comment on the quality of your argument (i.e., to evaluate the premises, the inferential process, and the conclusion).

4. What newspaper do you read regularly? Look at today's issue and find 5 arguments. Analyze these arguments, identifying premises, inferences, and conclusions. How many arguments did you find that are based on faulty premises? How many arguments used faulty inferences? Were there examples of solid arguments?

(b) the quality of the premises (i.e., whether they are acceptable, valid, true, and consistent). If the premises are unacceptable, discard the argument – there is no reason to proceed. If some premises are invalid, dismiss them and evaluate only valid premises. Use your knowledge, and, if required, additional resources in evaluating the truthfulness of each argument. If the argument contains multiple premises, check the premises for consistency; if inconsistency is detected, consider, if justifiable, eliminating inconsistent premises.

(c) the assumptions and qualifiers (both stated and unstated).

(d) the strength of any counterarguments.

Step 4: Complete the evaluation by judging the overall quality of the argument.

To conclude, logical arguments are an essential part of informational and persuasive communication. In this chapter we considered some of the many forms of valid logical arguments, and also some of the forms of invalid ones. It is essential that all students learn which are which.

8

Inference and Inferential Fallacies

If we were to select one performance component as most important of all, we might well select *inference*. Although people reason all the time, not all of these inferences or conclusions are correct or justified by the data. Philosophers and psychologists have attempted to classify and study the various kinds of erroneous inferences (rickety reasoning) that people can make. In classifying types of inferences, they refer to *fallacies*.

In the broader sense, fallacies are mistakes that occur in arguments and that affect the argument's strength. The Latin verb *fallere* signifies deception. Indeed, fallacious reasoning may be deceptive, because it comes across as sensible reasoning. However, in its modern meaning, fallacious reasoning refers to reasoning that is invalid or irrelevant because it accepts the premises without enough grounds to do so, or fails to use the relevant known facts. Fallacy is often hard to detect – it is simply an error in reasoning or falseness in an argument that seems sound.

There is no narrow, precise definition of fallacy. The concept of fallacy is closely linked to the concepts of intuition and counterintuition. Likewise, there is no universally accepted classification of fallacies. Aristotle drew up the first catalogue of fallacies and demonstrated that bad reasoning obeys certain patterns. The classification described here is by no means the only one or even necessarily the best one. This list is based on the work of many philosophers and psychologists.[1] These researchers' main argument in classifying and describing the fallacies is that rigorous study of logic and awareness of common fallacies should result in our intuition being less riddled with fallacious inferences.

FALLACIES OF RELEVANCE

Fallacies of relevance are committed when the premises of an argument have no bearing on its conclusion. The conclusion is irrelevant to the line of reasoning that led

---

[1] They include, for example, Amos Tversky and Daniel Kahneman (1974), Aaron Beck (1976), Irving Copi (1978), Ellen Langer (1989), Thomas Gilovich (1991), Marilyn Vos Savant (1995), Diane Halpern (1996), and Gird Gigerenzer, Peter Todd, and the ABC Research Group (1999).

up to it. Arguments of this type are referred to as *non sequiturs* (from the Latin *non sequitur*, meaning "it does not follow"). Consider an example of this fallacy:

> Joni is retiring from work. Her pension will be small, and her retired husband has little income. She told her husband she wants a convertible for Christmas. Her husband asked her why she thought she should get a convertible for Christmas when they couldn't afford it. Joni replied, "I deserve a convertible because I am about to retire."

Notice that Joni has created a cause-and-effect relationship that exists only in her head. At least from the standpoint of her husband and most others, her retirement in and of itself does not merit a new car, no matter how many other reasons there might be to get her one.

Here is another example of the fallacy of irrelevant conclusion. Can you say why this little scenario exemplifies this fallacy?

> Joseph was the prosecuting attorney in a case in which the defendant had been accused of murdering his mother. When asserting the defendant's guilt, Joseph argued, "Murder is a horrible thing to do. But to murder one's own mother deserves even swifter and harsher punishment."

There are many forms of fallacies of relevance; here we cover only a few of them.

AD HOMINEM ARGUMENTS

Inferences of the type *ad hominem* (meaning "against the person" in Latin) attempt to discredit a claim by attacking its proponents instead of providing a reasoned examination of the claim itself. There are five different types of *ad hominem arguments*.

Ad hominem abusive arguments attack a person's individual characteristics – age, character, family, gender, ethnicity, appearance, socioeconomic status, professional, or religious or political beliefs. In other words, arguments of this type imply that there is no reason to take a person seriously – the argument is against the person rather than against the person's position on an issue. Here is an example of an *argumentum ad hominem*.

> Mr. George picked up a new book on the history of the United States. He read in the "About the Author" portion of the flap that the author of the book was twenty-four years old. Mr. George put the book down, commenting, "No one who is twenty-four years old can write knowledgeably about their country's history."

Mr. George concludes that the author's age precludes her from writing a decent history. In fact, the book might be quite good. Mr. George has no way of knowing without reading it, or reviews of it, but instead chooses to focus on a characteristic of the author in making his judgment about the book.

Here is another example of an *argumentum ad hominem*. Can you see why it is an instance of this kind of fallacy?

Two women were testifying in a court case. One woman, who was a hairdresser, claimed she saw the defendant leaving the scene of the crime. The other woman, who was a prostitute, claimed that the defendant was with her during the time the crime occurred. One of the jurors thought, "I'll take the word of a hairdresser over the word of a prostitute any day."

Guilt by association arguments (also known as *poisoning the well* arguments) attempt to cast off a claim by attacking not the person claiming something, but the people who he or she spends time with on a regular basis. Another type of guilt by association argument is to challenge or doubt the reputation of those with whom the claimer shares opinions or beliefs. Here is an example of such an argument.

Mary advocates developing a huge condominium complex along the lakeshore. Mary has been seen more than once with known Mafia authorities and drug dealers. Mary is not trustworthy, and the development of the condominium complex should not approved.

In this argument, the premises are irrelevant to the conclusion; even if Mary hangs around with possible criminals, what she advocates may be a good thing for the town to do. The central deficit (fallacy) of the logic argument here is not whether Mary is the victim of a smear campaign or has bad taste in friends, but rather the failure to produce any premises ensuring the conclusion.

Tu quoque ("you too") arguments are constructed to refute a claim by attacking the claimer on the grounds that he or she has shown questionable conduct. The argument in this case attempts to show that behavior of the person making the claim is hypocritical or demonstrates a double standard. Consider the following example:

Tom believes that the community members should promote religious values. Tom does not go to church, does not read religious books, and does not celebrate religious holidays. Therefore, community members should not promote religious values.

Tom's actions have no bearing on the truth or falseness of his belief (even though he appears to be holding this belief hypocritically). Thus, this argument exemplifies a *tu quoque* fallacy.

Vested interest arguments attempt to dispute a claim by stating that its proponents are motivated by the desire to take advantage of a situation.

Mary advocates developing a huge condominium complex along the lakeshore. She does so because she is planning to use the condominium as a tax shelter to make a lot of money. We should not approve the development of the condominium complex.

In this argument, once again, the premises are not relevant to the conclusion. Developing a condominium complex may be justified independently of Mary's allegedly selfish intentions. Whether Mary is going to gain or lose personally by promoting the complex is immaterial. What counts here are the advantages and dis-advantages for the community of building the complex.

Circumstantial ad hominem fallacies attempt to refute a claim by arguing that its supporters endorse two or more conflicting propositions. The assumed implication is that we may therefore safely disregard one or all of those propositions.

> Emma claims that she could never be friends with someone who wasn't a vege-tarian. Emma also says that her boyfriend, who regularly eats beef and chicken, is her best friend. Therefore, it isn't important to worry about vegetarian concerns.

Note – the premises (whether consistent or not!) do not relate to the truth of the conclusion.

STRAW MAN ARGUMENTS

Straw man arguments attempt to refute a claim by replacing it with a less believable statement (the straw man) and then attacking the weaker claim rather than dealing with the original claim. An interesting aspect of this argument is that it may contain good reasons against the weaker claim, but these reasons will be irrelevant to the original claim.

> Jack firmly believed that 20 percent of the college's budget should go toward reinforcing every wall in every building on campus to make sure that the cam-pus would be completely safe during any type of natural disaster. When other students argued that there wouldn't be enough money left for other expenses, Jack said, "Obviously, you just don't care if the entire campus collapses and is completely destroyed."

The argument is a straw man because Jack is opposing a position that his oppo-sition does not really take. Other students don't believe that the campus's buildings should be unstable; they simply question the amount of money Jack wants to dedicate to this purpose. Jack has created a straw man, and knocked it down.

REPRESENTATIVENESS

The *representativeness* heuristic is used in making a judgment regarding the proba-bility of an uncertain event according to (a) how obviously the event is similar to or representative of the population from which it is obtained, and (b) the degree to which the event reflects the noticeable features of the process by which it is generated (such as randomness).

Consider some examples:

> All the families having exactly six children in a particular city were surveyed. In seventy-two of the families, the exact order of births of boys (B) and girls (G) was G B G B B G. What is your estimate of the number of families surveyed in which the exact order of births was B G B B B B?

Most people judging the number of families with the B G B B B B birth pattern estimate the number to be less than seventy-two. Actually, the best estimate of the number of families with this birth order is seventy-two, the same as for the G B G B B G birth order. The expected number for the second pattern would be the same because the gender for each birth is independent (at least, theoretically) of the gender for every other birth, and for any one birth, the chances of a boy (or a girl) are one out of two. Thus, any particular pattern of births is equally likely, even B B B B B B or G G G G G G.

Why do people believe some birth orders to be more likely than others? Tversky and Kahneman (1971) suggested that it is because they are using the representativeness heuristic. For example, people believe that the first birth order is more likely because, first, it is more representative of the number of females and males in the population, and, second, it looks more random than does the second birth order. In fact, of course, either birth order is equally likely to occur by chance.

Similarly, if asked to judge the probability of flips of a coin yielding the sequence – H T H H T H – people will judge it as higher than they will if asked to judge the sequence – H H H H T H. Thus, if you expect a sequence to be random, you tend to view a sequence that "looks random" as more likely to occur. Indeed, people often comment that the ordering of numbers in a table of random numbers "doesn't look random," because people underestimate the number of runs of the same number that will appear wholly by chance. Another example is the lottery – if you are given the choice between picking the number sequence 12–43–7–22–35 and the number sequence 1–2–3–4–5, which set would you be more likely to pick? Most people would pick the first set of numbers. Maybe you would, too, if you hadn't just read this section. But, of course, in a fair lottery, there *is no* cause-and-effect relationship between the particular numbers picked and the odds of winning.

Consider another example:

> Robert had a date set up with an actress. After he watched a play in which she had the lead role, they were planning to go to dinner. However, he sent a note to the actress after the play, saying, "You were so believable in your acting of that murder scene that I don't feel safe going out with you."

In this particular instance, Robert assumes that the actress's behavior in the play was representative of her behavior outside of it. But he has no logical basis for assuming that the actress's behavior in the play will represent her behavior outside the acting situation.

Can you say why the following scenario demonstrates this fallacy?

> Senator Charles was announcing the winners of the Golden Fleece Award for the biggest rip-off of taxpayers in 1981. Senator Charles said, "I bestow the Golden Fleece Award on Professor Dudley for his government-funded study of the nature of romantic love. As you may remember, we recently reviewed a study of the nature of romantic love, and it was absolutely worthless. Clearly, this study will be, too."

AD BACULUM ARGUMENT (APPEALS TO FORCE)

An *ad baculum* argument attempts to establish a conclusion by threat or intimidation. This type of reasoning error does not require much information and can be easily spotted in the following statement.

> The theory of relativity is correct, my dear, and if you don't think so, I'm going to break your kneecaps.

Once again, the premise is irrelevant to the justification of the conclusion. Threats and intimidation may be persuasive in many cases, but this type of persuasion does not have anything to do with any scheme of rational appraisal. Note that the reaction of "my dear" does not make any difference to the nature of the reasoning – even if "my dear" capitulates, the reasoning is still logically unacceptable.

AD VERENCUNDIAM ARGUMENT (APPEAL TO AUTHORITY)

Ad verecundariam arguments occur when we accept (or reject) a claim merely because of the prestige, status, or respect we have for its proponents (or opponents). The pattern of the fallacy of appeal to authority is to argue that a claim is true because an authority figure supports it. Authority figures can include, for example, doctors, judges, police officers, or professors. An argument that appeals to authority is a fallacy whenever that authority is not suitable to give evidence. Note that the fallacy is not in appealing to authority, but in appealing to authority that is not credible for a particular argument. Consider an example of this fallacy.

> Congress is presently trying to decide whether it has a right to take a legal stand on when a human life begins. During congressional debates on the matter, one representative was heard to say, "If the medical world, the religions, and all the philosophies cannot agree on when a human life begins, then it is the responsibility of the Congress to make that decision."

In this example, Congress is clearly in no better a position, and may well be in a worse position, to make the decision regarding when human life begins than doctors, clergy, or philosophers. Common examples of this fallacy occur in commercials (or public service announcements) when actors present their opinions on nonacting topics as though they are experts. Brad Pitt or Julia Roberts doesn't necessarily know any more about the environment or health care than any random person. But we may view them as authorities because of their fame. This fallacy is particularly common when an actor is famous for a role as an authority figure, such as if an actor from *Law & Order* did a commercial for a home security system or for a divorce lawyer.

Can you spot the appeal to authority in this example?

> Marvin was being interviewed by the admissions board of the law school he wished to attend the next year. One of the board members asked Marvin why he thought he would make a good lawyer. Marvin replied, "Well, my father is a

plumber, but he always wanted to be a lawyer. He's always told me I'd make a good lawyer, and I respect his opinion in this matter."

ARGUMENTUM AD POPULUM (APPEAL TO POPULARITY)

Ad populum arguments occur when we infer a conclusion merely on the grounds that most people accept it. The reasoning behind *argumentum ad populum* is, "If everyone else thinks this way, it must be right." The essence of this fallacy lies in our need to conform to popular views and conclusions. Consider an example of an *argumentum ad populum*:

> A state assemblyman, when asked why he went along with the new governor's social policies, replied, "The governor was elected by a large majority of the popular vote. Thus, it seems to me that the governor must know what she's doing."

A majority vote in no way guarantees that elected officials know what they are doing. Here is another example of an *argumentum ad populum*. Can you see why?

> Jackie's dad asked her why she wanted a computer for Christmas. She replied, "I want a computer because all my friends are getting them, and they sure know what they are doing."

ARGUMENTUM AD MISERICORDIUM (APPEAL TO PITY)

In this form of fallacy, an appeal to pity is invoked. This type of argument asks us to excuse an action on the grounds of unusual circumstances; it seeks forgiveness for mistakes or sympathy for someone who has behaved badly or broken a rule. Here is an example of the fallacy of appeal to pity:

> Cindy flunked her final exam in History, but she argued that she should be allowed to make up the test, as she was tired because she had to go to her uncle's birthday party.

"SHOULD" STATEMENT (APPEAL TO DUTY)

"I must do this," "I should feel that," and "They should do this" are examples of "should" statements. Such statements are irrational when they are used as the sole reason for behavior. Consider an example of the irrational use of a "should" statement:

> Cecil sat his teenage son down for a talk. Cecil told his son, "Everyone in our family is a success. You must be a success and carry on the family tradition."

This illustration provides a typical example of the use of "should" statements, and also demonstrates how children often have unrealistic expectations for themselves simply because of their parents' unrealistic expectations.

Here is another example of the commission of this fallacy. Can you spot it?

Part of Gordon's duties as the manager of a small apartment building was to shovel the snow from the front walk. One morning Gordon woke up with a fever and a horrible cold. He looked out the window and saw that five inches of snow had fallen the night before. Gordon thought, "With this cold it would be crazy for me to go out and shovel snow but it has to be done, so here I go."

ARGUMENT FROM IGNORANCE (APPEAL TO IGNORANCE)

This fallacy is committed whenever it is argued that something is true simply because it has not been proven false, or that it is false simply because it has not been proven true. Moreover, the fallacy of appeal to ignorance can be spotted when the same argument is used to support two different conclusions (for example, we cannot prove that ghosts do not exist nor can we prove that they do exist; therefore, this "lack of knowledge" can be used in the arguments of both believers and disbelievers in ghosts). Here is an example of an argument from ignorance:

The last paragraph of the experimental report stated that, despite elaborate experimental design and statistical procedures, Bexit's model had not been proven. Sally thought, "I really thought this model was the correct one, but it has failed to be proven in this study, so I guess it is not correct."

Sally jumped to the conclusion that because the model had not been found to be correct in this one case, it must be false. In science, however, as well as in other aspects of life, one failure to prove something to be true does not provide conclusive evidence that it is false.

Here is another example of an argument from ignorance. Can you spot it?

On Halloween night, Nate told his roommate, Sam, that he believed in goblins. Sam answered, "You must be kidding." Nate replied, "Well, no one can prove to me that goblins don't exist, so I believe in them."

PERSONALIZATION

If you see yourself as the cause of an event for which you were not primarily responsible, you have committed the fallacy of distorted personalization. Taking personally a statement that is not directed toward you is also an inappropriate personalization. Consider this example of a personalization:

Bernard's mother was recently committed to a psychiatric institution. Unfortunately, her family had a long history of mental illness. Bernard told his father, "Well, I am sure that I put Mom in there. What's worse, I'm sure that she knows that I am to blame."

In this example, Bernard personalizes the cause of an event for which, most likely, he was not responsible.

Here is another example of a personalization. Can you say why this particular fallacy applies in this instance?

> Janet's first-grade son came home one day with a note from his teacher that said that he was doing poorly in school. Janet said to herself, "I am a terrible mother because my son is doing so badly at school."

MAGNIFICATION OR MINIMIZATION

People sometimes magnify or minimize certain aspects of themselves. Sometimes, people can magnify their mistakes and minimize their accomplishments, which can lead to poor self-esteem. Other people overestimate themselves and minimize mistakes and maximize accomplishments. In either case, they are not using proper logic to evaluate them. Here is an example of this fallacy.

> Small College could not afford to hire another professor to teach twentieth-century literature, so they asked Professor Short, whose expertise was in eighteenth-century literature, to teach twentieth-century literature. Professor Short said, "Well, given that I'm one of the world's greatest experts on eighteenth-century literature, I have no doubt that I could teach the twentieth-century literature course just as well as I could teach the eighteenth-century literature course, which is perfectly."

In this instance, Professor Short may or may not be exaggerating his expertise in eighteenth-century literature, but he is almost certainly exaggerating his ability to teach the twentieth-century literature course.

Here is another example of a person committing the magnification/minimization fallacy. Can you see why?

> Marion was congratulating Donna on her recent prize for the best senior project in her class. Donna responded sincerely, "Oh, winning a prize means absolutely nothing. It has no value to me or to anyone else."

MENTAL FILTER

A person using a mental filter picks out one small aspect of a situation, often a negative aspect, and focuses on that one small aspect so that the bigger picture is distorted. It is as though all incoming events are perceived through a filter created by that small aspect of the situation. Consider an example of the use of a mental filter:

> Peg wanted to lose twenty pounds by Christmas vacation. The day before she was to leave for that vacation, she weighed herself and found that she was five pounds short of her twenty-pound goal. Peg told her roommate, "I am really mad at myself for losing only fifteen pounds, and not the full twenty pounds that I wanted to lose!"

In this example, Peg's obsession with losing the full twenty pounds prevents her from appreciating the fifteen pounds that she has lost. One risk that Peg faces in this case is that by losing sight of the big picture – losing weight – she may get discouraged and go back to poor eating habits.

Here is another example of the use of a mental filter. Can you spot it?

Walt asked Harriet why she refused to subscribe to the local newspaper, as it was the only source of local news and she had expressed to him such a great interest in local news. Harriet replied, "I hate newspapers that have comics sections, and even though I would like to learn about the local news, I refuse to read the newspaper because it has one."

IGNORATIO ELENCHI (MISSING THE POINT)

This fallacy occurs when the premises of an argument warrant a different conclusion from the one the arguer draws. Consider the following argument:

Inflation is a marker of economic problems. Last year inflation was running at the rate of 25 percent. This year the inflation rate is only 20 percent. The economy has recovered from its problems.

Given the premises, what follows is that the *rate* of inflation is decreasing. In other words, inflation still takes place, but it has slowed down. This dynamic, however, does not imply that the economy has recovered. It's actually the opposite – inflation still takes place and it is relatively high, suggesting that there are economic problems.

KNOWING THE UNKNOWABLE (ARGUMENTUM AD IGNORANTIUM – PREMISE NOT KNOWN TO BE UNTRUE)

In this type of fallacious reasoning, the reference is made to information that is impossible to know. For example, in their arguments people sometimes make references to magic (black or white). Is it possible to know whether magic exists? One of the most dramatic examples of *argumentum ad ignorantium* was the reasoning behind the witch trials in Salem, Massachusetts. If we do not know whether witchcraft exists, how can we prove that someone practices it?

THE FALLACY OF LABELING (NAME CALLING)

To label yourself or others is a distorted thought process when the label is unjustified by the circumstances, or when the label is inappropriately used as a reason for behavior or lack of behavior. Consider an example of unjustified labeling:

Harriet was on a twelve-hundred-calorie-per-day diet that allowed no sweets. One day, she succumbed to temptation and ate an entire quart of ice cream. Harriet thought, "How disgusting of me to eat a quart of ice cream. I am a pig."

Harriet has committed the fallacy of labeling because she has overreacted to her own weakness in succumbing to temptation. In fact, it is quite typical for people on low-calorie diets to succumb occasionally. By labeling herself a pig as a result of such failure to resist temptation, the chances are increased that she will not continue with the diet because of her low self-image.

Here is another example of someone committing the fallacy of labeling. Can you say why this fallacy applies in this instance?

Henry was a farmer's son from an obscure town in the Midwest. At college, Henry fell in love with the richest, most popular, most beautiful girl on campus. Henry often said to himself, "If only I weren't a hick farmer, then I'd have a chance with that beautiful, sophisticated girl."

EMOTIONAL REASONING

If we use our emotions or feelings as tangible evidence of a truth, then we are using emotional reasoning. "This is true because I feel it is true," is the motto of emotional reasoning. Here is an example:

Alice had a paper due in two days that she had not yet completed. She considered working on the paper Tuesday evening after dinner, but instead she picked up the newspaper and lay down on the couch, thinking, "I'm not really in the mood to work tonight, so I wouldn't get anything done anyway."

In this instance, Alice did not feel like working, so she jumped to the conclusion that she would get nothing done. She did not *try* to get something done. As a result, so she had no way of knowing whether once she started working, she might not find that she could, in fact, make progress on the paper.

Here is another example of the use of emotional reasoning. Can you see why?

Jeremy went to his girlfriend's house one evening only to find her very angry at him. He didn't know why. He asked her what he had done to make her angry, and she replied, "I don't remember what you did. But I know I'm mad, so you must have done something."

CIRCULAR REASONING

This type of fallacy is known as *petitio principii, begging the question*, or *circular reasoning*. The fallacy occurs when an argument assumes its own conclusion (i.e., when the conclusion appears as an assumption, albeit in different form). Unlike fallacies of relevance, this type of argument does not lack relevance, because there is nothing more relevant to the conclusion than the conclusion itself. Consider the following example of circular reasoning:

Murder is awful because it is just plain terrible.

The premise is *Murder is just plain terrible*, and the conclusion is *Murder is awful*. Would you not agree that these two sentences say essentially the same thing? In other words, the argument begs the question (that is where the name of this fallacy originated).

Now consider the following example:

> The death penalty is justified. Among normal human beings, there are always those abnormal ones who disrupt the public harmony and commit horrible crimes against other people. Therefore, it is to the advantage of normal people to get rid of the abnormal ones by putting them to death.

This passage argues for the conclusion that the death penalty is justified by assuming that it is okay to put "abnormal humans" to death. You should be able to see that these two statements say the same thing. The difference is that the conclusion is psychologically strengthened by the power of the other statement (the second premise – *Among normal human beings, there are always those abnormal ones who disrupt the harmony and commit horrible crimes against other people*).

Now consider the following argument:

> Miracles can't occur because they would defy the laws of nature.

Can you see the argument's circularity or endless loop?

A special case of circular argument is *circulus in probando* (vicious circle). In this kind of argument, one assumes what one wishes to prove. These are illustrations of *circulus in probando*.

> The story of the divine creation as told in the Book of Genesis must be true because God would not deceive us.
> The theory of relativity must be correct because we know it must be true.

In both of these cases, one is arguing circularly. One says that a certain book must be true, essentially because it must be true. The other says that a certain concept must be correct because it must be correct.

Question-begging epithets are phrases that bias (or prejudice) the argument. Examples of such phrases are: *white trash, bloody communists, godless socialists, rednecks*, and so on. The question-begging epithets are characteristic of *ad hominem* abusive attacks. If Chuck says, "Only a redneck would wear shoes without socks," and Mark is afraid of being seen as a redneck, then Mark will be sure to always wear socks with shoes. The opposite of *question-begging epithets* might be called *question-begging tributes*. In these circumstances, a very positive phrase (or a "tribute") is used. The assumption is that if you are on the side of the people using this phrase, then you qualify as that phrase, also. Because it is a positive phrase and a good thing to be, you are more likely to accept the argument. For example, in the movie *Moulin Rouge*, the main character, Christian, is asked if he is a bohemian. He doesn't know. Well, says one of his friends, are you for Beauty? For Truth? For Freedom? For Love?" Well, Christian must think to himself, I'm not going admit that I'm *against* any of these things. Therefore, Christian decides, he is a bohemian.

THE FALLACY OF EQUIVOCATION (FALLACY OF AMBIGUITY)

This fallacy occurs when the same words are used with different meanings. For example,

> People often visit psychotherapists when they are down. Down is often stuffed into jackets. Thus, people often go to psychotherapists when they are stuffed into jackets.

The key word here is *down*. The first two sentences are both individually correct. The problem arises when the third sentence is derived from the other two. The meaning of the term *down* has been switched so that the conclusion does not follow from the premises. Here is another example of the equivocation fallacy. Can you see why?

> Lisa's program has a bug in it – it keeps self-terminating in the middle of the run. Many bugs reside in flowers. Lisa's program resides in flowers.

One popular example of ambiguity is seen in roadside food markets and gas stations: big signs proclaiming, "Eat here and get gas." Many newspaper headlines can be confusing (or funny) because of semantic ambiguity. Ponder, for example, "Two sisters reunited after eighteen years in checkout line," "Enraged cow injures farmer with axe," or "Drunk gets nine months in violin case" (Lederer, 1989).

Such ambiguities can lead to fallacies when an expression's meaning shifts during the course of an argument. This can result in a misleading appearance of validity. The best way to deal with the fallacy of ambiguity is to rely on the context in interpreting the meaning of ambiguous words. However, despite some contextual clues, ambiguity can be quite troublesome.

THE FALLACY OF AMPHIBOLY

This fallacy is common to situations when one or more sentences (rather than a single word!) used are of ambiguous structure. For example, the sentence "*We are having my parents for dinner,*" even though of correct grammatical structure, might be "formally" misunderstood. An alien who does not know the customs of the Earth might be totally misled by this sentence and perceive the person delivering the sentence to be a cannibal.

Can you detect the fallacy of amphiboly in the following sentences?

> We went into the cave, saw dinosaurs' eggs, and took a few pictures. However, they were not developed.

The problem is amphibolous in that the phrase "were not developed" might be relevant to both the pictures and the eggs.

Here are two historical examples of amphiboly. The Russian Czarina Maria Fyodorovna saved a man's life (according to legend) because of a comma! Her husband, the czar, wrote out a death warrant: "Pardon impossible, to be sent to Siberia." His wife, however, misplaced the comma, so that the warrant read: "Pardon, impossible to be sent to Siberia." And the man was let go! Never argue with an English teacher who talks of the value of commas (Wallace, Wallechinsky, & Wallace, 1983). Another example – one that is also even more unlikely to have actually happened – is that J. Edgar Hoover, former director of the FBI, dictated a letter to his secretary to type up. When he looked at the final version, he didn't like her spacing and formatting – he was very keen on having exact margins. So he wrote on the top of the letter, "Watch the borders," and asked her to retype it. According to legend, border patrol guards near Mexico and Canada were on high alert for months (Brunvand, 1993).

THE FALLACY OF VAGUENESS

This fallacy refers to a situation in which the meaning is not clear (rather than to a situation in which meanings are multiple). Consider the following example.

> Hogwarts graduates prefer dandelion wine.
> Larry Lunky is a graduate.
> Therefore Larry prefers dandelion wine.

One cannot judge the validity of this argument because it is vague. Larry Lunky is a graduate, but is he a graduate of Hogwarts? It is not clear. Also, can we be sure that the Larry referred to in the last line is Larry Lunky, or might it be some other Larry? Without being sure of exactly what is being said, we cannot be certain that the argument is valid.

The fallacy of accent occurs when emphases are introduced into a statement in such a way that they produce multiple (and often misleading) interpretations. There are many examples of this fallacy – just open a newspaper or a magazine. Consider the following example:

> It has become clear during the trial that the policeman has been nursing a grudge against Barry Bennington. He and Bennington have had numerous fallings out. Little wonder that, given the chance, the policeman would take his opportunity for revenge. It is about time, therefore, that this officer has been brought to trial. A verdict in the case is imminent.

The reporter has chosen to accent the negative – to portray the policeman as guilty. It is not until the end we realize that there is still no verdict in the trial. But, through accenting, we are led to believe that the verdict will be against the policeman.

GARDEN PATH

A garden-path fallacy is one in which one is led down a road to believe one thing, only to learn later that one has been led astray. Consider an example:

> MARTIANS LAND!
> Conquer entire population.
> See them tonight on "Science Fiction Drama"

The first line of the headline might lead the reader to believe that Martians have landed. The second line seems to confirm this conclusion. The third line makes us realize we have been led down a garden path: No Martians have landed at all.

HASTY GENERALIZATION

We commit the fallacy of hasty generalization by considering only exceptional cases and quickly generalizing from those cases to a rule that actually fits only those exceptions. In other words, this fallacy occurs when an inference about an entire class of things (events) is made from insufficient knowledge of some of its members. Here is an example of hasty generalization:

> After she finished college, Cleo went for her first job interview. The interviewer told her that her academic work looked quite good, but that her résumé showed a lack of experience in the professional field, and that therefore his company couldn't hire her. Cleo went home thinking, "If that company won't hire me without experience, no company will."

In this instance, Cleo is rushing to the conclusion that just because one company didn't hire her, no other company will hire her either. In fact, such generalizations are typical of individuals who are on the job market and have an unsuccessful initial interview. Often, their hasty generalizations lead these people to become discouraged too early and to stop looking for a job prematurely.

Here is an example of another hasty generalization. What is the fallacy, and why is it a hasty generalization?

> Bill and a friend were discussing the governor of their state. Bill said, "The governor is a total failure because his economic programs have done serious damage to the state's economy."

Hasty statistical conclusions are most often the results of generalizing on the basis of biased, unrepresentative, inadequate sampling techniques or insufficient observations. This type of fallacy can commonly occur in the social sciences.

FALSE CAUSE

People often seek a cause for an event. If they rely heavy on coincidence or chance to identify the cause, then the fallacy of false cause has been committed. Consider an example of the fallacy of false cause in action:

> Jenny and Mark went into a restaurant at about 6 P.M., dressed rather casually. Although the restaurant was only about half full, the hostess seated Jenny and Mark in an obscure corner table near the kitchen. Jenny said to Mark, "She certainly doesn't want us seen in this restaurant, the way we're dressed. That's why she sat us in the corner."

In this instance, Jenny is assuming that it is her and Mark's clothing that has led to their being seated in an obscure corner. It is possible, of course, that Jenny is correct. However, there are other possible reasons why they might have been placed in an out-of-the-way corner. For example, all of the other tables may have been reserved, or the hostess simply did not give much thought to where she would seat them.

Here is another example of this fallacy. Can you see why this fallacy applies in this instance?

> Buck worked in a large office. He had applied for a promotion, but a woman was promoted instead of him. Buck said to himself, "It's obvious that the woman was promoted instead of me just because she is a woman."

False cause fallacies are linked to a number of logical mistakes, the two main types of which are confusing the cause and effect (see earlier examples) and not considering alternative causes. Another important instance of this fallacy is referred to as *post hoc*. In this fallacy, the causal relationship is inferred merely from two or more events happening close together in time. Consider the following example:

> Deirdre was hit by a car. I saw a suspicious green Chevy race pass by shortly after she was hit. The green Chevy must have hit Deirdre.

FAULTY ANALOGY

This inductive fallacy is associated with analogical reasoning. In a typical analogy, the assertion is made that x is similar to y, and that y is similar to z. The inference is, then, that x is similar to z. The faulty analogy occurs when the similarity is slight or not relevant. Consider the following example of a faulty analogy:

> At different points of time, all former colonies justly fought for their independence.
> Today the Alliance of Hot Dog Makers is fighting for its independence.
> The Alliance's cause is also just and worthy.

This analogy is extremely weak at best. Whereas the former colonies all over the world fought for their religious, financial, educational, and political freedom, the (imagined) Hot Dog Makers are fighting for the ability to sell processed meat.

THE FALLACY OF SUPPRESSED EVIDENCE

This type of fallacy can be observed when reasoning does not meet the requirement of total evidence. In other words, this fallacy occurs by ignoring evidence that would argue against the inferred conclusion. As an example, consider the following argument.

> In the Russian presidential elections in 2004, 60+ percent of the electorate voted.
> Maria is a twenty-two-year-old Russian woman.

> The probability that Maria participated in the Russian presidential elections of the year 2004 is 60+ percent.

As presented here, this conclusion has a fairly strong inductive probability. If, however, it is a known fact that the turnout of Russian young people in the 2004 presidential election was dramatically lower than that of the total electorate (only about one-third of Russians younger than twenty-five voted), then the evaluation of this argument will change substantially. In that case, it would be a bad argument and would commit the fallacy of suppressed evidence.

Now evaluate the following argument. Is any evidence suppressed?

> The man was run over by a car.
> Sandra does not have a driver's license.
> Sandra could not have run over the man.

The piece of evidence we really need to have here is whether Sandra was driving, not whether she has a driver's license. Many people drive even if they do not have a driver's license.

THE GAMBLER'S FALLACY

The gambler's fallacy is demonstrated by the following examples:

> I have not won the lottery recently.
> It is likely to happen soon.

And

> My computer has just been infected with viruses. I just needed to reformat my drive.
> Another virus attack is unlikely to happen again soon.

This type of reasoning is fallacious if the events discussed in the statements are more or less independent (e.g., winning a lottery on a given occasion is an independent event from any previous or any subsequent outcomes of lottery participation). The fallacy was named after the inclination of gamblers, who have had a run of bad luck, to think that the wheel of fortune will turn soon.

The most common example of gambler's fallacy is in gambling, of course. People who have had a losing streak in a chance game sometimes believe that their luck is due to change, even though each successive event is independent of previous events so that their luck is no more likely to change than to stay the same. A reverse example is in basketball. Many basketball players believe in the "hot hand" phenomenon – that after a "hot" player has a series of good shots, his or her chances at continuing to play improve. In fact, many studies (e.g., Koehler & Conley, 2003), have shown that hot playing in the immediate past has no relationship whatsoever on how well someone will perform in the future. Obviously, past behavior predicts future behavior – someone who is generally a better player will typically play better. But a quick run of good shots is more likely luck or circumstance.

SKILL, NOT CHANCE

In situations in which an outcome is controlled entirely and always by chance, it is fallacious to assume that any skill on the part of an agent is involved in the outcome. Many of us have committed this fallacy, trying to stress our participation in events that, in reality, had nothing to do with us. Consider an example of this fallacy:

> Joey had been practicing flipping coins for several days. His mother finally asked him why he was practicing. Joey explained, "I want to get into the Guinness Book of World Records as the person who can make a coin flip come up heads every time."

Of course, Joey's practicing will have no influence on how often a (fair) coin comes up heads. Here is another example of this fallacy. Can you spot the problem?

> Nancy put quarters into a slot machine until she had lost her ten-dollar roll. She was considering whether or not to buy more quarters from the casino office. She thought to herself, "I am sure that if I can get enough practice with this darn machine I'll eventually be able to start getting some more money out of it."

THE FALLACY OF COMPOSITION

The fallacy of compositions occurs when characteristics of one part of a thing are wrongly assumed to be true of the whole. In other words, we commit the fallacy of composition when we reason that what is true of parts of a whole is necessarily true of the whole itself. Consider the following example:

> When forming his panel of advisers, the newly elected governor chose the best person for each advisory position. The governor bragged to the press, "I'll have the most effective, efficient advisory panel any governor could have, because I have the best people on my panel."

In this instance, the governor is assuming that if everyone on his committee is maximally effective and efficient, this effectiveness and efficiency will carry over to the panel as a whole. However, even if each adviser works well individually, there is no guarantee that the individuals will work well collectively. They may, in fact, spend all their time arguing. One often sees the fallacy of composition when people are thinking about sports teams. They act as though the team will be as good as the sum of the individuals on the team, even though some sports teams work so poorly together that the individual talents largely go to waste. Indeed, the baseball team that wins the World Series is rarely the team that has the most future Hall-of-Famers.

Here is another example of the fallacy of composition. Can you spot the fallacy?

Jill went to Warren's apartment for a cocktail before they were to go out to dinner. Warren asked Jill if she would like beer or wine. Jill said, "Well, I like beer and wine equally well and really can't decide between them now, so why don't you put both beer and wine into my glass?"

THE FALLACY OF DIVISION

This fallacy is the opposite of the fallacy of composition. In composition, we invalidly attribute characteristics of the parts to the whole. In division, we invalidly attribute characteristics of the whole to the parts.

Mr. and Mrs. Smith were discussing their daughter's latest boyfriend. Mrs. Smith told Mr. Smith that this young man was a Republican who was presently working for the Republican caucus in the Congress. Mr. Smith commented, "Well, if he's a dedicated Republican that means he isn't a liberal, at least."

Mr. Smith is assuming that, because most or all of the Republicans he knows are not liberals, his daughter's boyfriend also will not be a liberal. However, the fact of the boyfriend's being a dedicated Republican in no way guarantees that he is not a liberal. On the contrary, a number of Republicans are, in fact, liberals. Another example might be assuming that a student majoring in business is particularly concerned with making money. Certainly, many students who major in business are concerned about making money, but there are many people who have much different reasons behind choosing a business major.

Here is another example of the fallacy of division. Can you say why this particular fallacy applies in this case?

The Arizona Angels are the best Little League team around. Jack Morton is one of the Arizona Angels. He must be one of the best Little League players in the state.

THE FALLACY OF THE UNDISTRIBUTED MIDDLE

This fallacy is a deductive-reasoning error. The reasoning takes the following form:

All A are B.
All C are B.
All A are C.

This argument is invalid because it rests on the belief that two terms are either a subset of or coincident with a third term (*All A are B and All C are B*) also must be a subset of or coincident with each other (*All A are C*). Consider an example:

All scientists are smart.
All accountants are smart.
All scientists are accountants.

Now consider another example. Can you recognize this form of argument in the statements below?

All little boys are children.
All little girls are children.
All little boys are little girls.

INVALID DISJUNCTION

The fallacy of *invalid disjunction* occurs in situations in which only two possible solutions are considered, even if there are many others that could be considered. Whenever you face a question that has many different responses and you select only two as being relevant, you have committed the fallacy of *invalid disjunction*. Here is an example of this fallacy:

> The curriculum committee wanted to give Professor Potts another two classes to teach per year. Professor Potts much preferred to do research rather than teach. She told the committee: "I can teach or I can do research. Take your pick."

In this instance, Professor Potts has set up an invalid disjunction. She is assuming that she can do either teaching or research, but not both.

Here is another example. Can you spot the invalid disjunction?

> Bob wanted to go to law school, but only at Clearview University. Thus, he applied only there, thinking, "If I don't get into Clearview University, I might as well not go to law school at all."

AVAILABILITY

People commit the fallacy of availability when they accept the first explanation, or an early explanation, that comes to mind for an event without considering other, less obvious or less readily available explanations. Consider an example of the fallacy of availability:

> Stewart owned a restaurant where he employed twenty-five people. One day, he noticed money missing from the cash register. Just after he noticed the missing money, he saw Frank, one of his employees, walking away from the area of the cash register with a puzzled expression on his face. Stewart shouted, "Frank, you stole money from the cash register!"

In this instance, Stewart concludes that Frank stole the money from the register because Frank had the misfortune to be the first possible culprit who came into Stewart's view. Stewart has no real evidence of Frank's guilt, but he jumps to an unwarranted conclusion because Frank happened to be readily available.

Consider another example of the fallacy of availability:

As Dawn and Barry took their seats for the symphony concert, they noticed that two children were sitting with their parents a couple of rows behind them. During the concert, Dawn and Barry could hear paper rustling behind them several times. Dawn whispered to Barry, "Those kids sitting behind us must be the ones who are rustling paper during the quiet points of the music!"

Sometimes, this fallacy can occur when you select the first thing that comes to mind, as opposed to the first thing that you see. For example, let's say that you ask Dave, who isn't familiar with baseball, to name the person with the highest single-season batting average. Dave might name the only baseball players he has heard of (e.g., Babe Ruth or Barry Bonds). Someone who is a casual fan might guess players they think of as exceptionally good hitters (e.g., Ted Williams). In each case, the players who initially come to mind are viewed as being more likely to be the correct answer. In fact, Hugh Duffy, an old-timer, has the highest batting average ever (.440 in 1894).

One phenomenon related to the availability heuristic is the mere exposure effect. This effect refers to the fact that people will tend, on average, to adopt a positive attitude toward something just by virtue of being exposed to it. If you've ever wondered why companies like Coca-Cola or McDonald's bother to advertise (who *hasn't* heard of them?), it's because you are more likely to feel good about the companies after you are exposed to their names or images frequently. It doesn't matter if it's a positive or neutral exposure, as long as it's not negative. Simply seeing a name or a face tends to make you like it more (Zajonc, 2001).

THE SLIPPERY SLOPE FALLACY

This fallacy occurs when the conclusion of an argument is based on an alleged chain reaction, suggesting that a single step in the wrong direction may result in a disastrous or otherwise undesirable outcome. Consider the following example:

The government spent more money this year than last year. Clearly, government spending is leading the country to bankruptcy.

Consider another example.

You drank a glass of wine last night. Keep that up and soon you will be a drunk.

It is important to note that these types of fallacies do not form an exhaustive list of possible reasoning fallacies, nor are they mutually exclusive. A given example of fallacious reasoning can often involve more than one kind of fallacy, or can be classified as exemplifying more than one. The important thing is to be aware of the kinds of fallacies people can commit, both in formulating your own reasoning and in evaluating the reasoning of others.

EXERCISE 8.1 PRACTICE IN DETECTING FALLACIES

Here are twenty-five vignettes presenting examples of everyday reasoning. Some of them involve fallacies, others do not. For each vignette, first determine whether the reasoning is valid or fallacious, and if it is fallacious, characterize the nature of the fallacy. Remember that there is often no unique characterization of a fallacy; hence, there may be more than one correct answer. Answers appear after the problems.

1. Jerry was fixing the first meal that he and his new wife would eat in their new house. He wanted it to be a very special meal, but he accidentally charred the steaks black, although he and his wife liked steaks rare. Jerry said, "I never do anything right!"

2. Some factory workers were sitting together at lunch discussing the dangerous working conditions at the factory. One worker commented that there wasn't much they could do about the conditions. Kay replied, "We may just be factory workers, but that doesn't mean we can't fight for our rights!"

3. Chris refused to eat his peas, because, he explained, they were green. When Jack questioned this reason for disliking peas, Chris explained, "My mother always made me eat a lot of green vegetables, and I came to dislike having green things at meals."

4. Nina was having a very hard time writing a paper based on some library research she had done. Her roommate was surprised that Nina was having trouble writing, because Nina had said she found some great sources in the library for her paper. Nina commented, "Even if I have the best possible references on this subject, the paper won't be particularly good unless I can tie them all together well."

5. Josh and Sandy were discussing the Mets and the Dodgers. Sandy asked Josh why he thought the Mets had a better chance of winning the pennant this year than the Dodgers. Josh replied, "Every player on the Mets is better than every player on the Dodgers, so the Mets must be the better team."

6. As a senior in high school, Jeff won a scholarship to a good college. Jeff had never intended to go to college. He wanted to work with his hands as a carpenter. But Jeff thought, "I really ought to take this opportunity to have a free college education, even if I never intended and don't really want to go to college."

7. The mayor of Kayville was recently asked why he thought violence on the streets had diminished since he was elected last year. He replied, "My administration promised to be tough on criminals. We obviously intend to keep that promise, and the criminals are backing off."

8. Adam's father was tried and convicted for embezzling funds from a charity for which he had worked. Adam does not want to go to his high school anymore because, he says, "Everyone at school knows about Dad's crime, and I am sure that they will think I am a crook, too."

9. Peter asked his girlfriend, Sarah, why she refused to go to a party with him. Sarah said, "I have a cold sore on my lip! I'm not going to any party looking like a disgusting freak!"

10. A medical researcher, Carol, had been taking hormone samples from thirty patients who had cancer of the liver. In three of the patients, she noticed unusually high concentrations of the hormone DNG. She reported to her supervisor, "I think I've found a significant link between DNG and liver cancer, based on this evidence from three cancer patients."

11. Tony and Leo were ambassadors from two different countries that often had political confrontations with each other. Although Tony and Leo often met on opposite sides of the negotiation table, they were good friends. When asked about this friendship, they said, "There is no reason we cannot be good friends even though we must argue with each other on behalf of our countries."

12. Ivan was in a car wreck last month, in which he was hurt only slightly. Now, he refuses to ride in a car, saying, "I was almost killed once. I'm not going to get into a car ever again."

13. Sheila was home on vacation from college. She knew her grandmother wanted to see her, but she did not enjoy visiting her grandmother, who was a constant complainer, and, besides, she had to finish a term paper. But Sheila thought, "I should want to go to see my grandmother."

14. Mike voted for the underdog candidate in the mayoral campaign. His father asked Mike why he had voted this way. Mike replied, "This candidate has never won an election in which he's run. I thought it was his turn, so I voted for him."

15. Josh was getting dressed to go out to dinner with a woman he liked a great deal. His mother suggested he wear his beige silk shirt. He declined, saying, "I wore that shirt the last time I went out with my former girl friend. She didn't like that shirt, and as a result, I never saw her again. I'm certainly not going to wear it again tonight."

16. Janice, a senior in high school, had consulted her vocational counselor and her math teacher for suggestions regarding colleges to which she should apply as a prospective math major. Janice thought, "My vocational counselor knows of math programs in general, and my math teacher can assess the merits of particular math programs, so I should consult them both."

17. Troy had been quite overweight most of his life. He finally lost a good deal of weight, and his friend was congratulating him on his weight loss. Troy commented, "Even though I lost weight, I still think of myself as a fat person, and I probably always will."

18. Sally was planning a trip to Las Vegas. She particularly liked the dice-throwing games, and was anxious to win enough by gambling to pay for her trip. A month before her trip, she began practicing throwing dice, thinking, "If I practice with the dice, I'll have a better chance of winning."

19. The professor asked Beth why she took all semester to do a term paper that had been due in late October. Beth answered, "Well, did you want me to hand in my paper in May or did you want me to do a good job?"

20. Carol had eaten caviar once, several years ago. She did not like the taste of caviar at all then. At a party she attended recently, Carol was offered a cracker with caviar on it. Carol thought, "Well, just because I didn't like caviar when I tried it a few years ago does not mean that I won't like it if I try it now."

21. Wayne was the organizer of a large conference for dentists. Everything seemed to be going smoothly at the conference. On the second day of the conference, Wayne overheard two dentists talking. One told the other that he thought the conference was extremely boring this year. Wayne thought, "It makes me feel pretty terrible to hear criticism from the speakers I brought to this conference."

22. There is no definite link between smoking and lung cancer, despite the surgeon general's report and years of scientific studies. Therefore smoking is not harmful to your lungs.

23. Mark knew that the winner of the international chess championships was often Russian. A Russian family moved in next door to Mark's house. Mark went next door one day, thinking, "If they are Russian, they can teach me how to play chess."

24. Twin brothers, Terry and Jerry, had both received their Ph.D.s in their respective fields. Terry had received his from a prestigious university, and Jerry had received his from a modest state university in their hometown. Jerry said to his wife one day, "I always feel inferior to Terry because he received his degree at a prestigious university and I didn't."

25. Beth, a movie star, refused to go to a photography session for her newest movie. When asked by her exasperated agent why, Beth answered, "Darling, I don't feel beautiful today. And if I don't feel beautiful, I don't look beautiful."

26. Nuclear weapons have not been used since 1945. Therefore, the danger of their use is currently very high.

Answers to Inferential-fallacy Problems

Keep in mind that there are other possible classifications for these fallacies. The important thing is for you to become aware of the kinds of fallacies people can commit, and of how to stop them in your own reasoning and in the reasoning of others.

1. Fallacious. Hasty generalization.
2. Valid.
3. Fallacious. Irrelevant conclusion.
4. Valid.
5. Fallacious. Composition.
6. Fallacious. "Should" statement.
7. Fallacious. False cause.
8. Fallacious. Personalization.
9. Fallacious. Magnification/minimization.

10. Fallacious. Hasty generalization.
11. Valid.
12. Fallacious. Hasty generalization.
13. Fallacious. "Should" statement.
14. Fallacious. Irrelevant conclusion.
15. Fallacious. False cause.
16. Valid.
17. Fallacious. Labeling.

18. Fallacious. Skill, not chance.
19. Fallacious. Invalid disjunction.
20. Valid.
21. Fallacious. Personalization.
22. Fallacious. Ignorance.
23. Fallacious. Division.
24. Fallacious. Magnification/minimization.
25. Fallacious. Emotional reasoning.
26. Fallacious. Gambler's fallacy.

SUMMING UP

It is very important to know common fallacies to avoid making them in your reasoning and to be able to detect them in other people's reasoning.

9

Knowledge-Acquisition Components

It is often said that the main thing separating humans from other animal life is our ability to learn and use language. (It is not, as you may think, our ability to create bad television shows.) By any standard, this ability is impressive. With only minor flaws, we regularly use a grammatical system that to this day linguists and psychologists do not fully understand. We apply this grammatical system to vocabularies that, for adults, are usually estimated to exceed fifty thousand words; for educated adults, they may exceed seventy thousand or eighty thousand words. The exceptional size of people's vocabularies becomes even more amazing when we consider that only a very small proportion of these words were ever directly taught. In our early school years, we are probably more likely to have formal instruction in spelling than in vocabulary, and the vocabulary that is directly taught is apt to be the vocabulary that is most likely to be forgotten. However we learn the tens of thousands of words in our vocabulary, it is clearly not primarily from direct instruction.

The skills we use to acquire our vocabularies would seem to be critical as building blocks of our intelligence. Psychologists have found vocabulary to be one of the best single indicators, if not the very best indicator, of a person's overall level of intelligence. The importance of vocabulary to the measurement of intelligence is shown by the fact that most major individual scales of intelligence – including the Wechsler tests, the Woodcock-Johnson tests, the Kaufman tests, and the Stanford-Binet – each contain vocabulary items as a centerpiece, and by the fact that many group-administered tests of intelligence also contain vocabulary items. Clearly, if someone wanted to understand and increase his or her intelligence, vocabulary would play a key role. He or she would want to understand the basis for vocabulary acquisition and then work on improving vocabulary-acquisition skills.

We (and many other psychologists) believe that people learn the meanings of most words as they see the words *in context*. In many cases, people may not even be fully aware of acquiring the new words' meanings. Suppose, for example, you were reading a book or a magazine, and saw a word that you either did not know or were only somewhat familiar with. At this point, you might consult a dictionary; most of us, however, are too lazy or busy to look up each word we don't know. In such instances, you might try to figure out the meaning of the word using the context surrounding the word. Often the surrounding context provides a wealth of information about the word in question. This chapter will focus on developing your skills in finding and using such contextual information.

In order to get better at learning words from their context, you need to improve three kinds of skills. First, you need to learn the processes required to figure out the meanings of unknown words. Second, you need to learn the kinds of information (or cues) to which these processes apply. Finally, you need to learn the variables that make this task more or less difficult. Let us turn now to each of these three kinds of skills.

LEARNING FROM CONTEXT

The Processes of Knowledge Acquisition

In learning the meanings of new words embedded in context, the reader has to separate helpful and relevant information in context from unneeded material. This extra information may actually get in the way of learning the words' meanings. A good reader will be able to combine the selected information into a meaningful whole. Past information about the nature of words can serve as a guide. Old information can be used to guide decisions about whether information will be useful, and how it should be used. The reader constantly seeks to connect the context of the unknown word to something with which he or she is familiar. Thus, we see that processing the available information requires three distinct operations: (a) locating relevant information in context, (b) combining this information into a meaningful whole, and (c) relating this information to what the reader already knows. These processes will be referred to from now on as selective encoding, selective combination, and selective comparison, respectively.

Selective Encoding

Selective encoding involves sifting out relevant from irrelevant information. When you read an unfamiliar word in context, you also can find many clues to its meaning. However, helpful information is mixed with useless information. You have to figure out which context cues are relevant, and which ones are not. This process isn't as difficult as it may sound. Most readers selectively encode information without even being aware that they are doing it. By becoming more aware of this process, you are in a better position to improve your use of it.

When you encounter an unfamiliar word, imagine the word to be the center of a network of information. In the sentence where the unknown word occurs, seek out cues concerning its meaning. Then expand your systematic search, checking the sentences surrounding the sentence containing the unknown word.

Consider the brief passage in Example 9-1.[1]

---

[1] Definitions of all unknown words in the boxes in this chapter are at the end of the chapter.

EXAMPLE 9-1

He first saw a *macropodida* during a trip to Australia. He had just arrived from a business trip to India, and he was exhausted. Looking out at the plain, he saw a *macropodida* hop across it. It was a typical marsupial. While he watched, the animal pranced to and fro. Sometimes it stopped to chew on the surrounding plants. Squinting because of the bright sunlight, he noticed a young *macropodida* securely fastened in an opening in front of the mother.

Even in this rather obvious example, there is much information to weed out. For instance, in order to figure out the meaning of the word *macropodida*, we need not know that the man in the passage was on a business trip, that he was tired, or that he squinted in the bright sunlight. Although such information may be quite relevant to the story as a whole, it is entirely irrelevant to our purpose of figuring out the meaning of the unknown word.

In the first sentence, there are two important cues: (1) the man saw a macropodida, so macropodidas must be able to be seen, and (2) the man saw the macropodida in Australia, so that macropodidas must be found in that continent. As we have seen, the second sentence does not contain any information relevant to the unknown word. The next sentence informs us that macropodidas hop and can be found on plains. In the fourth sentence, we learned that a macropodida is a marsupial; if you know that a marsupial is an Australian mammal that has a pouch for its young, then it's useful information. If you don't know what a marsupial is, then you can simply move on. In the fifth sentence, we find out something about what macropodidas eat. Finally, the last sentence informs us that mother macropodidas carry their young in openings on their front sides.

Normally, readers would not selectively encode all of the available information before proceeding to combine and compare the relevant facts. Usually, readers will shift from one process to another as they proceed through the paragraph. The listing of relevant data above is merely an attempt to show you the kinds of information that can be selectively encoded.

Example 9-2 contains a passage with a relatively low-frequency word embedded within it. Read the passage, and underline all portions of the text that seem to you to be relevant to figuring out the meaning of *sommelier*, the unknown word. Try to be conscious of how each underlined item relates to the target word. Then try to define *sommelier* before reading on.

As you may have noticed, there are many helpful pieces of information relating to the target word. The first thing we learn is that the sommelier serves some function at the biennial feast. Then, we are explicitly told that the sommelier is an elected position. In this same sentence, we learn that the position was wanted by all. From this statement, we can infer that the position is desirable. In addition, the sommelier should be intimately familiar with the wines, so a grower, producer, or merchant has always been chosen. We learn that the position is a great honor, and that the chosen

Once upon a time, there was a kingdom famous for the wines produced from its vineyards. The wines were as sweet and delicious as any to be found in the world. Naturally, the wines were highly popular with the citizens of the kingdom, and the wine critics liked them, too.

In a feast held every two years, all in the kingdom met to celebrate past successes and to ask the gods for their continued blessings. The honor of being elected the *sommelier* was wanted by all. Invariably, an expert wine taster was chosen from among the ranks of the growers, producers, and merchants. Product knowledge, exquisite manners, and a touch of savoir faire were the desired characteristics. The tradition had existed for generations and had survived unchanged through countless kings, until King Klingo arrived on the scene. Klingo displayed arrogance and a shortness that offended everyone in the good-natured land. As the day of the celebration drew near, people wondered if Klingo would promptly use his power to disrupt the wine feast. The people were not mistaken. Just as the elders were about to announce the newly elected *sommelier*, Klingo shouted, "The position of *sommelier* will be mine. As long as Klingo rules, Klingo will pour the wine."

person should have exquisite manners. At the very end of the passage, we learn that Klingo plans to make himself sommelier and plans to pour the wine. It is reasonable to infer, therefore, that serving wine is one function of the sommelier. In fact, a sommelier is a wine steward. Were you able to use the cues to figure out the meaning of this word?

Selective Combination

Selective combination involves combining selectively encoded information in such a way as to form an integrated, logical definition of the previously unknown words. Simply taking out the relevant cues is not enough to arrive at a tentative definition of a word: We must know how to combine these cues into an integrated representation of the word. When we encounter an unfamiliar word, we must selectively encode information about the meaning of the word before we can do anything else, but we usually do not selectively encode all of the relevant information before moving on to the selective combination of this information. The process of selective combination can begin just as soon as the second piece of information has been selectively encoded.

Typically, the available information can be combined in many ways, and, different persons will certainly produce slightly different combinations. Usually, however, there is one optimal combination of information that exceeds any other possibilities in its usefulness. You can imagine a similarity to a detective's job. First, detectives have to decide what the relevant clues are in figuring out who committed the crime (selective encoding). Once they have figured out some important clues, they begin to combine them selectively in such a way as to build a logical case against the suspect. Combining the clues in an improper way can result in a false lead, and ultimately, the arrest of the wrong suspect. Thus, just as the detective has to track down the individual who

EXAMPLE 9-3

There is no question that the *oont* is king of the Asian and African Deserts. The foul-tempered *oont* is widely used as a beast of burden by desert travelers, despite its many flaws. The *oont* has a strong, unpleasant odor, for example, and frequently bites, spits, and makes loud braying sounds. Sometimes it simply will quit on the job. Despite its strong, unpleasant odor, its loud noises, and its obnoxious habits of viciously biting, spitting when irritated, and quitting on the job, the foul-tempered *oont* is widely used as a beast of burden by desert travelers. The brown, shaggy animal seems similar to a cow in its cud-chewing, and its long neck may remind one of a giraffe. Its large, cushioned feet could be of the canine family, and its humped back vaguely resembles that of some breeds of buffalo. But although its appearance is a hodgepodge of other animals' traits, the *oont is* a remarkable creature. Perfectly suited to desert conditions, it can store vast quantities of water in its body tissues.

actually committed the crime, you have to track down the meaning of the word that is appropriate in the given instance or instances.

Consider how the process of selective combination can be applied to the *macropodida* example in Example 9-1. From the first sentence, we selectively encoded the fact that macropodidas are things we can see, and that they are found in Australia. Thus, we know that they are something that we can see when we go to Australia. The third sentence provided us with the knowledge that macropodidas can be found on plains, and with the knowledge that they hop. We thus now know that macropodidas are something that we can see hopping on the plains of Australia. Later, we learned that they are marsupials, that they eat plants, and that they carry their young in front openings. In sum, we now know that macropodidas are plant-eating marsupials that can be seen hopping on the plains of Australia, and that may be carrying young in openings in front of them.

We now have a fairly extensive network of information about the word macropodidas. Putting all the information together in a systematic manner yields a definition: A macropodida is a kangaroo.

Now read Example 9-3 and exercise your skills in selective combination. Locate the available cues in the passage (selective encoding), and then see if you can combine these cues into a meaningful definition or sentence describing the unknown word.

This is an easy passage on which to practice your skills, Not only is there a wealth of helpful cues, but these cues are easily combined as well. The first sentence tells us where *oonts* are found, in the Asian and African deserts. In the second through fourth sentences, we learn that the *oont* is unclean, loud, prone to biting and spitting, and quits on the job. Finally, we are told that the animal is used for transportation in the desert. In the fifth sentence, we learned that *oonts* are brown, shaggy, and that they are long-necked. We also learned that they chew the cud. Later, we learn that *oonts* have padded feet, humped backs, and the ability to store vast quantities of water in their bodies. We also learn that they are suitable for desert conditions. One way of combining concrete information such as this is to attempt to form a visual image of what the object, in this case an animal, could look like. Before too long, the visual image that you form, as you combine into it more and more information, is quite likely to look like a camel, which is exactly what an *oont* is.

Selective Comparison

Selective comparison involves relating newly acquired information to knowledge acquired in the past. As readers decide what information to encode and how to combine this information, what they already know about the topic can be quite useful as a guide. Any given bit of relevant information will probably be nearly useless if it cannot somehow be related to past knowledge. Without previous knowledge, the helpful hints that would normally lead readers to the definition of an unknown term will be meaningless, and readers will probably not even recognize the hints as relevant information. New information can be related to old information, and vice versa, by the use of similes, metaphors, analogies, and models. The goal, however, is always the same: to give the new information meaning by connecting it to old information that is already known.

Look again at the passage in Example 9-1 to analyze how selective comparison operates. In selective comparison, we try to establish how the new word is similar to and different from old words that we already have stored in memory. We may end up deciding either that the new word is a synonym for an old word that we already know, or that a new concept has to be constructed that expands on our old concepts. In the case of the macropodidas, the more information we have, the more restricted the range of things that it might be. Initially, it might be anything that we might see in Australia – a very large list of things. Later, we are able to reduce our list as we learn that a macropodida is something seen on a plain, and something that hops. We can restrict our list of possibilities further when we learn that it is a herbivorous marsupial. If our original list of things that are particularly characteristic of Australia included such items as aborigines, kangaroos, sheep, and eucalyptus trees, our developing list could no longer include all of these things. In fact, by the time we are done with the passage, the only item on this list that the passage could describe is the kangaroo. Thus, the process of selective comparison includes a whittling-down process whereby large numbers of possibilities are successively further reduced. Eventually, if only one possibility remains, that possibility is a likely synonym for the unknown word. If no possibilities remain, then we probably have to form a new concept that is related to, but is different from, all old concepts we have stored in memory.

Consider the sample passage in Example 9-4. The passage contains two unknown words. As you read the passage, try to be conscious of the background knowledge that you are bringing to bear on the passage. Create a list of possible meanings for each of the two unknown words, based on the selective comparisons that you make. As you progressively encode and combine more information, eliminate meanings from your lists that do not seem to fit the descriptions of each of the words.

This passage has two target words, each of which must be analyzed separately. Start with the word *oam*. The phrase "around the fire where the common meal was

EXAMPLE 9-4

Two ill-dressed people, one a wearied woman of middle years and the other a young man, sat around the fire where the common meal was almost ready. The mother, Tanith, peered at her son through the *oam* of the bubbling stew. It had been a long time since his last *ceilidh*, and Tobar had changed greatly. Where once he had seemed all legs and clumsy joints, he now was well formed and in control of his young body. As they ate, Tobar told of his past year, recreating for Tanith how he had wandered long and far in his quest to gain the skills he would need to be permitted to rejoin the tribe. Then, all too soon, their brief *ceilidh* ended, Tobar walked over to touch his mother's arm and quickly left.

almost ready" contains much helpful information. There is a fire, and a meal is being prepared. Based on our previous experience, we can figure out that the stew is bubbling because it is being cooked over a fire. At this point, we can hypothesize that the word *oam* means "steam" or "aroma." We can choose between these two possibilities using the information supplied by the verb *peered*. Again, if we relate what we already know to the new information being supplied by the text, we will realize that aromas are not peered through, but steam could be. "Steam" is the best definition of *oam*, the first target word.

The word *ceilidh* is more difficult to define. The first clause of the first sentence in which the word appears tells us that it had been "a long time since his last *ceilidh*." From the context, we can infer that a ceilidh is something that takes place. We already know from the beginning of the paragraph that two people are preparing to eat. Selectively comparing what we know with what the passage tells us might result in the preliminary guess that a ceilidh is a meal. This guess is quickly proven wrong, however. The passage goes on to inform us that since his last ceilidh, Tobar has grown into a man. Tobar would be very hungry indeed if he had grown into a man between his last meal and the present time. Fortunately, we learn from the passage that the distance between ceilidhs is one year. This information may be ascertained on the basis of the phrase, "Tobar told of his past year." Now our long-term memory is again activated as we search for events that would take place annually. Perhaps a ceilidh is a holiday feast or a birthday. A holiday feast is quickly ruled out. From previous experience, we know that feasts often have vast amounts of food and last for hours. This ceilidh is short and it is accompanied by a one-course meal. Birthday must also be eliminated as a possible meaning. It may fit the first use of the target word but it does not fit the second use. The last sentence of the text reads, "Then, all too soon, their brief ceilidh ended, Tobar walked over to touch his mother's arm and quickly left." Birthday cannot be the correct meaning because the word ceilidh relates to both mother and son. A ceilidh, then, is likely to be a visit. This is a difficult word to define on the basis of the passage, but if we selectively compare the available information to our store of previous information, the task is greatly facilitated. Now, use what you have learned

EXAMPLE 9-5

According to legend, on the night of Francesco Louis-Philippe's birth, there streaked across the midnight sky a *bolide* more blindingly magnificent than any seen before. Indeed, under his rule, the kingdom of Montaldo flared to sudden, brilliant prominence, only to be extinguished when it was overrun by the barbarous Guntherians. The constant state of warfare was a fact of life in the reign of King Louis-Philippe, and although the *spaneria* was a high price to pay, the nation overflowed with riches and national pride. Religious and political leaders took measures to ease the effects of the *spaneria* by relaxing the strict marriage laws requiring monogamy. All in all, the period was marked by a meteoric rise and decline: the many deaths, the many victories, and ensuing collapse. The Montaldans ruled the region until the armies of Guntheria destroyed them.

about selective encoding, selective combination, and selective comparison to try to define the two low-frequency words in Example 9-5.

Were you able to use selective encoding, selective combination, and selective comparison to figure out that a *bolide is* a shooting star (exploding meteor) and that a *spaneria is* a scarcity of men? Most people find *bolide* easier to figure out than *spaneria*.

Context Cues

In learning about the three processes of knowledge acquisition, you may have noticed that the various kinds of textual cues that trigger selective encoding, selective combination, and selective comparison tend to be systematic. Various kinds of cues occur again and again from one passage to another. You will find these processes easier to apply if you have in your mind a classification (or *taxonomy*) of the kinds of cues that are useful for figuring out meanings of new words. Although different classifications are possible, a particularly useful one distinguishes among eight types of cues: (a) setting cues, (b) value/affect cues, (c) property cues, (d) active property cues, (e) causal/functional cues, (f) class membership cues, (g) antonymic cues, and (h) equivalence cues. The explanations below will help you to recognize and to use these eight kinds of cues.

Setting Cues

Setting cues contain temporal (related to time), spatial (related to place), and situational information about the context in which the object or concept represented by an unknown word can be found. Examples of temporal setting cues are "in the afternoon," "every Monday," and "once upon a time." Examples of spatial setting cues are "at the intersection of Pine and Elm Streets," "on the roof," and "in Switzerland." Examples of situational cues are "at the Valentine's Day party," "during the last board meeting," and "while having dinner." In some cases, a single setting cue will provide information from two or more categories. For instance, "at dinner" suggests both a temporal frame of reference (evening) and a spatial frame of reference (at home or in a restaurant).

In judging a setting cue, you must first be sure that the cue relates information about the specific target word and not simply information about the general message conveyed by the context. In other words, you must be sure that the cue is relevant to defining the unknown word, rather than merely relevant to understanding the passage, in general.

Consider again the passage in Example 9-4. Consider how setting cues might help you in your use of selective encoding, combination, and comparison. This passage contains many setting cues. Start by analyzing the cues pertaining to the word *oam*. There are three setting cues in the first sentence, and the phrase, "around the fire where the common meal was almost ready," contains them all. "Around the fire" is a spatial cue because it tells where the action takes place. The words "common meal" provide a situational cue, and "almost ready" is a temporal cue. The trick now is to combine this information properly in order to arrive at the definition of *oam*.

Ceilidh is more difficult to define. The words "long time since" provide a temporal cue. Later, the clause "where once he had seemed all legs and clumsy joints, he now was well formed and in control of his supple young body" provides us with a rather complicated temporal cue that brings us up to date about Tobar. This clause tells us that the "long time" refers to a much longer period than mere days or weeks. Therefore, a *ceilidh* cannot be a synonym for a meal. We get another temporal cue in the words "told of his past year": It has been one year since his last *ceilidh*. The context also provides a situational cue. Whatever a *ceilidh* is, this one takes place at a meal, in the midst of an amiable conversation. There are other types of cues present in the passage that help to isolate the correct meaning, yet it is evident that the setting cues have conveyed a large amount of information about the word.

Now go over the passage in Example 9-5. Identify each of the setting cues pertaining to the target words that appear in the passage. Write a "T," a "P," or an "S" in the margin near each setting cue to indicate whether it provides time, place, or situational information. If a cue contains two subcategories of information, consider the primary message carried by the cue, and classify it accordingly.

Value/Affect Cues

Value/affect cues describe the evaluative implications and the emotional content of the concept represented by the unknown word. They hint at the positive or negative qualities of the concept, its desirability, and the emotions that it might evoke. Value/affect cues also include syntactic information that conveys expectations, such as "despite" or "regardless of." Examples of value/affect cues include: "Jane was glad that . . ."; "unfortunately . . ."; ". . . is complex"; ". . . is simpleminded."

Now return to the passage in Example 9-2. Several value/affect cues appear in this passage, although the unknown word – *sommelier* – cannot easily be defined simply on the basis of these cues. Let us see what the cues do tell us about the unknown word. Obviously, the position of *sommelier*, whatever it is, is desirable. It is an honor "coveted by all" to be elected *sommelier*. Moreover, we know that the position is

EXAMPLE 9-6

In our mobile society, where families are often spread across the states and neighbors are strangers, *eremophobia is* a constant complaint. Mental-health professionals treat the condition primarily through extended counseling sessions, but when anxiety and nervousness are pronounced, tranquilizers may be necessary. Often, not only the immediate sufferers but also those close to them may require counseling. Sufferers of *eremophobia* may exhibit intense dependency behavior, adversely affecting those close to them. For instance, an older couple lost all their children but one in a car accident. They then placed unreasonable demands for emotional support on the remaining child. He complained that his parents focused on him too much, to the point where the quality of his life had declined drastically.

important to the tradition of the celebration. King Klingo himself values the distinction highly.

Now read the passage in Example 9-6 and mark any value/affect cues that you are able to find. Finally, define the unknown word. Remember at all times to apply the operations of selective encoding, selective combination, and selective comparison.

State Property Cues

State property cues refer to descriptions of the state or condition implied by or associated with a word. They frequently include information that can be confirmed through the five senses, such as quantity, duration, and size. They may also, however, describe properties of the words that are not experienced directly through the senses. The cues are especially common in the form of adjectives. Examples of state property cues include: "smelled horrible," "could barely be seen," "is conscious."

Now return to Example 9-3. This paragraph is practically a list of state property cues. See how many can be identified. First, we are told that the *oont* is king of the desert. Then, we learn that the oont has a strong, unpleasant odor. The latter part of the passage contains several state cues concerning the oont's physical appearance. The oont is brown and shaggy, it has a long neck and humped back, and its feet are padded.

Now read the passage in Example 9-7 and mark any state property cues you are able to find. After you have done so, consider as well the setting cues and value/affect cues. See if you are able to define the unknown word. Remember to apply the operations of selective encoding, selective combination, and selective comparison.

Active Property Clues

Active property cues are the action-oriented counterparts of state property cues. They describe the dynamic properties of a word. Active property cues may describe something that the given person or thing does or has done to it. Some examples are "arose," "shines," "were burned by. . . ."

EXAMPLE 9-7

The *flitwite* was only one of the judicial remedies available to the justices of the Court of the King's Bench in the eleventh century, but it was perhaps the most important, Its frequent use added enormously to the treasury's funds, and new royal purchases were often financed by the issuance of an increased number *flitwites*. Even the most impartial of justices handed them down in multitudes, for the *flitwite* was as much a part of eleventh-century society as the civil tort is of our own. Medieval men and women related in direct and personal ways; therefore, conflict was likely to take the form of actual fighting. In a culture so preoccupied with lawsuits, the law must often deal with more subtle forms of conflict.

EXAMPLE 9-8

The ultimate goal of those seriously involved in raising livestock is to produce animals with a high percentage of top quality meat and a low percentage of waste. Recently, livestock breeders have successfully developed a new breed of turkey whose market potential lies in its high proportion of white meat to dark. The most efficient way to improve stock, practiced by an increasing number of ranches, is to hire a *thremmatologist* to advise in the purchase and mating of different breeds. The *thremmatologist* carefully researches the characteristics of each breed involved and then examines the bloodlines of the specific animals under consideration. The encouraging results of scientific monitoring are now giving rise to predictions that the age of made-to-order livestock is just around the bend.

Consider the passage in Example 9-8. First read the passage, and then see what active property cues you are able to find.

There are three groups of words in this passage that act as active property cues. A *thremmatologist* "advises in the purchase and mating of different breeds, researches the characteristics of the breeds, and examines the bloodlines of animals." These active property cues provide enough information to arrive at least at a tentative definition of the target word. In fact, a thremmatologist is a specialist in animal breeding.

Now read the passage in Example 9-9, marking any active property cues that occur. Also be aware of the other kinds of cues that have been discussed so far. Apply the processes of selective encoding, selective combination, and selective comparison to arrive at your best guess as to the meaning of the unknown word.

Causal/Functional Cues

Causal/functional cues are a stronger form of active property cues. They focus more on the goal of an unknown word. These cues describe causes, effects, functions, and purposes of the object or concept represented by the unknown word: what can cause the thing, what a thing can cause, what the thing is used for, and so on. These cues are related to active property cues in that they involve action, but the focus of the cue is

EXAMPLE 9-9

The students filed into the testing room, chattering nervously. When all were seated, the proctor began administering the dreaded Bumpus Memory Test. At exactly 9:00, the exam began. Not a whisper was heard as the students labored through the exam, deeply engaged in thought. Suddenly, a series of *rackarocks* shattered the silence, jolting everyone in the room. The proctor jumped to his feet and ran outside. He returned momentarily with two young pranksters, each held by the scruff of the neck. "Your parents are going to hear about this," he hollered above the laughter that now filled the air.

EXAMPLE 9-10

Vocabulary skills are a crucial foundation of well-spoken speech and concise writing. A good vocabulary is a powerful tool indeed, and the more words people command, the richer will be their mode of expression. We must realize, however, that learning a new word does not involve simply the acquisition of the term's formal meaning. Moreover, dictionary definitions frequently are not detailed enough to ensure proper usage. The goal must be to incorporate each new word into our active vocabularies. Words that lie gathering dust in the recesses of the mind serve no useful purpose, and a collection of half-learned words is bound to lead to *solecism*.

more on the effect that the action can cause than on the action itself. Some examples are "can cause a flood," "caused by a villain," "resulted in a mishap."

Consider now the passage in Example 9-10. Mark each causal/functional cue, and see if you can define the unknown word.

Although the target word, solecism, is difficult to define on the basis of the context, the causal/functional cue is clearly stated. It consists of the words "bound to lead to." The sentence in which the cue appears contains a cause-and-effect relation between half-learned words and solecism. The same sentence also contains a value/affect cue. We can deduce that solecism is not a good thing because half-learned words are undesirable. In this case, the causal/functional cues provide hints about the meaning of solecism – incorrect usage of words.

Now read the passage in Example 9-11, marking any causal/functional cues that may be present. Then define the two unknown words in the passage to the best of your ability. Be sure to use the other types of cues as well, and to apply to them selective encoding, selective combination, and selective comparison.

Class Membership Cues

Class membership cues deal with the relations between the unknown object or concept and various kinds of classes. They may identify classes or groups to which the unknown belongs. Alternatively, the unknown object or concept may itself be a class, in which case examples of the class members are given. Class membership cues can be negative.

EXAMPLE 9-11

The drug C-37 was first discovered at Henish Laboratories by Dr. Alex Whichard in the early 1970s. When the lozenge form of the drug was first approved for public use as a cough remedy, some claimed that a new age of medicine had arrived. Since then, however, serious side effects of the *lambative* have been noted, resulting in a call for the restriction of its use. The chief drawback is the *oscitancy* that it causes. Whereas some *oscitancy* is expected with any drug that functions as a relaxant, the effects of C-37 may be sudden and profound. Doctors have suggested that patients use the *lambative* in the confines of their homes and completely avoid alcohol, which intensifies any *oscitancy* the patient may be feeling.

EXAMPLE 9-12

The time immediately following the Holy Revolution was one of strict government control of personal and public affairs. Records available from this period contain no observable criticism of the regime, but it is unclear whether this was because of censorship or overwhelming popular support. On the surface, the country appeared to be turning moral principles into law with little effort. Each resident was required by statute to be *acapnotic*, and the tobacco industry was banned. The government also outlawed the use and production of alcohol, caffeine, marijuana, and dozens of other drugs. In addition, the new regime created a national department of *hamartiology* to advise on legislation concerning the prevailing morality. So successful was the new emphasis on righteous conduct that teenage delinquency virtually disappeared.

For instance, they may contrast the unknown with members of a distinct group – such as, "unlike butter, cream cheese, and peanut butter, _____". Examples of class membership cues include: "lions and tigers and _____"; "he put his books, notes, and _____ into his satchel"; "_____ is a typical mammal"; and "other _____ are bees, mosquitoes, and flies."

Now read the passage in Example 9-12, noting the two unknown target words. See if there are any class membership cues as you read the text.

Although there are no class membership cues for the second target word, *hamartiology*, there is one class membership cue for *acapnotic*. The sentence following the sentence with the target word reads, "the government also outlawed the use and production of alcohol, caffeine, marijuana, and dozens of other drugs." You can infer that tobacco is a member of the class of substances including alcohol, caffeine, and marijuana. The sentence also suggests that the use and production of tobacco have been similarly banned.

Dismantling the tobacco industry eliminates the production side and requiring everyone to be acapnotic eliminates the consumption side. Therefore, it seems reasonable to conclude that an acapnotic is a nonsmoker, which is in fact the meaning of the word. Hamartiology is the study of sin.

EXAMPLE 9-13

Having confidently entered the conference room expecting praise for a job well-done, the boy flinched under the unexpected blasting *animadversion* of his teacher. Had the paper been full of misused words, or had it wandered off the main point, such a harsh response would have been more understandable. For the boy had learned well the importance of avoiding sentence fragments, run-ons, *catachreses*, and other breaches of grammatical and semantic etiquette. And his skill at *diaskeasis* was not so rusty that he would allow obvious technical mistakes to occur. He was especially proud of his semantic abilities: Diction errors and *catachreses* rarely disgraced his papers. Unfortunately, the teacher was not attacking the written language, but rather the idea itself, and the boy had trouble accepting that his work could be so utterly rejected. He slowly collected his books and left the room, knowing the class would never be as enjoyable for him again.

EXAMPLE 9-14

Although the others were having a marvelous time at the party, the couple on the blind date was not enjoying the fun at all. A *pococurante*, he was dismayed by her earnestness. Meanwhile, she, who delighted in men with full heads of hair, eyed his substantial *phalacrosis* with disdain. When he failed to suppress an *eructation*, her disdain turned to disgust. He, in turn, was equally appalled by her noticeable *podobromhidrosis*. Although they both loved to dance, the disco beat of the music did not lessen either their boredom or mutual discomfort. Both silently vowed that they would never again accept a blind date.

Now read the passage in Example 9-13 and mark any class membership cues you can discover. At the same time, be alert for the other kinds of cues we have discussed, and remember to use these cues in your processes of selective encoding, selective combination, and selective comparison. After you have spotted the cues, see which of the three unknown words in the passage you can define.

Antonymic Cues
Antonymic cues are opposites of the target word. The presence of an antonymic cue almost always leads the reader directly to the meaning of the target word. Such cues are easy to identify and they usually define the target word with ease. Some examples are "different as night and _____"; "I'll be there come rain or _____"; "Wildly happy yesterday, she was unbearably _____ today."

Now read the passage in Example 9-14, identifying all antonymic cues. See if you can figure out the meaning of each of the four unknown words.

The passage contains two antonymic cues. Both of them are quite useful in helping to define the target words. The meaning of the word *pococurante* is illuminated by the clause "he was dismayed by her earnestness." Evidently, pococurantes do not take

EXAMPLE 9-15

The swampland is no place for the unprepared. The dangers are all too real. The insect-free life of the city is replaced by swarming clouds of poisonous mosquitoes; the warmth and dryness of the typical suburban dwelling is replaced by a perpetual musty dampness; and the firm, fertile land of meadows and pastures is replaced by wet, spongy soil and treacherous patches of *syrt*. You can sink into the stuff as easy as floating in the sea. Of course, the reward for facing these dangers is the opportunity to learn about life conditions in the early years of the earth's existence.

life too seriously. The second antonymic cue is even more of a giveaway. She likes a full head of hair, and she views this fellow's head unfavorably. Apparently, he is balding noticeably (much like one of the authors).

The remaining target words in the passage are not associated with antonymic cues, but let us see if we can discover any other types of cues that would help to define these target words. The words "fail to suppress" serve as an active property cue for the meaning of the target word *eructation*. It seems as though an eructation is something one would normally attempt to suppress in public. Burps and the passing of wind come to mind. The word *podobromhidrosis* is not as easy to pin down. The value/effect cues contained in the phrase "He . . . was appalled by" tells us that podobromhidrosis is undesirable, but there are no further cues to aid us in figuring out its meaning. In fact, a pococurante is an indifferent person, one who is nonchalant about things. A phalacrosis is a bald spot. An eructation is a burp, and people suffering from podobromhidrosis have smelly feet.

Now read Example 9-15, marking any antonymic cues that you are able to find. Also be aware of other kinds of cues that may help you to define the unknown word.

Equivalence Cues

Equivalence cues occur when a word is explicitly defined in context by the use of synonyms, restatements, or direct definitions. Equivalence cues are a type of class membership cue with the added feature that the "class" is identical to the meaning of the unknown word. Therefore, no additional inferences need to be drawn about similarities and differences between the meaning of the unknown word and the cue. An equivalence cue may appear before or directly after the target word, or it may appear some distance away. In the latter case, the reader must infer that the target word and the cue relate to each other. Some examples of equivalence cues are "A dog is a domestic canine" and "The president, or head of state, is . . . "

Read Example 9-16 and mark any equivalence cues that you can identify.

The word *cecity* appears twice in this passage, but there is only one equivalence cue. In the sentence after the second appearance of the word, the phrase "the onset of blindness" occurs. As the previous sentence refers to *cecity* as an affliction, we have been on the lookout for diseases, terminal conditions, and other health problems.

EXAMPLE 9-16

A stroll through the private gallery of Luis Roberto will soon convince anyone with a taste for art that the eighty-year-old master is a man to be watched. For fifty years, Don Luis painted only as a hobby but at age seventy, even in the face of impending *cecity*, Don Luis left the business world for a full-time career in art. His paintings glow with colors and forms that are alive, reaching off the canvas to pull the viewer into their play.

Healthy in every other respect, Don Luis is falling prey to *cecity*, an affliction he justifiably considers a demonic curse. The onset of blindness marks the beginning of the end for the giant talent. Don Luis compensates for his darkening world by painting as boldly with texture as he does with color and form. Bodies are literally piled onto one another, forcing themselves into one's vision and begging one to reach out a hand to touch them.

EXAMPLE 9-17

A four-year-old boy was found wandering around Center Park five days ago. Police reported that he seemed in good health despite being dazed, frightened, and hungry. An *ecchymosis* on his forehead suggested that he had fallen at some point. Fortunately, the rest of his body was free from other bruises or black-and-blue marks. The boy has brown hair, green eyes, and freckles. Any information leading to identification of his parents would be greatly appreciated by the Park Police.

Blindness would certainly be considered an affliction – especially by an artist. *Cecity*, then, means blindness.

Notice that there are other kinds of cues in the context. The first use of the term *cecity* is accompanied by the adjective "impending." This cue not only provides us with temporal information, it is also a value/affect cue. We may infer from the meaning of the word "impending" that *cecity* is undesirable.

We are later told, as related above, that *cecity* is an affliction. This is a stative property cue and also contains value/affect information. The use of the descriptive noun "affliction," informs us of the stative condition of *cecity*, and it reinforces the notion that it is undesirable. Finally, Luis Roberto considers *cecity* a "demonic curse." This is a pretty clear value/affect cue.

Now read the passage in Example 9-17. See if you can use equivalence and other cues to figure out the meaning of the unknown word.

You have now completed the description of the eight types of contextual cues. To refresh your memory, they are setting cues, value/affect cues, state property cues, active property cues, causal/functional cues, class membership cues, antonymic cues, and equivalence cues. You should be aware of the characteristics of each kind of cue. Should you feel at all unsure about the use of these cues in defining unknown words you encounter outside of this book, pick up a good novel and read until you come to an unfamiliar word. Then search for available cues. Almost invariably, you will find at least one. In the next section of the chapter, we will consider aspects of the unknown word and the surrounding text that make the knowledge-acquisition processes either easier or more difficult to apply to the recognition of the various kinds of contextual cues.

Mediators

Mediators are variables that make using knowledge-acquisition processes on contextual cues either easier or harder. Seven mediators that have been identified as particularly important in learning words from context are:

(a) the number of times the unknown word appears,
(b) the differing contexts in which the unknown word appears different times,
(c) the importance of the unknown word to understanding the surrounding paragraph,
(d) the helpfulness of the surrounding context in understanding the meaning of the word,
(e) the density of unknown words in the passage,
(f) the concreteness of the unknown word and of the surrounding context, and
(g) the usefulness of previously known information in understanding the passage or in understanding the meaning of the unknown word.

The following explanations are designed to teach you to recognize the mediators and to use them to your advantage when you encounter unfamiliar words. The explanations will draw on passages that you have previously analyzed, so that you will be better able to see how the mediators affect the application of the processes to the cues.

Number of Occurrences of an Unknown Word

Frequent occurrences of an unknown word in a given passage affect your ability to learn the word in several ways. First, the multiple occurrences are a signal that the word is important to the meaning of the context. Consequently, you are more likely to make a genuine effort to define the word. Second, each reappearance of the term provides more information about its meaning. In both of these cases, multiple occurrences are desirable. They offer an incentive to learn the word, and they provide the reader with more contexts. Occasionally, however, multiple occurrences will hinder the ability to define an unfamiliar word. For instance, you may have difficulty selectively combining the information obtained from the cues surrounding the separate appearances of the word.

When a passage contains multiple occurrences of an unknown word, the best strategy is to treat each occurrence separately. What does each use of the word tell you about the word's meaning? Do you think a single definition will work? If so, try to form an integrated definition of the word, given what you know. If a single meaning does not appear to satisfy all of the occurrences of the term, if may be that different senses of the word are required.

Now return to the passage in Example 9-7. Use this strategy to verify that the definition of the unknown word is suitable for each appearance of the word. What do the multiple occurrences tell you about the word?

This passage is not a particularly easy one. We learn from the first sentence that the *flitwite* was an important judicial remedy in the eleventh century. The context of the second occurrence tells us why the *flitwite* was important. Its "frequent use added enormously to the treasury's coffers." The context of the third use of the term informs us that regardless of the financial factors involved, *flitwites* were an important part of eleventh-century culture. As we read on, we learn that the *flitwite* appears to be a penalty for fighting. Based on what we know from the first two occurrences of the term, we can conclude that a *flitwite* is a monetary fine for fighting. Notice how our use of selective encoding and selective combination is brought on by the multiple occurrences of the unknown word. How do we know that a single definition is required? Notice that the first two uses of the term appear in consecutive sentences, the first and the second, and that the pronoun "its," which begins the second sentence, refers back to the word *flitwite* in the first sentence. Throughout the paragraph, the author always seems to be speaking about the same concept. Whatever else a *flitwite* may be, "a fine for fighting" is the only meaning required by this context.

In this passage, it is unlikely that *flitwite* is definable on the basis of only one appearance of the term. The reader probably needs all three occurrences to selectively encode, combine, and compare sufficient information to construct a definition. In the passage, the multiple occurrences fit together quite well, and each one adds a small bit of needed information.

Now return to the passage in Example 9-2. Decide whether the multiple uses of the target word do indeed fit with the single definition. Note how the multiple occurrences of the word help in its definition.

Variability of Contexts

Different types of contexts – for example, different kinds of subject matter or writing styles – are likely to supply a variety of information about the unknown word. A variability of contexts increases the likelihood that a wide range of hints and cues will be supplied about the term in question. This thus increases the probability that you will get a full picture of the scope of a given word's meaning. By contrast, if the word is simply repeated in the same context, seeing it over and over again won't be very helpful. Usually, variable contexts help in the construction of a definition. Sometimes, however, the multiple contexts may be hard to reconcile with each other. In this case, the additional information may be unhelpful.

Consider, for example, the passage in Example 9-16. In this passage, the target word *cecity* appears in two fairly divergent contexts. The first use of the word is surrounded by an only slightly helpful context. Based on the information contained in this context, we can figure out because of a value/affect cue that *cecity*, whatever it is, is undesirable. At this point, we might guess that the term meant either "senility" or "death," but we would probably not feel very confident about the preliminary definition. It is not until the second context, and the equivalence cue, that we can gain confidence that *cecity*, means "blindness." A quick check will verify that this definition fits the first occurrence of the word as well.

Now return to the passage in Example 9-4. Consider how variability of contexts and the different kinds of context cues provided help you to define the meaning of the word *ceilidh*.

Importance of the Unknown Word to Its Context

If knowing the meaning of an unfamiliar word is judged to be necessary to understanding its surrounding material, the reader is much more likely to invest an effort in figuring out what the word means than if the unfamiliar word is judged to he irrelevant to understanding the passage. In your day-to-day reading, it is not realistic to expect that you will invariably look up even, unfamiliar word that you encounter, or try to figure out the meaning of each new word. Therefore, it becomes important for you to be able to differentiate between those kinds that are more important to understanding the meaning of the passage and those that are less important.

Refer back to Example 9-9. First, briefly summarize the main idea of the passage. Would a lack of knowledge about the meaning of the target word hinder your ability to summarize the passage adequately? If so, it would seem that the word is important to understanding the meaning of the context as a whole. If not, then you could probably get by without figuring out or looking up the meaning of the unknown word.

As it turns out, this passage is fairly easy to summarize even without detailed information about the word *rackarocks*. A group of students is taking a standardized test that is suddenly disrupted by a disturbance created by a couple of jokesters. The meaning of rackarocks is relatively unimportant to the context in the passage because we do not need to know for sure that the word means firecrackers to understand that a disturbance is taking place. At the same time, understanding the meaning of the word helps us to understand the exact nature of the disturbance. Thus, the importance of the term to understanding the passage is probably best viewed as intermediate, relative to other words in other contexts.

Now consider the passage in Example 9-10. How important is understanding the meaning of the word *solecism* to understanding the meaning of this passage?

Helpfulness of the Context

The helpfulness of the context to understanding the meaning of an unfamiliar word is an important mediator. If the context in which the word appears is filled with easily interpretable hints and cues, then it is easier to define the word. By contrast, the absence of contextual cues can make defining an unknown word next to impossible. The helpfulness of contextual cues is affected by the position of the cues in the passage. If a given cue occurs close to the target word, then there is a better chance that the cue will be recognized as relevant to the unknown word's meaning. In contrast, a cue separated from the target word by a large portion of the text may go unrecognized. Yet such a cue may still be useful for figuring out the meaning of the word. It is thus important to look not only at the contexts immediately surrounding the unknown word, but at contexts at a greater distance as well. Finally, it is important to understand that cues may occur both before and after the target word. If you stop reading as soon as you encounter an unfamiliar term, you will not give yourself a chance to find any cues that appear after the word itself. By reading at least somewhat beyond the word, you will be less likely to overlook cues that appear after the word's occurrence.

Consider, for example, the unknown word in Example 9-3. Notice that there are many helpful cues in this passage, and that they occur both before and after each appearance of the word. Moreover, some of them occur at some distance from the unknown word. Now look again at Example 9-17. Where do the context cues for defining *ecchymosis* appear? Which ones appear before the appearance of the word, and which appear after? Which are close in proximity to the word, and which are at some distance?

Density of Unknown Words in a Passage

The density of unknown words in a passage can affect the ability to define unfamiliar words. If readers are confronted with a high density of previously unknown words, they may be unwilling or simply unable to use the available cues to best advantage. Moreover, when the density of unknown words is great, it can be difficult to discern which cues refer to which words. Some unknown words may actually get in the way of defining other unknown words.

When you are confronted by a passage containing several unfamiliar words, it is important not to panic or become discouraged. Often, if you crack the code and define even one of the difficult terms, the remaining terms will become much easier to understand. Resist the temptation to give up, and force yourself to read a substantial portion of a given paragraph or passage before trying to figure out the meaning of the unknown terms.

Consider again the passage in Example 9-13. There are three unknown words here, and only the first is relatively easy to define. The boy was expecting praise, but he received *animadversion* instead. Figuring out that *animadversion* is harsh criticism will make easier the task of defining the subsequent two unknown words. As you figure out the meaning of each word, even if tentatively, it will help you with the others. At times, if you figure out the later unknown words, you may have to go back and revise your tentative definition of the unknown words that occurred earlier in the passage. Now consider again the passage in Example 9-14. Notice that there are four unknown words in this passage, and that their occurrences in close proximity make defining each word relatively more difficult. Consider how selective encoding, selective combination, and selective comparison applied to the context cues in this passage can help in your definition of each of the unknown words.

Concreteness of the Unknown Word and Its Context

The concreteness of the unknown word and of the context is another important mediator. Concrete words are words referring to concepts that can be perceived by the senses. Abstract words refer to those things that are not tangible, physical qualities or entities. Although it is convenient to refer to words as being either concrete or abstract, these attributes actually occur on a continuum. "Chair," "person," and "briefcase" are examples of concrete words. "Illness" and "warmth" are examples of words that straddle the line between concreteness and abstractness, and "freedom," "creativity," "communism," and "religion" are examples of abstract terms. It is usually easier to define concrete terms than abstract ones, because concrete terms have more straightforward definitions. Abstract terms are often difficult to define to the satisfaction of any large number of people. For example, what, exactly, does "freedom" mean?

As you read, it may be helpful to keep in mind whether you are working with a concrete or an abstract unknown word. First, the level of concreteness or abstractness of the concept the word represents may help you in deciding what information in the context is applicable to defining the word. Second, knowledge about the relative concreteness or abstractness of the term governs how "solid" a definition you may be able to give. The concreteness of the surrounding context also affects your ability to infer a word's meaning. In most cases, the greater the concreteness of the context, the easier it will be to define the word in question. If the passage is very abstract, you may have to compromise slightly in the quality of your definition.

Consider, for example, the word *thremmatologist* in Example 9-8. In this passage, we are dealing with a concrete context and a relatively concrete target word. Moreover, the context is relatively helpful. The cues are easily located and comprehended. In contrast, consider the meaning of the word *spaneria* and the surrounding context cues in Example 9-5. Here, the context that helps to define *spaneria* is more abstract, and the word itself has a more abstract meaning. As a result, it becomes more difficult to define this word.

Usefulness of Previously Acquired Information

Whenever people read, they generally attempt to connect the ideas described in the text to things they already know about the subject of the text, using the process of selective comparison. Sometimes, background knowledge can be very helpful in illuminating the meaning of a text and of an unknown word. Inevitably, the usefulness of selective comparison hinges on the relevance of past knowledge to understanding the situation presented in a new passage. In some cases, you may have a considerable amount of knowledge to bring to bear on the passage, but it simply may not be very helpful in identifying the meanings of unknown words; in other cases, this knowledge may provide the critical information you need for defining one or more unknown words.

In using prior knowledge, ask yourself what sorts of situations you are familiar with that are relevant to the context in which the unknown word appears; also, ask yourself whether the target word seems similar to any other words or combinations of words that you have experienced before. This type of conscious brainstorming can often force you to retrieve relevant information from way down in your memory, and thus serve as a basis for unearthing the critical clue in defining a new word.

Consider again the passage in Example 9-11. This passage has two target words, *oscitancy* and *lambative*. *Lambative* is simply a synonym for the word "lozenge." You need only a moderate amount of previous knowledge to figure out the meaning of this word. Even if you did not realize that lambative referred to a lozenge, you probably guessed that a lambative was a medicine or a cough remedy. Oscitancy presents a different story, however. Previous knowledge is quite useful. We learn that oscitancy is a side effect of C-37. But what kind of side effect? We learned that it is a common problem with relaxants. Have you ever used relaxants? How did you feel when you were under their influence? We also learned that the oscitancy potentially created by C-37 is exacerbated by alcohol. Have you ever combined cough medicine with a few alcoholic drinks? How did it make you feel? Probably you felt very sleepy. Defining this word will be easier for people with some experience with cough remedies and particularly for those people who have mixed alcohol and cough remedies. In this case, previous knowledge is almost a necessity for figuring out the meaning of the word. Consider also how previous knowledge can help you in defining the meaning of the word *syrt*, which appears in Example 9-15.

You have now learned about three kinds of entities that can help you figure out the meanings of unknown words. When you encounter an unknown word in context, attempt to apply the processes of selective encoding, selective combination, and selective comparison to each of the eight kinds of contextual cues described in this chapter. Keep in mind, as you attempt to define the unknown word or words that the mediators described earlier will make your job either easier or harder. Being aware of these mediators and attempting to use them to your advantage can facilitate your application of the processes to the context. If you have any doubts about how well this method can work, pick up a good novel and read until you come to an unfamiliar word. Use your knowledge about the processes, contextual cues, and mediating variables to aid you in defining the word. You may be pleasantly surprised with the result.

STRATEGIES FOR MEMORIZING

The emphasis in this chapter has been on learning meaningful material from context. Occasionally, however, you may need to memorize lists, facts, or basically unrelated strings of information. Maybe you have an exam coming up that emphasizes memorization, or perhaps you need to remember a shopping list. It is useful to have a set of strategies for memorizing these kinds of materials. These strategies are also called mnemonics. This section describes several different mnemonics.

Categorical Clustering

Suppose you need to memorize a small shopping list. How can you increase the chances that when you get to the supermarket, you will actually remember what you wanted to buy?

One helpful technique that you may already use is categorical clustering. In this technique, you group things together by the category they are in. For example, suppose you need to buy apples, milk, Cheerios, grapes, yogurt, Wheaties, Swiss cheese, grapefruit, and lettuce. Rather than trying to memorize the list in unordered fashion, it helps to memorize by categories:

Fruits – apples, grapes, grapefruit
Dairy Products – milk, yogurt, Swiss cheese
Cereals – Cheerios, Wheaties
Vegetables – lettuce

Organizing the list by categories will help you remember the items when you get to the supermarket. Make sure you also know the number of categories you have memorized, so that if one is missing, you will know that you need to remember another category of things to buy.

Here is a list of things to buy at the hardware store. Use categorical clustering to help you learn the list: "screws, hammer, mousetraps, box of nails, pliers, bug spray, saw, thumbtacks, flypaper." Remember to count categories so that you know how many different kinds of things you will need to buy.

Interactive Imagery

Interactions within a List of Words

Sometimes the list you need to remember does not fit nicely into convenient categories. In such cases, you will need a more general method to help you remember the list. Suppose, for example, that you need to remember a list of basically unrelated words: cat, table, pencil, hook, mirror, radio, Kansas, rain, electricity, stone. A useful technique for learning such lists is to generate *interactive image*. For example, you might imagine a *cat* sitting on a *table* holding a *pencil* in its paw and writing in a *book*, with *rain* pouring over *Kansas* (as pictured from a map) that lands on a *radio* that is sitting on a *stone*, which generates *electricity*, reflected in a *mirror*. The number of items you wish to place in any one interactive image will depend on what you find comfortable when you have to remember the words. Generally, however, the interactive images will facilitate your recall of the list of words.

Pegwords

Sometimes it is easier to use a pegword system for remembering a list of words. In this system, each word is associated with a word on a previously memorized list, and an interactive image is created between the two words. The following list is frequently used:

One is a bun.   Six is a stick.
Two is a shoe.   Seven is heaven.
Three is a tree.   Eight is a gate.
Four is a door.   Nine is a dime.
Five is a hive.   Ten is a hen.

Once you memorize this list, you can use it over and over again as a basis for learning new lists.

Consider, for example, the previous list. The first word is *cat*: You might visualize a cat eating a delicious bun. The second word is *table*: You might imagine a shoe atop a tall table. The third word is *pencil*: You might visualize one large branch of a tree that ends with a sharp pencil point. The fourth word is *book*: You might imagine a door that is in fact the cover of a book with which you are familiar. The fifth word is *mirror*: You might imagine bees in a hive looking at themselves in a mirror. Then go on forming interactive images for each of the words in the list. When you need to remember the words, you first recall the numbered images and then recall the words when you visualize them in the interactive images. This technique has the advantage of facilitating recall of the order of the words as well as of the words themselves.

These techniques help facilitate recall because it is easier to remember interactive images than to remember words. Now, try applying each of the two techniques described above (interactive images within the list and pegwords) to the following two lists of words:

1. *gorilla, dictionary, word, teacher, pear, sinister air, lunch, red, tooth*
2. *rock, ocean, tail, pretty, eraser, love, radiator, plug, television, rose*

Method of Loci

Yet another technique for memorizing words that makes use of interactive imagery is called the *method of loci*. This technique dates from ancient times, when it was used by orators who wished to remember key concepts for their speeches. The idea is simple: Visualize a walk around an area you know well. It might be your college campus, or the neighborhood in which you grew up. Along this walk there should be some major landmarks with which you are familiar – your own house, a neighborhood park, a stream, and so on. Decide in advance on the mental walk you will take and the landmarks you will visualize along the way.

Later, when you need to memorize a list of words, take the mental walk, depositing each word to be memorized along the walk at one of the distinctive landmarks. Visualize an interactive image between the new word and the landmark. For example, consider the following short list of words: *computer, ink, bird, heart, snow*. Suppose the first five landmarks on your mental walk are dormitory, a small stream, a clump of trees, a clock tower, and the building in which English classes are held. You might imagine a large *computer* in the lobby of your dormitory, *ink* (rather than water) flowing down the stream, a *bird* singing in the clump of trees, a *heart* beating the seconds where the clock normally is, and *snow* covering the English building. When you wish to remember the list, take your mental walk, and pick up the words you have learned from each of the landmarks along the walk.

Here is a new list of words. Use the method of loci with a familiar route to memorize and then recall the list of words: *rug, grave, blue, kangaroo, television, crate, briefcase, car, laugh, wheat.*

Verbal Mnemonics

We already discussed this concept briefly on page 84. Here, we will go into more detail.

Acronyms

These techniques make use of verbal rather than imagery-based encodings for words you wish to remember. An acronym is a word or expression each of whose letters stand for a certain other word or concept. For example, suppose you want to remember the list *Indian, roast, crater, hanger, pain*. You might form the acronym CHIRP, with the first letter of each word to be memorized represented by one of its letters: Crater, Hanger, Indian, Roast, Pain. One popular real-life example is HOMES, a mnemonic used to remember the great lakes of Michigan: Huron, Ontario, Michigan, Erie, and Superior. Another is ROY G. BIV, which stands for the colors of the rainbow – Red, Orange, Yellow, Green, Blue, Indigo, and Violet. This technique is useful if the first letters of the words to be memorized actually can be formed into a single word, or something close to one. It is less useful if the letters just don't happen to form into a word (although, as in Roy G. Biv, it doesn't have to always be a "real" word). It is also important to note that you have to remember what each letter stands for; one of us regularly has students who write out the relevant acronym on an exam but nevertheless do not remember the correct answer.

Acrostics

In an acrostic, one forms a sentence rather than a single word to help one remember the new words. For example, the list above might be remembered by the sentence "Children hop in roadsters punctually." There are many common real-life acrostics. If you have ever taken piano lessons, you may already know "Every good boy does fine," which stands for all of the treble notes (E, G, B, D, F). Another popular one is "My very elegant mother just sat upon nine pins," which is a way of remembering the correct order of the planets (from closest to the sun to furthest) – Mercury, Venus, Earth, Mars, Jupiter, Saturn, Uranus, Neptune, and Pluto (no longer considered a planet).

Rhymes

Sometimes you can remember a series of words or a set of rules through rhymes. For example, if you are trying to remember how many days are in March, you can remember a mnemonic rhyme that begins, "Thirty days hath September/April, June, and November/All the rest have thirty-one . . . " (The rest of the rhyme discusses the odd nature of February.) Similarly, the fates of the six wives of Henry VIII can be remembered with

> Divorced, Beheaded, Died,
> Divorced, Beheaded, Survived

There's one rhyme that many of us used to learn to speak English – the Alphabet song ("A, B, C, D," etc.). How many of you thought that ellemenno (LMNO) was its own letter?

Use an acronym, acrostic, or rhyme to memorize the words in each of the following two lists:

1. *normal, baseball, story, intelligence, laundry, engine, gate, soap*
2. *terror, hotel, pavement, relish, curtain, seer, wood, lesson*

To summarize, a variety of methods – categorical clustering, interactive imagery between words in the list, pegwords, the method of loci, acronyms, acrostics, and rhymes – can help you memorize lists of words. Using these methods is usually much easier than rote memorization.

SUMMING UP

We've discussed in this chapter knowledge-acquisition components that can help you learn new information and better remember old information. The next chapter will focus exclusively on new things – specifically, how well you can cope with novelty.

Definitions of Unknown Words in Examples

acapnotic:	a nonsmoker.
animadversion:	harsh, adverse criticism.
bolide:	a shooting star; an exploding meteor.
catachresis:	incorrect use of a word or phrase.
cecity:	blindness.
ceilidh:	a visit; a private conversation.
diaskeuasis:	editorial revision.
ecchymosis:	a bruise or contusion; a black-and-blue mark.
eremophobia:	fear of loneliness.
eructation:	a belch.
flitwite:	a fine for fighting.
hamartiology:	the study of sin.
lambative:	medicine in lozenge form.
macropodida:	kangaroo.
oam:	steam.
oont:	a camel.
oscitancy:	drowsiness.
phalacrosis:	baldness; a bald spot.
pococurante:	a nonchalant or indifferent person.
podobromhidrosis:	smelly feet.
rackarock:	an explosive; a firecracker.
solecism:	incorrect usage of words.
sommelier.	a wine steward.
spaneria:	a scarcity of men.
syrt:	quicksand, bog.
thremmatologist:	a specialist in animal breeding.

10

Coping with Novelty

An important aspect of intelligence is the ability to cope with the unknown and the unexpected. Often, new tasks and situations are the ones that most require us to exercise our intelligence. Coping with novelty can take different forms. Sometimes, the novelty is understanding a new task or situation. Other times, the novelty is knowing what to do in a new kind of task or situation. One of the most important mental skills for dealing with novelty is insight.

INSIGHT

In this section of the chapter, we will provide a brief description of the phenomenon of insight and talk about theories that attempt to characterize it.

People have been interested in the nature of *insight* for many years. It is easy to see why. The greatest discoveries in scientific history were often discovered by insight. Think of Copernicus realizing that the Sun rather than the Earth is the center of the solar system, or Galileo understanding that two objects will fall from a height at the same rate of speed regardless of their weights. On a more day-to-day basis, think of the insights that you have had into your own life. Perhaps you realized that you were truly in love, or that you wanted to change your major and pursue psychology as a career. It would be to everyone's advantage to understand the mental processes underlying insight.

The Nature of Insight

Conventional views of insight fall into two basic camps – the special – process views and the nothing-special views (Perkins, 1981; Sternberg & Davidson, 1995). According to *special-process* views, insight is a process that is different from ordinary types of information processing. Among these views are the ideas that insight results from extended unconscious leaps in thinking, that it results from greatly accelerated mental processing, and that it results from a short-circuiting of normal reasoning processes.

These views are appealing and seem to make sense. However, they appear to carry with them at least three problematical aspects.

First, they do not really pin down what insight is. Calling insight an "unconscious leap" or a "short-circuiting" makes insight sound like pretty much a "black box" of unknown contents. Even if one of these theories were correct, just what insight is would remain to be identified. Second, virtually all the evidence in support of these views is anecdotal rather than experimental. For each piece of anecdotal evidence to support one of these views, there is at least one corresponding piece of evidence to refute it. Finally, as they stand, the positions are probably not pinned down sufficiently to allow experimental tests. As a result, it is not clear that the positions could even be proven right or wrong. This characteristic may be responsible for there being so little research. If something cannot ever be proven right or wrong, there is less of a temptation to study it.

According to the *nothing-special* views, insight is merely an extension of ordinary perceiving, recognizing, learning, and conceiving. This view, most forcefully argued by David Perkins (1981), Patrick Langley and Randolph Jones (1988), and Robert Weisberg (1995, 2006), would look at past failures to identify any special processes of insight as being a result of the (alleged) fact that there is no special process of insight. Insights are merely significant products of ordinary processes. We can understand the kind of frustration that would lead Perkins and others to this view: After repeated failures to identify a construct experimentally, the theorist can easily be tempted to ascribe the failure to the nonexistence of the construct. We cannot find what is not there! But it is not clear to us that we should yet be ready to abandon the notion that there is something special about insight. Arguments for the nothing-special views have been arguments by default. In other words, because we have not identified any of these processes, we are to believe that they have no independent existence. Such arguments would be unacceptable if we were able to make a positive case for the existence of insight processes.

The Triarchic View of Insight

The view of insight that we prefer (Davidson & Sternberg, 1984; Sternberg & Davidson, 1982) is that insight consists of not one but three separate but related psychological processes:

1. *Selective encoding.* Selective encoding involves sifting out relevant information from irrelevant information. Significant problems generally present us with large amounts of information, only some of which is relevant to problem solution. For example, the facts of a legal case are usually both numerous and confusing: An insightful lawyer must figure out which of the myriad facts are relevant to principles of law. Similarly, a doctor or a psychotherapist must sift out those facts that are relevant for diagnosis or treatment. Perhaps the occupation that most directly must employ selective encoding is that of the detective: In trying to figure out who has perpetrated a crime, the detective must figure out what the relevant facts are. Failure to do so may

result in the detective's following up on false leads, or in having no leads to follow up on at all.

2. *Selective combination.* Selective combination involves combining what might originally seem to be isolated pieces of information into a unified whole that may or may not resemble its parts. For example, the lawyer must know how the relevant facts of a case fit together to make (or break) the case. A doctor or psychotherapist must be able to figure out how to combine information about various isolated symptoms to identify a given medical (or psychological) syndrome. A detective, having collected the facts that seem relevant to the case, must determine how they fit together to point at the guilty party rather than at anyone else.

3. *Selective comparison.* Selective comparison involves relating newly acquired information to old information that you already have. Problem solving by analogy, for example, is an instance of selective comparison: The solver realizes that new information is similar to old information in certain ways (and dissimilar from it in other ways) and uses this information better to understand the new information. For example, an insightful lawyer will relate a current case to past legal precedents; choosing the right precedent is absolutely essential. A doctor or psychotherapist relates the current set of symptoms to previous case histories in his or her own or in others' past experiences. Again, choosing the right precedents is essential. A detective may have been involved in or know about a similar case where the same method was used to commit a crime. Drawing an analogy to the past case may be helpful to the detective both in understanding the nature of the crime and in figuring out who did it.

It should be evident that the processes of insight that are being proposed here are the same as the processes of knowledge acquisition proposed in the last chapter. Is insight, then, really nothing at all special, but merely a mundane extension of knowledge-acquisition skills? We do not believe this to be the case. What seems to separate insightful use of selective encoding, selective combination, and selective comparison from ordinary use of these processes is that it is not at all obvious how or where they should be applied. By contrast, the nature of the problem in learning vocabulary from context is very clear: The task is to define the unknown word. Moreover, the kinds of clues that are useful in defining an unknown word are very specific. Therefore, with practice, the finding and use of these clues can become fairly routine. In insightful selective encoding, selective combination, and selective comparison, it is not obvious how to apply these processes. Often it is not even obvious that they are appropriate in the first place.

We therefore agree with Perkins and others taking the position that the processes of insight are the same as ordinary cognitive processes. However, the circumstances of their application are different. It is much more difficult to apply selective encoding, selective combination, and selective comparison in an insightful way than it is to apply them in a routine way. Thus, we do not agree with Perkins that insightful processing differs from noninsightful processing only in terms of the way the product is evaluated.

INSIGHT PROBLEMS

Selective Encoding

Consider the following problem. As you do so, think about how selective encoding can help you to solve the problem.

> Many scientists have offered explanations for the total extinction of dinosaurs and other creatures sixty-five million years ago. One of the facts agreed on by most geologists is that the earth was struck by a huge asteroid or comet approximately ten kilometers in diameter. The data that support this theory rest on the fact that a thin layer of iridium, an element found mainly in meteors, is present in geological strata throughout the world. (Scientists know that the iridium itself did not cause the extinction of dinosaurs and plants, but it is simply proof that some catastrophic event involving meteors took place.)
>
> The scientists explain that an asteroid crashed into the earth and caused huge amounts of dust and dirt to fly into the atmosphere. The dust blocked the sunlight, according to scientists, for approximately three months to a year, which caused the land to cool. Many animals died from starvation and from the cold.
>
> One of the misunderstood things, until now, is the reason why the ocean ecology died. The ocean mass – which was then even larger than it is now – did not change temperature as drastically as did the earth. In view of the evidence, scientists have come up with an explanation. What might that explanation be?

In order to find relevant information, you might want to go through the following steps, at least mentally: First, restate the problem. A meteor crash killed many animals. What information in this description of the event might show why a meteor crash also would kill ocean animals and plants?

Second, list all the information in the problem. In this problem, such information would include the following facts: (a) dinosaurs and other animals died suddenly sixty-five million years ago; (b) the earth was struck by a huge asteroid ten kilometers in diameter; (c) a layer of iridium, mainly an element from meteors, is embedded throughout the earth; (d) when the meteor crashed, huge amounts of dust and dirt were thrown into the atmosphere; (e) dust blocked sunlight for three months to a year; (f) the land cooled; (g) the ocean mass was much larger than the land mass; and (h) the temperature change was not important to the ocean.

Third, eliminate items of information that are likely irrelevant in solving the problem. In this case, information about the land, dinosaurs, and animals, the earth's being struck by the asteroid, and the layer of iridium is probably not directly relevant to this problem.

Fourth, consider the information that is relevant to solving the problem. In this problem, such information would include facts that might explain the results of the crash of the meteorite: that it threw large amounts of dust out into the atmosphere, that the dust blocked sunlight for three months to a year, that the land cooled in the darkness, and that the ocean temperature change was not important.

Fifth, think about whether or not you might be able to gather more information from the given relevant information. For example, the fact that large amounts of dust were thrown into the atmosphere would result in air pollution and blockage of sunlight. What effect might a blockage of sunlight have on the ocean ecology? What effect might pollution have on this ecology? What effect might the death of the plant life in the seas, as a result of a lack of sunlight, have on the total food chain on which all animals in the sea depend?

ARITHMETICAL AND LOGICAL WORD PROBLEMS

In this section of the chapter, we will review the role of selective encoding in arithmetical and logical word problems. To begin, consider the following problem:

> You have black socks and blue socks in a drawer, mixed in a ratio of four to five. Because it is dark, you are unable to see the colors of the socks that you take out of the drawer. How many socks do you have to take out of the drawer to be assured of having a pair of socks of the same color?

This problem is a good example of the importance of selective encoding. People who answer the problem incorrectly tend to focus on information in the problem that is actually irrelevant, namely, that the sock colors are mixed in a ratio of four to five. There are at least three reasons why this information might *seem* to be relevant, at first reading. First, people often assume that all the numbers given us in a mathematical problem will be relevant to solving that problem. This assumption, however, is incorrect. Second, there are so few numbers in this particular problem that people would assume that each hint given would be relevant, even if they did not always make this assumption. Third, people often start to solve problems of this kind by figuring out how to use the numbers given in the problem before they even consider whether the information is relevant to the solution of the problem. Thus, people who answer the problem incorrectly often do so because they are misled by the irrelevant information in it.

The correct answer is "three." Consider the possibilities. If the first sock is blue and the second sock is blue, you immediately have a pair. Similarly, if the first sock is black and the second sock is black, you also immediately have a pair. At worst, the first sock will be blue and the second sock black, or vice versa. In this case, it will take a third sock to create a pair of one color or the other.

In some cases, the use of selective encoding is on a fairly large scale, and the need for it may therefore suggest itself immediately, at least to some people. In other cases, selective encoding may need to be applied only on a very small scale, but its application may nevertheless determine the correct answer to a problem, as in the following:

> A teacher had twenty-three pupils in his class. All but seven of them went on a museum trip and thus were away for the day. How many of them remained in class that day?

This problem again requires selective encoding for its correct solution. People frequently read the problem and immediately subtract seven from twenty-three to obtain sixteen as their answer. But this answer is incorrect. The critical word in the problem is "but." It is not the case that seven students went on the museum trip but rather that "all but seven" went on the trip. Thus, the fact that there are a total of twenty-three students in the class actually becomes irrelevant, even though it is one of only two numbers in the problem. The correct answer to the problem is actually the single number in the problem that is relevant to the problem's solution, namely, seven.

EXERCISE 10.1

Each of the following arithmetical or logical word problems requires selective encoding for its solution. First list the relevant information for solving each problem (selective encoding). Then solve each problem. Answers appear after the problems.

1. According to the U.S. Constitution, if the vice president of the United States should die, who would be the president?

2. A man who lived in a small town in America married twenty different women in that same town. All of them are still living, and he never divorced any of them. Yet he broke no laws. How could he do this?

3. A man was putting some finishing touches on his house and realized that he needed something that he did not have. He went to the hardware store and asked the clerk, "How much will 150 cost me?" The clerk in the hardware store answered, "They are 75 cents apiece, so 150 will cost you $2.25." What did the man buy?

4. Fifteen percent of the people in a certain town have unlisted telephone numbers. You select two hundred names at random from the local phone book. How many of these people can be expected to have unlisted telephone numbers?

5. In the Thompson family, there are five brothers, and each brother has one sister. If you count Mrs. Thompson, how many females are there in the Thompson family?

6. A taxi driver picked up a fare at the Hyatt Regency Hotel who wanted to go to the airport. The traffic was heavy, and the taxicab's average speed for the entire trip was just forty miles per hour. The total time of the trip was eighty minutes, and the customer was charged accordingly. At the airport, the taxi driver picked up another customer who wanted to be taken to the same Hyatt Regency Hotel. The taxi driver returned to the hotel along the same route that he had used just before, and traveled with the same average speed. But this time the trip took an hour and twenty minutes. Can you explain why?

7. A clothing store ordered eighty new dresses. Each dress cost the manager $40. The total bill was $3,200. After he had placed the order, the store manager discovered that had he ordered one hundred or more dresses, he would have received a 10 percent discount. If the manager had ordered five more dresses, how much more would he have had to pay?

8. One day, a woman hailed a passing taxicab. On the way to her destination, she chattered incessantly. The taxi driver got annoyed. In desperation, he finally said, "Lady, I can see in the mirror that you are trying to talk to me. I'm very sorry, but I cannot hear a single word you are saying. I am extremely hard of hearing, and my hearing aid has not worked all day." When the woman heard this, she stopped talking, feeling very sorry for the driver. But after she got out at her destination, paid her fare, and watched the cab drive away, she suddenly realized that the driver had lied to her. How did she know that the driver had lied?

9. Susan gets in her car in Boston and drives toward New York City, averaging fifty miles per hour. Twenty minutes later, Ellen gets in her car in New York City and starts driving toward Boston, averaging sixty miles per hour. Both women take the same route, which extends a total of 220 miles between the two cities. Which car is nearer to Boston when they meet?

10. Howard is given a choice of three doors and must open one of them. Behind Door #1, there are raging fires. Behind Door #2, there are a hundred assassins with knives and guns. Behind Door #3, there are lions that haven't eaten in three years. Which door would be safest to open?

Answers to Arithmetical and Logical Word Problems

(1) The president. The death of the vice president has no effect on who is the president.

(2) The man is a minister. The critical word in this problem is "married." The man married the various women, but he did not himself become married to them.

(3) The man was buying house numbers. His address is 150, so he needs three numbers for a total cost of $2.25.

(4) None. Unlisted numbers do not appear in the phone book.

(5) Two. The only females in the family are the mother and her one daughter, who is the sister to each of her brothers.

(6) Eighty minutes and one hour and twenty minutes are the same amount of time.

(7) $200.00. Because the store manager still was not buying one hundred or more dresses, he received no discount.

(8) The lady knew that the taxicab driver was lying because he had taken her to the destination that she had orally asked him to take her to.

(9) Each car is at the same distance from Boston when they meet, as the cars are immediately next to each other.

(10) Door #3. If the lions hadn't eaten in three years, they would be dead.

A famous problem requiring careful selective encoding requirements is the following:

An airplane crashes on the U.S.-Canadian border. In what country are the survivors buried?

The correct solution to this problem requires careful reading and selective encoding of the word "survivors." Unless you read the problem very carefully, you will not come up with the correct answer that survivors are not buried.

INFORMATION-EVALUATION PROBLEMS

Selective encoding is also important for finding solutions to information-evaluation problems. In this type of problem, it is important to determine which pieces of information are relevant out of all the possible information that might be available. To illustrate, consider the following problem:

> How do desert animals withstand the heat of the desert?
> a. Most desert animals cannot tolerate temperatures above 150 degrees Fahrenheit.
> b. Desert animals are often nocturnal, and live inside burrows (underground tunnels) during the day.
> c. A typical burrow does not get any hotter than 80 degrees Fahrenheit.
> d. The burrows of desert animals have high relative humidity, which comes from the animals' own water vapor.
> e. The burrows prevent animals from becoming dehydrated.

Notice that among the facts available, there is one that are irrelevant to finding the solution to the problem – (d). The important strategy in finding solutions to this problem is to avoid being distracted by irrelevant information.

EXERCISE 10.2

In each of the following problems, you are presented with a question and a number of facts. Mark each fact as either relevant (R) or irrelevant (I) for answering the questions. In some cases, pieces of information may be relevant only when considered in conjunction with each other. In such cases, both pieces of information should be marked as relevant. You should therefore read all of the statements before marking any of them as relevant or irrelevant. Answers appear after the problems.

1. How much work is performed in pulling on a stuck drawer?
  a. Many people think studying involves hard work.
  b. To the scientist, work is a measurable physical quantity in the same sense that length and height are measurable.
  c. Work can be accomplished in pushing a car up a hill.
  d. To qualify as a form of work, a force must push an object for a distance.

2. Why do television sets with cable connections get better reception than televisions with antennae?
  a. Televisions flash pictures on a screen at a rate of thirty pictures per second and so produce the effect of continuous motion.
  b. At the broadcast station, a television image must be analyzed into two hundred thousand electrical charges.

    c. Each of the two hundred thousand charges is discharged thirty times per second and transmitted to the viewers.

    d. The picture can be transmitted by a coaxial cable, which travels directly from the broadcast source to the viewer.

    e. Most television pictures are transmitted by waves (high-frequency short waves) similar to those used by radio stations.

    f. High-frequency short waves can travel only in straight lines; they cannot bend to follow the earth's surface. Their range is limited to the visual horizon.

3. Why are protective laboratory goggles made from Plexiglas?

    a. Ultraviolet rays and X-rays pass through Plexiglas, but heat rays do not.

    b. Plexiglas is widely used in surgery for artificial limbs.

    c. Plexiglas has better transparency than ordinary glass.

    d. Plexiglas can withstand heat as high as 100 degrees Centigrade.

    e. Plexiglas resists water, caustic alkalis, dilute acids, gasoline, and mineral oil.

    f. Plexiglas can be used to replace defective heart valves.

4. Why is it necessary to add detergent to water in order to wash clothes?

    a. The combination of detergent and water allows the detergent to penetrate between the clothes and the dirt.

    b. One hundred pounds of domestic washing is soiled with between two and four pounds of dirt.

    c. Most dirt cannot be dissolved by water alone.

    d. One hundred pounds of domestic washing usually has 0.9 pounds of protein-free organic matter (waxes, alcohol), 0.3 pounds of protein (hair, skin), 0.15 pounds of grease and sweat, as well as sand and dust.

5. Why does only a fraction of an iceberg show above water?

    a. Icebergs are huge ice mountains that float.

    b. They are brilliantly lit and majestic.

    c. Icebergs may provide a source of fresh water.

    d. When water freezes into ice, it expands in size and becomes less dense. Ice is a little lighter than water.

    e. Icebergs have posed a great danger to ships in the past.

    f. Icebergs break off from the polar icecap.

6. Where do space satellites get the electricity to run their electronic equipment?

    a. Weather satellites, communication satellites, and probes are unmanned.

    b. The storage batteries of U.S. satellites are kept charged by current generated in solar cells.

    c. Satellites can alter their courses with control jets when they receive commands from earth monitoring stations.

    d. In 1965, the space probe Mariner 4 took twenty-one pictures of the planet Mars from a distance of six thousand miles.

7. Are cameras limited to taking pictures only of things that can be seen by the human eye?

    a. Cameras can photograph heat waves.

    b. An infrared camera can take pictures in complete darkness.

c. X rays can photograph the inside of the human body partly because X-rays are only one hundred angstroms in length.

Answers to Information-Evaluation Problems*

1.		2.		3.		4.		5.		6.		7.	
a.	I	a.	I	a.	R	a.	R	a.	R	a.	I	a.	R
b.	I	b.	I	b.	I	b.	I	b.	I	b.	R	b.	R
c.	I	c.	I	c.	R	c.	R	c.	I	c.	I	c.	R
d.	R	d.	R	d.	R	d.	I	d.	R	d.	I		
		e.	R	e.	R			e.	I				
		f.	R	f.	I			f.	I				

* Alternative answers are acceptable if you can provide a compelling justification.

MYSTERY PROBLEMS

It was said earlier that a classic situation for insights is the situation faced by a detective trying to solve a crime. Selective encoding can be particularly important in detective work. Let us consider the following mystery story and solve it, using selective encoding as a primary basis for solution.

Trying to fight his seasickness, Detective Ramirez went through the long corridor that led to the cabin of the late Mr. Saunders. Once he got to the cabin, Detective Ramirez saw Mr. Saunders's body slumped over the dresser. A small gun lay in one of his hands. Approaching the dresser, Ramirez could see some loose papers on it. Among them was a suicide note. In the suicide note, Mr. Saunders explained why he had suddenly decided to end his life. A pen without its cover was also on the dresser.

While reading the suicide note, Ramirez thought he would never understand how a famous writer such as Saunders could have committed suicide. Saunders was Detective Ramirez's favorite mystery writer, so Saunders's death upset him very much.

Ramirez shifted his eyes from the note to Saunders's body, which was lying on its left side. Saunders had been a tall man in his forties with fair complexion and blond hair that somehow masked a long scar on his right cheek. The body was dressed in a well-cut dark suit that showed the writer's taste for the good things in life. "What a loss," Ramirez thought.

A noise in the background reminded Ramirez that there were two more people in the cabin besides him: the ship's captain and Mr. Saunders's nephew, Mr. Prince, who was the one who had discovered the body. Detective Ramirez asked Prince to tell him everything he had heard or seen regarding the incident.

"We came back to Mr. Saunders's cabin shortly after the captain's reception was over," said Mr. Prince. "Mr. Saunders – my uncle – told me he wanted to be alone. He wanted to take some notes for his next book. So I left the cabin and went directly to my own cabin, which is next door."

"What happened after that?" asked Detective Ramirez.

"Shortly after I left, I heard a shot," Mr. Prince continued, "and when I came in, I saw my uncle's body slumped on the dresser. I called his name but I did not get any reply, so I went closer to see why he did not answer and then I noticed the bullet through his left temple."

"Did you touch anything?" asked Detective Ramirez.

"No, I did not. I left everything the way it was."

Ramirez was certain that the apparent suicide was in fact a murder. He said to Mr. Prince, "You'd better tell me the whole truth." How did Detective Ramirez know that Mr. Saunders's death was murder, not suicide?

The basis on which Ramirez concluded that Mr. Saunders was murdered was based on one relevant fact – Mr. Prince could not have known his uncle had a bullet through his left temple unless he had moved the body. Mr. Saunders fell on his left side and the wound was not visible. In fact, Ramirez noticed Saunders's right cheek, which has a scar on it. This example illustrates the importance of selective encoding in the detective work – the main task is to "discover" the most relevant fact among a number of facts available.

EXERCISE 10.3

Now try to solve the following three stories on your own. Note that the answers appear after the problems (but do not look at them before you try your best to solve the problems).

1. Detective Ramirez was about to go to bed after one of those very hot summer days in New York. He had already put his pajamas on when the clock struck nine and the phone rang. It was the police chief inspector, named Smith, who asked Ramirez to go immediately to a very old house on the city outskirts. It was raining so it took Ramirez a while before he got to the house.

As soon as Detective Ramirez met Inspector Smith, he asked him what the problem was.

"This is Mr. Brown," said Smith, "he can explain everything better than I can."

"Well?" said Ramirez to a very nervous man who seemed to be in shock.

"We came back from the movies around 7:00 P.M. My wife went directly to our bedroom while I stayed in the library doing some work. One hour later, I went upstairs to go to bed and I found our bedroom locked. I tried to get some response from my wife but I did not succeed. I thought she had forgotten to unlock the door and was taking a bath so I went back to the library and worked half an hour more. When I went back upstairs and again got no response, I started to worry and called the police," said Mr. Brown.

"Show us the room," said Ramirez.

Once upstairs, Ramirez tried to force the door but he could not do it. He asked Brown if there was another way to enter the room. Mr. Brown called one of the servants and asked him to take Detective Ramirez outside the house and show him a window on the second floor. Once outside, Ramirez put a ladder up to the window and climbed up. When he finally entered the room, he could barely see enough to find the switch to turn on the light. He then opened the door to let Smith in. Mrs. Brown's body was slumped over a fine desk. There was a suicide note under the dead woman's hand. The handwriting was erratic and the lines sloped down to one side. The pen was still firmly grasped in the woman's hand. The woman explained why she had taken her life, yet it was difficult to figure out what she said due to her messy writing. Just at that moment the oldest son arrived. When he saw the police there, he asked at once what was going on. The police officer told him there had been a death. His mother had committed suicide. When the young man heard this, he rushed up and found Detective Ramirez, Inspector Smith, and Mr. Brown reading the note. They were talking about the difficulty of reading the woman's handwriting.

"If only she had written a more legible note," said Inspector Smith. To which the young man replied: "Mother could never see very well in the dark."

Ramirez lit a cigar, looked at the young man, and asked him where he had been for the last three hours. Between sobs, the young man said to Ramirez, "I was in a nearby movie theater. I left home around 6:30 P.M. to get to the movie on time. Once the movie ended, I came home and found this terrible event." Ramirez looked at the young man and said, "I would like you to come with me to police headquarters. I do not believe this was suicide; I think it was murder." Why did Ramirez suspect Brown's son?

2. Sitting in his office, Detective Ramirez was ready to question Mr. Haggerty about his friend's death. At that moment the phone rang. It was the coroner. He called Detective Ramirez to report the cause of Mr. Lynch's death.

"The body has bruises everywhere, but Lynch died from a blow on the back of his head," said the coroner to Detective Ramirez. As soon as Ramirez hung up the phone, Mr. Haggerty started to tell in his very soft voice his version of what had happened to his friend, Mr. Lynch. "Last night we were coming back from a party riding our motorcycles. It was raining very hard so we could hardly see where we were going. The only thing that prevented the rain from blinding us was our helmets. The streets were getting very slippery, so we had to ride very carefully to avoid an accident. We had downed a few drinks at the party and Lynch had a few more than I did. He said he was getting tired of driving in the rain and getting all wet so he was going to go faster to get home sooner. I told him it was very dangerous to go faster; it was better to take it easy. But he did not listen to what I said and started to go faster and faster. I tried to make him listen to reason but he paid no attention. Suddenly we got on a steep downhill street and Lynch tried to slow down, but his motorcycle spun around and he flew over the handlebars, hitting his head against a telephone pole. I got off my motorcycle and knelt down to help him, but he was already dead." Detective Ramirez smiled as he booked Mr. Haggerty as a murder suspect.

Why did Detective Ramirez arrest Mr. Haggerty?

3. It was 4:00 in the afternoon when Detective Ramirez was on his way to a hotel located on Casanova Avenue. A few minutes before, somebody had phoned

Ramirez to inform him of a death in the hotel. As soon as Ramirez arrived, he asked the hotel manager to tell him what he knew. "This afternoon at around 3:45 P.M. one of the maids told me about the incident."

"Could you tell me where to find this maid? I would like to ask her some questions," said Ramirez. "Sure, I will send for her right away," the manager said. As soon as Ramirez met the maid, he asked her to explain everything she knew about the incident. "Very well, sir! Usually, room 44 is one of the first rooms I clean after lunch, but today the 'Do not disturb' sign hung on the doorknob. I could hear the radio playing softly. So I went ahead and cleaned the other rooms. At 3:30 P.M., the sign was still there, so I started to wonder if maybe Ms. Rose was sick or had forgotten to remove the sign. I knocked on the door and there was no answer. Everything was quiet. I used my key to open the door and there I saw her, lying on her bed. She was very pale and her eyes were lifeless. I got scared and ran downstairs to tell the manager about it." Ramirez asked the manager to tell him what he knew about the event. "Well . . . when the maid came to inform me about the incident, both of us went upstairs to room 44 and there she was, lying on her bed, dead."

"Could you please take me to the room?" asked Ramirez.

"Sure I can! Follow me," said the hotel manager.

As soon as Detective Ramirez entered Ms. Rose's room he saw her lying on her bed, dead. Everything was quiet and there was no sign of any violent struggle or damage caused by somebody breaking into the room. Everything seemed to be in perfect order. Some details in the room gave Detective Ramirez some indication of the dead woman's personality. There were flowers in a vase on a small table beside the window. There were some magazines and newspapers on a chair facing the small table. There was a big picture of the deceased on the bureau. In Ms. Rose's right hand there was a covered bottle of sleeping pills; only two were left. It looked like a typical suicide.

Touching the deceased's body, Detective Ramirez said, "This woman has been dead for hours." He asked the hotel manager, "Did you remove anything in this room?"

"No, we did not remove anything at all!"

"There is something odd here and I am going to find what it is," said Ramirez. He called the police chief on his cell phone. "Chief, I'm going to be here longer than I thought. We're looking at a possible murder here."

Why does Detective Ramirez think there was something odd going on?

Answers to Mystery Problems

1. How does Mr. Brown's son know that the lights were off in his parents' bedroom at the time his mother was writing the note?

2. It would be impossible to hold a conversation such as the one Haggerty described, while riding motorcycles with helmets on in a hard rain, especially because Haggerty has a soft voice.

3. Ms. Rose had been dead for hours, so someone must have turned off the radio that the maid heard after lunch but not at 3:30.

You have now completed various kinds of exercises on the process of selective encoding. The emphasis in these exercises was on your improving your ability to separate relevant from irrelevant information. In the next section, we will consider the problem of how to selectively combine information once you have decided it is relevant for problem solution.

Selective Combination

Let us start by saying that selective combination refers to the process of putting pieces of information together in new ways. In this section, we will go through a number of examples to illustrate selective combination in action.

Arithmetical and Logical Word Problems

Consider the following problem

> There were one hundred politicians at a meeting. Each politician was either honest or dishonest. We know the following two facts: First, at least one of the politicians was honest. Second, for any two politicians, at least one of the two was dishonest. How many of the politicians were honest and how many were dishonest, and what are the respective numbers of each?

In this particular problem, selective encoding of information is not particularly difficult. Indeed, the relevant clues – that at least one politician was honest and that for any two politicians, at least one was dishonest – are even emphasized. The problem is to figure out how to combine these clues.

The first clue tells you that there is at least one honest politician, and from this clue, you can infer that there are possibly ninety-nine dishonest politicians. Of course, there may be fewer than ninety-nine dishonest politicians. The second clue tells you that, if you take any two politicians, you are guaranteed that at least one of them (and possibly both of them) will be dishonest. Combining these two clues gives you an answer to the problem. The second clue tells you that if you take the honest politician in the first clue and match that politician with any other of the ninety-nine politicians, at least one of the two politicians will be dishonest. Now, because you know that the politician from the first clue is honest, it follows that the other ninety-nine must be dishonest. There is no other way of guaranteeing that at least one politician in each pair will be dishonest. You can conclude, then, that there is one honest politician and there are ninety-nine dishonest politicians.

Now, consider another selective combination problem that many people find to be quite difficult, despite its deceptively simple appearance:

> I bought one share in the Sure-Fire Corporation for $70. I sold that share for $80. Eventually, I bought back the share for $90, but later sold it for $100. How much money did I make?

As in the preceding problem, the information that is relevant for solution is quite obvious. Indeed, all of the numerical information in this problem is relevant. The question is, how does one combine it? There are actually two ways to arrive at the answer. The first involves considering the first buying-selling sequence. When the share of stock is sold the first time, I make a profit of $10. When I sell the share the second time, I again make a profit of $10. My total profit, therefore, is $20. Another way to solve the problem involves simply adding up the amount of money I pay in purchasing shares – $70 + $90 = $160 – and subtracting that sum from the total amount of money involved in my selling of the shares – $80 + $100 = $180. The difference, again, is $20, my profit on the transactions.

EXERCISE 10.4

Each of the following problems requires selective combination for its solution. Although there may be other difficulties to each problem, the primary one is that of figuring out how to combine pieces of information in the problem (selective combination). See if you can solve each problem. Answers appear after the problems.

1. How many pets do I have if all of them are birds except two, all of them are dogs except two, and all of them are cats except two?

2. Mr. Lester has a small outdoor grill that is just big enough to hold two T-bone steaks. Mr. Lester's wife and son are starved. Mr. Lester's problem, therefore, is to broil three steaks – one for each of the three members of the family – in the shortest possible amount of time. Mr. Lester says to his wife and son, "I know that it takes thirty minutes to broil both sides of one steak because each side takes fifteen minutes. Since I can cook two steaks at the same time, thirty minutes will be enough time to get two steaks ready. Another thirty minutes will be needed to broil the third steak, so that I can finish the whole job in an hour." How can Mr. Lester complete the cooking of all three steaks in just forty-five minutes?

3. Jeannie failed to show up for school time and again. Although she always came in with notes from her mother, the school's attendance officer became suspicious and called the mother. As the attendance officer had suspected, the notes were fakes. The attendance officer called Jeannie into his office for an explanation. Unfortunately for the attendance officer, Jeannie had an explanation for why she had no time for school.

"I sleep 8 hours a day. That makes 8 × 365 or 2,920 hours. There are 24 hours per day, so that's the same as 2,920 divided by 24 or about 122 days. Saturday and Sunday, of course, are not school days. That amounts to 104 days per year. As you know, we have 60 days of summer vacation. Now, I need 3 hours per day for meals-that's 3 × 365, or 1,095 hours per year. Now, if you divide 1,095 by 24, that gives you 45 days per year. Finally, I need at least 2 hours a day for recreation. That comes to 2 × 365 or 730 hours. If you divide 730 by 24, you come out with about 30 days per year." Jeannie jotted down these figures and added up the total:

Sleep	122
Weekends	104
Summer	60
Meals	45
Recreation	30
Sum	361

"As you can see," said Jeannie, "that leaves me with just four days to be sick, and I haven't even yet considered the school holidays we get per year! So you can scarcely fault me for having been out as many days as I have been."

The attendance officer didn't know how to respond to Jeannie, and was ready, in desperation, to let her go. Can you find the error in Jeannie's calculations, helping out yourself even if you are unwilling to help out the poor attendance officer?

4. You have three crates of china. One is labeled "cups," one is labeled "saucers," and one is labeled "cups and saucers." Unfortunately, each label is on a wrong box. By taking only one piece of china from one box, how can you label each box correctly?

5. You are at a party of truth-tellers and liars. The truth-tellers always tell the truth, and the liars always lie. You meet a new friend. He tells you that he just heard a conversation in which a girl said she was a liar. Is your new friend a liar or a truth-teller?

6. If a doctor gave you thirty pills and told you to take one every thirty minutes, how long would they last?

7. You have a new kind of bread dough that doubles in size every hour. When you first put the dough into a large bowl, it covers only the bottom of the bowl. It takes twelve hours to fill the bowl completely. How many hours does it take for the bowl to become half full?

8. A potted plant costs $15. The plant costs $10 more than the pot. How much is the pot worth?

9. A recipe calls for four cups of water. You have only a three-cup container and a five-cup container. How can you measure out exactly four cups of water using only these two containers?

10. You and I have the same amount of money. How much money must I give you so that you have $10 more than I have?

11. A boy and a girl are talking. "I'm a boy," said Person A. "I'm a girl," said Person B. If at least one of them is lying, which is the boy and which is the girl?

12. If you go to sleep at 8:00, having set your old-fashioned, nondigital alarm clock so that you will wake up at 9:00, how many hours will you sleep?

Answers to Arithmetical and Logical Word Problems

(1) The information that all of the pets except two are birds immediately tells you that the total number of pets is two plus the number of birds. The further information that all of the pets are dogs except two tells you that the total number of pets is equal to two plus the number of dogs. And finally, the information that all of the pets are cats except two tells you that the total number of pets is two plus the number of cats. Since you are told of three kinds of pets that the pet owner has, you have exhausted your "degrees of freedom." Aside from the birds, there must be one dog and one cat. Aside from the dogs, there must be one bird and one cat. Aside from the cat, there must be one dog and one bird. So, if there is one of each pet, the total number of pets is three.

(2) Suppose we label the steaks A, B, and C. In the first round of cooking, which takes fifteen minutes, Mr. Lester can cook side 1 of steak A and side 1 of steak B. In a second round of cooking, which also takes fifteen minutes, Mr. Lester can cook side 2 of steak A and side 1 of steak C, temporarily taking steak B off the flame. In a third round of cooking, which again takes fifteen minutes, Mr. Lester can complete the job by putting back on the grill steak B and cooking side 2 of that steak, and also cooking side 2 of steak C. In this more efficient way of cooking the three steaks, there are always 2 steaks on the flame, so that the job can be completed in forty-five minutes rather than in the full hour.

(3) Jeannie is assuming, in her calculations, that the various partitions of her time are independent and therefore additive. Her additive logic would work only if time spent in sleep was distinct from time spent on weekends, if these two times were distinct from time spent during the summer, if these three times were distinct from time spent during meals, and if all these times were distinct from times spent during recreation. But, clearly, the times spent on these various activities are overlapping. As a result, they cannot simply be added up.

(4) The correct answer is to take a piece of china from the "cups and saucers" crate. Relabel the crate correctly (that is, if you pull out a cup, put the "cup" label on the crate, and if you pull out a saucer, put the "saucer" label on the crate). Then reverse the two labels that are left. A common mistake people make in this problem is to try taking the one piece of china from the crate labeled "cups" or the crate labeled "saucers." This procedure will not tell you what is in any of the crates. For example, if you happen to get a cup from the crate marked, "saucers," you would not know whether the crate contained only cups or whether it contained cups and saucers. However, because you know that every crate is mislabeled, you know that both cups and saucers cannot be in the crate labeled "cups and saucers." Whatever you draw from this crate is what the crate contains, and because all the boxes are mislabeled, you need simply switch the two remaining labels and the problem is solved.

(5) Your new friend is clearly a liar. If the girl about whom the friend was talking were a truth-teller, she would have said that she was a truth-teller. If she were a liar, she would have said that she was a truth-teller also. Thus, regardless of whether the girl was a truth-teller or a liar, she would have said that she was a truth-teller. Since your friend has said that she said she was a liar, your friend must be lying, and hence must be a liar.

(6) The pills would last fourteen hours, thirty minutes. The thing to remember is that in the first hour, you take three pills, one at the start of the hour, one after the half hour, and one after an hour. Thus, you finish the complete set of thirty pills after fourteen hours, thirty minutes, rather than after fifteen hours. The pill you take at the start of the first hour is not available at the beginning of the fifteenth hour.

(7) The correct answer is eleven hours. Because the dough doubles in size every hour, the bowl is half full the hour before it is completely full. The best way to solve this problem is to work backward from the last hour (hour 12) rather than forward from the first hour.

(8) $2.50. This answer meets all of the conditions of the problem. If the pot is worth $2.50, the plant is worth $12.50. The plant is thus worth $10 more than the pot. (A common mistake that people make in this problem is to assume that the plant costs $10. It does not: It costs $10 more than the pot. To find out how much the pot costs, first subtract $10 from $15. Then split the $5 in half. This gives you $2.50, what the pot is worth.)

(9) Fill the five-cup container with water. Pour as much of the contents as you can into the three-cup container. Now spill out the contents that you just poured into the three-cup

container. You now have two cups in the five-cup container. Pour the contents of the five-cup container into the three-cup container. Now fill the five-cup container again. Pour as much of the contents in the five-cup container as you can into the three-cup container. This container will take only one cup. You now have four cups left in the five-cup container.

(10) $5 (as long as you both start out with a minimum of $5). If we both start out with $10, and I give you $5, then you will have $15, $10 more than the $5 I now have left.

(11) Person A is the girl and Person B is the boy. If at least one of them is lying, then both of them must be lying. Suppose Person A is lying. Then Person A is actually a girl rather than a boy. Because we know that the situation involves a boy talking to a girl, then Person B must actually be a boy, and hence Person B must be lying. The identical logic applies if one starts off by assuming that Person B is lying.

(12) The alarm will go off in one hour.

Conceptual Projection Problems

In these problems, you must predict states of the future from limited information. Consider first some "otherworldly" problems.

> On the planet Kyron, in a faraway galaxy, there are four kinds of unisex humanoids:
>
> A TWE is a Kyronian who is born a child and remains a child throughout its lifetime.
> A NEL is a Kyronian who is born an adult and remains an adult throughout its lifetime.
> A BIT is a Kyronian who is born a child and becomes an adult.
> A DEK is a Kyronian who is born an adult and becomes a child.

Your task will be to analyze two pieces of information given to you about a particular Kyronian, and to decide whether these two pieces of information describe a TWE, NEL, BIT, or DEK. The two pieces of information will be a description of the Kyronian in the year of its birth, 2008, and a description of the Kyronian twenty-one years later, in the year 2029. The description of the Kyronian in the year 2008 will appear to the left, and the description in the year 2029 will appear to the right. Each description may take either of two forms. The description may be verbal, consisting of any of the words TWE, NEL, BIT, or DEK; or the description may be pictorial, consisting of either

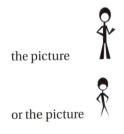

the picture

or the picture

In order to make these judgments, you will need to know two additional facts. First, when a Kyronian is first born, it is not possible to distinguish a TWE from a BIT, or a NEL from a DEK. The reason for this is that at birth, both a TWE and a BIT appear to be children, and both a NEL and a DEK appear to be adults. It is only after one has an opportunity to see what effect, if any, the aging process has had, that one can distinguish a TWE from a BIT, or a NEL from a DEK. Second, after twenty-one years, it is possible to make these distinctions, because a BIT has changed from a child to an adult, and a DEK has changed from an adult to a child. A TWE and a NEL look exactly as they did at birth.

The kinds of judgments you will be making are of four types:

1. The first category of judgment involves two pictures. You will be presented first with a picture of a Kyronian at birth in 2008, then a picture of the same Kyronian in the year 2029, and finally with three alternative verbal descriptions. Your task will be to judge which of the three verbal descriptions correctly identifies the kind of Kyronian depicted in the pictures. For example, you might be presented with the following problem:

(circle one):   DEK   NEL   BIT

The correct answer to this problem is DEK, because the pictures depict a Kyronian who was born an adult and became a child.

2. The second category of judgments involves a verbal description of a Kyronian at birth in 2008, and a picture of the same Kyronian twenty-one years later in the year 2029. Your task is to judge which of three verbal descriptions correctly identifies the kind of Kyronian depicted in the verbal description and the picture. There is one important thing for you to realize in this kind of problem. Because it is not possible to tell at birth whether the individual is a TWE or a BIT, on the one hand (because both appear as children), or a NEL or a DEK, on the other (because both appear as adults), the verbal description for 2008 can be counted on only to identify correctly the physical appearance of the Kyronian; it may or may not correctly predict the appearance of the same Kyronian twenty-one years later. It is simply not possible, in 2008, to know what the Kyronian will look like twenty-one years later. Thus, if you are told that the Kyronian is a TWE, you can be assured that the Kyronian appears to be a child; you cannot be certain that twenty-one years later the Kyronian will still appear to be a child; if the Kyronian is actually a BIT, it will appear to be an adult. Similarly, if you are told the Kyronian is a BIT, you cannot be sure it is not actually a TWE. The same principle applies to NEL and DEK. If you are told that the Kyronian appears to be a NEL or a DEK in 2008, you can be sure only that the Kyronian appears to be an adult. You cannot he sure of what the Kyronian will look like in 2029. To summarize, the verbal description in 2008 will always correctly describe the Kyronian's physical appearance in 2008, but it may or may not correctly predict the Kyronian's physical appearance in 2029.

Consider two examples:

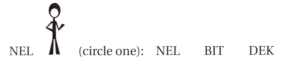

NEL   (circle one):   NEL   BIT   DEK

The correct answer is NEL, because the Kyronian appears to be an adult in 2008, and appears to be an adult in 2029 as well. NEL thus correctly predicted the Kyronian's physical appearance in 2029.

DEK   (circle one):   DEK   NEL   BIT

The correct answer is again NEL, because the Kyronian appears to be an adult in both 2008 and 2029. In this example, DEK failed to predict correctly the physical appearance of the Kyronian in 2029. As always, however, the description of physical appearance was correct for 2008.

3. The third category of judgment involves a picture of a Kyronian in the year 2008, followed by a verbal description of the same Kyronian in the year 2029. Your task is to indicate which of two pictures correctly describes the physical appearance of the Kyronian in the year 2029. Watch out for the case in which the verbal description of the Kyronian in the year 2029 is *inconsistent* with the picture of the Kyronian in the year 2006. In this event, you choose as your answer the letter I. An inconsistency is different from a misprediction of physical appearance. An inconsistency represents an important situation – a contradiction in terms. Consider two example problems:

TWE   (circle one):   I

Here, the correct answer is , because the Kyronian was born as a child and remained a child throughout its lifetime. Note that the verbal description is consistent with the picture.

BIT   (circle one):   I

In this example, the correct answer is I. The picture depicts an adult Kyronian in 2008, but a BIT is born in 2008 as a child. Because this situation is impossible, the picture and verbal description are inconsistent.

4. The fourth category of judgments involves two verbal descriptions of a Kyronian, one in 2008 and the other in 2029. The verbal descriptions are followed by two alternative pictures and the letter I. Your task is to select the picture that correctly depicts in 2029 the Kyronian described in the two verbal descriptions, or else to indicate that the two verbal descriptions are inconsistent with each other (I). There are two important things for you to realize in this kind of problem. First, remember that

verbal descriptions in 2008 always accurately represent the physical appearance of the Kyronian in 2008, but may or may not accurately predict the Kyronian's physical appearance in 2029. Second, it is possible for two verbal descriptions to be inconsistent. Two verbal descriptions are inconsistent if one describes a Kyronian being born as an adult, and the other describes the Kyronian being born as a child, or vice versa. This is not simply a case of misprediction; it is an impossibility. Consider some examples of this kind of problem:

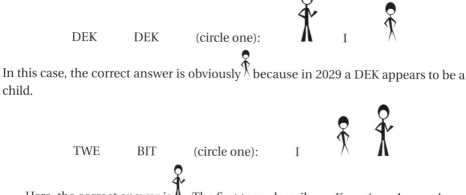

DEK   DEK   (circle one):   I

In this case, the correct answer is obviously ⚊ because in 2029 a DEK appears to be a child.

TWE   BIT   (circle one):   I

Here, the correct answer is ⚊. The first term describes a Kyronian who was born a child; it incorrectly predicts that the Kyronian will remain a child. In fact, the second term shows that the child becomes an adult.

NEL   TWE   (circle one):   I

Here, the correct answer is I, because the first term describes a Kyronian born as an adult, and the second term describes a Kyronian born as a child. This is impossible, and hence the two verbal descriptions are inconsistent.

EXERCISE 10.5

Like the sample problems earlier in this chapter, the problems presented in Exercise 10.5 are in two parts. The left side contains the two pieces of information from 2008 and from 2029. The right side consists of three response choices. If the evidence from 2029 is a picture, the response choices are verbal descriptions. If the evidence from 2029 is a verbal description, the response choices will be pictures plus a letter "I" (representing a response of "Inconsistent"). Answers appear after the problems. Remember,

A TWE is a Kyronian who is born a child and remains a child throughout its lifetime.
A NEL is a Kyronian who is born an adult and remains an adult throughout its lifetime.
A BIT is a Kyronian who is born a child and becomes an adult.
A DEK is a Kyronian who is born an adult and becomes a child.

		A	B	C
1.	DEK		I	
2.	TWE		I	
3.			TWE	BIT	NEL
4.	BIT		BIT	DEK	TWE
5.	TWE		BIT	TWE	NEL
6.	DEK			I
7.	BIT			I
8.	BIT	BIT		I	
9.	NEL			I
10.	NEL			I
11.	BIT	DEK		I	
12.	TWE	BIT			I

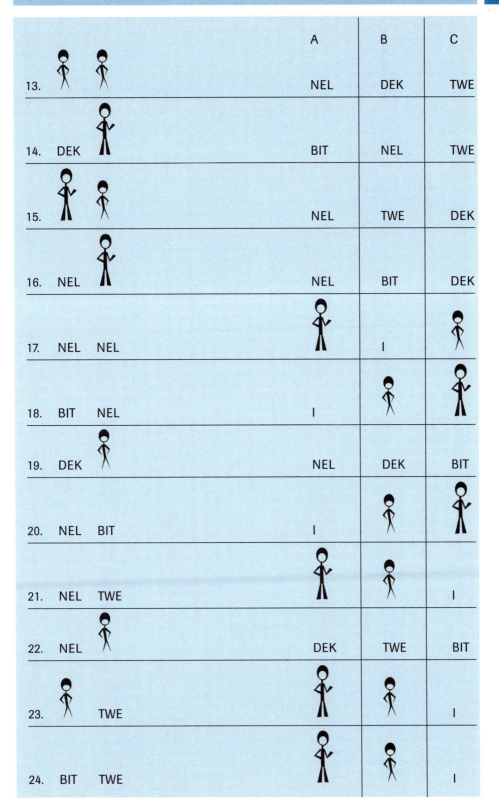

			A	B	C
13.			NEL	DEK	TWE
14.	DEK		BIT	NEL	TWE
15.			NEL	TWE	DEK
16.	NEL		NEL	BIT	DEK
17.	NEL	NEL		I	
18.	BIT	NEL	I		
19.	DEK		NEL	DEK	BIT
20.	NEL	BIT	I		
21.	NEL	TWE			I
22.	NEL		DEK	TWE	BIT
23.		TWE			I
24.	BIT	TWE			I

		A	B	C
25.	TWE	DEK	NEL	BIT
26.	BIT	BIT	TWE	DEK
27.		NEL	TWE	DEK
28.	NEL DEK			I
29.	DEK NEL	I		
30.	DEK TWE		I	
31.	DEK DEK			I
32.	BIT		I	
33.	TWE DEK			I
34.	TWE NEL		I	
35.	DEK BIT			I
36.	TWE TWE		I	

Answers to Conceptual Projection Problems

1. A	7. A	13. C	19. B	25. C	31. A
2. B	8. C	14. B	20. A	26. A	32. B
3. B	9. C	15. C	21. C	27. A	33. C
4. C	10. B	16. A	22. A	28. B	34. B
5. B	11. B	17. A	23. B	29. C	35. C
6. C	12. A	18. A	24. B	30. B	36. C

SELECTIVE COMPARISON

Selective-comparison problems require you to relate new information to old information. Analogies are good examples of such problems, because they require you to draw on prior knowledge. Analogies also require you to infer a relation. You then use that relation to complete a new analogy. However, most analogies are not particularly novel. We will try to present some analogies that we believe truly are new.

Novel Analogies

Most analogies rely on information that is already known. Any facts used in solving analogies are those that you already know. It is possible to create novel analogies by choosing small aspects of the world around us to change. You then must use new information to solve the analogy correctly. Consider the analogy below. In solving this analogy, assume that the statement given before the analogy is true, whether or not it is actually true. Then solve the analogy taking this assumption into account. Sometimes the assumption will be true in the real world; other times, it will be false. Sometimes the assumption will affect the solution you reach; other times, it will not. The important thing is to assume the statement is true, even if it is not true in the real world, and then to use the assumption, where needed, to solve the analogy.

OCEANS are sweet.
PICKLES are to SALT as OCEANS are to
DEPTH   SUGAR   CANDY   JUICE   BLUE

The correct answer is "sugar." Notice that the first statement is unrealistic (oceans are not sweet; if anything, they are salty). However, the target analogy (PICKLES are to SALT) suggests the relationship of an ingredient (one of the key ingredients of a pickle is salt). Thus, the correct answer is sugar – if anything makes oceans sweet, it is sugar.

Now try the problems presented in Exercise 10.6.

EXERCISE 10.6

1. VILLAINS are lovable.
HERO is to ADMIRATION as VILLAIN is to
CONTEMPT   AFFECTION   CRUEL   KIND

2. CHOWDER is sour.
CLAM is to SHELLFISH as CHOWDER is to
SOUP   STEAK   LIQUID   SOLID

3. LAKES are dry.
TRAIL is to HIKE as LAKE is to
SWIM   DUST   WATER   WALK

4. SPARROWS play hopscotch.
TROUT is to SCALY as SPARROW is to
FEATHERY   BUMPY   EAGLE   CANARY

5. CHERRIES are fruits.
EGG is to YOLK as CHERRY is to
PASTURE   BONE   ORCHARD   PIT

6. KITES are pretty.
WAGON is to PULL as KITE is to
PUSH   FLY   HANDLE   TAIL

7. ELEPHANTS are enormous.
MOUSE is to TINY as ELEPHANT is to
TRAMPLE   LAZY   HUGE   SLEEP

8. HUTS provide shelter.
CASTLE is to LARGE as HUT is to
IGLOO   POOR   SMALL   TENT

9. SOLDIERS wear boots.
GANGSTER is to REVOLVER as SOLDIER is to
UNIFORM   SWORD   RIFLE   SHIELD

10. DEER attack tigers.
LION is to COURAGEOUS as DEER is to
TIMID   AGGRESSIVE   COUGAR   ELK

11. BASEBALL is a game.
TENNIS is to RACKET as BASEBALL is to
CLUB   BAT   STRIKE   PUTT

12. CARPENTERS are green.
TAILOR is to CLOTH as CARPENTER is to
WALL   PAINT   CABINET   WOOD

13. COBRAS drink lemonade.
ROBIN is to BIRD as COBRA is to
DESERT   LIZARD   SNAKE   JUNGLE

14. NEEDLES are flat.

THIMBLE is to BLUNT as NEEDLE is to

SHARP   SMOOTH   STAB   BRUISE

15. PRESIDENTS give speeches.

CAPITOL is to PLACE as PRESIDENT is to

PERSON   DETECTIVE   AGENCY   GOVERNMENT

16. CLOCKS last forever.

CALENDAR is to DATE as CLOCK is to

TIME   PLACE   TICKING   HUMMING

17. PIGS climb fences.

GOLDFISH is to BOWL as PIG is to

ROUND   CAGE   DIRTY   GRACEFUL

18. RADISHES are fruit candies.

PRETZEL is to SALTY as RADISH is to

BITTER   CHOCOLATE   SALAD   SWEET

19. ELVES are tiny.

GIANT is to TALL as ELF is to

SHORT   FAT   BOY   MAN

20. RACCOONS eat meat.

MAN is to HANDS as RACCOON is to

COAT   TOES   PAWS   SHOE

21. PADDLES are oars.

RUDDER is to STEER as PADDLE is to

PROPEL   MELT   WOOD   WAX

22. CARS are machines.

JET is to PILOT as CAR is to

HOUSE   ENGINE   DRIVER   GARAGE

23. GRANITE is edible.

IRON is to METAL as GRANITE is to

SOLID   FOOD   TASTY   HARD

24. WAITRESSES serve meals.

FLIGHT ATTENDANT is to PLANE as WAITRESS is to

BUS   RESTAURANT   MENU   SCHEDULE

25. TOENAILS can do acrobatics and walk tight ropes.

LION TAMER is to WHIP as TOENAIL is to

BALLS   TRAPEZE   FIRE   FEET

26. DENIM is blue.

STEEL is to METAL as DENIM is to

FLIMSY   TILE   FABRIC   STURDY

27. LAMBS are frisky.

CALF is to cow as LAMB is to

SHINY   DUCK   WOOLLY   SHEEP

28. HAMSTERS are active.
DOLL is to TOY as HAMSTER is to

PET   PICTURE   LIVING   QUIET

29. DENTISTS wear coats.
MECHANIC is to ENGINE as DENTIST is to

PLEASANT   CAST   PAINFUL   TOOTH

30. MAPLES are purple.
ROSE is to PETALS as MAPLE is to

LEAVES   SYRUP   SUGAR   BARK

31. MOUNTAINS are invisible.
CANYON is to LOW as MOUNTAIN is to

FALL   STEEP   CLIMB   HIGH

32. TRAINS carry passengers.
HOUSE is to BUILDING as TRAIN is to

WAREHOUSE   BOX   STATION   VEHICLE

33. GOLF is a sport.
WALTZ is to DANCE as GOLF is to

BATTLE   GAME   CART   CADDY

34. SAINTS are demons.
SINNER is to BAD as SAINT is to

GOOD   HELL   HEAVEN   WICKED

35. LEMONS are animals.
LIME is to GREEN as LEMON is to

YELLOW   ORANGE   GROW   PICK

36. MILK is a liquid.
CHEESE is to THICK as MILK is to

JUICE   TASTY   THIN   CEREAL

37. SHAMPOO is black.
SOAP is to BODY as SHAMPOO is to

HAIR   RUG   WASHED   STAINED

38. CATS scratch things.
PERSON is to FINGERNAIL as CAT is to

BRUSH   FUR   KNIFE   CLAW

39. THUNDER is silent.
LIGHTNING is to VISIBLE as THUNDER is to

QUIET   FEEL   INAUDIBLE   NOISY

40. DIAMONDS are fruits.
PEARL is to OYSTER as DIAMOND is to

MINE   TREE   RING   PIE

41. MOTHS kill people.
HORNET is to DANGEROUS as MOTH is to

HARMLESS   SCORPION   DEADLY   BUTTERFLY

42. LOVE is wonderful.
KISS is to ACTION as LOVE is to
IMAGINARY   DEGREE   FEELING   REAL

43. CANTALOUPES are fruits.
ZUCCHINI is to SQUASH as CANTALOUPE is to
NUT   MELON   EAT   CRACK

44. OVENS produce heat.
REFRIGERATOR is to COLD as OVEN is to
STOVE   COOL   SINK   HOT

45. OXYGEN is pink.
BLOOD is to HEART as OXYGEN is to
LIVER   LUNG   DRY   DAMP

46. SAPPHIRES are junk.
CARNATION is to FLOWER as SAPPHIRE is to
JEWEL   SPARKLING   MINERAL   DULL

47. LIONS chase foxes.
BEE is to INSECT as LION is to
AMPHIBIAN   JUNGLE   MAMMAL   LAND

48. LIFE JACKETS prevent drowning.
PARACHUTE is to SKY as LIFE JACKET is to
SEA   DITCH   FLOATING   COVERING

49. GOATS are robots.
CHICKEN is to HATCHED as GOAT is to
BORN   FARM   BUILT   FACTORY

50. CHINESE drink tea.
GERMAN is to EUROPEAN as CHINESE is to
ENGLISH   ASIAN   CHINA   JAPAN

51. ZEBRAS are wildlife.
LEOPARD is to SPOT as ZEBRA is to
STRIPE   STAR   SHOOT   HOLD

52. KIDNAPPERS are thirsty.
HOSTAGE is to VICTIM as KIDNAPPER is to
POLICEMAN   CRIMINAL   RANSOM   JAIL

53. GHOSTS are athletes.
WEREWOLF is to MONSTER as GHOST is to
DRAMA   SPIRIT   HAUNT   ACT

54. GUITARS are instruments.
BUGLE is to BLOW as GUITAR is to
TYPE   STRUM   OFFICE   CONCERT

55. PIANOS make music.
HAMMER is to TOOL as PIANO is to
BENCH   INSTRUMENT   KEYS   LEGS

56. GREYHOUNDS are fast.
FOXHOUND is to HUNT as GREYHOUND is to
SPEEDY   CRAWL   RACE   SLOW

57. BALLS are flat.
POLE is to CYLINDER as BALL is to
SPHERE   CIRCLE   BOUNCE   THROW

58. APPLES are vegetables.
CARAMEL is to CHEWY as APPLE is to
SOFT   CRISP   SAUCE   STEW

59. TOASTERS write cookbooks.
SPATULA is to UTENSIL as TOASTER is to
WRITER   GADGET   BREAD   BOOK

60. EARTH is hollow.
SUN is to STAR as EARTH is to
PLANET   MOON   SPINNING   FALLING

Answers to Novel Analogies

1. AFFECTION	16. TIME	31. HIGH	46. MINERAL
2. SOUP	17. CAGE	32. VEHICLE	47. MAMMAL
3. WALK	18. SWEET	33. GAME	48. SEA
4. FEATHERY	19. SHORT	34. WICKED	49. BUILT
5. PIT	20. PAWS	35. YELLOW	50. ASIAN
6. FLY	21. PROPEL	36. THIN	51. STRIPE
7. HUGE	22. DRIVER	37. HAIR	52. CRIMINAL
8. SMALL	23 FOOD	38. CLAW	53. SPIRIT
9. RIFLE	24. RESTAURANT	39. INAUDIBLE	54. STRUM
10. AGGRESSIVE	25. TRAPEZE	40. TREE	55. INSTRUMENT
11. BAT	26. FABRIC	41. DEADLY	56. RACE
12. WOOD	27. SHEEP	42. FEELING	57. CIRCLE
13. SNAKE	28. PET	43. MELON	58. CRISP
14. SMOOTH	29. TOOTH	44. HOT	59. WRITER
15. PERSON	30. LEAVES	45. LUNG	60. PLANET

SELECTIVE ENCODING, COMBINATION, AND COMPARISON

Now combine the use of the three insight skills – selective encoding, selective combination, and selective comparison – in solving these scientific insight problems. Let us work together on the following example.

A scientist is doing a study for the Department of Energy to see if some clothes keep people warmer than other clothes. This is his description of the experiment: Two women are walking along a road. The sun is shining brightly overhead, throwing shadows behind the women. The women are the same height and weight. One wears a white dress and the other wears a black dress. The dresses are identical except for color: They are both cotton and are the same style and length. The woman in the black dress is comfortable, and the woman in the white dress is cold. The scientist concluded, based on these facts, that dark-colored clothes help a person to keep body heat, whereas light-colored clothes let the body heat disappear. The Department of Energy fired the scientist. What did he do wrong?

In finding an answer to this problem, we have to take into consideration all information that might be relevant and ignore the irrelevant information. The most relevant piece of information that needs to be encoded is the color of the women's dresses. The scientist did not take into account the effect of solar radiation. Sunshine made the woman in dark clothes warm because dark colors tend to absorb heat. The woman in white was cooler because light colors tend to reflect heat.

EXERCISE 10.7

Below there are a number of scientific insight problems. Please go through these problems and try to find solutions to them. Note that the answers to these problems are given at the end of the exercise.

1. Dr. Smith was reading the newspaper when she saw an article called "Plants Have Feelings, Too." It reported that a scientist had conducted an experiment to see if plants had feelings. The scientist decided that plants conveyed their feelings not by smiles or frowns, but by electromagnetic waves. To test this theory, she connected the plants to machines that measured the waves, and had different people approach the plants and talk to them. The scientist was pleased to discover that Person A, who spoke kindly to the plants, registered one way on the machine, whereas Person B, who abused the plants, registered in a different way. She concluded that plants responded to different human actions in different ways.

Dr. Smith wanted to test this theory. She repeated the experiment, but this time she attached the machines to plants and to empty Styrofoam cups. At the end of the experiment, she was surprised. Sure enough, the plants responded to different people in different ways. But so did the Styrofoam cups!

Dr. Smith was mystified; but slowly, an incredible idea began to form in her mind. "I can't believe this discovery," she said. "I've . . . I've learned that Styrofoam cups have feelings!"

Unfortunately, Dr. Smith had made the wrong conclusion. What conclusion would you draw?

2. Christopher Wood, a doctor at Class Act University, was hiking along a riverbank. In the middle of the river were some boulders that blocked the water. Looking down, Dr. Wood saw that when the current hit the boulders, it split. In the process of breaking, a couple of things happened – some water actually went rippling upstream a little way, and some eddies went wandering off downstream, but most of it went rushing downstream. As the water eddies moved out from main current, the water slowed down, and dropped whatever rocks and dirt it was carrying. Along the banks, these deposited particles began to build up the riverbank.

On Monday, Dr. Wood went into the laboratory. He was studying atherosclerosis, a condition in which the arteries (especially those carrying blood to the brain) grow thicker, decreasing the flow of blood. He decided to look at the carotid arteries, where atherosclerosis usually takes places.

Using special sonar equipment, he looked at the vessels in a patient. Focusing in on the point where the two carotid arteries split off from one artery, he noticed a strange thing. At the fork, the blood started to move in a funny way. And it was just beyond this point that he saw the unusual but deadly thickening of the artery walls.

Suddenly he said, "Aha!"

What do you think he realized?

3. When a jet airliner is flying at a cruising altitude of thirty-five thousand feet, it leaves behind it a white wake, which is a white trail that traces its path. High in the sky where the jets travel, conditions are very cold. Jet aircraft derive the energy that keeps them flying from the combustion of fuel (petroleum). In chemical terms, petroleum is a hydrocarbon, that is, for the most part, a combination of carbon and hydrogen. When the fuel is burned, the oxygen from the air combines with the carbon and the hydrogen, releasing energy and leaving a gas that is a combination of carbon and oxygen (carbon dioxide) and water. When a jet flies, streaming out carbon dioxide and water vapor behind it, the carbon dioxide is as invisible as the oxygen and nitrogen of which the air itself is composed. What is the white trail?

4. Every morning, millions of microscopic crustaceans in the world's lakes and oceans migrate to very deep water. And late each afternoon, they surface again. For them, this is an expensive round trip to commute, requiring enormous amounts of energy and time. Students of migration have wondered for years what such zooplankton gain by spending their days in cold, dark waters, where food is scarce, and where they cannot reproduce quickly.

To find out, two scientists spent a year observing two species, *Daphnia hyalina* and *Dapbnia galeata*. Both species spend the night near the surface, but in the morning, *D. hyalina* departs for the depths, rejoining *D. galeata* only when shadows lengthen in early evening.

All day long, *D. galeata* enjoys the benefits of warmth and abundant food near the lake's surface, while, far below, *D. hyalina is* deprived. Under such conditions, one would expect *D. galeata* to thrive and multiply until it drove its neighbor out.

Not so, the scientists report. Even though *D. galeata* grows and reproduces faster, its population is equaled – and often outnumbered – by *D. hyalina*.

Can you think why?

5. Dr. Wallace learned from a friend that he could grow living creatures by boiling the seeds of pumpkins. He was surprised, because he had been taught that living creatures reproduced themselves; now, if this friend was right, he could grow microorganisms and animals and birds from scratch. The doctor was excited, because he knew he would be famous if the discovery was true. He decided to test it. He took a flask and carefully cleaned it so no organisms were left alive. Next, he added water and the pumpkin seeds, and boiled them to make sure he killed the germs. Finally, he put a plastic stopper in the bottle and sealed it so no organisms could get in. Suddenly, he realized he'd made a mistake. If he wanted something to grow, he had to give it air! So he took out the plastic stopper and put in a cork, which let air through. Two days later, there were lots of microorganisms swimming in the water. Dr. Wallace knew he had successfully grown them from pumpkin seeds, and rushed out to tell his friends of his great discovery.

Unfortunately, Dr. Wallace made a big mistake. What was it?

6. There is at least one known instance of a jet fighter pilot shooting his own plane out of the air, using his own guns. Amazing as it seems, aeronautical engineers have made it possible for a supersonic jet fighter to catch up with the fire from its own guns with sufficient speed to shoot itself down. If a plane flying at one thousand miles per hour fires a burst from twenty-millimeter guns, the shells leave the plane with an airspeed of about three thousand miles per hour.

Why won't a plane that continues to fly straight ahead fly into its own bullets?

7. Scientists have noticed that on rainy days following hot, dry summer days, the air takes on a fresh, clean, spring smell. What causes that? To some extent, the falling rain washes pollutants out of the air. But that is not the main reason. Think about the following facts from the reports of two Australian scientists, Dr. Bear and Dr. Thomas, and see if you can get the answer.

a. Air is full of plant vapor in the form of invisible oils and essences.

b. These substances – pinene, myrcene, isoprene, and linalool – are the substances you smell when you get close to living plants.

c. Clay is a major component of toothpastes and antacids (Maalox, DiGel, and so on) and one of its primary characteristics is its ability to act as a sponge, absorbing many times its weight in liquids.

d. On hot days, the clay is baked dry of any water. What it does then is to absorb the scents of plants from the air, so the scents are trapped and pulled out of the air.

What do you think happens when it starts to rain that makes the air smell so fresh?

8. Napoleon surrendered to the British in 1815. The British sent him in exile to the island of St. Helena because they wanted to eliminate any possibility that he would rebuild his army. Napoleon and a few attendants were sent to Longwood House, a moldy, damp place that, as their only concession to the once-powerful emperor, the British repapered in green and gold wallpaper.

Over the past few years, Dr. Stan Forshufrud has studied the medical accounts of Napoleon's last months at St. Helena. The scientist developed a theory that Napoleon was deliberately and systematically poisoned by his enemies with arsenic. Napoleon's symptoms were classic for arsenic poisoning: shivering, swelling of the limbs, and repeated gastric upsets. Napoleon's companions in exile also suffered from these symptoms.

Another scientist, Dr. David Jones, has been studying the uses of arsenic over the years. This is his report:

By 1800, a popular and cheap dye, "Scheele green," was used in paints, fabrics, and wallpapers. The dye contained arsenic. As long as the wall-paper, fabric, or paint was dry, it was quite harmless. But once it got wet from condensation, rising damp, or whatever – it could go moldy. To survive on the wallpaper, the mold must somehow get rid of the arsenic. Many molds convert it to a vapor.

What do you think might have caused Napoleon's death?

9. In 1960, Dr. Wooton, a doctor and professor of medicine at the University of Tennessee, was surprised to see a young man walk into his office. The young man was orange. Dr. Wooton was even more surprised when the man said that his problem was a stomach pain, but made no mention of his color. Quickly, Dr. Wooton recalled various medical disorders that could cause skin color to change: liver damage turned a victim yellow, heart disease turned a victim blue, pituitary disease turned a victim paper-white. But he couldn't imagine what turned a person orange.

After examining the patient, Dr. Wooton discovered that he had an abnormal pancreas, which could mean cancer. He scheduled the young man for tests at the hospital, and took a detailed history. One of the doctor's questions was, "When did you turn orange?" The man said he hadn't realized he was turning orange, because it happened so gradually. The doctor found nothing else unusual in the man's background, except for his diet. He ate lots of vegetables – carrots, rutabaga, squash, beans, spinach – as well as oranges and eggs, and he drank gallons of tomato juice each day.

The man went to the hospital and had tests performed. They showed that his stomach pain was not cancer, but a simple cyst that could be easily removed. It was not responsible for the strange color of his skin.

Dr. Wooton did more research into the problem of the man's skin color, and finally found documented proof that food could change a person's color. Foods like carrots, oranges, and eggs contain carotene, which turn a person yellow, but not orange. Then he found reports that tomatoes contain lycopene, a red dye. But tomatoes were not known to turn a person orange. What do you think caused the man to turn orange?

10. Copernicus was standing on the beach, watching the sailing ships come in and leave. He noticed a strange thing about the ships that were coming in from the sea. As a ship moved closer, he could see the very tip of it. Then he could see the masts, and finally, the body. "How odd," he thought. "It looks as if the ship is actually rising from the ocean. But I know it isn't-it simply confirms my suspicions that the earth is round, and not flat." How did Copernicus reach this conclusion?

11. Many lepidopterists (people who study butterflies) believe that male butterflies are brightly colored and vividly patterned in order to appeal to the female. Robert Silberglied tested this belief by changing the colors of a male butterfly's wings. He found that females did not discriminate against the males with incorrectly colored wings.

Instead, he has proposed another theory. It is based on the fact that, because butterflies are so fragile and easily injured, they have developed characteristics that allow them to avoid physical fights. In addition, to support his theory, Silberglied reported the well-known fact that territorial birds can intimidate their enemies without ever touching them.

What do you suppose Silberglied's theory is?

12. Heaters, air conditioners, and refrigerators are very similar machines. What each of them does is to pump heat from one place to another. Heat pumps move heat from air that is outside a house into the inside of a house (even when it is cold outside, the air still has some heat). Air conditioners move heat from inside a house to the outside of a house. Refrigerators take heat from inside a refrigerator and move it outside of the refrigerator.

On a hot afternoon, if you opened the door of your refrigerator, do you think it would significantly cool off your kitchen? Why?

13. Dr. Eureka and his fellow scientists suspected that germs caused diseases and that they could live and travel on the air or in living creatures. But they had a problem: They thought that each kind of germ caused a different kind of disease, but they could never grow one kind of germ by itself without a lot of other kinds of disease germs appearing.

Still, Dr. Eureka wanted to try the experiment again. He took a test tube and cleaned it carefully. Then he prepared a soup that the germs liked to eat and put it in the test tube. Finally, he took a germ and put it in the liquid. He placed the test tube in a warm place so the germ could grow.

A week later he came back and discovered that some other germs had somehow gotten in, and now all the germs were swimming together, completely mixed. Oh, well, he thought, I guess my samples will always be contaminated.

Then, while he was sadly walking around his lab, he found half a baked potato he'd left lying on his desk after lunch the previous week. On it were little dots, each a different color. Looking at the potato closely, he realized that the little dots were germs – but they hadn't gotten mixed in together: Each kind sat on its own part of the solid potato surface. He had perfect samples of individual kinds of germs.

Suddenly, he slapped his forehead and said, "How stupid can we be? It's easy to keep germs from mixing together: This potato tells us what's wrong with our soups!" What's the difference between the potato and the soup?

14. According to Pasteur's account, he once placed under the microscope a drop of sugar solution that was in the process of changing into butyric acid. The drop contained bacteria, which were at first rapidly mobile. Then he observed the odd fact that, while the bacteria at the center of the drop continued to move, those at the edge that were more exposed to air came to a standstill. From this simple observation, Pasteur made an important discovery. What was it?

Answers to Scientific Insight Problems

(1) When Dr. Smith's Styrofoam cups registered on the machine, she should have known that something else other than the plants was causing the vibrations. Instead, she misinterpreted the evidence offered by the "control" condition. The machine registered for irrelevant reasons.

(2) Dr. Wood realized that what was happening in the blood vessel was probably similar to what happened to the river: The fork or branching of the artery acted like the boulder in the river.

(3) The white trail is the water vapor, which begins to condense once it hits the cold upper atmosphere.

(4) Fish feed during the day and because *D. galeata* remains near the surface during the day, it is much more visible and convenient prey than *D. hyalina*, which departs to the depths during the same time.

(5) Dr. Wallace allowed microbes that travel in the air to get into the flask when he opened it and when he continued to allow air to move in and out.

(6) Gravity pulls the bullets down; thus, unless a pilot consciously dives to run into the bullets, they will not hit the plane.

(7) When it rains, the clay begins to absorb the water. Much like a soapy sponge that has water falling on it, the clay begins to release some of what it has absorbed (the scents). Then the falling rain actually washes the scents out of the clay and releases them into the air.

(8) Napoleon's death was caused by arsenic poisoning from the arsenic that was present in the wallpaper. Because of the dampness of the house, the wallpaper became wet and moldy. The mold's exudation, which contained arsenic, was mixed with the air that Napoleon was breathing constantly.

(9) Carotene, which is yellow and which is present in carrots, oranges, and eggs, and lycopene, a red dye present in tomatoes, combined in the patient's blood to produce the orange color.

(10) Copernicus's reasoning was that if the earth were flat, he would have seen the entire ship appear at once, instead of watching it appear bit by bit, as it did.

(11) Silberglied's theory is that bright colors tend to intimidate the predators of butterflies, and therefore serve as a defense.

(12) No, it would not cool off the kitchen to open the refrigerator. Heat from the room would move inside it, only to be pumped back into the room.

(13) The potato is solid. Therefore, when germs land on it, they remain in the same place. The soup is liquid, and when germs land in it they can move around without difficulty.

(14) Pasteur's important discovery was that air can affect certain bacteria, either immobilizing or killing them.

SUMMING UP

Dealing with novelty and using insight are essential components of problem solving, because virtually any problem, by the virtue of definition, imposes on its solver some ambiguity that needs to be overcome in order to find the solution. Both responses to novelty and insight are important psychological phenomena in their own right, but they are probably better known as components of creativity. What, exactly, is creativity? We will discuss this question in the next chapter.

11

Deciding for Creativity

Creativity is another aspect of dealing with novelty. What is creativity? Your first thought may be that it is something different – "thinking outside of the box." Certainly, this is an important part of creativity. But psychologists view creativity as being a little more complex than just being something new. Creativity is traditionally defined as something that is novel, good, and appropriate for the task. If you are asked a math question on a midterm and you draw a picture of an elephant, then this is doing something in a different way but not necessarily a *creative* way (Kaufman & Sternberg, 2007). Research suggests that, to a large extent, people can become creative if they decide that is what they want to do (Chen, Kasof, Himsel, Dmitrieva, Dong, & Xue, 2005).

Creativity can occur anywhere. Consider, for example, the following story: A politician and his wife decide to eat dinner in a fancy French restaurant in Washington, DC. The waiter approaches their table and asks the wife what she would like as an appetizer. "The garlic bread," she tells the waiter. "And the main course?" the waiter asks. "The steak," responds the politician's wife. "And the vegetable?" asks the waiter. "He'll have the same," responds the politician's wife.

Some people think that only the "greats" can be creative – the Darwins, the Mozarts, the Picassos, the Shakespeares. But we do not believe that this is true. Instead, creativity is a decision that anyone can make. The politician's wife decided, through her cutting remark, for creativity.

People decide for creativity every day. Maybe it's when you think of an unusual example in a class paper. Or when you try to figure out a way to keep your dog from jumping over the backyard fence, or find the quickest method of doing the dishes. Perhaps you keep a journal or play guitar or program flash computer games. These are all ways of deciding for creativity; it is possible to be creative in many different ways (Baer & Kaufman, 2005). People who decide to be creative are like good investors: They decide to buy low and sell high in the world of ideas.

INVESTING IN CREATIVITY

An investment theory of creativity (Sternberg & Lubart, 1995a; Sternberg & Lubart, 1995b; Sternberg, Lubart, Kaufman, & Pretz, 2005) asserts that creative thinkers are like good investors: They buy low and sell high. Whereas investors do so in the world of finance, creative people do so in the world of ideas. Creative people generate ideas that are like undervalued stocks (stocks with a low price-to-earnings ratio), and both the stocks and the ideas are generally rejected by the public. When creative ideas are proposed, they often are viewed as bizarre, useless, and even foolish, and are summarily rejected. The person proposing them often is regarded with suspicion and perhaps even with disdain and derision.

Creative ideas are both novel and valuable. But they are often rejected because the creative innovator stands up to vested interests and defies the crowd. The crowd does not maliciously or willfully reject creative notions. Rather, it does not realize, and often does not want to realize, that the proposed idea represents a valid and advanced way of thinking. Society generally perceives opposition to the status quo as annoying and offensive, and as reason enough to ignore innovative ideas (Aljughaiman & Mowrer-Reynolds, 2005).

Evidence abounds that creative ideas are often rejected (Sternberg & Lubart, 1995a). Initial reviews of major works of literature and art are often negative. Toni Morrison's *Tar Baby* received negative reviews when it was first published, as did Sylvia Plath's *The Bell Jar*. The first exhibition in Munich of the work of the Norwegian painter Edvard Munch opened and closed the same day because of the strong negative response from the critics. Some of the greatest scientific papers have been rejected not just by one but by several journals before being published. For example, John Garcia, a distinguished biopsychologist, was immediately denounced when he first proposed that a form of learning called classical conditioning could be produced in a single trial of learning (Garcia & Koelling, 1966).

From the investment view, then, the creative person buys low by presenting a unique idea and then attempting to convince other people of its value. After convincing others that the idea is valuable, which increases the perceived value of the investment, the creative person sells high by leaving the idea to others and moving on to another idea. People typically want others to love their ideas, but immediate universal applause for an idea often indicates that it is not particularly creative.

Creativity is as much a decision about and an attitude toward life as it is a matter of ability. Creativity is often obvious in young children, but it is harder to find in older children and adults because their creative potential has been suppressed by a society that encourages intellectual conformity (Beghetto & Kaufman, 2007).

KINDS OF CREATIVITY

Another aspect of creativity that you might consider is what kinds of creativity there are. Are there different ways to be creative? We have developed the "propulsion" model of creativity to account for different types of creativity (Sternberg, 1999a; Sternberg, Kaufman, & Pretz, 2002; Sternberg, Kaufman, & Pretz, 2003). According to this theory, there are eight different ways to be creative:

Types of Creativity that Accept Current Paradigms and Attempt to Extend Them

1. *Replication.* The individual or group attempts to show that a field is in the right place. The individual intends to keep the field where it is rather than moving it. Think of a scientific study whose sole goal is to show that an earlier experiment can be reproduced, or maybe a romance novel that is quite similar to earlier novels, having only different main characters and a new setting.

2. *Redefinition.* The person or group attempts to redefine where a field is. The current status of the field thus is seen from different points of view. An example might be the concept of "found poetry" – the ability to write a poem from such nonliterary source materials as instructions on how to shampoo your hair or the quotations of Donald Rumsfield.

3. *Forward Movement.* The person or group attempts to move the field forward in the direction it already is going. For instance, most successful websites are a result of someone's nudging the domain a little bit further and applying an Internet sensibility. Amazon's success was to introduce the concept of online book sales, eBay created online auctions, and Travelocity created an online travel agency. Most new commercial products, such as a new version of a cereal that adds sugar frosting on top of the existing cereal, represent forward movements.

4. *Advance Forward Movement.* The individual or group attempts to move the field forward in the direction it is already going, but by moving it beyond where others are ready for it to go. For example, many of Leonardo da Vinci's inventions, such as the flying machine, were so far ahead of their time that they could not be built during his lifetime. Indeed, the same concept applies today. When e-mail was first introduced, many people were slow to catch on. Now, almost everyone has an e-mail address!

Types of Creativity that Reject Current Paradigms and Attempt to Replace Them

5. *Redirection.* The individual or group attempts to redirect the field from where it is toward a different direction. An example of redirection in rap/hip-hop music can be found in the early work of the group Run-D.M.C. Early rap did not appeal to mainstream audiences. Then Run-D.M.C. actively moved the field in a way that would appeal to the mainstream. They added guitar riffs and more melody to their songs to make the rap songs sound more like more mainstream rock-and-roll. They collaborated with famous rock bands such as Aerosmith (for the hit song "Walk this Way"). As a result, they appealed to an entire audience (Aerosmith's many fans) that might otherwise not have been inclined to listen to rap music. Thanks in part to Run-D.M.C.'s influence, rap/hip-hop is one of the most popular musical styles today.

6. *Reconstruction/Redirection.* The individual or group attempts to move the field back to where it once was (a reconstruction of the past) so that the field may move onward from that point, but in a different direction. Many very conservative

politicians, who hark back to a better and simpler age, exemplify reconstruction/redirection. These politicians believe that the field of politics – indeed, perhaps, the world as a whole – would be better served by undoing the last several decades of domestic and foreign policy and starting over from scratch.

7. *Reinitiation.* The individual or group attempts to move the field to a different as yet unreached starting point and then to move from that point. Einstein's work in physics, in which he showed that Newtonian physics represented only a limiting case of physics, is an example of reinitiation. His theory of relativity provided brand-new ideas about space and time.

8. *Integration.* The individual or group attempts to integrate two formerly diverse ways of thinking about phenomena into a single way of thinking about a phenomenon. The television show *Star Trek* was an example of integration. *Star Trek* was based on a similar concept as the western show *Wagon Train* – strong and resilient men and women triumphed over an assortment of different types of people. *Star Trek* used humans and Vulcans, and had them triumph over a variety of different alien species.

Think about your own favorite television shows, movies, books, and songs. Where would their creators fit as creative contributors? Which types of contributors do you think would have the most lasting impact?

BALANCING SYNTHETIC, ANALYTIC, AND PRACTICAL ABILITIES

Creative work requires applying and balancing three abilities – synthetic, analytic, and practical (Sternberg, 1985; Sternberg & Lubart, 1995a; Sternberg & O'Hara, 1999; Sternberg & Williams, 1996). All of these abilities can be developed (Gelman & Gottfried, 2006; Moran, & John-Steiner, 2003; Runco, 2004).

Synthetic ability is what we typically think of as creativity. It is, as we have discussed, the ability to generate novel and interesting ideas. Often the person others call creative is a particularly good synthetic thinker who makes connections between things that other people do not recognize spontaneously.

Analytic ability is typically considered to be critical thinking ability. A person with this skill analyzes and evaluates ideas. Everyone, even the most creative person, has better and worse ideas. Without well-developed analytic ability, the creative thinker is as likely to pursue bad ideas as to pursue good ones. The creative individual uses analytic ability to work out the implications of a creative idea and to test it.

Practical ability is the ability to translate theory into practice and abstract ideas into practical accomplishments. An implication of the investment theory of creativity is that good ideas do not sell themselves. The creative person uses practical ability to convince other people that an idea is valuable. For example, every organization has a set of ideas that dictate how things, or at least some things, should be done. When an individual proposes a new procedure, he or she must sell it by convincing others that it is better than the old one. Practical ability is also used to recognize ideas that have a potential audience.

Creativity requires these three abilities. The person who is only synthetic may come up with innovative ideas, but cannot recognize or sell them. The person who is only analytic may be an excellent critic of other people's ideas, but is not likely to generate creative ideas. The person who is only practical may be an excellent salesperson, but is as likely to promote ideas or products of little or no value as to promote genuinely creative ideas.

Anyone can develop his or her own creativity by finding a balance among synthetic, analytic, and practical thinking. A creative attitude is at least as important as are creative thinking skills (Schank, 1988; Selby, Shaw, & Houtz, 2005). You can use the following twelve strategies to develop creativity in yourself and in others around you.

TWELVE WAYS TO DECIDE FOR CREATIVITY

1. Redefine Problems

Redefining a problem means taking a problem and turning it on its head. Many times in life individuals have a problem and they just don't see how to solve it. They are stuck in a box. Redefining a problem essentially means extricating oneself from the box. This process is the synthetic part of creative thinking.

A good example of redefining a problem is summed up in the story of an executive at one of the biggest automobile companies in the Detroit area. The executive held a high-level position, and he loved his job and the money he made on the job. However, he despised the person he worked for, and because of this, he decided to find a new job. He went to a headhunter, who is someone who finds jobs for people. The headhunter assured the executive that a new job could be easily arranged. After this meeting, the executive went home and talked to his wife, who was teaching a unit on redefining problems as part of a course she was teaching on Applied Intelligence. The executive realized that he could apply what his wife was teaching to his own problem. He returned to the headhunter and gave the headhunter his boss's name. The headhunter found a new job for the executive's boss, which the boss – having no idea of what was going on – accepted. The executive then got his boss's job. The executive decided for creativity by redefining a problem.

2. Question and Analyze Assumptions

Everyone has assumptions. Often, one does not know he or she has these assumptions because they are widely shared. Creative people question assumptions and eventually lead others to do the same. Questioning assumptions is part of the analytical thinking involved in creativity. When Copernicus suggested that Earth revolves around the sun, the suggestion was viewed as preposterous because everyone could see that the sun revolves around Earth. Galileo's ideas, including the relative rates of falling objects, caused him to be banned as a heretic. When an employee questions the way that his boss manages the business, the boss does not smile. The employee is questioning assumptions that the boss and others simply accept – assumptions that they do not wish to open up to questions.

Sometimes it is not until many years later that society realizes the limitations or errors of their assumptions and the value of the creative person's thoughts. The momentum of those who question assumptions allows for cultural and technological advancement.

Society tends to make a mistake by emphasizing the answering and not the asking of questions. The good student is perceived as the one who can quickly come up with the right answers. The expert in a field thus becomes the extension of the expert student – the one who knows and can recite a lot of information. As John Dewey (1933) recognized, how one thinks is often more important than what one thinks. Schools need to teach students how to ask the right questions (questions that are good, thought-provoking, and interesting) and lessen the emphasis on rote and by-the-book learning.

3. Do Not Assume That Creative Ideas Sell Themselves: Sell Them

Everyone would like to assume that their wonderful, creative ideas will sell themselves. But, as Galileo, Edvard Munch, Toni Morrison, Sylvia Plath, and millions of others have discovered, they do not. On the contrary, creative ideas are usually viewed with suspicion and distrust. Moreover, those people who propose such ideas may be viewed with suspicion and distrust as well. People are comfortable with the ways they already think; indeed, most people have a particular interest in their existing way of thinking. Because of this, it can be extremely difficult to convince people to change their current way of thinking.

Thus, you need to learn how to persuade other people of the value of your ideas. This selling is part of the practical aspect of creative thinking. If you do a science project, it is a good idea to present it and demonstrate why it makes an important contribution. If you create a piece of artwork, you should be prepared to describe why you think it has value.

4. Enjoy Idea Generation

Creative people demonstrate a "legislative" style of thinking: They like to generate ideas (Isaksen & Gaulin, 2005; Sternberg, 1997). The environment for generating ideas can be constructively critical, but it must not be harshly or destructively critical. You need to acknowledge that some ideas are better than others. You should explore your ideas with your friends. You should meet with your teachers or parents to identify and encourage creativity in your ideas. When you have an idea that does not seem to have much value, do not just criticize it. Rather, think about new approaches. Ideally, you can use a new approach that uses and improves your older ideas. People should be praised for generating ideas, even if some of the ideas are silly or unrelated. People also should be encouraged to identify and develop their best ideas into high-quality projects.

5. Recognize That Knowledge Is a Double-Edged Sword and Act Accordingly

Some years ago, one of us was visiting a very famous psychologist who lives abroad. As part of the tour he had planned for the author, he invited the author to visit the local zoo. The two professors went past the monkey cages, and saw the monkeys engaged in what could euphemistically be called "strange and unnatural sexual behavior." The author, of course, looked away. However, the host did not do the same. After observing the monkeys for a short amount of time, the author was astounded to hear his host analyze the sexual behavior of the primates in terms of his theory of intelligence. The author realized at that time, as he has many times since, how knowledge and expertise can be a double-edged sword. With all his expertise, the psychologist had become rigid in his thinking.

However, one cannot be creative without knowledge. Quite simply, one cannot go beyond the existing state of knowledge if one does not know what that state is. Many students have ideas that are creative to them, but not to the field. How many times have you had a good idea, only to find out that someone beat you to it? Those with a greater knowledge base can be creative in ways that those who are still learning the basics of the field cannot be. If you want to be a creative guitar player, you have to know the basic chords and finger positions. If you want to be a creative writer, you need to know basic grammar and to have read the classics.

At the same time, those who have an expert level of knowledge can experience "tunnel vision," or narrow thinking. Experts can become so stuck in a way of thinking that they become unable to remove themselves from it (Frensch & Sternberg, 1989; Simonton, 2000). Such narrowing does not just happen to others. It happens to everyone, including the senior author of this book. For example, at one point in his career, every theory he proposed seemed to have three parts. (Of course, there were *three* good reasons for this . . .) At that point, he was "stuck on threes." Learning must be a lifelong process, not one that ends when a person achieves some measure of recognition. When a person believes that he or she knows everything there is to know, he or she is unlikely to ever show truly meaningful creativity again.

The upshot of this is that we tell our students that the teaching-learning process is a two-way process. Teachers have as much to learn from their students as the students have to learn from the teachers. Teachers have knowledge the students do not have, but students have flexibility the teachers do not have – precisely because they do not know as much as the teachers do. A creative teacher will not just teach his or her students but also learn from them.

6. Identify and Surmount Obstacles

Buying low and selling high means defying the crowd. And people who defy the crowd – people who think creatively – almost inevitably encounter resistance. The question is not whether one will encounter obstacles; that obstacles will be encountered is a fact. The question is whether the creative thinker has the resilience to continue on. We have often wondered why so many people start off their careers doing creative work and then vanish from the radar screen. We think we know at least one reason why: Sooner or later, they decide that being creative is not worth the resistance and punishment. The truly creative thinkers pay the short-term price because they recognize that they can make a difference in the long term. But, as we have discussed, it is often a long while before the value of creative ideas is recognized and appreciated.

One example of having to wait for ideas to be recognized occurred in our own experience. When the senior author was very young, he became interested in intelligence and intelligence testing as a result of poor scores on intelligence tests. As a seventh grader of the age of thirteen, he decided it would be interesting to do a science project on intelligence testing. He found the Stanford-Binet Intelligence Scales in the adult section of the local library and he started giving the test to friends. Unfortunately, one of his friends tattled to his mother, who reported him to the school authorities. The head school psychologist threatened to burn the book that contained the test if he ever brought it into school again. He suggested that the senior author find another interest. Had the senior author done so, he never would have done all the work he has done on intelligence, which has meant a great deal to his life, and, he hopes, something to the world. Indeed, this book would never have been written. The psychologist's opinion presented a major obstacle, especially to an early adolescent. However, because the author surmounted that obstacle, he has been able to do research on intelligence, which has been very fulfilling for him.

7. Take Sensible Risks

When creative people defy the crowd by buying low and selling high, they take risks in much the same way as do people who invest. Some such investments simply may not pan out. Moreover, defying the crowd means risking the crowd's anger. But there are levels of sensibility to keep in mind when defying the crowd. Creative people take sensible risks and produce ideas that others ultimately admire and respect as trend setting. In taking these risks, creative people sometimes make mistakes, fail, and fall flat on their faces.

We emphasize the importance of sensible risk-taking because we are not talking about risking life and limb for creativity. To help students learn to take sensible risks, teachers can encourage them to take some intellectual risks with courses, activities, and teachers – to develop a sense of how to assess risks.

Nearly every major discovery or invention entailed some risk. When a movie theater was the only place to see a movie, someone created the idea of the home video machine. Skeptics questioned if anyone would want to see videos on a small screen. Another initially risky idea was the home computer. Many wondered if anyone would have enough use for a home computer to justify the cost. These ideas were once risks but are now ingrained in our society.

The senior author took a risk as an assistant professor when he decided to study intelligence, as the field of intelligence has low prestige within academic psychology. When he was being considered for tenure, it came to his attention that his university was receiving letters that questioned why it would want to give tenure to someone in such a marginal and poorly respected field. He sought advice from a senior professor, Wendell Garner, telling Garner that perhaps he had made a mistake in labeling his work as being about intelligence. Indeed, he could have done essentially the same work but labeled it as being in the field of "thinking" or of "problem solving" – fields with more prestige. Garner's advice was that the senior author had come to Yale wanting to make a difference in the field of intelligence. He had made a difference, but now he was afraid it might cost him his job. He was right: He had taken a risk. But Garner maintained that there was only one thing that he could do – exactly what he was doing. If this field meant so much to him, then he needed to pursue it, just as he was doing, even if it meant losing his job. He did not lose his job, but other risks he has taken have not turned out as well. When taking risks, one must realize that some of them just will not work, and that is the cost of doing creative work. Indeed, choosing to study creativity is itself a risk, as it is often less respected than other areas that seem more prestigious, scientific, or relevant (Plucker, Beghetto, & Dow, 2004).

Few students are willing to take risks in school, because they learn that taking risks can be costly. Perfect test scores and papers receive praise and open up future possibilities. Failure to attain a certain academic standard is perceived as deriving from a lack of ability and motivation and may lead to scorn and lessened opportunities. Why risk taking hard courses or saying things that teachers may not like when that may lead to low grades or even failure? Indeed, how many of you have received a lower grade because you argued for a stance that the teacher disagreed with? Good teachers will recognize creative and high-quality work, even if it does not reflect their own beliefs. Unfortunately, there are some teachers who are unable to do this.

Furthermore, teachers may inadvertently encourage students to only learn to "play it safe" when they give assignments without choices and allow only particular answers to questions. The father of one of the authors once took a test that asked for the main reasons underlying World War I. The father gave a detailed and creative answer about three central reasons. When the test was returned, the teacher had given the father a 75 percent, because four reasons were discussed in class, and only three were mentioned in the answer. It is perfectly appropriate for the rules and "correct" answers to be valued on a test, of course. But when the rules and "correct" answers as expected by the teacher become the *only* thing valued on a test, a teacher is not encouraging or rewarding sensible risk-taking.

8. Tolerate Ambiguity

People like things to be in black and white. People like to think that a country is good or bad (ally or enemy) or that a given idea works or does not work. The problem is that there are a lot of grays in creative work. Artists working on new paintings and writers working on new books often report feeling scattered and unsure. They often need to figure out whether they are even on the right track. Scientists often are not sure whether the theory they have developed is exactly correct. These creative thinkers need to tolerate the ambiguity and uncertainty until they get the idea just right (Amabile, 1996).

A creative idea tends to come in bits and pieces and develops over time. However, the period in which the idea is developing tends to be uncomfortable. Without time or the ability to tolerate ambiguity, many may jump to a less than optimal solution. When a student has almost the right topic for a paper or almost the right science project, it's tempting for teachers to accept the near-miss. To help students become creative, teachers need to encourage them to accept and extend the period in which their ideas do not quite come together. Students need to be taught that uncertainty and discomfort are a part of living a creative life. Ultimately, they will benefit from their tolerance of ambiguity by coming up with better ideas.

9. Develop Self-Efficacy

Many people reach a point where they feel as if no one believes in them. We reach this point frequently, feeling that no one values or even appreciates what we are doing. Because creative work often doesn't get a warm reception, it is extremely important that creative people believe in the value of what they are doing. This is not to say that individuals should believe that every idea they have is a good idea. Rather, individuals need to believe that, ultimately, they have the ability to make a difference.

The main limitation on what students can do is what they think they can do. All students have the capacity to be creative and to experience the joy associated with making something new, but first they must be given a strong base for creativity. Sometimes teachers and parents unintentionally limit what students can do by sending messages that express or imply limits on students' potential accomplishments (Beghetto, 2006). Instead, these adults need to help students believe in their own ability to be creative. For example, one of us was an aspiring creative writer when he was a child. He would write short stories that were usually quite bad and ask his mother to read them. His mother critiqued the stories using very high standards – instead of telling him that his story was good for a ten-year-old, she gave him feedback and comments to make the story even better. The author grew up feeling that he was capable of writing stories that could be publishable with enough work and effort (and, eventually, he published many short stories). It was essential to have a mentor (in this case, his mother) who made him feel that there were no limits to what he could accomplish.

We have found that probably the best predictor of success among our students is not their ability, but their belief in their ability to succeed. If students are encouraged to succeed and to believe in their own ability to succeed, they very likely will find the success that otherwise would elude them.

10. Find What You Love to Do

It sounds so simple – love what you do. Yet it's absolutely true. You need to find what excites you in order to unleash your best creative performances. Your teachers and parents, in turn, need to remember that this may not be what really excites them. People who truly excel creatively (whether at work or at play) almost always genuinely love what they do. Certainly, the most creative people are intrinsically motivated in their work (Amabile, 1996; Ivcevic & Mayer, 2007). Less creative people often pick a career for the money or prestige and are bored with or hate their job. Most often, these people do not do work that makes a difference in their field. Finding what you really love to do can be time-consuming and even painful. In the long run, it almost always pays off.

We often meet students who are pursuing a certain field not because it is what they want to do, but because it is what their parents or other authority figures expect them to do. We always feel sorry for such students. We know that although they may do good work in that field, they almost certainly will not do great work. It is hard for people to do great work in a field that simply does not interest them.

Of course, taking this attitude is easier said than done. When Sternberg's son, Seth, was young, Sternberg was very happy that his son wanted to play the piano. He plays the piano, and was glad that his son wanted to play the piano, too. But then Seth stopped practicing and ultimately quit, and the elder Sternberg felt badly. A short time thereafter Seth informed the author that he had decided that he wanted to play the trumpet. The author reacted very negatively, pointing out to Seth that he had already quit the piano and probably would quit the trumpet, too.

The elder Sternberg then found himself wondering why he had been so harsh. How could he have said such a thing? But then he quickly understood it. If someone else's child wanted to play the trumpet, then that was fine. But the elder Sternberg could not imagine any Sternberg child playing the trumpet. It did not fit his ideal image of a Sternberg child. The elder Sternberg realized he was being narrow-minded and doing exactly the opposite of what he had told everyone else to do. It's one thing to talk the talk, another to walk the walk. He backpedaled, and Seth started playing the trumpet.

Eventually, he did, in fact, quit the trumpet. Finding the right thing is frustrating work! But Seth eventually did find the right thing. As a college student, he already had started two businesses. Seth was doing what was right for him. Whether it was right for his father really did not matter.

11. Delay Gratification

Part of being creative means being able to work on a project or task for a long time without immediate rewards. Students must learn that rewards are not always instant and that there are benefits to delaying gratification. In the short term, people are often ignored when they do creative work or even punished for doing it.

Many people believe that they should reward children immediately for good performance, and that children should expect rewards. This style of teaching and parenting emphasizes the "here and now" and often comes at the expense of what is best in the long term.

An important lesson in life – and one that is intimately related to establishing the inner discipline to do creative work – is to learn to wait for rewards. The greatest rewards are often those that are delayed.

We can relate to the concept of delayed gratification, as one of the greatest rewards of Sternberg's own life has yet to come. Some years ago, Sternberg contracted with a publisher to develop a test of intelligence based on his theory of intelligence (Sternberg, 1985). Things were going well until the president of the company left and a new president took over. Shortly after that, the project was canceled. The company's perception was that there was not enough of a potential market for a test of intelligence based on his theory of analytical, creative, and practical abilities. Sternberg's perception was that the company and some of its market was stuck in the past, endlessly replicating the construction and use of the kinds of tests that have been constructed and used since the turn of the century.

Whoever may have been right, Sternberg and Grigorenko (two of your authors) ultimately decided that if we wanted to make this test work, we would have to publish it ourselves, not through a conventional publisher. Some years later, we are still working to find a way that the test can be used by others. It is a difficult exercise in delay of gratification. But we try to practice what we preach, and so we wait for the day when the test will see the light of day and make a difference to children's lives.

As demonstrated by this example, hard work often does not bring immediate rewards. Children do not immediately become expert baseball players, dancers, musicians, or sculptors. And the reward of becoming an expert can seem very far away. Children often succumb to the temptations of the moment, such as watching television or playing video games. The people who make the most of their abilities are those who wait for a reward and recognize that few serious challenges can be met in a moment. Ninth-grade students may not see the benefits of hard work, but the advantages of a solid academic performance will be obvious when they apply to college.

12. Find an Environment That Fosters Creativity

You need to find an environment that fosters and rewards creativity (Cropley, 2006). Otherwise, no matter how many of the other decisions you make, you may find it ultimately very difficult to decide for creativity.

The teachers most people probably remember from their school days are not those who crammed the most content into their lectures. The teachers most people remember are those teachers whose thoughts and actions served as a role model. Most likely, they balanced teaching content with teaching students how to think with and about that content. For example, one of us will never forget the teacher who started off a seventh-grade social studies class by asking whether students knew what social studies was. Of course, everyone nodded his or her head. The class then spent three sessions trying to figure out just what it was.

You can stimulate your own creativity by cross-fertilizing in your thinking – in other words, thinking across subjects and disciplines. The traditional school environment often has separate classrooms and classmates for different subjects and seems to influence students into thinking that learning occurs in discrete boxes-the math box, the social studies box, and the science box. However, creative ideas and insights often result from integrating material across subject areas, not from memorizing and reciting material.

If you want to do creative work, you need to *allow yourself the time to think creatively*. This society is a society in a hurry. People eat fast food, rush from one place to another, and value quickness. Indeed, one way to say someone is smart is to say that the person is *quick* (Sternberg, 1985), a clear indication of our emphasis on time. This is also indicated by the format of the standardized tests used – lots of multiple-choice problems squeezed into a brief time slot. If you have a paper to write, do not wait until the last minute. Rushing through it will almost certainly not allow you the time to think creatively. Most creative insights do not happen in a rush (Gruber & Davis, 1988; Runco, 2004). You need time to understand a problem and to toss it around.

To be creative, you need to allow yourself to make mistakes. Buying low and selling high carries a risk. Many ideas are unpopular simply because they are not good. People often think a certain way because that way works better than other ways. But, once in a while, a great thinker comes along – a Freud, a Piaget, a Chomsky, or an Einstein – and shows us a new way to think. These thinkers made contributions because they allowed themselves and their collaborators to take risks and make mistakes.

Many of Freud's and Piaget's ideas turned out to be wrong. Freud confused Victorian issues regarding sexuality with universal conflicts. Piaget misjudged the ages at which children could perform certain cognitive feats. Their ideas were great not because they lasted forever, but, rather, because they became the basis for other ideas. Freud's and Piaget's mistakes allowed others to profit from their ideas.

Although being successful often involves making mistakes along the way, schools are often unforgiving of mistakes. Errors on schoolwork are often marked with a large and pronounced X written in red ink. When a student responds to a question with an incorrect answer, some teachers pounce on the student for not having read or understood the material, which results in classmates laughing. In hundreds of ways over the course of a school career, children learn that it is not all right to make mistakes. The result is that they become afraid to risk the independent (and sometimes flawed) thinking that leads to creativity.

Being creative requires you to take responsibility for both successes and failures. To take responsibility means you need to (1) understand your own creative process, (2) criticize your ideas when appropriate, and (3) take pride in your best creative work.

You can enhance your creative output through creative collaboration. Creative performance often is viewed as a solitary occupation. You may picture the writer writing alone in an apartment, the artist painting in a solitary loft, or the musician practicing endlessly in a small music room. In reality, people often work in groups. Collaboration can spur creativity.

You also need to learn how to imagine things from other viewpoints. An essential aspect of working with other people and getting the most out of collaborative creative activity is to imagine yourself in other people's shoes. Individuals can broaden their perspective by learning to see the world from different points of view.

Creativity comes from a person-environment fit. What is judged as creative is an interaction between a person and the environment (Connell, Sheridan, & Gardner, 2003; Csikszentmihalyi, 1999; Gardner, 1999; Sternberg, 1999a; Sternberg & Lubart,

1995a; Sternberg et al., 2005). The very same product that is rewarded as creative in one time or place may be scorned in another.

In the movie *Dead Poets' Society*, a teacher who the audience might well judge to be creative is viewed as incompetent by the school's administration. Similar experiences occur many times a day in many settings. There is no absolute standard for what constitutes creative work. The same product or idea may be valued or devalued in different environments. The lesson is that individuals need to find a setting in which their creative talents and unique contributions are rewarded, or they need to modify their environment.

One of the authors once had a student to whom he gave consummately bad advice concerning environment. She had two job offers. One was from an institution that was very prestigious, but not a good fit to the kind of work she valued. The other institution was a bit less prestigious, but was a much better fit to her values. The author advised her to take the job in the more prestigious institution, telling her that if she did not accept the job there, she would always wonder what would have happened if she did. Bad advice: She went there and never fit in well. Eventually she left, and now she is at an institution that values the kind of work she does. Now we always advise students to go for the best fit.

SUMMING UP

We have described twelve relatively simple things anyone can do to help foster creativity. But the important thing to remember is that the development of creativity is a lifelong process, not one that ends with any particular high school or university degree (Beghetto & Kaufman, 2007; Cohen, 1989; Rostan, Pariser, & Gruber, 2002). Once a person has a major creative idea, it is easy for that individual to spend the rest of his or her career following up on it. It is frightening for that person to contemplate that the next idea may not be as good as the last one, or that success may disappear with the next idea. This fear often results in people becoming complacent and the creativity process being halted.

Sometimes, as experts, people become too content with their own knowledge and stop growing. People can be victims of their own expertise. They can become entrenched in ways of thinking that worked in the past, but not necessarily in the future. Being creative means that people need to step outside the boxes that they – and others – have created for themselves, and continue to do so throughout their entire life.

Creativity is an essential component of learning and problem solving, because virtually any problem, by the virtue of definition, imposes on its solver some ambiguity that needs to be overcome in order to find the solution. In talking about creativity, we have provided you with twelve pieces of advice on how to develop creativity in yourself and in others around you.

Automatizing Information Processing

WHAT IS AUTOMATIZATION?

Think about what happens when you read a newspaper or a magazine article. Unless the article is unusually technical or poorly written, the chances are that you can understand it fairly easily. You are probably barely aware of the mental processing you are doing while you are reading, despite the enormous complexity of the reading process. Because you are, most likely, a skilled reader (at least, in comparison to young children), you can concentrate on absorbing the new facts and ideas in the article. You don't have to pay attention to things such as what the individual letters of each word are, how the words are pronounced, how the words fit together to form sentences, what the words mean, and so on. If you were in early elementary school, however, you would not be able to devote as much attention to absorbing the main facts and ideas of the article. Rather, you would have to concentrate on some of the basic processes – such as letter and word encoding, figuring out meanings of words, and so on – that are required for basic reading comprehension.

Stated in another way, as an adult reader, you have *automatized* – or made automatic – the lower level information processing involved in reading. As a result, you are able to devote most of your mental resources to understanding the higher-level information contained in a text. Young children have not fully automatized the processes of reading. Hence, they must devote relatively more of their attention to lower-level processing at the expense of higher level processing. Young children do not have the mental resources left over to comprehend fully the article that easily and effortlessly can be comprehended by an adult. Whereas we have already briefly covered this topic, we will now explore the question of automatization in more detail.

Consider another example of automatization. When you drive, you very likely are able to listen to the radio and even carry on a conversation as well. If you are driving by yourself, you may find yourself listening to the radio and even thinking about your activities for the day as you both drive and listen to the radio. You are able to devote so many mental resources to listening, talking, and thinking about matters other than road conditions and the state of your automobile. Why? It is because, for you, driving has long ago become automatic. But try to remember back to when you were first learning to drive. You probably had to devote your full attention to studying the road and working on not getting into an accident. If you learned how to drive standard shift, you may have found that just paying attention to shifting seemed to require more attention than you could possibly spare, given the necessity of watching out for where you were going and what was getting in your way. When you were first learning to drive, you would not have been in a position to carry on a serious conversation and still be able to watch the road. As in the case of reading, your automatizing of information processing (in this case about how to drive) has freed the mental resources you once needed to devote fully to driving for other mental tasks, such as carrying on a conversation or thinking about your activities for the day.

If you are a touch typist on the computer (i.e., you type the "correct" way), you will have observed the same course of development. When you first learned to type without looking at the keys, you may well have thought seriously about each keystroke, trying to ensure that you hit the right key. Your typing when you first learned was probably slow and effortful. If you have since become an efficient touch typist, however, you no longer need to devote much attention to individual keystrokes. On the contrary, you may be practically unaware of them. Efficient touch typists find that when they see a string of words, they automatically type in the correct letters. They hardly realize at all what their fingers are doing. The process of typing has become so automatized that the touch typist is not even fully aware, at a conscious level, of which keys are where on the keyboard. If someone were to ask the touch typist the letter that corresponds to a key in a certain position, the typist would probably have great difficulty in answering correctly. Many touch typists would be unable to fill in the letters on a blank keyboard. Yet they can rapidly type a paper without thinking about which keys are where. Again, a process that was once highly conscious, effortful, and controlled has become effortless, subconscious, and automatic.

These examples show that performance in almost any kind of cognitive or motor skill can become faster and more accurate with practice. Practice seems to bring about a noticeable change in the kind of processing a person does on a given task. Several investigators have actually proposed that there are two distinct forms of information processing. Walter Schneider and Richard Shiffrin (1977) have referred to these two types of processing as *controlled* and *automatic* processing. Controlled processing is:

(a) comparatively slow
(b) sequential in nature (executed one step after another)
(c) effortful
(d) under conscious control
(e) limited by short-term memory, and
(f) requires little or no training to develop.

In contrast, automatic processing is:

(a) relatively fast
(b) executed in parallel (many different operations are done at once)
(c) almost effortless
(d) not limited by short-term memory capacity

(e) for the most part subconscious, and

(f) requires extensive practice to develop.

Tasks such as reading, playing the piano, and driving require largely controlled processing when they are first learned, but later require primarily automatic processing.

Reading, driving, and typing illustrate the transition of three kinds of information processing from controlled to automatic. They also show the trade-offs between coping with relative novelty and automatization. People who are able to automatize information processing efficiently have more mental resources ("brain" power, so to speak) left over for other things. In contrast, people who have a hard time automatizing information processing may find themselves simply lacking the mental resources to cope with relative novelty. Even if they have the mental powers needed to cope with relative novelty, they will be so busy dealing with the basic aspects of a given task that they will be unable to devote enough attention to the novel aspects of the task or situation.

This trade-off between dealing with novelty and automatizing information processing has important implications for distinguishing between fast learners and slow learners. Fast learners are often those who can automatize information processing with relatively little effort. Their efficient automatization leaves them with plenty of "brain power" left over to process the new in a given task or situation. Slow learners may have difficulty with the automatization of information processing. As a result, they may have few resources left over to cope with relative novelty.

According to this view, slow learners are often not people who simply have little "brain power." On the contrary, they even may be superior in knowledge-acquisition or other processes discussed earlier in this book. Some slow learners may thus be in a paradoxical situation of being highly intelligent according to conventional tests yet learning slower than their classmates. Such people are referred to as having a learning disability. Some learning disabilities, therefore, can result in part from inefficiency in the automatization of information processing (Samuels, 1999; Sternberg & Wagner, 1982).

Fortunately, difficulties in automatization are often limited to specific media or symbol systems. For example, individuals with a reading disability are often quite effective in learning in other areas, such as numerical computation or reasoning. Individuals with a mathematical disability are often highly effective readers, and may be fine reasoners in domains other than mathematics. In short, inefficiency of automatization is often limited only to certain domains of information processing, rather than being general to all domains.

IMPLICATIONS OF AUTOMATIZATION FOR INTELLIGENCE THEORY AND TESTING

This view has important implications both for understanding and for measuring intelligence. Consider, for example, findings about intelligence that have emerged from studies of intellectual functioning.

One finding that consistently emerges is that speed of performing elementary cognitive tasks is often correlated with performance on standard intelligence tests (Sternberg & Pretz, 2004). To many psychologists, these correlations have seemed surprising. Imagine a reaction-time task in which a light goes on and the individual must rapidly press a button corresponding to that light, which turns it off. Why should basic speed on this task correlate with intelligence test performance? The choice reaction-time problems are about as simple as problems can get, whereas the problems on intelligence tests are usually much more complex. The present view suggests that such a correlation is because of the importance of automatization in intelligent performance, overall, and from the degree to which the choice reaction-time test measures automatization. Why should the speed with which someone can name a single letter of the alphabet, or compare whether two letters have the same name, correlate with intelligence test scores? Again, the present theory would suggest that the two tasks correlate because of the role of automatization in intelligence.

Theorists such as Arthur Jensen (1982, 1998) and Earl Hunt (1980) have suggested that such tasks correlate with measured intelligence because of the importance of speed of mental functioning in intellectual ability. They may be correct, in part. But efficiency of automatization seems to play at least as much of a role in these statistical correlations as sheer speed. In tasks such as choice reaction time, letter identification, and letter comparison, subjects are usually given large numbers of test trials, for which their reaction time is measured. Some may rapidly automatize performance on these tasks, whereas others may not. The rate and amount of automatization that eventually takes place may tell us more about intelligence than the sheer speed with which simple tasks such as choice reaction time are processed.

The point of view expressed above has certain implications for fully understanding the nature of bias in mental testing. Traditional forms of analysis of test bias may insufficiently take into account the roles of relative novelty and automatization. Suppose that the exact same test items are given to two groups of people. One group of people is highly familiar with the kinds of items that appear on the test. Indeed, they may barely need to read the directions in order to get started solving the test items. For them, performance on the given type of task is probably at least somewhat automatized before the test even begins, so that the individuals in this group will have ample mental resources left over to deal with the novelty in the test items in the test situation.

For another group of people, however, the test items may be quite unfamiliar. These people may have to read the instructions quite carefully, and even then may need substantial practice before they reach the level of automatization that members of the other group started off with. Members of this group will begin with relatively few mental resources left over to deal with the novelty in the test items and stimuli. As a result, the test will be measuring performance that is at quite different levels on the experiential continuum for the two groups. Each group may have the same mental structures and use the same mental processes and strategies. However, the members of the second group will be at a clear disadvantage. They will be hampered by their previous unfamiliarity with the kinds of items appearing on tests, or even with the kinds of past experiences that would enable them rapidly to automatize performance on these items. As a result, the test will not really be measuring the same thing for the two groups of people.

An example of how familiarity with the test items can impact scores can be seen in different types of tasks used on current intelligence tests. If general information (i.e., knowing who discovered electricity) is measured verbally or by having people write out answers, there are often large differences between European Americans and African Americans. If, however, the same type of information is tested using pictures and photographs, these differences are greatly reduced. Similar results are found when testing reading comprehension, with students acting out written instruction, such as "peel a banana" (Kaufman, 1994). It is quite amazing to think that the way that you ask people to answer a question can matter so much. Yet it makes sense when you consider the importance of familiarity with a test's format. If you are trying to find out how much someone knows about the world or about history, you might be only testing how comfortable he or she is with writing or speaking. In sum, understanding intelligence requires more than simply understanding the various kinds of components discussed in the previous part of the book (metacomponents, performance components, and knowledge-acquisition components). A full theory of intelligence must therefore take into account not only mental processing, but people's level of experience with the tasks and situations that require this mental processing. Dealing with novelty and automatizing information processing as you gain more experience with tasks and situations constitute two important aspects of intellectual skills.

INCREASING THE EFFICACY OF AUTOMATIZATION

We can reach the conclusion that the ability to automatize information processing quickly and well is an important, if not obvious, part of intelligence. As we have seen, people who are able to automatize will have more resources available for other new things in their lives. In general, automatization lets people take in more of the world, and learn more.

How can people increase the efficiency and quality of their automatized information processing? Surprisingly, there has been relatively little research on this topic. Fortunately, however, one researcher, Walter Schneider (Schneider & Shiffrin, 1977; Schneider, 1982), has devoted a portion of his career to discovering the principles that lead to rapid automatization. The discussion in this section is based largely on his work, in which he has participants perform relatively simple tasks over thousands of times, and observes the course of automatization. Here are some of the main findings from his research.

First, Schneider has found that consistency in information processing is a necessary condition for the development of automatization. In other words, when we practice a task that we wish to automatize, we need to develop a strategy that can be used consistently throughout the task. At least in initial learning, it is also important that the task be fairly standard. In other words, a task like juggling involves the same basic motions and concepts and would be ideal for starting out. In contrast, a poor choice might be something like playing soccer, in which you would have to run, kick, aim, and do many other actions that required different physical and mental actions. Schneider has found that task performance improves based on the number of times you perform the task and the degree of consistency in your performance. This can be expressed as number of trials X degree of consistency.

Second, Schneider has found that the key to becoming better at automatizing a process is to do it correctly and accurately. This may seem like an obvious statement, but it actually goes against an important principle in learning – which is that you learn by your mistakes. Errors teach us what *not* to do next time. Indeed, making mistakes and learning from these mistakes can often result in finding new and interesting solutions to a process. But the best way to automatize a process is to perform it as mistake-free as possible. Note that, in automatization your goal is not to learn what to do (as in learning from your mistakes), but, rather, to learn how to do it (as efficiently as possible).

Third, although the development of a full level of automatization can take anywhere from two hundred to two thousand (or even more) trials of performance on a task, automatization can begin much more quickly. Sometimes it can set in at as few as ten trials, so long as those trials involve consistency in strategic performance. In other words, you could not expect to completely automatize a task without a great deal of experience with that task. However, you can expect to see at least *some* results fairly quickly if you follow the principles discussed in this chapter and if you are able to develop a consistent strategy for task performance.

Fourth, there may be some degree of "consolidation time" in our automatization of information processing. You have probably noticed that when you are learning how to do something new, whether it be typing, throwing a football, playing the piano, or doing a difficult math problem, you reach a point where you are just not improving any more. You may even notice that you start to make a number of mistakes. The best thing to do when this happens is to stop for a while, or at least to slow down for a short period of time. Often, learning has taken place and is continuing to take place, but it needs time to consolidate. In other words, your performance may not fully reflect your learning. So take a break, and then go back to the task.

Fifth, it helps to learn the task that we wish to automatize while trying to do it faster. Schneider has found that people learning a task need to be pushed, at least a bit, to perform faster. In other words, it is not enough that you merely perform the task again and again. You also have to push yourself to speed up. So, for example, if you wish to increase your typing speed, you have to work at it consciously and not just expect that typing lots and lots of papers will result in the speedup you desire.

Sixth, automatization is likely to be more rapid if we are able to devote our full attentional resources to the task at hand. The more we are distracted, the less attention we can devote to the task. As a result, we are less likely to be able to efficiently automatize our performance. So when you decide that you would like to increase your automatization of performance on a given task, try to devote as much of your attention as you can to that task – at least during the periods when you are trying to improve your performance on it. If you're learning to juggle, don't practice with the television on (especially if you're juggling sharp objects).

Seventh, automatization of performance can be substantially influenced by the context in which that performance occurs. Consider, for example, bowling. Nate may learn to bowl and get quite good at it, figuring out how to knock over the most pins and make the process automatized. However, if Nate finds himself in a different bowling alley, or using a different bowling ball, or even bowling in different circumstances, he may end up taking much longer to line up his shots, knock down fewer pins, and generally bowl worse. So, you need to realize that automatization does not necessarily generalize right away. If you wish to perform a certain task automatically under many different circumstances, then at some point you will have to practice that task under a variety of circumstances. Automatization can be expected to generalize only if you help it along in this way.

Eighth, automatization and generalization require that learning be done at the appropriate level of the task being learned. Consider, for example, that you are learning to play the piano. Initially, you will learn with easy pieces (such as "Three Blind Mice" or "Mary had a Little Lamb"), and you may actually become quite good at them. But eventually, you must move on to harder material (such as classical or jazz). Similarly, in learning to drive, you would probably be at a disadvantage if your initial learning were on a busy rush-hour street in New York or Mexico City or Rome. Eventually, though, if you will have to negotiate such traffic, it will be important for your training to include it. One of us learned to drive in suburban California – a fairly easy place to drive, with wide roads, many traffic lights, and constantly sunny weather. When he moved to the East Coast, he was initially unprepared to figure out how to suddenly deal with jug handles, unprotected left-hand turns, single-lane roads, and driving in snow and heavy rain. Indeed, for almost any task that will eventually be automatized, it is necessary to start with easy subtasks and to move on to more difficult ones. The difficulty of the subtask has to gradually increase in an appropriate way for one's level of expertise.

Ninth, motivation is often more important to automatizing information process-ing than is any other single variable. The automatization of processing often requires many, many trials of repeated practice. It is very easy for motivation to flag under these circumstances. After a certain point, the task can become repetitive and boring. It is therefore important to build in ways of motivating yourself. Such ways might include considering the future benefits of automatized processing (such as being able to type quickly or to play the piano well in concerts), evaluating your progress (by plotting a graph of the speed at which you are performing the task at different points in time), or considering how much more enjoyable it will be to you to perform the task quickly and easily rather than slowly and effortfully. Many people never automatize task performance simply because they have lost the motivation to do so.

Tenth and finally, it may help you more to think of yourself as your own "coach" rather than as your own "teacher." The practice required to automatize performance is more like that required for sports or music or dance than for the kind of academic learning required in school. Relatively few school-based activities require repeated performance on a single type of task, whereas a number of extracurricular activities do. Viewing yourself as a coach rather than as a teacher may put you more in the correct frame of mind for the task at hand.

AUTOMATIZATION: SOME PRACTICE PROBLEMS

As you can see from this discussion, there is no one general skill of automatized information processing. Automatization occurs at different rates in different domains. It may be present to a high degree in one kind of performance, but entirely absent in another. Thus, any practice in task automatization must necessarily be limited in scope and domain.

The following practice exercises are intended to help you automatize performance on four tasks in the domain of letter and symbol recognition. As you perform these tasks, keep in mind the findings of Walter Schneider as described above. You will need a clock or watch with a second hand.

LETTER COMPARISON

In the letter-comparison task, you will be presented with four sets of letter pairs. Each set contains eighty pairs of letters. Your task is to scan these pairs of letters rapidly and in order, and to indicate whether each pair of letters has the same name or a different name. For example, the following pairs are composed of letters with the same name: AA, Dd, fF, nn. The following pairs are composed of letters with different names: BK, Nb, gF, hz. For each pair, indicate as quickly as you can whether the letters are the same (S) or different (D). Time yourself as you work through each set of these letter pairs. See if you can improve your speed. Try not to make mistakes. Answers appear after the last set. This task is based on Posner and Mitchell (1967).

LETTER-COMPARISON TASK

Set 1

1. j o	17. O S	33. O T	49. Q Q	65. y s
2. i n	18. w W	34. r R	50. N n	66. L E
3. k k	19. L i	35. b c	51. E z	67. C C
4. l v	20. R r	36. U u	52. m i	68. E F
5. q x	21. T t	37. Q r	53. F F	69. d d
6. D D	22. F W	38. x g	54. V v	70. A P
7. v Y	23. B b	39. a a	55. K H	71. E E
8. P P	24. R u	40. Z Z	56. S s	72. c W
9. x X	25. i P	41. R R	57. T T	73. A A
10. f F	26. s k	42. V r	58. o g	74. F o
11. N N	27. e e	43. E J	59. C y	75. z Z
12. r t	28. T t	44. N n	60. h h	76. t F
13. K I	29. r s	45. G G	61. l u	77. k k
14. c C	30. V E	46. f u	62. i n	78. d D
15. L I	31. h h	47. J g	63. o o	79. N N
16. h h	32. s S	48. a c	64. f f	80. x B

(Problems continued on next page)

Set 2

1. u R	17. A A	33. I K	49. c b	65. a C
2. f f	18. f E	34. D D	50. Z z	66. X x
3. P i	19. Y y	35. e r	51. D d	67. B B
4. s Y	20. k k	36. t F	52. E L	68. j o
5. W e	21. l v	37. N n	53. c c	69. L l
6. h h	22. n N	38. r V	54. H c	70. H K
7. M E	23. q x	39. m m	55. T t	71. c C
8. q Q	24. G G	40. J E	56. l u	72. u m
9. E E	25. s i	41. Q r	57. i n	73. t T
10. x B	26. N N	42. k k	58. O O	74. G m
11. a a	27. E z	43. S s	59. g x	75. P P
12. O F	28. i I	44. t F	60. e E	76. R P
13. T O	29. W w	45. F E	61. S O	77. F F
14. I I	30. a y	46. r S	62. T T	78. y C
15. s S	31. J j	47. d d	63. r h	79. W w
16. V E	32. V v	48. T t	64. u u	80. i g

Set 3

1. f O	17. c c	33. x q	49. c b	65. n X
2. I I	18. A n	34. y Y	50. O d	66. W w
3. s i	19. B B	35. a q	51. n n	67. O S
4. E E	20. R P	36. u m	52. u R	68. h r
5. f T	21. v V	37. g G	53. f f	69. r R
6. E E	22. D D	38. E F	54. M w	70. C c
7. i g	23. e w	39. c c	55. a a	71. Z j
8. k k	24. z E	40. l l	56. T t	72. v l
9. f t	25. V I	41. T O	57. F K	73. Z z
10. z Z	26. c C	42. s S	58. s S	74. E V
11. F f	27. R r	43. h j	59. U u	75. O o
12. s s	28. T T	44. Q q	60. i n	76. H C
13. p I	29. u u	45. P P	61. I K	77. v V
14. G G	30. K H	46. g x	62. e r	78. X x
15. x b	31. r V	47. Q r	63. N N	79. j o
16. E L	32. J J	48. s S	64. I i	80. F F

Set 4

1. N n	7. u u	13. n N	19. J j	25. O f
2. E z	8. T T	14. E J	20. u f	26. Z z
3. m i	9. g i	15. V v	21. P A	27. t F
4. D D	10. C y	16. R P	22. E E	28. k k
5. V v	11. a y	17. Q Q	23. e W	29. E e
6. H K	12. G G	18. a c	24. I I	30. x B

(Problems continued on next page)

31. N	N	41. f	F	51. O	o	61. V	E	71. E	E
32. s	y	42. N	N	52. q	x	62. h	h	72. P	i
33. f	f	43. r	t	53. l	v	63. s	S	73. u	R
34. o	o	44. K	I	54. k	k	64. T	O	74. B	b
35. f	E	45. c	C	55. i	n	65. e	E	75. G	F
36. l	u	46. L	I	56. j	o	66. c	b	76. T	t
37. d	d	47. r	r	57. x	X	67. S	s	77. r	S
38. F	E	48. S	O	58. P	P	68. r	Q	78. T	t
39. C	C	49. w	W	59. Y	q	69. x	g	79. c	c
40. E	L	50. L	l	60. D	D	70. a	a	80. k	s

Answers to Letter-Comparison Task

Set 1

1. D	17. D	33. D	49. S	65. D
2. D	18. S	34. S	50. S	66. D
3. S	19. D	35. D	51. D	67. S
4. D	20. S	36. S	52. D	68. D
5. D	21. S	37. D	53. S	69. S
6. S	22. D	38. D	54. S	70. D
7. D	23. S	39. S	55. D	71. S
8. S	24. D	40. S	56. S	72. D
9. S	25. D	41. S	57. S	73. S
10. S	26. D	42. D	58. D	74. D
11. S	27. S	43. D	59. D	75. S
12. D	28. S	44. S	60. S	76. D
13. D	29. D	45. S	61. D	77. S
14. S	30. D	46. D	62. D	78. S
15. D	31. S	47. D	63. S	79. S
16. S	32. S	48. D	64. S	80. D

Set 2

1. D	11. S	21. D	31. S	41. D
2. S	12. D	22. S	32. S	42. S
3. D	13. D	23. D	33. D	43. S
4. D	14. S	24. S	34. S	44. D
5. D	15. S	25. D	35. D	45. D
6. S	16. D	26. S	36. D	46. D
7. D	17. S	27. D	37. S	47. S
8. S	18. D	28. S	38. D	48. S
9. S	19. S	29. S	39. S	49. D
10. D	20. S	30. D	40. D	50. S

(Answers continued on next page)

51. S	57. D	63. D	69. S	75. S
52. D	58. S	64. S	70. D	76. D
53. S	59. D	65. D	71. S	77. S
54. D	60. S	66. S	72. D	78. D
55. S	61. D	67. S	73. S	79. S
56. D	62. S	68. D	74. D	80. D

Set 3

1. D	17. S	33. D	49. D	65. D
2. S	18. D	34. S	50. D	66. S
3. D	19. S	35. D	51. S	67. D
4. S	20. D	36. D	52. D	68. D
5. D	21. S	37. S	53. S	69. S
6. S	22. S	38. D	54. D	70. S
7. D	23. D	39. S	55. S	71. D
8. S	24. D	40. S	56. S	72. D
9. D	25. D	41. D	57. D	73. S
10. S	26. S	42. S	58. S	74. D
11. S	27. S	43. D	59. S	75. S
12. S	28. S	44. S	60. D	76. D
13. D	29. S	45. S	61. D	77. S
14. S	30. D	46. D	62. D	78. S
15. D	31. D	47. D	63. S	79. D
16. D	32. S	48. S	64. S	80. S

Set 4

1. S	17. S	33. S	49. S	65. S
2. D	18. D	34. S	50. S	66. D
3. D	19. S	35. D	51. S	67. S
4. S	20. D	36. D	52. D	68. D
5. S	21. D	37. S	53. D	69. D
6. D	22. S	38. D	54. S	70. S
7. S	23. D	39. S	55. D	71. S
8. S	24. S	40. D	56. D	72. D
9. D	25. D	41. S	57. S	73. D
10. D	26. S	42. S	58. S	74. S
11. D	27. D	43. D	59. D	75. D
12. S	28. S	44. D	60. S	76. S
13. S	29. S	45. S	61. D	77. D
14. D	30. D	46. D	62. S	78. S
15. S	31. S	47. S	63. S	79. S
16. D	32. D	48. D	64. D	80. D

VISUAL SEARCH

This task, which has been studied by William Estes (1982) and others, requires you to search a string of letters for a target letter. If you find the target letter in the string of letters, you indicate this with a "Y" (Yes). If you do not find the target letter in the string of letters, you indicate this with an "N" (No). In this task, unlike the previous task, the case of the letter *does* matter. In other words, the case of the letter (capital or lower) in the target must match the case of the letter in the subsequent letter string. For example, if you see the target letter K followed by the letter string g H N p K, you should indicate "Y." But if you see the target letter z followed by the letter string c A Z P u, you should indicate "N."

Eight sets of visual-search items follow. Each set contains forty items. The items become progressively more difficult in terms of the number of letters in the letter string following the target. Try to increase the speed with which you scan the letter strings as you progress through the successive sets of exercises. Answers appear after the last set.

VISUAL SEARCH TASK
Set 1

1. f	K	n	p	C	21. p	B	P	I	N
2. B	L	x	B	r	22. T	m	v	E	Y
3. n	e	p	b	n	23. J	K	o	b	j
4. V	R	S	T	O	24. e	r	e	x	c
5. t	b	t	n	q	25. g	m	T	S	u
6. I	Y	o	M	p	26. N	C	S	Q	W
7. c	m	W	c	l	27. f	i	h	n	f
8. P	S	K	P	Y	28. A	F	C	v	p
9. v	t	L	N	v	29. y	h	y	e	a
10. m	f	r	e	p	30. A	K	D	L	G
11. g	S	g	L	u	31. p	O	F	v	M
12. S	L	R	Y	M	32. F	W	c	F	k
13. l	n	c	l	x	33. G	l	c	p	O
14. O	E	s	F	R	34. h	i	j	e	h
15. x	v	T	I	d	35. m	c	g	M	F
16. B	N	E	B	V	36. d	u	r	m	w
17. J	t	O	J	f	37. v	g	U	s	n
18. n	l	f	c	d	38. R	M	R	G	T
19. K	A	r	G	n	39. t	C	h	t	M
20. E	A	F	H	E	40. F	v	R	N	o

Set 2

1. P	J	m	A	h	3. E	M	C	G	E
2. c	o	m	c	y	4. x	b	O	m	P

(Problems continued on next page)

5. l	w l c k	23. R	E u M k
6. H	K E D Z	24. i	m j d i
7. V	P o V y	25. Q	C A F N
8. f	m k z v	26. c	h U s c
9. A	f V A r	27. b	i T H d
10. C	T L J E	28. K	M U l k
11. k	a R f M	29. r	Y o M q
12. H	M r T z	30. s	o l f p
13. s	a F s N	31. C	T P O C
14. L	M e L x	32. B	i G H q
15. f	r m c k	33. T	N A J D
16. g	n Z g d	34. d	s t c r
17. S	R o E j	35. E	p E F k
18. c	m i c g	36. o	T S u r
19. R	Z D R F	37. L	O M T Y
20. f	R m k D	38. P	r W P u
21. w	b t w k	39. y	k b o t
22. Y	D Y O E	40. a	J d a M

Set 3

1. M	L q M g	21. p	s O N b
2. s	T N T W	22. F	h e F W
3. O	C n k O	23. Q	N I W Q
4. c	T m A I	24. h	z h i o
5. r	p Y m F	25. M	Z b M s
6. B	S G B I	26. d	u r m w
7. j	d R k j	27. e	v A W d
8. n	e f l c	28. M	G T M Z
9. K	e R G n	29. t	b t E R
10. F	S F T O	30. R	f A o V
11. e	l I A n	31. W	T G W D
12. B	m k B H	32. q	v S M u
13. m	q l m e	33. J	y m J O
14. V	O T R D	34. u	c p u l
15. t	r x u t	35. g	o m T S
16. m	Q i T d	36. E	A R S W
17. c	m c S t	37. f	p f i v
18. L	S W B O	38. A	F r M k
19. v	t L v N	39. s	m s p i
20. k	x m o r	40. B	H Y T D

(Problems continued on next page)

Set 4

1. M	L	R	q	T	u	c	21. U	M	T	U	S	O	L
2. p	c	a	x	t	m	y	22. c	t	M	a	f	C	i
3. i	v	O	S	x	b	l	23. n	i	c	d	s	e	m
4. T	S	N	E	T	M	G	24. v	t	L	o	v	Q	r
5. B	G	S	n	d	r	m	25. F	T	I	D	F	S	A
6. a	u	F	v	M	s	P	26. Y	l	u	Y	k	C	E
7. f	r	u	t	f	m	z	27. A	I	C	L	O	N	R
8. N	B	c	G	d	s	j	28. g	m	p	g	t	e	n
9. J	E	B	G	J	N	A	29. e	S	n	T	l	o	R
10. t	h	U	m	B	t	p	30. P	u	R	n	O	p	A
11. n	b	p	e	n	i	z	31. G	C	T	W	G	Q	R
12. a	o	M	S	v	l	B	32. e	u	K	l	A	r	c
13. K	R	O	x	K	g	l	33. A	m	Q	s	R	i	e
14. J	O	T	M	I	S	B	34. R	K	o	B	G	f	q
15. v	l	u	v	r	x	m	35. b	y	e	r	b	s	u
16. d	m	T	s	U	O	q	36. M	Q	D	M	E	J	G
17. X	A	r	S	i	T	m	37. h	m	l	q	v	s	h
18. L	B	W	U	L	F	R	38. f	k	B	v	q	P	R
19. s	p	l	w	b	h	m	39. q	L	N	q	a	r	F
20. p	M	A	H	P	T	X	40. g	i	t	s	o	m	x

Set 5

1. P	V	R	n	y	f	z	21. S	T	I	D	S	F	M
2. t	m	b	E	U	t	n	22. B	g	n	S	d	R	q
3. m	E	T	M	V	G	H	23. f	i	c	d	s	m	b
4. e	r	L	O	s	Q	p	24. r	M	a	z	O	T	r
5. g	m	g	p	t	d	h	25. T	N	G	W	T	P	Y
6. N	J	O	d	F	m	v	26. x	r	Y	l	S	m	a
7. f	p	l	t	f	v	r	27. A	C	s	F	r	A	T
8. A	L	U	M	C	N	J	28. o	r	e	n	s	y	t
9. Y	w	D	i	Y	k	E	29. M	T	U	A	R	M	W
10. a	U	x	r	M	C	s	30. Q	r	M	T	o	W	a
11. p	O	R	V	F	P	K	31. e	f	x	m	t	i	r
12. s	w	m	i	l	h	u	32. c	n	L	e	P	c	z
13. q	K	c	e	P	r	n	33. P	F	S	W	R	O	L
14. h	v	s	h	l	a	f	34. f	S	M	f	E	n	q
15. D	R	S	M	U	D	H	35. Y	h	U	o	n	G	A
16. u	d	m	T	S	i	p	36. b	x	u	g	b	i	l
17. l	v	r	x	m	l	b	37. J	O	T	V	I	R	F
18. R	G	o	B	U	h	p	38. n	e	b	p	n	t	i
19. A	v	S	M	u	y	B	39. K	R	o	X	g	K	h
20. W	T	C	R	I	W	S	40. a	G	c	P	n	E	w

Set 6

1. T	v p M A j q p h
2. c	s f p r c y o m
3. B	E M C B A R W Z
4. h	t b O m P s Q y
5. m	l a w g k r m o
6. Z	H O D U C Y K E
7. V	y P o N r X f e
8. l	f r m k z s q t
9. F	A e R I m F V l
10. J	C T L J E B O H
11. k	a R f M i T Y l
12. E	h A m C O R t d
13. a	S l Q R m c a B
14. I	T I L M R E C D
15. e	f r m k c p t l
16. z	G n z D r M Q k
17. W	g E R I s i h p
18. n	c m a e g n f j
19. S	L I R M Z S K D
20. o	f R m K d A s L
21. r	h w s q t b r o
22. M	Y U R F D O A G
23. I	R e Z j a T I u
24. s	m i r l a o g d
25. Q	J U R C F T B Q
26. d	C h U s n O r t
27. g	b l T H s g D r
28. K	s M u L P r E i
29. y	h g E r V O s X
30. s	t o l d i r m a
31. P	R 0 T C P A X Y
32. R	h i G R o v A C
33. T	S W J A D M R N
34. c	d n e s t c r z
35. H	E S p N m a T I
36. f	o m T S u r A c
37. Y	L C O M T Y B U
38. R	p z I W s U L B
39. q	y m k o b u q r
40. m	A l J d m K s P

Set 7

1. a	w E n P c G S h
2. K	H K g X O R b y

(Problems continued on next page)

3. n		i	t	n	p	b	e	f	z
4. R		p	h	U	B	o	G	s	M
5. b		l	i	x	u	b	g	q	r
6. Y		A	G	n	o	U	h	d	t
7. f		q	n	E	f	S	K	X	o
8. P		L	O	R	W	S	F	A	X
9. c		z	P	L	c	e	N	v	a
10. e		r	z	t	m	x	f	g	i
11. q		A	w	O	t	M	r	g	n
12. M		W	R	M	A	O	T	Y	U
13. o		t	y	s	n	e	r	h	g
14. B		T	A	f	r	B	c	S	O
15. x		a	m	S	D	i	K	g	E
16. T		G	W	Y	T	P	N	Q	V
17. r		M	a	X	u	t	r	C	N
18. f		b	m	s	k	d	u	h	z
19. b		Q	r	D	s	N	G	i	p
20. S		M	F	T	D	I	S	W	Q
21. W		S	T	C	W	R	I	G	O
22. A		S	M	y	V	g	k	e	J
23. J		F	R	I	V	O	T	Z	N
24. l		b	m	x	l	r	v	h	k
25. u		p	I	S	t	m	d	o	v
26. D		H	D	U	M	R	S	L	E
27. h		f	a	l	h	s	v	r	p
28. q		n	R	p	E	C	k	y	L
29. s		u	h	l	i	m	w	e	j
30. P		K	F	V	P	O	R	U	N
31. a		s	C	M	r	x	U	l	v
32. Y		E	k	i	D	Y	w	h	S
33. A		J	N	C	M	U	L	R	P
34. f		r	v	f	t	l	p	o	y
35. N		v	M	F	d	o	J	s	U
36. g		h	d	g	m	o	w	f	r
37. e		p	r	O	L	s	Q	z	K
38. M		H	G	V	M	E	X	L	R
39. t		n	t	U	E	b	K	f	O
40. P		z	f	N	Y	o	g	i	r

Set 8

1. e		K	l	A	n	P	u	r	c	G	o
2. K		g	m	q	R	O	x	K	d	i	l
3. n		m	q	l	e	p	b	n	i	a	r
4. J		B	X	H	V	I	M	O	R	S	T
5. b		m	e	v	x	u	s	b	r	h	y

(Problems continued on next page)

6. X	Y	o	M	P	q	i	l	S	r	A
7. o	M	s	t	p	C	F	o	X	E	n
8. L	P	I	M	R	O	F	U	S	W	B
9. s	c	t	L	N	e	B	o	R	s	A
10. g	p	e	r	f	x	m	o	s	t	i
11. m	S	L	q	r	H	t	O	u	B	C
12. U	A	E	R	Y	M	T	U	S	O	L
13. p	o	r	e	n	c	a	x	t	m	y
14. C	T	m	A	l	C	s	f	R	i	p
15. i	r	P	Y	l	v	o	S	t	X	B
16. T	V	Z	S	E	N	T	M	G	Y	P
17. v	t	O	L	d	R	m	A	x	v	Q
18. n	f	l	e	i	c	d	s	b	o	m
19. B	s	A	r	G	N	h	d	R	m	T
20. F	N	O	M	E	F	A	S	T	I	D
21. G	P	S	I	W	G	B	Q	C	R	T
22. A	e	b	l	Q	i	0	u	M	S	v
23. R	y	m	K	o	B	U	g	f	q	p
24. v	c	l	u	v	r	x	a	q	i	m
25. d	o	m	T	S	u	I	l	p	R	a
26. M	A	R	M	Q	E	D	B	X	I	J
27. h	r	p	i	h	m	t	v	s	l	q
28. q	F	r	m	k	C	B	v	e	o	p
29. f	s	w	i	m	p	l	u	y	b	h
30. p	B	L	T	H	A	M	C	O	R	P
31. a	l	P	u	s	O	F	q	M	T	v
32. Y	h	o	W	D	l	u	C	Y	k	e
33. A	R	N	I	C	O	P	L	U	M	S
34. f	e	z	p	l	t	i	v	r	u	f
35. N	Z	s	M	B	c	g	D	F	j	O
36. g	j	u	r	m	g	p	t	d	e	n
37. e	A	g	U	s	n	t	L	O	p	r
38. J	M	R	V	T	E	B	J	A	N	G
39. t	C	h	U	m	b	t	E	R	n	p
40. P	c	f	A	z	V	R	n	O	H	Y

Answers to Visual Search Task

Set 1

1. N	8. Y	15. N	22. N	29. Y	36. N
2. Y	9. Y	16. Y	23. N	30. N	37. N
3. Y	10. N	17. Y	24. Y	31. N	38. Y
4. N	11. Y	18. N	25. N	32. Y	39. Y
5. Y	12. N	19. N	26. N	33. N	40. N
6. N	13. Y	20. Y	27. Y	34. Y	
7. Y	14. N	21. Y	28. N	35. N	

Set 2

1. N	8. N	15. N	22. Y	29. N	36. N
2. Y	9. Y	16. Y	23. N	30. N	37. N
3. Y	10. N	17. N	24. Y	31. Y	38. Y
4. N	11. N	18. Y	25. N	32. N	39. N
5 Y	12. N	19. Y	26. Y	33. N	40. Y
6. N	13. Y	20. N	27. N	34. N	
7. Y	14. Y	21. Y	28. N	35. Y	

Set 3

1. Y	8. N	15. Y	22. Y	29. Y	36. N
2. N	9. N	16. N	23. Y	30. N	37. Y
3. Y	10. Y	17. Y	24. Y	31. Y	38. N
4. N	11. N	18. N	25. Y	32. N	39. Y
5. N	12. Y	19. Y	26. N	33. Y	40. N
6. Y	13. Y	20. N	27. N	34. Y	
7. Y	14. N	21. N	28. Y	35. N	

Set 4

1. N	8. N	15. Y	22. N	29. N	36. Y
2. N	9. Y	16. N	23. N	30. N	37. Y
3. N	10. Y	17. N	24. Y	31. Y	38. N
4. Y	11. Y	18. Y	25. Y	32. N	39. Y
5. N	12. N	19. N	26. Y	33. N	40. N
6. N	13. Y	20. N	27. N	34. N	
7. Y	14. N	21. Y	28. Y	35. Y	

Set 5

1. N	8. N	15. Y	22. N	29. Y	36. Y
2. Y	9. Y	16. N	23. N	30. N	37. N
3. N	10. N	17. Y	24. Y	31. N	38. Y
4. N	11. N	18. N	25. Y	32. Y	39. Y
5. Y	12. N	19. N	26. N	33. N	40. N
6. N	13. N	20. Y	27. Y	34. Y	
7. Y	14. Y	21. Y	28. N	35. N	

(Problems continued on next page)

Set 6

1. N	8. N	15. N	22. N	29. N	36. N
2. Y	9. Y	16. Y	23. Y	30. N	37. Y
3. Y	10. Y	17. N	24. N	31. Y	38. N
4. N	11. N	18. Y	25. Y	32. Y	39. Y
5. Y	12. N	19. Y	26. N	33. N	40. Y
6. N	13. Y	20. N	27. Y	34. Y	
7. N	14. Y	21. Y	28. N	35. N	

Set 7

1. N	8. N	15. N	22. N	29. N	36. Y
2. Y	9. Y	16. Y	23. N	30. Y	37. N
3. Y	10. N	17. Y	24. Y	31. N	38. Y
4. N	11. N	18. N	25. N	32. Y	39. Y
5. Y	12. Y	19. N	26. Y	33. N	40. N
6. N	13. N	20. Y	27. Y	34. Y	
7. Y	14. Y	21. Y	28. N	35. N	

Set 8

1. N	8. N	15. N	22. N	29. N	36. Y
2. Y	9. Y	16. Y	23. N	30. Y	37. N
3. Y	10. N	17. Y	24. Y	31. N	38. Y
4. N	11. N	18. N	25. N	32. Y	39. Y
5. Y	12. Y	19. N	26. Y	33. N	40. N
6. N	13. N	20. Y	27. Y	34. Y	
7. Y	14. Y	21. Y	28. N	35. N	

DIGIT-SYMBOL PAIRING

This task presents you with a key that pairs a set of symbols with a set of digits.

Following this key, you will find 120 symbols. Your task is to indicate the appropriate digit for each symbol. For example, you might see the following pairings:

$$+ \quad - \quad x \quad \backslash$$
$$1 \quad 2 \quad 3 \quad 4$$

Following this set of pairings, you would see 120 of those four symbols, which you are to match as quickly as possible with the appropriate digit.

What follow are eight sets of different pairings of digits with symbols. Each set of items contains from four to eight pairings followed by 120 symbols. As you work through these sets, try to increase your speed while maintaining perfect or near-perfect accuracy. Answers appear after the last set.

DIGIT-SYMBOL PAIRING TASK

		^	(	+	"
Set 1	KEY:	1	2	3	4

1.	(	21.	+	41.	+	61.	+	81.	+	101.	+
2.	^	22.	"	42.	"	62.	"	82.	"	102.	"
3.	"	23.	^	43.	^	63.	^	83.	^	103.	^
4.	+	24.	"	44.	(	64.	"	84.	"	104.	(
5.	^	25.	+	45.	+	65.	+	85.	+	105.	"
6.	+	26.	"	46.	(	66.	"	86.	^	106.	+
7.	"	27.	^	47.	"	67.	^	87.	(	107.	(
8.	^	28.	"	48.	+	68.	+	88.	+	108.	^
9.	(	29.	+	49.	"	69.	(	89.	"	109.	"
10.	"	30.	^	50.	^	70.	"	90.	^	110.	+
11.	^	31.	(	51.	(	71.	+	91.	(	111.	"
12.	+	32.	(	52.	"	72.	"	92.	+	112.	^
13.	"	33.	+	53.	+	73.	(	93.	"	113.	(
14.	(	34.	"	54.	^	74.	^	94.	^	114.	+
15.	^	35.	^	55.	(	75.	"	95.	+	115.	"
16.	"	36.	+	56.	+	76.	(	96.	"	116.	^
17.	(	37.	"	57.	"	77.	"	97.	(	117.	+
18.	^	38.	^	58.	^	78.	+	98.	^	118.	(
19.	+	39.	"	59.	(	79.	"	99.	"	119.	"
20.	^	40.	(	60.	+	80.	^	100.	+	120.	^

		[	\	;	-
Set 2	KEY:	1	2	3	4

1.	;	18.	;	35.	[	52.	[	69.	;	86.	[
2.	\	19.	-	36.	-	53.	-	70.	[	87.	-
3.	-	20.	\	37.	;	54.	;	71.	\	88.	;
4.	\	21.	\	38.	\	55.	-	72.	-	89.	[
5.	;	22.	-	39.	-	56.	\	73.	\	90.	\
6.	[	23.	[	40.	;	57.	[	74.	;	91.	;
7.	;	24.	;	41.	\	58.	;	75.	[	92.	[
8.	-	25.	\	42.	[	59.	\	76.	-	93.	-
9.	\	26.	[	43.	;	60.	-	77.	\	94.	;
10.	-	27.	-	44.	-	61.	\	78.	;	95.	\
11.	;	28.	;	45.	;	62.	;	79.	[	96.	[
12.	[	29.	[	46.	\	63.	[	80.	;	97.	\
13.	;	30.	;	47.	-	64.	-	81.	\	98.	-
14.	\	31.	\	48.	[	65.	\	82.	-	99.	\
15.	[	32.	[	49.	;	66.	;	83.	;	100.	;
16.	-	33.	\	50.	\	67.	[	84.	[	101.	\
17.	\	34.	;	51.	;	68.	-	85.	\	102.	;

(Problems continued on next page)

103.	-	106.	\	109.	-	112.	\	115.	\	118.	[
104.	;	107.	;	110.	;	113.	[	116.	-	119.	\
105.	-	108.	[	111.	[	114.	-	117.	\	120.	[

		#	$	|	}
SET 3	KEY:	1	2	3	4

1.	}	21.	}	41.	}	61.	#	81.	}	101.	$
2.	|	22.	$	42.	#	62.	}	82.	#	102.	#
3.	#	23.	|	43.	|	63.	$	83.	#	103.	}
4.	$	24.	}	44.	}	64.	|	84.	|	104.	|
5.	|	25.	#	45.	#	65.	}	85.	}	105.	#
6.	}	26.	|	46.	}	66.	#	86.	#	106.	$
7.	#	27.	}	47.	$	67.	|	87.	$	107.	}
8.	$	28.	#	48.	#	68.	$	88.	#	108.	|
9.	}	29.	$	49.	|	69.	}	89.	}	109.	$
10.	|	30.	|	50.	}	70.	|	90.	#	110.	#
11.	#	31.	}	51.	|	71.	$	91.	$	111.	}
12.	$	32.	$	52.	$	72.	#	92.	|	112.	#
13.	|	33.	|	53.	}	73.	}	93.	}	113.	$
14.	#	34.	#	54.	#	74.	|	94.	#	114.	}
15.	$	35.	}	55.	$	75.	}	95.	$	115.	#
16.	}	36.	|	56.	|	76.	|	96.	}	116.	$
17.	#	37.	#	57.	}	77.	$	97.	#	117.	}
18.	}	38.	$	58.	#	78.	#	98.	$	118.	|
19.	$	39.	}	59.	|	79.	}	99.	|	119.	#
20.	|	40.	|	60.	$	80.	|	100.	}	120.	$

		{	&	@	*	~
SET 4	KEY:	1	2	3	4	5

1.	*	16.	*	31.	~	46.	&	61.	&	76.	*
2.	@	17.	&	32.	&	47.	*	62.	~	77.	~
3.	~	18.	~	33.	{	48.	@	63.	@	78.	@
4.	&	19.	{	34.	*	49.	~	64.	{	79.	*
5.	{	20.	*	35.	~	50.	@	65.	@	80.	@
6.	*	21.	*	36.	@	51.	*	66.	~	81.	*
7.	&	22.	{	37.	&	52.	{	67.	*	82.	@
8.	*	23.	@	38.	*	53.	&	68.	{	83.	~
9.	@	24.	&	39.	~	54.	~	69.	~	84.	@
10.	~	25.	@	40.	{	55.	*	70.	@	85.	~
11.	*	26.	*	41.	*	56.	~	71.	&	86.	@
12.	{	27.	*	42.	@	57.	@	72.	~	87.	{
13.	&	28.	{	43.	~	58.	&	73.	*	88.	*
14.	~	29.	@	44.	{	59.	{	74.	~	89.	&
15.	@	30.	*	45.	*	60.	&	75.	{	90.	@

(Problems continued on next page)

91.	*	96.	*	101.	*	106.	@	111.	{	116.	&
92.	~	97.	@	102.	&	107.	~	112.	&	117.	{
93.	&	98.	*	103.	{	108.	&	113.	~	118.	&
94.	~	99.	~	104.	~	109.	~	114.	*	119.	~
95.	{	100.	@	105.	*	110.	*	115.	@	120.	{

		=	?	%	!	<
SET 5	KEY:	1	2	3	4	5

1.	%	21.	!	41.	%	61.	%	81.	%	101.	=
2.	<	22.	?	42.	?	62.	<	82.	!	102.	%
3.	?	23.	<	43.	=	63.	!	83.	<	103.	?
4.	!	24.	%	44.	!	64.	?	84.	=	104.	=
5.	=	25.	=	45.	<	65.	=	85.	<	105.	%
6.	!	26.	%	46.	=	66.	<	86.	%	106.	?
7.	%	27.	?	47.	%	67.	!	87.	?	107.	=
8.	?	28.	!	48.	?	68.	?	88.	!	108.	%
9.	<	29.	=	49.	%	69.	=	89.	<	109.	!
10.	%	30.	<	50.	!	70.	!	90.	%	110.	?
11.	<	31.	?	51.	=	71.	<	91.	=	111.	<
12.	?	32.	%	52.	<	72.	?	92.	!	112.	%
13.	%	33.	=	53.	=	73.	%	93.	?	113.	=
14.	!	34.	?	54.	%	74.	?	94.	%	114.	<
15.	<	35.	%	55.	!	75.	!	95.	<	115.	!
16.	=	36.	?	56.	?	76.	=	96.	=	116.	=
17.	!	37.	!	57.	=	77.	<	97.	!	117.	?
18.	%	38.	%	58.	%	78.	%	98.	%	118.	!
19.	<	39.	<	59.	?	79.	<	99.	!	119.	%
20.	!	40.	=	60.	!	80.	!	100.	<	120.	<

		\	[	,	=	x	o
SET 6	KEY:	1	2	3	4	5	6

1.	o	14.	x	27.	,	40.	[	53.	=	66.	=
2.	x	15.	\	28.	\	41.	x	54.	,	67.	[
3.	=	16.	o	29.	,	42.	o	55.	o	68.	,
4.	,	17.	=	30.	[	43.	=	56.	x	69.	[
5.	[	18.	,	31.	=	44.	[	57.	\	70.	=
6.	\	19.	\	32.	\	45.	,	58.	o	71.	o
7.	[	20.	x	33.	o	46.	\	59.	[	72.	\
8.	,	21.	,	34.	x	47.	x	60.	,	73.	x
9.	o	22.	\	35.	,	48.	o	61.	o	74.	=
10.	x	23.	x	36.	[	49.	=	62.	x	75.	,
11.	[	24.	o	37.	=	50.	[	63.	=	76.	\
12.	=	25.	=	38.	\	51.	=	64.	x	77.	o
13.	o	26.	[	39.	,	52.	\	65.	o	78.	,

(Problems continued on next page)

79.	x	86.	[	93.	[	100.	x	107.	o	114.	\
80.	[	87.	x	94.	o	101.	\	108.	,	115.	o
81.	=	88.	[	95.	=	102.	,	109.	[	116.	x
82.	,	89.	,	96.	\	103.	=	110.	x	117.	,
83.	\	90.	=	97.	x	104.	[	111.	\	118.	[
84.	x	91.	\	98.	=	105.	x	112.	o	119.	=
85.	=	92.	x	99.	,	106.	=	113.	=	120.	\

		-	8	/	=	v	]		
SET 7	KEY:	1	2	3	4	5	6		

1.	-	21.	-	41.	v	61.	-	81.	=	101.	/
2.	/	22.	v	42.	8	62.	=	82.	/	102.	=
3.	=	23.	/	43.	-	63.	v	83.	=	103.	]
4.	v	24.	8	44.	=	64.	8	84.	-	104.	-
5.	v	25.	]	45.	-	65.	]	85.	v	105.	/
6.	/	26.	=	46.	/	66.	=	86.	=	106.	v
7.	v	27.	v	47.	v	67.	/	87.	-	107.	8
8.	=	28.	]	48.	8	68.	v	88.	]	108.	=
9.	-	29.	-	49.	-	69.	=	89.	v	109.	-
10.	/	30.	v	50.	/	70.	-	90.	8	110.	/
11.	8	31.	8	51.	=	71.	/	91.	/	111.	]
12.	v	32.	]	52.	v	72.	8	92.	8	112.	v
13.	/	33.	v	53.	/	73.	/	93.	]	113.	]
14.	]	34.	]	54.	]	74.	v	94.	=	114.	8
15.	/	35.	=	55.	-	75.	/	95.	/	115.	/
16.	-	36.	v	56.	8	76.	=	96.	-	116.	8
17.	8	37.	-	57.	v	77.	]	97.	v	117.	=
18.	v	38.	/	58.	/	78.	-	98.	/	118.	-
19.	-	39.	=	59.	]	79.	]	99.	=	119.	]
20.	v	40.	[	60.	-	80.	8	100.	-	120.	/

		/	t	[	;	z	\	=	]
SET 8	KEY:	1	2	3	4	5	6	7	8

1.	\	12.	]	23.	/	34.	;	45.	=	56.	]
2.	/	13.	t	24.	;	35.	/	46.	]	57.	=
3.	=	14.	/	25.	z	36.	z	47.	;	58.	/
4.	z	15.	\	26.	]	37.	]	48.	t	59.	z
5.	t	16.	=	27.	t	38.	=	49.	=	60.	]
6.	]	17.	]	28.	]	39.	\	50.	]	61.	=
7.	/	18.	z	29.	[	40.	t	51.	/	62.	]
8.	;	19.	t	30.	/	41.	\	52.	\	63.	/
9.	=	20.	/	31.	z	42.	;	53.	z	64.	t
10.	\	21.	=	32.	=	43.	]	54.	;	65.	/
11.	z	22.	[	33.	t	44.	[	55.	t	66.	;

(Problems continued on next page)

67.	z	76.	=	85.	z	94.	[	103.	]	112.	z
68.	t	77.	;	86.	;	95.	/	104.	z	113.	;
69.	=	78.	t	87.	t	96.	\	105.	;	114.	t
70.	[	79.	=	88.	]	97.	t	106.	[	115.	;
71.	;	80.	\	89.	/	98.	=	107.	\	116.	/
72.	=	81.	=	90.	t	99.	z	108.	t	117.	\
73.	t	82.	/	91.	;	100.	=	109.	=	118.	]
74.	/	83.	;	92.	z	101.	/	110.	=	119.	[
75.	]	84.	=	93.	]	102.	=	111.	]	120.	\

Answers to Digit Symbol Pairing Task

Set 1

1. 2	21. 3	41. 3	61. 3	81. 3	101. 3
2. 1	22. 4	42. 4	62. 4	82. 4	102. 4
3. 4	23. 1	43. 1	63. 1	83. 1	103. 1
4. 3	24. 4	44. 2	64. 4	84. 4	104. 2
5. 1	25. 3	45. 3	65. 3	85. 3	105. 4
6. 3	26. 4	46. 2	66. 4	86. 1	106. 3
7. 4	27. 1	47. 4	67. 1	87. 2	107. 2
8. 1	28. 4	48. 3	68. 3	88. 3	108. 1
9. 2	29. 3	49. 4	69. 2	89. 4	109. 4
10. 4	30. 1	50. 1	70. 4	90. 1	110. 3
11. 1	31. 2	51. 2	71. 3	91. 2	111. 4
12. 3	32. 2	52. 4	72. 4	92. 3	112. 1
13. 4	33. 3	53. 3	73. 2	93. 4	113. 2
14. 2	34. 4	54. 1	74. 1	94. 1	114. 3
15. 1	35. 1	55. 2	75. 4	95. 3	115. 4
16. 4	36. 3	56. 3	76. 2	96. 4	116. 1
17. 2	37. 4	57. 4	77. 4	97. 2	117. 3
18. 1	38. 1	58. 1	78. 3	98. 1	118. 2
19. 3	39. 4	59. 2	79. 4	99. 4	119. 4
20. 1	40. 2	60. 3	80. 1	100. 3	120. 1

Set 2

1. 3	8. 4	15. 1	22. 4	29. 1	36. 4
2. 2	9. 2	16. 4	23. 1	30. 3	37. 3
3. 4	10. 4	17. 2	24. 3	31. 2	38. 2
4. 2	11. 3	18. 3	25. 2	32. 1	39. 4
5. 3	12. 1	19. 4	26. 1	33. 2	40. 3
6. 1	13. 3	20. 2	27. 4	34. 3	41. 2
7. 3	14. 2	21. 2	28. 3	35. 1	42. 1

(Answers continued on next page)

43. 3	56. 2	69. 3	82. 4	95. 2	108. 1
44. 4	57. 1	70. 1	83. 3	96. 1	109. 4
45. 3	58. 3	71. 2	84. 1	97. 2	110. 3
46. 2	59. 2	72. 4	85. 2	98. 4	111. 1
47. 4	60. 4	73. 2	86. 1	99. 2	112. 2
48. 1	61. 2	74. 3	87. 4	100. 3	113. 1
49. 3	62. 3	75. 1	88. 3	101. 2	114. 4
50. 2	63. 1	76. 4	89. 1	102. 3	115. 2
51. 3	64. 4	77. 2	90. 2	103. 4	116. 4
52. 1	65. 2	78. 3	91. 3	104. 3	117. 2
53. 4	66. 3	79. 1	92. 1	105. 4	118. 1
54. 3	67. 1	80. 3	93. 4	106. 2	119. 2
55. 4	68. 4	81. 2	94. 3	107. 3	120. 1

Set 3

1. 4	21. 4	41. 4	61. 1	81. 4	101. 2
2. 3	22. 2	42. 1	62. 4	82. 1	102. 1
3. 1	23. 3	43. 3	63. 2	83. 1	103. 4
4. 2	24. 4	44. 4	64. 3	84. 3	104. 3
5. 3	25. 1	45. 1	65. 4	85. 4	105. 1
6. 4	26. 3	46. 4	66. 1	86. 1	106. 2
7. 1	27. 4	47. 2	67. 3	87. 2	107. 4
8. 2	28. 1	48. 1	68. 2	88. 1	108. 3
9. 4	29. 2	49. 3	69. 4	89. 4	109. 2
10. 3	30. 3	50. 4	70. 3	90. 1	110. 1
11. 1	31. 4	51. 3	71. 2	91. 2	111. 4
12. 2	32. 2	52. 2	72. 1	92. 3	112. 1
13. 3	33. 3	53. 4	73. 4	93. 4	113. 2
14. 1	34. 1	54. 1	74. 3	94. 1	114. 4
15. 2	35. 4	55. 2	75. 4	95. 2	115. 1
16. 4	36. 3	56. 3	76. 3	96. 4	116. 2
17. 1	37. 1	57. 4	77. 2	97. 1	117. 4
18. 4	38. 2	58. 1	78. 1	98. 2	118. 3
19. 2	39. 4	59. 3	79. 4	99. 3	119. 1
20. 3	40. 3	60. 2	80. 3	100. 4	120. 2

Set 4

1. 4	6. 4	11. 4	16. 4	21. 4	26. 4
2. 3	7. 2	12. 1	17. 2	22. 1	27. 4
3. 5	8. 4	13. 2	18. 5	23. 3	28. 1
4. 2	9. 3	14. 5	19. 1	24. 2	29. 3
5. 1	10. 5	15. 3	20. 4	25. 3	30. 4

(Answers continued on next page)

31. 5	46. 2	61. 2	76. 4	91. 4	106. 3
32. 2	47. 4	62. 5	77. 5	92. 5	107. 5
33. 1	48. 3	63. 3	78. 3	93. 2	108. 2
34. 4	49. 5	64. 1	79. 4	94. 5	109. 5
35. 5	50. 3	65. 3	80. 3	95. 1	110. 4
36. 3	51. 4	66. 5	81. 4	96. 4	111. 1
37. 2	52. 1	67. 4	82. 3	97. 3	112. 2
38. 4	53. 2	68. 1	83. 5	98. 4	113. 5
39. 5	54. 5	69. 5	84. 3	99. 5	114. 4
40. 1	55. 4	70. 3	85. 5	100. 3	115. 3
41. 4	56. 5	71. 2	86. 3	101. 4	116. 2
42. 3	57. 3	72. 5	87. 1	102. 2	117. 1
43. 5	58. 2	73. 4	88. 4	103. 1	118. 2
44. 1	59. 1	74. 5	89. 2	104. 5	119. 5
45. 4	60. 2	75. 1	90. 3	105. 4	120. 1

Set 5

1. 3	21. 4	41. 3	61. 3	81. 3	101. 1
2. 5	22. 2	42. 2	62. 5	82. 4	102. 3
3. 2	23. 5	43. 1	63. 4	83. 5	103. 2
4. 4	24. 3	44. 4	64. 2	84. 1	104. 1
5. 1	25. 1	45. 5	65. 1	85. 5	105. 3
6. 4	26. 3	46. 1	66. 5	86. 3	106. 2
7. 3	27. 2	47. 3	67. 4	87. 2	107. 1
8. 2	28. 4	48. 2	68. 2	88. 4	108. 3
9. 5	29. 1	49. 3	69. 1	89. 5	109. 4
10. 3	30. 5	50. 4	70. 4	90. 3	110. 2
11. 5	31. 2	51. 1	71. 5	91. 1	111. 5
12. 2	32. 3	52. 5	72. 2	92. 4	112. 3
13. 3	33. 1	53. 1	73. 3	93. 2	113. 1
14. 4	34. 2	54. 3	74. 2	94. 3	114. 5
15. 5	35. 3	55. 4	75. 4	95. 5	115. 4
16. 1	36. 2	56. 2	76. 1	96. 1	116. 1
17. 4	37. 4	57. 1	77. 5	97. 4	117. 2
18. 3	38. 3	58. 3	78. 3	98. 3	118 4
19. 5	39. 5	59. 2	79. 5	99. 4	119. 3
20. 4	40. 1	60. 4	80. 4	100. 5	120. 5

Set 6

1. 6	6. 1	11. 2	16. 6	21. 3	26. 2
2. 5	7. 2	12. 4	17. 4	22. 1	27. 3
3. 4	8. 3	13. 6	18. 3	23. 5	28. 1
4. 3	9. 6	14. 5	19. 1	24. 6	29. 3
5. 2	10. 5	15. 1	20. 5	25. 4	30. 2

(Answers continued on next page)

31. 4	46. 1	61. 6	76. 1	91. 1	106. 4
32. 1	47. 5	62. 5	77. 6	92. 5	107. 6
33. 6	48. 6	63. 4	78. 3	93. 2	108. 3
34. 5	49. 4	64. 5	79. 5	94. 6	109. 2
35. 3	50. 2	65. 6	80. 2	95. 4	110. 5
36. 2	51. 4	66. 4	81. 4	96. 1	111. 1
37. 4	52. 1	67. 2	82. 3	97. 5	112. 6
38. 1	53. 4	68. 3	83. 1	98. 4	113. 4
39. 3	54. 3	69. 2	84. 5	99. 3	114. 1
40. 2	55. 6	70. 4	85. 4	100. 5	115. 6
41. 5	56. 5	71. 6	86. 2	101. 1	116. 5
42. 6	57. 1	72. 1	87. 5	102. 3	117. 3
43. 4	58. 6	73. 5	88. 2	103. 4	118. 2
44. 2	59. 2	74. 4	89. 3	104. 2	119. 4
45. 3	60. 3	75. 3	90. 4	105. 5	120. 1

Set 7

1. 1	21. 1	41. 5	61. 1	81. 4	101. 3
2. 3	22. 5	42. 2	62. 4	82. 3	102. 4
3. 4	23. 3	43. 1	63. 5	83. 4	103. 6
4. 5	24. 2	44. 4	64. 2	84. 1	104. 1
5. 5	25. 6	45. 1	65. 6	85. 5	105. 3
6. 3	26. 4	46. 3	66. 4	86. 4	106. 5
7. 5	27. 5	47. 5	67. 3	87. 1	107. 2
8. 4	28. 6	48. 2	68. 5	88. 6	108. 4
9. 1	29. 1	49. 1	69. 4	89. 5	109. 1
10. 3	30. 5	50. 3	70. 1	90. 2	110. 3
11. 2	31. 2	51. 4	71. 3	91. 3	111. 6
12. 5	32. 6	52. 5	72. 2	92. 2	112. 5
13. 3	33. 5	53. 3	73. 3	93. 6	113. 6
14. 6	34. 6	54. 6	74. 5	94. 4	114. 2
15. 3	35. 4	55. 1	75. 3	95. 3	115. 3
16. 1	36. 5	56. 2	76. 4	96. 1	116. 2
17. 2	37. 1	57. 5	77. 6	97. 5	117. 4
18. 5	38. 3	58. 3	78. 1	98. 3	118. 1
19. 1	39. 4	59. 6	79. 6	99. 4	119. 6
20. 5	40. 6	60. 1	80. 2	100. 1	120. 3

Set 8

1. 6	5. 2	9. 7	13. 2	17. 8	21. 7
2. 1	6. 8	10. 6	14. 1	18. 5	22. 3
3. 7	7. 1	11. 5	15. 6	19. 2	23. 1
4. 5	8. 4	12. 8	16. 7	20. 1	24. 4

(Answers continued on next page)

25. 5	41. 6	57. 7	73. 2	89. 1	105. 4
26. 8	42. 4	58. 1	74. 1	90. 2	106. 3
27. 2	43. 8	59. 5	75. 8	91. 4	107. 6
28. 8	44. 3	60. 8	76. 7	92. 5	108. 2
29. 3	45. 7	61. 7	77. 4	93. 8	109. 7
30. 1	46. 8	62. 8	78. 2	94. 3	110. 1
31. 5	47. 4	63. 1	79. 7	95. 1	111. 8
32. 7	48. 2	64. 2	80. 6	96. 6	112. 5
33. 2	49. 7	65. 1	81. 7	97. 2	113. 4
34. 4	50. 8	66. 4	82. 1	98. 7	114. 2
35. 1	51. 1	67. 5	83. 4	99. 5	115. 4
36. 5	52. 6	68. 2	84. 7	100. 7	116. 1
37. 8	53. 5	69. 7	85. 5	101. 1	117. 6
38. 7	54. 4	70. 3	86. 4	102. 7	118. 8
39. 6	55. 2	71. 4	87. 2	103. 8	119. 3
40. 2	56. 8	72. 7	88. 8	104. 5	120. 6

COMPLEX VISUAL SEARCH

This task resembles the earlier visual search task except that it is more difficult and challenging. A task very similar to this one was used by Schneider and Shiffrin (1977) in their original studies of controlled and automatic information processing. In this task, you will find a set of two to four target letters followed by forty items arrayed in a variety of physical patterns. Your task is to indicate for each of the forty items whether any of the target letters appears in the visual array. If one or more of the target letters do appear, you should indicate this with a "Y" (Yes). If none of the letters appear, you should indicate this with an "N" (No). If, for example, the target letter string is (a b c) and the following array is

```
        n
c
    h        p   u
```

you should indicate a "Y" If, by contrast, the target letters are h and q, and you see the visual array

```
a           d
                c
    e    f
```

you should indicate an N.

Note that this task is more challenging than the previous task because of two variations. First, the number of targets is greater; second, the letters to be compared to the targets are shown in two dimensions rather than just one. As you work through the twelve sets of items, try to increase your speed while maintaining perfect or near-perfect accuracy. Answers appear after the last set.

COMPLEX VISUAL SEARCH

SET 1
TARGET LETTERS: (r, j)

1. q   p
    s
    d
	2. n o
	           j
	   v
		3. b r
		   z z

4. m
   y
     e
       f
	5. o
	   p
	   x
	   r
		6. u q
		
		   b o

7.   a
      o
    u
   r
	8. v b
	      j
	
	    g
		9. x
		   n I o

10. b   c
    t   w
	11. u p
	    l
	       p
		12. k k d
		           g

13.   v
   f   m
    p
	14. r s
	         v
	   g
		15. z u
		    o
		    f

16. b   q
    d
    n
	17. a b c
	
	   e
		18. w
		    w
		     u u

19. h   a
    r   v
	20. g
	     v
	   b
	d
		21. r p
		   s z

22. t   b
   j   p
	23. k w
	      u s
		24. j
		   k
		     z q

25.   p   o
   d   l
	26. w
	  x
	  y
	   I
		27. y
		   o
		      u
		   v

28.   e   p
  r   e
	29. y
	    z x q
		30. w w d
		       r

(Problems continued on next page)

31.   f   a
    j   v

32.   h   g
        s   r

33.   t
     r
         d
           b

34.   t   y j
   l

35. o   u
    r   z

36. x   w
     z   e

37.   q
  w   p
     j

38   y
   d   s   r

39. w o   p
   r

40. p   p
   g   h

SET 2

TARGET LETTERS: (u e)

1.   o   s
    c
  n

2. I   p
    z u

3.   v e   a
         c

4. m   v   s
  x

5.   p
  d
       g
  u

6. o   n   d
         p

7. b   x
   r t

8. I
   o r n

9. m   c
    x   v

10.   f f
 s
 c

11. o r   b
     c

12. i o u
     q

13.   g
 z w p

14.   a z
 n e

15. b   b
   e d

16. y
  o
   a
    u

17.   s
  a
    e
 b

18. p q
 u e

19. o k
  u k

20. z
  y
  p
 r

21.   r t
 r
 m

22. w w
 v b

23. t y i
    e

24.   q
   r
  u
 w

(Problems continued on next page)

25.
              r
  t   e   y

26.
    h   j   l
       u

27. u
        z
          g
      d

28.
       p
  g   e
   b

29.
     p q s
   h

30. c   d
  d
  g

31.
    w
  x   y
   b

32.
     s d
  g
     e

33.
    q c
  w
  m

34. c b a
  e

35.
     f f
    j
  u

36. n m
  v h

37.
     p
  g v
 r

38. m m
   b z

39.
       i
  q   h
     k

40.
   e o
  d f

SET 3
TARGET LETTERS: (t l)

1.
   m
 w
    z
   t

2. r   l
  v x

3.   u y t
   c

4.   a
   s
 s
   a

5.
   i
  o
   p
 t

6. q s
 u
   k

7. m x z
   l

8.   o
 l   d f

9.   r z
 k
    t

10. q
   s
  l
 m

11.   d c
  w
    m

12.   b x
  l f

13. v   l
   d s

14.   u
 p o t

15. b a s
 r

(Problems continued on next page)

16. w   e   17.   l   18.   m
        c   k   g   h   b
                                     v   d w

19.   i   20.   m b   21.   n
    a   d   n t   m   o
            n   p

22. z   23.   p   24.   d
    j   o   w   e
    r   a   l
    v   f

25.   j   26.   o   27.   a   v a
           l   i   s
       r   d
           r   b

28.   q   r   29. h   f   30. w   c
                a   d   x   i   s   t

31. b   s   32.   f   u   c   33.   n
    i   t   l   d
                                                                  b
                                                              x

34.   s   g   35.   w   36.   w
                 b   f   c
       d   l   m   w
                                                            a

37.   p   38.   i   39.   q   w
                 f   e   d
       e   t   r   e
             m

40. w
          e
       g
       d

SET 4
TARGET LETTERS: (h z)

1. w   e   r   2.   t   a   3.   i
         s   y   s   j   z   d
         h   w   e   b   d   f   u

(Problems continued on next page)

4.
```
              w
    s
              g
  a
            a  q
```

5. d z x
```
            s  v  b
```

6.   u   y
```
        w
              b  v  a
```

7.   s   n
```
          x        w
     q        d
```

8.   v m j
```
                c
        i        o
```

9.   p
```
        d     h
              s     n     m
```

10. a   b   c   d
```
     z     k
```

11.   e   e
```
        f        f
        g        h
```

12.   t   y
```
              w        n     q
              r
```

13.   b   n
q
```
          c  x
```

14.   i   f g
```
        h     t
              v
```

15.   u
```
        e     g  f
                j  a
```

16. z   b   p
```
          d     n
        s
```

17.   m   x
```
              c
        w        z
              c
```

18.   i   e
```
              c  v
        k        a
```

19.   s
```
   w
          w
                z
   q
```

20.   w t y
```
        f  g  h
```

21. i   n s a
```
           n
           e
```

22.   r   y
```
   b     s     e
              h
```

23.   w   z   x
```
        w              v
              j
```

24.   e
```
           v
              f
        e
              t  y
```

25.   t   o
```
     r     r
   z
        b
```

26.   p
```
        p     u
           w     n  m
```

27.   a
```
     s        s
        s        h
        o
```

28.   s
```
          r        w
        s  z        l
```

29.   v   c
```
        x  z
                  m
              v
```

30.   d f g
```
              a
        c
           h
```

31.   a   p
```
           l  v
        z  e
```

32.   x c v
```
                p
        m  n
```

33.   i v q
```
              a  f  z
```

(Problems continued on next page)

34.
```
                    j
              d   m
        p     l   u
```

35.
```
                w   e
        s   n
                z   c
```

36.
```
    c     b   n
                    e   a   l
```

37.
```
    s           m
            b
        r           k
            e
```

38.
```
          b   v
        f           n
          k   j
```

39.
```
                w       i
                        m
                m
                    y
            a
```

40.
```
              r   t
      k
        l
          q
              c
```

SET 5
TARGET LETTERS: (o k)

1.
```
          l   m       n
                  n
        w               z
```

2.
```
        p       n
        s       k
        b       x
```

3.
```
                  c       a
                s       z
            b       o
```

4.
```
      a
    d
        e
    k
          f   g
```

5.
```
            l           q
                    s   o
            l       r
```

6.
```
                v   b
        v   c
                i   d
```

7.
```
    s           v       h
        q           o
            r
```

8.
```
          m   v   b
                    k
        g       b
```

9.
```
              b       x
          h           n
              x   z
```

10.
```
    o           p   b
        s
          d
              a
```

11.
```
                      s
            d           h
                      u
            k       b
```

12.
```
        s               y
                  m
            c   n   v
```

13.
```
    b   m   v   c

        x
        t
```

14.
```
    d           f
              u
        g   f       x
```

15.
```
          n       h   b
              c           o
              z
```

16.
```
    s       c       n
          a       v       n
```

17.
```
s       d   s
        g
        f
        k
```

18.
```
          c           n
          f   s   b
          o
```

(Problems continued on next page)

19. c o	20. w r a	21. s f
a d	y v c	a
f g		o r
		t

22. w	23. z z	24. f d
p t	g	a o
n	h	v x
a d	k p	

25. e y	26. o	27. s s
v u	b	a k p
k r	l	r
	m	
	q e	v

28. b j	29. l	30. z
f	g h	d f
k l	k l	a g h
c	v	

31. w i	32. j	33. c v
x b v	l	a o g p
	h	
f	e w t	

34. d	35. p q	36. u i
f	l j	s t
s		d g
l a	o y	
c		

37. w r	38. e t u	39. s f
j l	k	a g m
	b	x
v x	m	

40. p w		
m		
b		
d		
v		

(Problems continued on next page)

SET 6
TARGET LETTERS: (a b)

1. q   u
      r   t
      f   r
        b

2.   p   t   y
                       u
              a   l
              z   m

3.   d   f
              l k
                  b   d
                  i
            q

4.   f   h j
    d   k
      s x c

5.   g   y
       v   n
       x   z
       m   n

6. w s   g   h
       x   c   b   k

7.   s   f   v
    d   p
        a i   o

8. f   g
       p   d
       g   r
       k   d

9. r   q   v   z
    s
    d
    l
    u

10.   p
              r
          i
        j
      n   f h   g

11. b   n   m
                 c   v n
              u
              x

12. q   w
                  d s
           d   b
                  x z

13. q   s
        m   g
          b   l
            x
              a

14. e   r   n
              f
         w   p
            s   h

15.   o   e
           u y
           g h
           w k

16.   e   v   k
       a   c   x
           n   m

17.   e r
         q   w
                    m
            s   z
            l p

18.   p i
          k
                    m
          c x
              n   b

19.   q
    s   z   x s
       d   m
      r   s
          n

20.   f g   h
       i o p
                       l
                       z

21.   f   r t
           q   s   g j
           c

22.   e   y
         a   g
           l k
    w o

23.   t
           f   e
         u   d
         y   I
      i

24.   r   y   i
       j   k
                u
       o   w

(Problems continued on next page)

25.	26.	27.

q   a
  w
d   p
  h
  i   y
	c x
	     f g
	 d t
	   l o
		r u f
		z h l
		        l
		
		          b

28.	29.	30.

t   i
f   g
    d
 	
    k
 a k
	t i
	p u
	    m n
	        g
		k v
		   t u
		 g q g
		   s s
		    m

31.	32.	33.

c v b
 	
w s v c
	e i
	   o u
	    m n
	r w
		e w y u
		   s x a n

34.	35.	36.
o i j d s x z n	s f d a l z x n	z c b q r n m k

37.	38.	39.
r t c i l v b n	s d f j k n m l	s x c n x a m p

40.		

u
i
   i
d
   y		

SET 7

TARGET LETTERS: (g m)

1.	2.	3.

w   d f
w c
    v b
	n
	f g
	s j
	a z x
		e q
		t l
		  n
		s d z

4.	5.	6.

q
a y w s
c b
  z
	r
	   d
	  k
	a e y u
		r v
		 e k
		  n b
		i n m

(Problems continued on next page)

```
7.  y  e  r  t  y        8.  j     r              9.  q  w  q
    s                        d     l                     k
    d                        d     m                     a  e
    x                        e     n                   v    z

10. u     i     o        11.          f     l       12.            j  k
    s     h     g                           k                    g     f
          b                  r        t                  s  w  r     y
    b                          x  z      m

13. r     v     p     w  14.          j     l       15.       f     x     q
                             m     s                   j  e              m
          a                               v                      v     c
    z     v     m              f  c  n  h

16.          d  x     n  17.    t  u  i           18.          w     a
               x                s  c                             m
       m                        d  s  l                       d     a
       f                                                 x  c  s
    z        b

19.             e     y u 20.          q     i  z  21.             w
    a     s        c         v  b  x                          f     g
    x                                    d   s              s           l
    g                                                   a              c
                                                              w

22.          w     o      23.       a  d     f    24.          c     b
    q              j                s  x  z                a     s     k
       d  s                                m                 c     n  f
    z              z                b

25.          y  u         26.          a     d    27.                   a
    d  g                     n                z       c                 d
    n  h                              b                                 v
  z x                           c  v     m                   z
                                                                 n
                                                               b
                                                             z

28.       q  p            29.    f     h     q    30.    s     q
    s     j                  h                          s  h
       b                                    m           m        l
  x     n     g                 v  c     s              x  v
```

(Problems continued on next page)

31.
```
        a           z
              j
              n
              v
     c    b    l
```

32.
```
              z    c
         l  k
                 m    b
            n
                      v
```

33.
```
        a    f       h
     s    n    g
                v  d
```

34.
```
   o    p
      n    c
  j    l
      c    s
```

35.
```
           u    i
      y  t  r
            b  n  f
```

36.
```
t    b    l       p
       c    d    a
                 m
```

37.
```
u    i    p
      n
  b           v
     b  c
```

38.
```
p    t    w
        b
        v
  s  x    z    q
```

39.
```
           z  n  m
      a  s  d
           p
```

40.
```
                   o
                 u
              y
            v
          c
        m
    q  a
```

SET 8
TARGET LETTERS: (a x t)

1.
```
w                r
         e
      a
```

2.
```
         y    i
   m
            n
```

3.
```
r    y
b    x
```

4.
```
c
   n
     m
       t
```

5.
```
        x        u
              g
         s
```

6.
```
w    t
g
c
```

7.
```
v       b
   x
   c
```

8.
```
d
g
j
k
```

9.
```
           c    h
        v    x
```

10.
```
           n
        m
     a
  p
```

11.
```
g       t
   b       o
```

12.
```
t
      r
                p  s
```

13.
```
              s  f
   x    c
```

14.
```
      w    r
   v
        c
```

15.
```
              q
        e    r
              g
```

(Problems continued on next page)

16. c
  f

17. w p
   b
     a

18.   s p
 k
      x

19. z   n m
    c

20. n   o
  x
    u

21.   e t
   s   b

22.   q
 f n
  a

23. w t
  r e

24. q   a z
  v

25. d   b
 b
 f

26.   q
  e t h

27.   u
      c
     m
   n

28. a   p
  m
 j

29.   m x
     k l

30.   u p
 r   t

31.   l z
 d f

32.   n
  r l
  v

33. y
   n
    x
     p

34.   u
 m n
    c

35.   i
 a d
    j

36. q   g
   b v

37.   n
 p
   m
 k

38.   t y
  f
     v

39. s v n
      n

40.   o
  u
  c
 r

SET 9
TARGET LETTERS: (u c p)

1.   e d
 z   x

2.   w
  j
    k
   v

3.   v p
 l
   o

(Problems continued on next page)

```
4.          a      c   | 5.                 o   | 6.       q      a
   n                   |              d         |     f         u
   m                   |         x              |
                       |                        |
7.              n  v   | 8.                 p   | 9.             i
   s                   |         l      k       |            u
   b                   |                j       |         m
                       |                        |         v
10.       w            | 11.      i      p      | 12.            r
      d      i         |         l              |        u    t
         n             |             y          |               m
                       |                        |
13.    e       g    h  | 14.             q      | 15.   q          y
          b            |        g               |            i
                       |            f           |            p
                       |          d             |
16.               d    | 17.             u      | 18.        r
          z            |             k          |              l  w
             n         |            b           |
   w                   |        f               |        s
19.    a      x        | 20.      w    o        | 21.      z    b
                       |                        |            c
        c              |      p                 |     f
        v              |               m        |
22.        y    i      | 23.      g             | 24.            u
       h               |      r                 |         m
     s                 |      l                 |      r
                       |      f                 |                  j
25.            g       | 26.      e             | 27.           g
      f        i       |      i                 |                  p
                       |             p          |        a
           j           |               o        |     s
28.        y  u        | 29.      l    p        | 30.      u  o
   j                   |      k                 |
           m           |          j             |      a
                       |                        |          k
31.        a      p    | 32.      i    t        | 33.      i  y  e
   l                   |          f             |
           i           |        g               |      r
```

(Problems continued on next page)

34.   t   w
  d
       b
	35. a
	    c
	       d
	       f
		36. q w
		       f

37. e   f
    l
  d
	38. a
	   s
	     l
	   g
		39. r t
		       c
		  s

40. q
    g
 j
    m		

SET 10

TARGET LETTERS: (r b a)

1. q   i
  u
q   o
  b
	2. u
	   t e
	  c
	 g r
		3. o u
		   b n
		f g

4.   d
q   d
  f r
   n
	5. g
	a v
	 n
	 z
	 c
		6. i
		   g k
		 p u
		   a

7. e w e
    m
  w
  z
	8. q s
	    k
	 c b
	   m
		9. y e w
		k d y

10. f
 t o
e   y
  p
	11. z x
	 l
	   r
	n m
		12. r
		 l k
		 v
		 c
		    o

13.   y
  o
 u
x
 i
d
	14. u
	h l o w
	   e
		15. t e
		 b v
		   p
		   w

(Problems continued on next page)

```
16.  a        d          17.                  j      18.        q    l
         s                              m                   r      l
         d                                   v                            p
         j                              l                        o
         x                          y       o

19.    z     c     x      20.                 o      21.    w        s     n
       s     g     h               r   t     u  p                      o
                                       j                                      i
                                                                    r

22.          q     a      23.             i   o     24.             i   u
       k  l                          j  h  g                   s        l
               d     z                    m                  z              d
                                          l

25.                x   b  26.        p      o  e    27.    u          q
       s                n         w   a     s                      j
               l                                          z        x
                     f                                        v

28.                  w    29.        i        t    30.     a         z
              m                  k         d                   f        l
       z             v           h                                        d  s
          b  c                         x

31.    i        n         32.             o  r     33.             v    c
       k                         e     l                                 f
       c                             e   s                  g
          b                                                   d     n
          g

34.       q  w           35.          w   e        36.                    y
          c                       g                                n   q
       d  s                         j                      c
          h                     a                             z  x

37.          s     c      38.        q             39. z      x  v
       f                                   l                z
          j     k                          l                   x
       s                        l                              v
                                l       a

40.    l     t
       e     w
             r
       m
```

(Problems continued on next page)

SET 11
TARGET LETTERS: (i o u)

1.   w s c
   e
  a
    o
	2. p
	    z
	            j
	        d s
	   r
		3. i
		  f g
		     m n
		      d

4. t   y
  g   h
  s   a
	5. w
	       e
	     d
	    g
	   u
	  f
		6. w
		  h j
		   f d
		   o

7.   q   t
  u
 f   v z
	8. s a
	  c c
	     n
	  a
		9. w r y
		        t
		  d u

10. d   g z
  f
    v   b
	11. e n m
	    r
	    k
	    i
		12. q
		     q p
		  n b x

13. w
   c
    o
     n
      s
	14. r e
	    f d
	         m
	     n l
		15. i p
		   m
		         l
		  k m

16.   g h
   v   b
  s   u
	17. e k
	  m b s a
		18. y t w
		     m
		        d
		  a

19.   q
     v
 x
  s x z
	20. h b
	  m
	  n
	    b c
		21. d
		  s
		  a
		  u
		  d
		  n

22.   p l
   n b
 k
 c
	23. y t
	  k j
	  n b
		24. b c
		    v
		  z x
		    d

(Problems continued on next page)

25. y h g
    m
    i
    b

26.   h   d
      l
   o   c
      p

27.   a   q
      n b
  c   x

28.   g f
 m   l
  b x

29.   p r
 k d
    v t

30.   d s z
   f
  d
 l

31.   q
    i
    e   y
 w   t

32.   y   r
      h
 x   c   n

33.   a   v
   o   m
 c   n

34.   v k
 b g
  j
  t

35.   h t
    u   s
  p   b

36. a   c
 f
    j
 v
 i

37.   e
   p
 r   t
   n   m

38. y w q   u
    m
    v

39. t   r q
 g
   d   o

40.   a q
   m
  i
d   e

SET 12
TARGET LETTERS: (t g i f)

1.   s   a
     h
     c
 z   s

2.   i   h
  p o
  b   m

3.   b d
   l w g
 n

4. a   h
    i
 d   j
  l

5.   e   w
  s   a
  m v

6.   t   y
     l
  k   r
   w

7.   i
  e   o
 u
z   z

8.   o   x
 o u   y
    b

9.   y
  j   k
  f   m
   v

(Problems continued on next page)

10.
```
                d
    s   a   e
                f
            c
```

11.
```
                        o
            v  n  x  p  r
```

12.
```
            y
    h  d      o
        k
        e
```

13.
```
                v
    b              t
        c            p
            x
```

14.
```
        i        d
    l  p  u  w
```

15.
```
    s   a
    o   p
    f   a
```

16.
```
            n
        m
      c
          z
            a
                q
```

17.
```
            u
    m  n
            p
                k
            j
```

18. y   r
```
        s
        o
        w
        y
```

19.
```
            u
        c
            g
      r      a    s
```

20.
```
                h
    k  l
        y  e  w
```

21.
```
            w      t
        r  e
            a          o
        k
```

22.
```
                h
    d    h  k
            o  p
        j
```

23.
```
            y        j
            h          p
                  o
        d
```

24.
```
                n      m
            v      b
          c    d
```

25.
```
            m  e
        n
      v    c  x  d
```

26.
```
                i
        m          u  r
            s
```

27.
```
                y   m
        f              k
    v            n  m
```

28.
```
        u
    j  g  h
        x   z
```

29.
```
                    p  u  y
        l  x  e
```

30.
```
            u
            s      d
          x    z
            g
```

31.
```
            p
    k        h
        n        n
          l
```

32.
```
      i     e
    l      s
                m  n
```

33.
```
                    g   d
            b  v
            m
                    l
```

34.
```
        j
    m  b  i
            z
      c
```

35.
```
                u      y
        k  s  a
                l
```

36.
```
                p
        h
                v
      j
                c
      z
```

(Problems continued on next page)

37. 　　　　　j　e
　　　m　b
　　　　d
　　c

38. 　　　　k　x
　　l　　　　d
　　　m　　　f

39. 　　　　v　l
　　a　z
　　　b　n
　　　　　n　g

40. 　　　　u
　j　　　　　l
　m　　　b
　n

Answers to Complex Visual Search

Set 1

1. N	2. Y	3. Y	4. N	5. Y	6. N
7. Y	8. Y	9. N	10. N	11. N	12. N
13. N	14. Y	15. N	16. N	17. N	18. N
19. Y	20. N	21. Y	22. Y	23. N	24. Y
25. N	26. N	27. N	28. Y	29. N	30. Y
31. Y	32. Y	33. Y	34. Y	35. Y	36. N
37. Y	38. Y	39. Y	40. N		

Set 2

1. N	2. Y	3. Y	4. N	5. Y	6. N
7. N	8. N	9. N	10. N	11. N	12. Y
13. N	14. Y	15. Y	16. Y	17. Y	18. Y
19. Y	20. N	21. N	22. N	23. Y	24. Y
25. Y	26. Y	27. Y	28. Y	29. N	30. N
31. N	32. Y	33. N	34. Y	35. Y	36. N
37. N	38. N	39. N	40. Y		

Set 3

1. Y	2. Y	3. Y	4. N	5. Y	6. N
7. Y	8. Y	9. Y	10. Y	11. N	12. Y
13. Y	14. Y	15. N	16. N	17. Y	18. N
19. N	20. Y	21. N	22. N	23. N	24. Y
25. Y	26. N	27. N	28. N	29. N	30. Y
31. Y	32. Y	33. N	34. N	35. Y	36. N
37. N	38. Y	39. N	40. N		

Set 4

1. Y	2. N	3. Y	4. N	5. Y	6. N
7. N	8. N	9. Y	10. Y	11. Y	12. N
13. N	14. Y	15. N	16. Y	17. Y	18. N
19. Y	20. Y	21. N	22. Y	23. Y	24. N
25. Y	26. N	27. Y	28. Y	29. Y	30. Y

(Problems continued on next page)

31. Y	32. N	33. Y	34. N	35. Y	36. N
37. N	38. N	39. N	40. N		

Set 5

1. N	2. Y	3. Y	4. Y	5. Y	6. N
7. Y	8. Y	9. N	10. Y	11. N	12. N
13. N	14. N	15. Y	16. N	17. Y	18. Y
19. Y	20. N	21. Y	22. N	23. Y	24. Y
25. Y	26. Y	27. Y	28. Y	29. Y	30. N
31. N	32. N	33. Y	34. N	35. Y	36. N
37. N	38. Y	39. N	40. N		

Set 6

1. Y	2. Y	3. Y	4. N	5. N	6. Y
7. Y	8. N	9. N	10. N	11. Y	12. Y
13. Y	14. N	15. N	16. Y	17. N	18. Y
19. N	20. N	21. N	22. Y	23. N	24. N
25. Y	26. N	27. Y	28. Y	29. N	30. N
31. Y	32. N	33. Y	34. N	35. Y	36. Y
37. Y	38. N	39. Y	40. N		

Set 7

1. N	2. Y	3. N	4. N	5. N	6. Y
7. N	8. Y	9. N	10. Y	11. Y	12. Y
13. Y	14. Y	15. Y	16. Y	17. N	18. Y
19. Y	20. N	21. Y	22. N	23. Y	24. N
25. Y	26. Y	27. N	28. Y	29. Y	30. Y
31. N	32. Y	33. Y	34. N	35. N	36. Y
37. N	38. N	39. Y	40. Y		

Set 8

1. Y	2. N	3. Y	4. Y	5. Y	6. Y
7. Y	8. N	9. Y	10. Y	11. Y	12. Y
13. Y	14. N	15. N	16. N	17. Y	18. Y
19. N	20. Y	21. Y	22. Y	23. Y	24. Y
25. N	26. Y	27. N	28. Y	29. Y	30. Y
31. N	32. N	33. Y	34. N	35. Y	36. N
37. N	38. Y	39. N	40. N		

Set 9

1. N	2. N	3. Y	4. Y	5. N	6. Y
7. N	8. Y	9. Y	10. N	11. Y	12. Y
13. N	14. N	15. Y	16. N	17. Y	18. N
19. Y	20. Y	21. Y	22. N	23. N	24. Y
25. N	26. Y	27. Y	28. Y	29. Y	30. Y
31. Y	32. N	33. N	34. N	35. Y	36. N
37. N	38. N	39. Y	40. N		

(Problems continued on next page)

Set 10

1. Y	2. Y	3. Y	4. Y	5. Y	6. Y
7. N	8. Y	9. N	10. N	11. Y	12. Y
13. N	14. N	15. Y	16. Y	17. N	18. Y
19. N	20. Y	21. Y	22. Y	23. N	24. N
25. Y	26. Y	27. N	28. Y	29. N	30. Y
31. Y	32. Y	33. N	34. N	35. Y	36. N
37. N	38. Y	39. N	40. Y		

Set 11

1. Y	2. N	3. Y	4. N	5. Y	6. Y
7. Y	8. N	9. Y	10. N	11. Y	12. N
13. Y	14. N	15. Y	16. Y	17. N	18. N
19. N	20. N	21. Y	22. N	23. N	24. N
25. Y	26. Y	27. N	28. N	29. N	30. N
31. Y	32. N	33. Y	34. N	35. Y	36. Y
37. N	38. Y	39. Y	40. Y		

Set 12

1. N	2. Y	3. Y	4. Y	5. N	6. Y
7. Y	8. N	9. Y	10. Y	11. N	12. N
13. Y	14. Y	15. Y	16. N	17. N	18. N
19. Y	20. N	21. Y	22. N	23. N	24. N
25. N	26. Y	27. Y	28. Y	29. N	30. Y
31. N	32. Y	33. Y	34. Y	35. N	36. N
37. N	38. Y	39. Y	40. N		

SUMMING UP

In this chapter, we have discussed the process of automatization and discussed ways that you can improve how fast you make a process automatic. In particular, we have given extensive examples of simple and complex tasks that you have hopefully been able to make yourself perform automatically. Learning and becoming an expert at this process can help free up valuable mental resources to use on other activities.

In the next chapter, we will turn to a different aspect of intelligence: practical intelligence.

Practical Intelligence

By her fourth year in college, Mary had managed to anger and annoy nearly every professor in the philosophy department. This was especially problematical, given that philosophy was her major. Her course papers were certainly acceptable, and there was nothing wrong with her senior thesis. However, it was clear that no one liked to have her around. When she applied to the graduate program, members of the department were dismayed. They finally decided that she did not have the right "values" for a career as a philosopher. No one overtly admitted the true reason for the negative decision on her application to graduate school: No one liked Mary.

Tom went to his literature class after a long night spent doing the reading for the class. The topic of discussion was Dostoevsky's *Crime and Punishment*. The class discussion started with an analysis of the protagonist, Raskolnikov. John, a classmate, repeatedly made remarks that obviously impressed the professor. Tom was frustrated: He knew not only that John had not read the book but also that John had spent the previous night at a party. John always seemed to have a way of saying the things people wanted to hear, whether or not those things had any substance.

Dr. Worthley was tired after a long day seeing patients, and on arriving at her home, turned on the television. As soon as the screen lit up, she became frustrated: There, on the screen, was Dr. Johnston being interviewed on yet another talk show. Dr. Worthley and her professional colleagues were convinced that Dr. Johnston's diet plan was useless in the long run for losing weight, and that it also had harmful side effects. Despite this fact, Dr. Johnston seemed to consistently be able to get on television to talk about both his diet and himself.

The department chairman thumbed through the course evaluations of his teaching staff. The pattern of ratings depressed him. As usual, Mr. Agar had received highly favorable ratings from the students in his classes. The chairman had attended a number of Mr. Agar's lectures: They were extremely entertaining, but, in the chairman's opinion, lacking substance. Mrs. Novina's lectures, by contrast, were rather dry – yet they were carefully organized and full of both substance and informed ideas. Mrs. Novina, however, had once again received only mediocre ratings from her students. Despite her quality as a teacher, she simply failed to spark the enthusiasm of the students, and it showed in her ratings.

WHAT IS PRACTICAL INTELLIGENCE?

Each of these anecdotes illustrates a pervasive but little understood aspect of our daily lives: intelligence as it operates in real-world contexts, or *practical intelligence*. In school, there is tremendous interest in and concentration on the teaching of academic knowledge and skills. Students are taught academic knowledge; they are tested on it; they are graded on it; and their admission to further educational programs depends on it. Ultimately, their ability to find well-paying and professional jobs will be largely determined by it. Despite the overwhelming emphasis we place on academic knowledge and skills, we all know just how important practical knowledge and skills are in our daily lives. However useful academic intelligence may be, most of us know people whose professional or personal life has been greatly affected, for better or for worse, by their practical intelligence. These anecdotes are just a few examples of how high or low practical intelligence can affect real-world outcomes.

Although there is no universally accepted definition, practical intelligence can be defined as intelligence as used in real-world contexts. It acts through efforts by individuals to adapt to, shape, and select environments. In adaptation, people seek to accommodate to the environment to get the best fit between themselves and the environment. For example, you might try to fit yourself to the requirements of a new job. In shaping, people seek to accommodate the environment to themselves for the same reason. For example, you might try to change the requirements of a new job to suit yourself. In selection, people seek a new environment to which they would be a better fit. This is usually done after deciding that a present environment is unsuitable and probably cannot be changed so as to be suitable. For example, you may decide that you are better off finding a new job. In everyday life, we often call practical intelligence "common sense," although what constitutes common sense may vary from one society or culture to another, and may vary even within societies and cultures.

DEVELOPING YOUR PRACTICAL INTELLIGENCE

This discussion should indicate that there are many forms of practical intelligence. Indeed, an entire book could be devoted to exercises designed to test or improve how practically intelligent you are across different domains. The exercises in this chapter represent only a small portion of the possible skills that might be assessed and developed. For the most part, these exercises are taken from our own investigations of practical intelligence.

Adaptive Behavior Checklist

Sternberg, Conway, Ketron, and Bernstein (1981) conducted a survey in which they asked people to list behaviors that they believed to be distinctively characteristic of either particularly intelligent persons or of particularly unintelligent ones. Analysis of these behaviors revealed that they fell into three general classes: practical problem-solving skills, verbal skills, and social competence. The researchers then refined the checklist of behaviors so that it could be used as an instrument for self-evaluation. A person can rate the extent to which each of a set of behaviors characterizes himself or herself, and then compare this self-characterization to the characterization people have given for a highly intelligent person. Berg and Sternberg (1985) have conducted a similar survey for adults of systematically varying ages from thirty to seventy years old. The behaviors obtained can differ from one culture to another (Grigorenko et al., 2004; Sternberg & Kaufman, 1998; Yang & Sternberg, 1997).

Below you will find a listing of some of the behaviors that have emerged from this research: Rate on a scale of 1 (low) to 9 (high) the extent to which each of these behaviors characterizes your typical performance. In general, higher ratings are associated with better performance.

BEHAVIORAL CHECKLIST

1. Practical problem-solving ability
   a. Reasons logically and well
   b. Identifies connections among ideas
   c. Sees all aspects of a problem
   d. Keeps an open mind
   e. Responds thoughtfully to others' ideas
   f. Sizes up situations well
   g. Gets to the heart of problems
   h. Interprets information accurately
   i. Makes good decisions
   j. Goes to original sources for basic information
   k. Poses problems in an optimal way
   l. Is a good source of ideas
   m. Perceives implied assumptions and conclusions
   n. Listens to all sides of an argument
   o. Deals with problems resourcefully
2. Verbal ability
   a. Speaks clearly and articulately
   b. Is verbally fluent
   c. Converses well
   d. Is knowledgeable about a particular area of subject matter
   e. Studies hard
   f. Reads with high comprehension
   g. Reads widely
   h. Writes without difficulty
   i. Sets aside time for reading
   j. Displays good vocabulary
3. Social competence
   a. Accepts others for what they are
   b. Admits mistakes

    c. Displays interest in the world at large

    d. Is on time for appointments

    e. Has social conscience

    f. Thinks before speaking and doing

    g. Displays curiosity

    h. Does not make snap judgments

    i. Makes fair judgments

    j. Assesses well the relevance of information to a problem at hand

    k. Is sensitive to other people's needs and desires

    l. Is frank and honest with self and others

    m. Displays interest in the immediate environment

DECODING NONVERBAL CUES

One important aspect of your everyday life is the ability to decode the nonverbal messages that people send to you. Such messages, transmitted during the course of a conversation, may in some cases correspond to what a person is saying, but in other cases, they may not. Often, the nonverbal messages are a better indication of a person's true feelings than the verbal messages that they accompany. It is therefore quite important to be able to decode such messages.

On the following pages, you will find thirty pictures of pairs of individuals. The first twenty pairs are of male-female couples. Ten of the couples are genuinely involved in romantic relationships; the other ten are not. Your task is to guess which couples are involved in relationships, and which are not. In the second set of pictures, you will see sets of two individuals, one of whom is the other's supervisor/boss. Your task is to guess who is the supervisor/boss of the other individual.

You may want to do these tasks without first being told what kinds of nonverbal cues are indicative of the true situation. Answers appear after the pictures.

PICTURES OF MALE-FEMALE COUPLES. WHICH ARE REAL COUPLES? [FIGURE 13–1]

5.

6.

7.

8.

9.

10.

11.

12.

13.

14.

15.

16.

17.

18.

19.

20.

WHO ARE THE SUPERVISORS, AND WHO ARE THE SUPERVISEES? (FIGURE 13–2)

1.

2.

3.

4.

5.

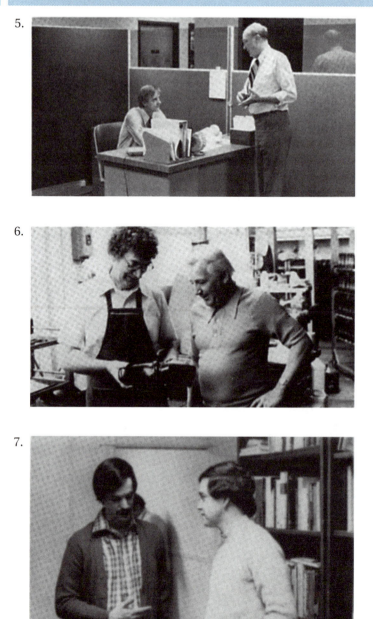

6.

7.

8.

9.

10.

Answers: Couples (FIGURE 12-1)

R = Real Couple; F = Fake Couple

1.	F		5.	R		9.	R		13.	F		17.	R
2.	R		6.	R		10.	R		14.	F		18.	F
3.	F		7.	F		11.	R		15.	F		19.	F
4.	F		8.	R		12.	F		16.	R		20.	R

Answers: Supervisor-Supervisee (FIGURE 12-2)

L = Supervisor on the left; R = Supervisor on the right

1.	L		3.	R		5.	R		7.	R		9.	R
2.	L		4.	R		6.	R		8.	L		10.	L

Consider first the couples task. What kinds of things should you look for in deciding whether each pair of individuals is a genuine or a fake couple? Sternberg and Smith (1985) found several nonverbal clues to be diagnostic. The things to look for are these:

1. *Relaxation.* The individuals constituting the genuine couples look, on the average, more relaxed with each other.
2. *Angle of bodies.* Individuals constituting genuine couples tend to lean toward each other more than do individuals in fake couples.
3. *Positioning of arms and legs.* Individuals in genuine couples tend to position their arms and legs more naturally than do individuals who are just posing.
4. *Tenseness of the hands.* Individuals in fake couples tend to have hands showing tenseness and discomfort, whereas individuals in real couples do not show these symptoms.
5. *Match in socioeconomic class.* Individuals in genuine couples appear to be a better match in socioeconomic class than do individuals in fake couples. One generally guesses socioeconomic class from clothes and physical appearance.
6. *Distance between bodies.* The individuals in fake couples are generally at a greater physical distance from each other than are the individuals in real couples.
7. *Amount of physical contact.* Individuals in real couples generally show more physical contact with each other than do individuals in fake couples.
8. *General similarity.* Individuals in real couples generally tend to be more similar in appearance, including such factors as dress, age, and ethnicity.

In the supervisors task, the variables that predict which individual is the supervisor (and which the supervisee) are these:

1. *Direction of eye gaze.* The supervisor tends more to gaze directly at the supervisee, whereas the supervisee tends more to look away.

2. *Formality of dress.* The supervisor tends to be more formally dressed.
3. *Age.* The supervisor tends to be the older of the two individuals.
4. *Tenseness of hands.* The supervisor's hands tend to be more relaxed than those of the supervisee.
5. *Socioeconomic class.* The supervisor tends to be the individual who appears to be of the higher socioeconomic class.

Everyday Situations

Below are twenty everyday situations. After each situation, you are presented with three options that represent different ways of handling the situation. One of these options represents a solution of adaptation – you try to fit yourself to the environment. A second option represents a solution of shaping – you attempt to fit the environment to yourself. The third option represents a solution of selection – you decide to leave that environment altogether. You should consider the available information, and decide which of these kinds of solutions is best. Questions to ask yourself include:

1. Given who you are, could you behave in ways that are adaptive to the situation, or could you change yourself to be more adaptive?
2. If not, could the environment be shaped so as to conform better to who you are? In other words, can you see ways of changing the situation so as to make it more suitable for yourself?
3. If you do not see ways of adapting yourself or of shaping the situation, might it be better to find a new environment altogether? If so, what kinds of alternative environments might be available to you?

Note that in problems such as these, there is no one right or wrong answer. On the contrary, the "right" answer will depend upon the individual, the situation, and the interaction between the two. Your goal, therefore, ought to be to find the course of action that is right for you. Thinking about the options of adaptation, selection, and shaping, about the constraints that exist in your own personality and abilities, and about the way your personality and abilities interact with the situation will help you to make a more practically intelligent decision in situations such as those presented here. A key to the answers appears after the problems.

EXERCISE 13.1

REAL-WORLD PROBLEMS

1. The nation of Dragonia is characterized by cruel leadership, an elitist society, brutal repression of any dissent, and general intolerance. Life in this small nation is boring, predictable, and dangerous. The small upper class controls the government and military, whereas everyone else lives as second-class citizens who work in factories or farms.

You are a young person born to the upper class who has just completed your education at a respected university in Europe. On returning to Dragonia, do you:

a) accept the calling of your birth, resolving to perform your duties to the best of your ability?

b) criticize the culture of elitism and try to create a fairer order?

c) decide that you cannot live in such a world and move to a large city elsewhere, where you can live in relative freedom and obscurity?

2. Your old, beat-up Honda is about to die on you. To avoid the inevitable breakdown, you decide to purchase a new car, a Mercedes, no less. The local dealership has many new models, and it has a good reputation. After describing to the salesman just what you have in mind, you find out that the price is much higher than you expected. Do you:

a) decide to haggle and bargain for the absolute lowest price possible?

b) resign yourself to buying a different type of car?

c) buy the car of your dreams, knowing that you will have to get a second job to supplement your income?

3. Television reception in your area is poor because of a nearby mountain range. The reruns of *Star Trek: The Next Generation*, your favorite show, are hardly worth watching, because of all the double images and static interference. Given that you value your free time highly, do you:

a) continue watching your favorite show in its current, hard-to-watch form?

b) buy a satellite dish to improve the reception?

c) take up video games?

4. As you are putting on your brand new suit from Brandt Brothers, you notice that there is a large stain on the inside lining of the jacket. Because you are proud of your appearance, do you:

a) wear another suit and take the spotted one to the cleaners?

b) realize that the stain cannot be seen with the jacket on, and, therefore, decide the stain is harmless?

c) return the suit to Brandt Brothers and select a new one?

5. Your sixteen-year-old son arrives home four hours after midnight curfew, at 4:00 A.M. He has clearly drunk too much alcohol and immediately goes to sleep. As a concerned parent, do you:

a) grab him as soon as he wakes up the next day in order to discuss the meaning of responsibility, discussing the importance of keeping his curfew and not getting drunk?

b) take your son out of public school, and send him to private school where he will find more mature friends?

c) say to yourself that boys will be boys, and a sixteen-year-old can take care of himself?

6. All semester long, your class in cognitive psychology has been your most difficult and demanding. Two weeks before the final, you come down with a severe case of the flu. The illness robs you of a week of valuable study time, forcing you to cram for several exams in one week. Faced with the prospect of ruining your 4.0 GPA, do you:
a) pull off a superhuman series of all-nighters?
b) ask the professor if you can reschedule your exam?
c) drop some courses, as the pressure is just too great?

7. Aunt Gertrude gives you a shirt for Christmas that is not quite your style. Poor Aunt Gertrude is always giving the most hideous gifts, and this one is no exception: an ugly, plaid, 100 percent polyester nightmare. In this delicate situation, do you:
a) exchange the shirt for one that you like better?
b) take Aunt Gertrude aside to discuss the type of gift that in the future you would like to receive?
c) hang the shirt in the back of your closet and resolve to wear it at the next Halloween party you attend?

8. Your best friend, Jill, always cheats when the two of you play tennis. She automatically calls any ball out that falls even remotely near a line. In the face of this inexplicable ridiculousness, do you:
a) refuse to play tennis with her? After all, you have plenty of other tennis partners who do not cheat.
b) figure that tennis is only a game to be enjoyed and decide to tolerate her foolishness, knowing in your heart that you are a better player?
c) take Jill aside and tell her that you know that she is cheating, and make her promise to play fairly?

9. You are having dinner at an expensive restaurant. After a wonderful appetizer, you get your main course – a steak for two – that arrives quite overdone. Do you and your partner:
a) eat the dish, although it is obviously way below par?
b) demand that the waiter take it back?
c) leave the dish essentially untouched, and vow never to return to the restaurant?

10. Your assigned seat on Flight 114 from Rome to Paris on some no-name discount airline is next to a very addicted smoker. You had thought the no-name airline was nonsmoking, but you were wrong. The area around your seat is shrouded in a cloud of smoke, and your allergies are troubling you. To remedy the situation, do you:
a) go to the bathroom every time he lights up?
b) ask him not to smoke?
c) call for the stewardess and demand a new seat?

11. The cafeteria at your work serves terrible food. Everyone in the company agrees that the food is horrible, but nobody can agree on a solution. Do you:
a) buy prepackaged food that can't be ruined?
b) petition for a new, improved food service?
c) eat at the diner down the street?

12. You are a construction worker on a large project in the city. Your foreman is a real jerk who randomly punishes the workers, supposedly for slacking off. No one likes him, but what can you do? Do you:
a) look for another place to work?
b) do your best to tolerate the downside of the job?
c) take the foreman out for a beer (or three), and when he loosens up, explain the nature of your problems with him?

13. The beautiful house you just bought needs a fresh coat of paint. Unfortunately, all of the companies that submit bids are very high-priced. In light of the fact that the house really does need painting, do you:
a) call the companies back and attempt to bargain down the price?
b) accept the fact that the job is going to be expensive, bite the bullet, and hire the most reputable of the companies?
c) have your two teenage sons paint the house? The job will be second-rate, but still adequate.

14. Imagine that you are a high school math teacher. One morning, you discover that the eraser for the blackboard is missing. In light of this event, do you:
a) send one of the students to hunt for another one?
b) wipe the board with your hand?
c) decide to use the overhead projector instead?

15. You are the president of a large, democratic country. Suddenly, your nation is rocked by a scandal involving one of your most trusted advisors. Do you:
a) understand that an occasional mistake is bound to occur, and decide to support your struggling advisor to the fullest?
b) call your advisor to your office, scold him severely, warn him that any further bad behavior will lead to his being fired, and tell him that you plan to discipline him publicly?
c) fire him immediately, as your administration must not be associated with even the slightest degree of corruption?

16. Your son gets his birthday wish: a cute cocker spaniel puppy. Eight months later, the dog is not house-trained, jumps on the bed when he's not supposed to, and is a general nuisance. Do you:
a) tell your son he had better do something about the dog, and fast?
b) proceed to train the dog yourself?
c) sell the dog?

17. You are considering flying to Florida for a winter vacation. Unfortunately, the plane fare is more than you expected. Do you:
a) shop around for the lowest fare?
b) decide to drive?
c) spend the extra money? After all, you are going on vacation.

18. With three kids and New York City prices, you are having trouble making ends meet in your current job. Do you:
a) make do as well as you can?

b) ask the boss for a raise?

c) look for a new position?

19. You are currently in the midst of a midlife crisis. Your children disappoint you, your spouse is a bore, and your job is depressing. In order to improve the quality of your life, do you:

a) try to find a good psychiatrist?

b) explain to your family what you are going through, and tell them they must do their share to help improve the situation?

c) leave home to start fresh, possibly with a younger man or woman?

20. Because there is virtually no free parking near your workplace, you are gradually building a collection of parking tickets. In view of this situation, do you:

a) let the tickets mount up, figuring you will pay them at some point?

b) start parking in one of the overpriced garages?

c) go to court, and try to convince the judge that you should not have to pay the fines?

Answers to Real-World Problems

1.	a) adaptation		8.	a) selection		15.	a) adaptation
	b) shaping			b) adaptation			b) shaping
	c) selection			c) shaping			c) selection
2.	a) shaping		9.	a) adaptation		16.	a) shaping
	b) selection			b) shaping			b) adaptation
	c) adaptation			c) selection			c) selection
3.	a) adaptation		10.	a) adaptation		17.	a) shaping
	b) shaping			b) shaping			b) selection
	c) selection			c) selection			c) adaptation
4.	a) shaping		11.	a) adaptation		18.	a) adaptation
	b) adaptation			b) shaping			b) shaping
	c) selection			c) selection			c) selection
5.	a) shaping		12.	a) selection		19.	a) adaptation
	b) selection			b) adaptation			b) shaping
	c) adaptation			c) shaping			c) selection
6.	a) adaptation		13.	a) shaping		20.	a) adaptation
	b) shaping			b) adaptation			b) selection
	c) selection			c) selection			c) shaping
7.	a) selection		14.	a) shaping			
	b) shaping			b) adaptation			
	c) adaptation			c) selection			

Tacit Knowledge

Tacit knowledge is knowledge that we pick up from our experience, often without realizing that we have learned it. It is usually not explicitly taught. The tacit knowledge needed for success varies from one job or life course to another. However, practically intelligent people tend to be those who are good at putting themselves in other people's shoes. In other words, they tend to know how to use the knowledge they have to make right decisions. They are able to apply this knowledge to a broad range of types of tasks. The tacit-knowledge items here require you to solve the kinds of problems you often encounter in a college or university setting. Draw on your full knowledge of such a setting in order to answer these questions. The questions tap into quite important abilities – the ability to manage yourself, to manage others, and to manage tasks. After you have answered the questions, the answer key will tell you the kind of responses that students are more and less likely to give.

Situation 1: You are enrolled in a class you are not excited about – it is hard, and not very interesting! However, you do care about your grade. Fortunately, so far, you have been doing fine. The class has a short paper due tomorrow, but every time you tried to work on the paper, something else got in the way. You planned to finish the paper today, but you just received a phone call from your friend Alan, who reminded you that today his soccer team is playing and he expects you to come to see the game. Most of your friends will be there, and you would love to go.

Given this situation, rate the quality of the following choices in response to the situation:

1	2	3	4	5	6	7
Not a very good choice			Average			A very good choice

_____ a) Go to the game, but bring a note pad with you so that you can write down ideas for the paper during the game.

_____ b) Go to the game and stay for the first half; then go back to work on your paper.

_____ c) Tell Alan that you will work on the paper for an hour and will come to see him play afterward.

_____ d) Go, enjoy yourself, and then stay up all night to work on the paper.

_____ e) Go to the game and then come up with an excuse so that you can get permission to turn in the paper late in case you cannot finish it on time.

_____ f) Tell Alan you would like to go to the game but really need to study for your class.

Situation 2. Melanie, a student in your language class with whom you are not very close, is having problems and is likely to flunk the class and be on academic probation. Even though you do not know Melanie well, you like her and would like to become friends. Her academic problem is not something you have talked about directly, but you know from other people that her grades are really poor. You know that she is smart, but she does not have the right study skills and wastes a lot of time studying in a way that is not efficient.

Given this situation, rate the quality of the following choices in response to the situation:

1	2	3	4	5	6	7
Not a very good choice			Average			A very good choice

_____ a) Wait for Melanie to approach you before offering any advice.

_____ b) Tell her how you study, and why you think it would help her to do the same.

_____ c) Suggest to several people in the class to get together and share ideas about study strategies. Make a point of inviting Melanie.

_____ d) Encourage her to ask the teacher for help.

_____ e) Talk to your teachers or a counselor about her.

_____ f) Offer to study together for this class.

_____ g) Try to help her with homework assignments to improve her grades.

_____ h) Try to think of situations that develop language skills (e.g., find a native speaker who could talk to the student and help her to gain a momentum in the development of basic language skills).

Popularity of Responses

Situation 1   (a) Average
              (b) Popular
              (c) Popular
              (d) Unpopular
              (e) Unpopular
              (f) Popular

Situation 2   (a) Popular
              (b) Popular
              (c) Popular
              (d) Average
              (e) Unpopular
              (f) Average
              (g) Unpopular
              (h) Average

Conflict Resolution

Presented here are six stories involving three different kinds of conflicts: between individuals in personal relationships, between individuals in organizations, and between countries. Read each story, then read the seven styles of conflict resolution that follow the story. Rate the desirability of each style of conflict resolution from 1 (poor) to 10 (excellent). In other words, how desirable is each of the proposed strategies for resolving the conflict presented in the story? In general, these conflict resolution situations have no one "correct" solution. It is worth remembering, however, that more intelligent people tend to try to reduce conflict. A key that lists styles of conflict resolution appears after the problems.

EXERCISE 13.2 CONFLICT-RESOLUTION PROBLEMS

1. A recent purchase for the local university's economics department has turned out to be a source of conflict among the faculty, students, and staff. The controversy centers on a new powerful computer system complete with many essential software packages. The department bought the new computer with hopes that the machine would help the efficiency of the economics department. Unfortunately, this has not happened. If anything, the new computer system has been a source of hard feelings, departmental division, and worse efficiency. Part of the problem revolves around the dual function of the university's economics department, which prides itself on being both "a foremost research institution" and "a high quality place of teaching and learning." The department has been divided into two subdivisions to meet its various commitments and interests, one focused on research and the other on teaching. Consequently, there has been intense competition between the two factions for use of the new computer.

The research subdivision needs the computer and its associated software for its various research projects. These projects are extensive and require software that is only on the computer. The research subdivision justifies this use of the computer as "necessary if the department is to maintain its reputation as a major research institution." Furthermore, the research contracts with the local government bring in a major portion of the operating budget for the economic department. Without the research contracts, the department would have to make drastic cutbacks in its existing program.

The faculty and students of the economics department's teaching subdivision also have extensive need for the computer. This group uses the computer for many different class projects. The software on the computer is used to help teachers prepare PowerPoint and grade student exams. The education group sees its work as no less important than that of the research group. In fact, many of the faculty believe the teaching subdivision should receive first priority. Without their share of time on the computer, the education group knows it could not continue to attract high-quality teachers and students. And without the students' tuition money, the department would find it impossible to carry on either teaching or research.

In other words, both subdivisions of the department need each other to carry on the work each wishes to accomplish. At a recent department meeting, it was determined to be impossible to obtain another computer until at least next year because of the high cost of a new computer.

At the meeting of the research group, the following different options were considered:

_____ a. The research group could try to get the education group's budget reduced if the education group does not comply with the needs of the research group.

_____ b. The research group could decide to take no action at this time and wait to see what the education group will do.

_____ c. The research group could make sure that the education group cannot use the computer by signing up to use the computer well in advance, even if there is no immediate use for the machine.

_____ d. The research group could bring in a third party, like a university decision-making board, and plead the group's case before the board.

_____ e. The research group could be openly critical of the function of the education group to the other members of the economics department, hoping to receive support for the research group's position.

_____ f. The research group could accept the fact that there is a scarcity of resources and try to make the best of the situation.

_____ g. The research group could voluntarily reduce its own use of the computer by only using the machine for its most essential projects.

2. Bill and Sue Martin have been married for the past fourteen years and have two children, a boy, thirteen, and a daughter, twelve. For the past five years, Bill has been working as a car salesman in town. Although his income has so far been steady, he works on commission and sales have been down. He has been working longer hours but he has not been making more money. Sue works as a sales clerk in a local department store to help supplement the family's income.

The Martin family lives in what was originally a two-bedroom house. During the early years, the boy and the girl shared the same bedroom, while the parents had the other bedroom. As the children grew older, the Martins realized that they either would need a larger home, or they would need to add another bedroom to their present home. Because it was clear that the family could not afford a new home, the Martins spent a moderate amount to build an extra bedroom in the basement for their son. This way, each of the children could have a separate room and some privacy. This seemed like the most workable solution to the family's space problem.

Then, about six months ago, Mrs. Martin's father died, leaving Mrs. Martin's mother, Mrs. Jones, all alone with little financial support. The elderly Mrs. Jones had severe problems adjusting to her husband's death. She totally isolated herself from family and friends and preferred to spend her days alone in her small apartment. The older woman's physical and mental health quickly began to get worse. Mrs. Martin tried to help her mother as much as possible, but as the months passed, it became increasingly clear that Mrs. Jones could no longer manage living alone.

Mrs. Martin approached her husband about the possibility of her mother moving in with the family. Mr. Martin, who had never gotten along with his mother-in-law, was totally against the idea. Mr. Martin pointed out the family's space problem. If the mother moved in, the now-teenage children would again have to share a room. Moreover, someone would always have to be at home to supervise Mrs. Jones to make sure she was all right. Because both Mr. and Mrs. Martin work full time, this necessity would pose difficulties for the family. Finally, the added friction between Mr. Martin and the mother-in-law might make the situation intolerable.

Mr. Martin suggested that the family look into the possibility of a nursing home for Mrs. Jones. The family could afford only a limited-care facility, but at least

Mrs. Jones would have a safe place to stay and someone to look after her. Mrs. Martin was especially against putting her mother in a nursing home. She had heard the horror stories about bad things that happened at these places. Furthermore, Mrs. Martin had always been close to her mother and wanted her mother nearby.

The Martins further considered hiring a full-time nurse to look after the mother, but this option was quickly ruled out for financial reasons. Mrs. Martin is the only child in the family, and there are no other relatives to take care of Mrs. Jones. The only true possibilities are for Mrs. Jones to move into the Martins' home, or to have Mrs. Jones move into a nursing home. Because Mr. Martin is set against the mother moving in, and Mrs. Martin is set against her mother moving into a nursing home, what should Mr. Martin do?

_____ a. Mr. Martin might seek an outside counselor to help the family solve its dilemma.

_____ b. Mr. Martin could be openly critical of both the wife and mother-in-law for forcing him to have the mother-in-law stay in the house.

_____ c. Mr. Martin could just accept the mother-in-law's moving into the house and try to make the best of a difficult situation.

_____ d. Mr. Martin could refuse to pay anything in support of the mother-in-law while she stays in the house.

_____ e. Mr. Martin could decide to take no action and wait to see what would happen.

_____ f. Mr. Martin could physically bar the mother-in-law from entering the house against his wishes.

_____ g. Mr. Martin might agree to a trial period with the mother-in-law in the house and try to be as kind and positive as possible.

3. The two nations of Uvolo and Mboka share a common border. Although the two nations have had friendly relations for a number of years, there has been a recent conflict over how to best use the area's major natural resource, the Kilo River. Both Uvolo and Mboka depend heavily on the Kilo for crop irrigation, hydroelectric power generation, transportation, and a sustained water supply for the two countries' ever-growing populations.

The problem centers on Mboka, which is upriver from Uvolo and controls the source of the Kilo River. Mboka has experienced a big population increase within the last ten years. To support this increase, Mboka has needed to use more and more water from the Kilo. Farms have been planted where there was once only desert. Huge dams have been built for hydroelectric power generation and flood control. Large factories that use millions of gallons of water per day have been built near the border with Uvolo, increasing the pollution flowing into the river. Subsequently, the amount of water flowing into Uvolo has decreased by at least 50 percent. The water that does flow is so polluted that without a very expensive water treatment process, it is almost unusable for human consumption and crop irrigation.

Recently, Uvolo's health ministry published a report noting a significant increase in illnesses from people drinking the polluted water. In addition, the agricultural ministry in Uvolo has found initial evidence that vast crop damage and drought will happen without some significant change in the present situation.

On hearing this evidence, the Uvolon government filed a formal protest to the government of Mboka demanding a change in that government's present water policies. The Mbokan government, although concerned about the plight of the Uvolons, maintains that where the Kilo flows within their borders, it is their property to be used as they best see fit. Thus, there will be no change in their policies.

The Mbokans maintain that they are not the cause of Uvolo's problem, but cite Uvolo's inefficient farming methods as the cause of their agricultural dilemmas. Mboka also argues that Uvolo's health conditions were poor long before Mboka's present water management policies. Mboka also claims that it must be Uvolon factories causing the pollution problem because Mbokan factories use the most technologically advanced pollution control devices. Given Mboka's unwillingness to share responsibility for the water problems along the Kilo, what should Uvolo do?

_____ a. Uvolo could take action to destroy Mboka's dams and factories along the border.

_____ b. Uvolo could accept the situation as it is even though the situation is not perfect.

_____ c. Uvolo could try to take its case to the World Court or another international body to cause a change in Mboka's policies or win some compensation.

_____ d. Uvolo could decide to take no action at this time and to wait and see what Mboka will do.

_____ e. Uvolo could try to find a solution without the help of Mboka by searching for another source of water other than the Kilo River.

_____ f. Uvolo could break off diplomatic ties and denounce Mboka before the world community in order to persuade Mboka to change.

_____ g. Uvolo could cease all trade with Mboka and try to convince other nations to do the same until Mboka changes its water management policies.

4. Tom and Kathy Clark just recently celebrated their tenth wedding anniversary. Unfortunately, what should have been a happy occasion was ruined by a bitter disagreement between the couple. Within the last year, Kathy has become more and more unhappy about the amount of time Tom spends away from home.

Tom runs his own accounting firm in New Providence. From the beginning, he has worked long hours, often several nights a week. Tom must work late each night, especially during tax time between December and April. In addition to his regular hours at work, Tom is involved in extra commitments that keep him away from home several nights a week. On Tuesday evenings, Tom attends meetings of the local school board, which he enjoys serving on very much. Another important activity for Tom is his Thursday evening Bible study at the local church. Several times, Tom has invited Kathy to attend his various activities and has offered to pay for a sitter for the children. Each time, Kathy has declined.

As a result, with such a full and active schedule, Tom feels he needs to have free time on Wednesday night to play racquetball at the local YMCA with his friends. This is Tom's only opportunity for exercise during the week. Unlike his friends, Tom does not go out drinking after the games, but goes right home to Kathy and the children. He often arrives home only after the family has already gone to bed. The couple has three children, all in school. Kathy is worried that the children will soon be grown up and will never have a chance to spend much time with their father.

Tom feels that he cannot cut anything out of his present schedule if he is to provide for his wife and children, do community service, practice his religious faith, and allow himself some leisure time for his physical health. Tom loves his family and hopes they understand this. He tries to spend as much quality time as possible with the family during the weekends. Moreover, because Tom offers to have Kathy come with him to the various activities, he feels he has taken the initiative to spend time with her. Each time Kathy says no because she has her own friends and activities. Although Kathy has tried to be understanding of her husband's needs, she is starting to resent the amount of time Tom spends away from home. To supplement the family's income, Kathy is working part-time as a library assistant at the high school while the children are in school. Kathy also feels pressured for time, but her children must take top priority. Kathy is tired of nagging Tom about his schedule, but nothing seems to change his habits. Kathy has come to the end of her patience and realizes that something has to change if she is to be happy. Kathy considered the following solutions:

_____ a. Kathy might try criticizing Tom's behavior in front of family, friends, and Tom's professional colleagues to get him to spend more time at home.

_____ b. Kathy could spend the money she makes at the high school on herself and the children only and not let Tom benefit from her extra income.

_____ c. Kathy might try to find some counseling for the couple to work out an agreement that is satisfying to both.

_____ d. Kathy could decide to take no action at this time and wait to see what Tom will do.

_____ e. Kathy could accept the situation with Tom as it is even though the situation is far from perfect.

_____ f. Kathy might try being extra nice to Tom, hoping this would convince him to spend more time with the family.

_____ g. If Tom continues to spend most of his evenings away from home, Kathy might consider a separation and possible divorce from Tom to show him she is serious about his being with the family.

5. The nations of Omat and Qarah are two small countries sharing a common border. A geological survey conducted in the late 1960s indicated the existence of a rich field of petroleum deposits right along the border between the two countries.

From the early 1970s, the nation of Omat has aggressively exploited the oil field by building hundreds of oil wells along the common border with Qarah. Sales from the oil brought Omat huge sums of capital, which has been used to develop local industry and thereby upgrade that standard of living for the people of Omat. The government of Qarah, on the other hand, decided not to use any of their oil reserves, but instead wanted to let the oil lie in reserve at least until the year 2020, when the oil could be sold for a higher price and also be used to assure domestic supplies to local industrial development. Qarah felt it would not need the oil money until then. In the meantime, Qarah, unlike Omat, planned to depend on its long established tradition of an agriculturally based economy for the improved livelihood of its people.

Late in 2005, Qarah commissioned another survey to determine just how vast their oil reserves were, in order to begin planning for their use around the year 2020. Much to the shock of the people of Qarah, the commission reported that the oil reserves were rapidly diminishing each year and that, within five to ten years, there would be no oil left at all. The commission attributed this rapid depletion of Qarah's oil reserves to the aggressive oil exploitation of neighboring Omat. Although Omat was only drilling for oil on their side of the border, apparently, the oil field was subterraneanly connected and drilling on one side of the border was depleting reserves on the other side. Upon receiving the commission's report, the government of Qarah sent an immediate protest to the government of Omat and demanded an immediate cessation of drilling until some sort of solution could be mutually agreed upon. Omat responded that "although our people are sympathetic to the plight of Qarah, a cessation of drilling would be impossible because of long-standing oil contracts with the United States and Western Europe. Moreover, our own economic health depends on the continued flow of oil from our land." Furthermore, Omat stated, "because we have been scrupulous in making sure our drilling has been conducted only within our territory, we can in no way be held responsible for your regrettable situation. But out of respect for your present plight, our nation is willing to reduce slightly our oil production on a temporary basis." Given Omat's reply, what should Qarah do?

_____ a. Qarah could try to get other nations on its side by openly criticizing Omat's practices.

_____ b. Qarah could just accept the present situation and try to make the best of it.

_____ c. Qarah could take action to destroy Omat's oil fields unless Omat immediately stops its oil production.

_____ d. Qarah could decide to take no action at this time and wait to see what Omat will do.

_____ e. Qarah could stop all trade with Omat and try to convince other nations to do the same.

_____ f. Qarah could go to the World Court or some other international body and state its case against Omat.

_____ g. Qarah could try to build up its other resources and try to buy its oil from Omat

6. Since its establishment in 1945, World Press International (WPI) has been a leading wire news service. WPI has continued to enhance its reputation as an accurate and reliable source of world and national news stories for newspapers, radio, and television. For years, no other news wire service could compete with WPI until recently, when the National Wire Service (NWS) appeared on the scene.

NWS was founded in 1972 by wealthy newspaper owner R. William Hastings. With the new company's substantial financial backing, it was, in a short time, able to gather a news network rivaling the longer established WPI.

Because of the two company's similar functions, they immediately found they were sharing a variety of news sources and lines of communication. More heated than their competition for news stories was the competition between the two companies in their search for customers.

The board of directors of WPI became alarmed at the increasing number of customers NWS was attracting. Even some of WPI's long-established customers were switching over to the new service. Since the companies charged the same amount of money for their services, a possible reason for the turnover was NWS's aggressive sales and promotional practice. WPI's directors knew something had to be done to meet their competition from NWS, or their company would soon be out of business.

The WPI board met to consider its options. Because the problems facing the company were so severe, it was determined that even extreme measures had to be considered. Here are some of the possibilities the board considered:

_____ a. WPI could just accept the present situation even though it is not perfect.
_____ b. WPI might try secretly sabotaging NWS's news transmission lines and news reporting networks.
_____ c. WPI might temporarily reduce its prices to bring some of its old customers back from NWS.
_____ d. WPI could try to find problems with NWS and then make those flaws known to NWS customers.
_____ e. WPI might consider offering to merge with NWS.
_____ f. WPI could try to find a third party to mediate some of the disagreements between NWS and WPI.
_____ g. WPI could decide to take no action at this time and wait to see what NWS will do.

"Answers" to Conflict-resolution Problems

The seven suggested modes of conflict resolution were the same in each of the six stories, although of course specifics of each proposed solution were tailored to the individual parties and conflict situations. The seven modes of conflict resolution were:

(a) *physical action*, in which the target party attempts to get its way through physical force or coercion directed at the other party;

(b) *economic action*, in which the target party attempts to get its way through economic pressure directed at the other party;

(c) *wait and see*, in which the target party decides to wait things out and see if the situation improves;

(d) *accept the situation*, in which the target party decides to accept the situation as it is and make the best of it;

(e) *step-down*, in which the target party attempts to defuse the conflict by reducing or removing its demands on the other party;

(f) *third-party intervention*, in which the target party seeks some outside third party to mediate the conflict,

(g) *undermine esteem*, in which the target party seeks to undermine the esteem in which the opposing party is held by other parties outside the conflict situation.

Options (c), (d), (e), and (f) tend to defuse conflicts; (a), (b), and (g) tend to exacerbate them.

1. a. economic
    b. wait and see
    c. physical
    d. third-party
    e. undermine esteem
    f. accept situation
    g. step-down

2. a. third-party
    b. undermine esteem
    c. accept situation
    d. economic
    e. wait and see
    f. physical
    g. step-down

3. a. physical
    b. accept situation
    c. third-party
    d. wait and see
    e. step-down
    f. undermine esteem
    g. economic

4. a. undermine esteem
    b. economic
    c. third-party
    d. wait and see
    e. accept situation
    f. step-down
    g. physical

5. a. undermine esteem
    b. accept situation
    c. physical
    d. wait and see
    e. economic
    f. third-party
    g. step-down

6. a. accept situation
    b. physical
    c. economic
    d. undermine esteem
    e. step-down
    f. third-party
    g. wait and see

SUMMING UP

This chapter has reviewed some of the literature on the assessment of practical intelligence, and also has presented four kinds of exercises intended to develop your skills in exercising practical intelligence. Practical problems, unlike academic ones, often have no single right or wrong answer. Indeed, the mistake people often make is looking for the certainty that just does not exist in practical situations. Practical situations of any importance almost always involve some elements of risk, uncertainty, and ambiguity. You are probably often aware that you are not sure whether you made the right decision or done the right thing, even after the decision is made. What, then, can you do to improve your responses to practical situations? The following guidelines may be helpful:

1. Consider the possibility, in real-life decision-making situations, of using what Irving Janis called a decisional balance sheet. In the decisional balance sheet, you write out each possible course of action. For each course of action, you then list each possible outcome, both positive and negative. You also list the possible effects the courses of action will have on yourself and on others. The object is to determine which course of action has the highest number of potentially good outcomes associated with it. Sometimes, it may be useful to estimate how good are the good outcomes and how bad are the bad outcomes on some kind of rating scale. The reason for this is that although one possible course of action may appear to yield more "good" outcomes, these outcomes may not be incredibly good. In contrast, a different course of action may result in a smaller number of good outcomes, but they may all be wonderful.

2. Be sure to consider as much information as possible, and fully to consider the consequences of this information. A common mistake that people make is to act impulsively on the basis of incomplete information. A key element of intelligence is the ability to not act impulsively and to instead delay your response and be more reflective. Of course, there are times to act impulsively and times to act reflectively. If you see a large object in the middle of the road while you are driving, it is obviously best to act quickly. But when the stakes are high, and the time for thought is available, it is best to be reflective. Be sure to use all of the information at your disposal in making a decision. You also should seek as much information as you can from available sources.

3. Consider the relative strengths of the three basic strategies for coping with real-world problems: adaptation, shaping, and selection. Very often, you will believe your options in a situation to be more limited than they really are. For example, many times people assume that they have to adapt to a situation, when actually they may be able to shape it. At other times, people may assume that their only options are either to adapt to the situation or to try to shape it, but they do not recognize the real possibility of getting out of it altogether. The practically intelligent person knows when to persist, but also when to quit. When considering how to solve an everyday problem, consider solutions that involve courses of action that involve adaptation, shaping, or selection.

4. Most important, choose solutions to problems that realistically take into account who you are and what you are facing. You should draw on your own experience and the advice of others when you try to solve the problems that confront you on a day-to-day basis. But when you do this, remember to take your own character and abilities into account. Solutions that work for others may not work for you, and solutions that may have worked for you in the past may not work for you in the present. You must use the present time and place as your frame of reference when you analyze your own past experience. By doing so, you will find that you are best able to utilize your practical intelligence.

Why Intelligent People Fail (Too Often)

Everyone fails sometimes. Indeed, it is doubtful that we could ever learn if we never failed at anything. The sign of intelligence is not the absence of mistakes, but, instead, learning from those mistakes so that they are not made again and again (Dweck, 1999; Sternberg, 2000; Sternberg, 2002). An intelligent person can be forgiven for making mistakes, but perhaps not for making the same ones over and over again.

Almost all of us know supposedly intelligent people who make mistakes too often and who fail at what they do too often. It is as though their intelligence doesn't mean anything when they have to actually live in the real world. Clearly, intelligence is not enough for successful performance in the everyday world, no matter how broadly intelligence is defined. People can come into the world with the best brains in the world, grow up with every intellectual advantage, read all kinds of books (like this one) about how to become smarter – and still make a mess of their lives. Unless they can overcome the stumbling blocks that can get in the way of ideal intellectual performance, they may find that their intelligence is of little value.

This chapter discusses twenty stumbling blocks that can get in the way of even the smartest individuals. For the most part, these stumbling blocks are not strictly intellectual ones. If people can keep these sorts of problems under control, however, then they can focus on developing their intelligence with the knowledge that it will lead to better performance in the real world. As you read the twenty stumbling blocks, it may become more and more clear to you why there is a limit to how much standard achievement tests like the SATs can actually predict real–world performance.

1. *Lack of motivation*. It barely matters what talents people have if they are not motivated to use them. In many environments, motivation counts at least as much as intellectual skills in being successful. The reason that motivation is so important is that people within a given environment – for example, a college classroom – often represent a relatively narrow range of ability. Most college students are smart. The same group of people, however, represent a much broader range of motivation. Motivation thus becomes a key source of individual differences in success.

For some people, motivation will come from external sources – they will be driven by the need for approval, recognition, money, grades, and so on. For others, motivation will be internal, getting satisfaction in a job well done and from the enjoyment of a task. Most people will be both internally and externally motivated to different extents and depending on the circumstance. If you are working at McDonald's and making French fries, the odds are that you are motivated by your paycheck. You may enjoy what you do but it may not be the primary reason why you do it. In contrast, if you are writing poetry, the odds are that you are motivated by enjoyment. Most people don't get rich from writing poetry.

Whatever the source of the motivation, it is critical to using your intelligence to be successful. In general, it is better for motivation to be internally generated. People who are internally motivated tend to be more likely to succeed in school and to be creative (e.g., Baer & Kaufman, 2005; Church, Elliot, & Gable, 2001). In addition, external motivators can go away. If you're working hard at school to get good grades, you may encounter trouble when you're in a job where there is no steady feedback to receive. Internally motivated individuals are more likely to be able to stay motivated regardless of what happens around them.

Motivation is a state of mind, not a trait. People are not just highly motivated or not. They become motivated through their interactions with tasks and situations. We all need to find our own motivation. Many people find that, if they set their minds to it, almost any intellectual pursuit can become interesting. Often, things are not interesting because we tell ourselves they will not be. If we tell ourselves they will be, we may find that they become interesting.

2. *Lack of impulse control.* There are times in life when people need to act impulsively, for example, in running away from a sudden danger. But, on average, impulsive behavior tends to hurt intellectual work, not help it. In one of his earliest books, L. L. Thurstone (1924) claimed that a key feature of intelligent people is their ability to control impulsive responses. Many years later, a comparative psychologist, David Stenhouse (1973), independently came to the same conclusion. Being regularly impulsive gets in the way of optimal intellectual performance because people are unable to use their full intellectual resources on a problem. Although endless reflection is also clearly undesirable, people should not let themselves get carried away by the first solution that occurs to them in attempting to solve a problem. Better solutions may come up after further thought.

3. *Lack of perseverance and excessive perseverance.* Some people, despite all their intelligence, give up too easily. If things do not immediately go their way, or if their initial attempts at something fail, they drop whatever they are doing. They thereby lose the opportunity to complete these tasks – and, perhaps, succeed. It is as though the smallest bit of frustration is enough to keep them from trying. At the other extreme are people who continue working on a problem long after they should have quit. They keep plugging away even after it should have become clear to them that they are going to be unable to solve the problem, at least at that time. Alternatively, they may basically have solved the problem, but they then go on to solve it again and again. One can see in certain scholarly careers the existence of this tendency. The scholar does an important piece of work, perhaps as a Ph.D. thesis, and then follows up the work with additional studies that address smaller points. At some point, people in the field generally expect that scholar to move on to another problem, or at least

to a different approach to the same problem. Instead, the scholar continues to do what to most people appears to be the same research, over and over again. There may be minor changes in or additions to the research, but from the point of view of practically anyone but the scholar, the scholarly contribution essentially ceased long ago.

Excessive perseverance can be seen in many fields – some musicians and singers explore the same issues and ideas in every album and stick to the same musical styles. Others keep changing and evolving. This happens in life, as well. Almost everyone knows someone who has tried to go out with someone and was turned down. Some people in this situation keep asking out the person again and again, despite the rejection. It is as though the person is unable to stop in a relentless quest. He or she continues to pursue a goal long after it has become obvious to everyone else that no progress has been made.

4. *Using the wrong abilities*. Many people have a point in their lives at which they realize that they are either in the wrong job, or that they are going about their current job incorrectly. It is as though the work they are doing requires one set of abilities, and they are trying to do it with a different set of abilities. This phenomenon, of course, can happen for college or graduate school as well. For example, one of us had a father who initially went to medical school. He realized after a year that his skills were not well matched to medical school and that he wasn't enjoying his classes. The intelligent thing to do in this situation is to find another career to pursue – and this is, indeed, what the father did; he ended up becoming a (successful) psychologist.

Switching schools or changing careers is not easy. Often your family or your friends will have certain expectations of you, and it is reasonable to worry that people will be disappointed. You may be disappointed yourself – perhaps you always dreamed of being a doctor or a lawyer and are coming to the realization that this isn't the best path for you. If you are in a job that you realize is not a good fit, it can be downright scary to think about starting over or trying to succeed in a different area. Yet the ultimate benefit that can be accrued – the enjoyment and success of a career or school that *is* a good fit – will likely make the hassle and fears worth it in the end.

5. *Inability to translate thought into action*. Some people are very good at coming up with solutions to their problems. Indeed, they may actually seem to have a solution for everything in their lives as well as in the lives of other people. Yet when it comes time to translate their thought into action, they are unable to do it. In the words of the psychologist E. R. Guthrie (1935), they become "buried in thought." No matter how good their ideas, they rarely seem to be able to do anything about them. In order fully to capitalize on our intelligence, we must have not only good ideas, but also, the ability to do something about these ideas. We must be able to translate thought into action. Almost everyone knows of people who have made an important decision for their lives, but seem unable to act on it. Having decided to get married, for example, they cannot set a date. When it comes to action, paralysis sets in. Even if these people have a high level of intelligence, they are unable to benefit from it. At times, we are all like this. The problem we face is to do something about it and to act when appropriate rather than remaining buried in thought.

6. *Lack of product orientation.* Some people seem very concerned about the process by which things are done, but not nearly as concerned about the resulting products. Yet it is primarily on the basis of what we produce that our accomplishments are judged, whether in school or in later life. We have all known people who have done really outstanding research that should have an important impact on the field. When it comes to writing up their research, though, they do a clearly second- or third-rate job. They were very involved in the process of the research, but then they lost their involvement and enthusiasm once it was time to turn that process into a final product. As a result, their contributions are not seen as being as important as they potentially could be. Their full level of intelligence is not reached.

7. *Inability to complete tasks and to follow through.* The one certain prediction about "noncompleters" is that whatever they begin they will not finish. Nothing in their lives ever seems to draw quite to a close. Perhaps they are afraid to finish things for fear that they will not know what to do next. Or they may overwhelm themselves with the details of a project, becoming so hopelessly enmeshed that they are unable to progress. The lives of these people often seem to embody Zeno's paradox. In this paradox, a man wishes to get from point A to point B. In order to travel this distance, he has to cover half the distance. In order to travel the remaining half of the distance, he has first to cover half of that distance, leaving one quarter of the total distance remaining. But in order to travel *that* distance, he first has to cover half of that. In the paradox, the man always goes half the remaining distance without ever arriving. Similarly, in the situations that life presents, some people seem unable to reach the end.

8. *Failure to initiate.* Other people seem unwilling or unable to initiate projects; they are always trying to decide what to do. Often, this inability to initiate results from fear of commitment. These people are afraid to become too committed to anything, and as a result they are unwilling to start anything. Consider, for example, the problem of a student trying to decide on a thesis topic. Some students fail to complete graduate school because they can never commit themselves to a topic. A thesis requires a large investment of time and energy, and some students are simply unwilling to make this commitment. Many people act this way in interpersonal relationships. They never seem to want to let their relationships develop into a strong commitment. As a result, they go through life in a series of superficial relationships, unable to start anything more substantial that runs the risk of leading to such a commitment. John Adams, the second president of the United States, was quoted as saying, "There are only two creatures of value on this earth – those who have commitment, and those who require the commitment of others."

9. *Fear of failure.* Fear of failure seems to start early in life. To some extent, we have seen fear of failure at work in our students. They often are very capable, but sometimes seem to be unwilling to risk failure. Many people do not reach their full intellectual potential because of their fear that they will fail at what they do. In college, they may not take the difficult courses that they need because they do not expect to do well in them. As a result, they may do well in the courses they take, but later have no use for those courses. Later on, as lawyers or doctors or scientists or business

executives, they may not undertake the projects that could really make a difference to their careers because of their fear that the projects will not succeed. Indeed, they may not even enter the occupation of their choice because of their fear that they will not succeed in it. Or they may not continue with a personal relationship, not because of how it is going, but because of their fear of how it might go.

In some cases, fear of failure may be realistic. If the consequences of failure are high enough, fear of failure can be quite adaptive. For example, the whole strategy of nuclear prevention depends on fear of failure. The theory is that no country will start a nuclear war because of the fear that it will be a disaster for them as well as for their opponents. Thus, there are times at which it is quite reasonable not to take risks. But there are other times when we must take risks. Being unwilling or unable to do so may lose you opportunities that may never return.

10. *Procrastination*. Procrastination seems to be a universal fact of life. We all, at some time or another, procrastinate. We put off for later the things we know should be done now. Indeed, one of us just checked the baseball scores before returning to work on this paragraph! Procrastination becomes a serious problem only when it is someone's typical way of doing things. Some students tend always to be looking for little things to do so as to put off the big things. They always manage to get their daily reading and assignments done, but they seem to procrastinate forever in undertaking the large-scale projects that can really make a difference. It is easy to become consumed in daily trivia that can gobble up all of one's time – answering e-mail, doing errands, and so on. This type of focus may result in short-term success but often results in long-term failure. Those who tend to procrastinate often have to force themselves to undertake the big things. Otherwise, they would be unable to do them without pressure, whether legitimate or self-imposed.

11. *Misattribution of blame*. Some people feel they can do no wrong, and are always looking for others to blame for even the slightest misfortune. Others are always blaming themselves for everything, regardless of their role. Misattribution of blame can seriously limit one's intellectual self-realization. For example, we once observed a student who was very able and competent in research. The professors thought she was terrific, and yet she always blamed herself for anything that went wrong. It reached the point where she felt that she could do nothing right. Eventually, she left the program. Another student was exactly the opposite. She managed to always blame others for things that went wrong in her graduate career. Although it was clear to nearly everyone around her that she was just not working very hard, she always had an excuse for why things were not getting done. The excuse tended to involve what other people had done to prevent her from working and reaching her goals. If there is blame to be placed, it is important to know where to place it. Misattribution of blame closes the door to self-improvement, and prevents us from using our talents to the fullest.

12. *Excessive self-pity*. We all pity ourselves sometimes. When things do not go just right, it is difficult not to do so. But constant self-pity can be very harmful. When one of our students entered our program, he had certain clear disadvantages in terms of preparation and obviously felt sorry for himself. At that point, others felt sorry for him, too. But, after a while, people became annoyed and even angry at his constant

self-pity. After a point, everyone expected him to pull himself up by his bootstraps and make a go of things. But the self-pity never seemed to end. A vicious circle ensued in which as he became sorrier and sorrier for himself, others became less and less sorry. Finally they wanted to have little to do with him. He seemed to spend more time feeling sorry for himself than making the effort needed so that he no longer would have to feel sorry! Self-pity is not only useless for getting work done, but, after a certain point, it tends to put off those who might otherwise be most helpful.

13. *Excessive dependency.* In most of the tasks people face, they are expected to have a certain degree of independence. Often, people's home lives may not prepare them for the independence that will later be expected of them. Once they enter a career, they are expected to fend for themselves, and to rely upon others only to a very small degree. Many students seem not to learn this. They expect others either to do things for them or constantly to show them how to get things done. Without this help, they are at a total loss. The result is that they often have to seek jobs that require less responsibility, or else they never do as well as they otherwise might have. In school, as well as in work, do not expect either your professors or your fellow students to get things done for you. If you want to get them done, the best way to do so is either to do them yourself or to take responsibility for having someone else get them done. Don't expect others to take the responsibility that you yourself must take.

14. *Wallowing in personal difficulties.* Everyone has personal difficulties, but their extent differs widely from one person to another. Some people have repeated tragedies in their lives, others seem to lead charmed existences and almost never encounter difficulties. During the course of your life, you can expect some real joys, but also some real sorrows. The important thing is to try to keep both the joys and the sorrows in perspective. Some people let their personal difficulties greatly interfere with their work. Others seem to be completely unaffected. Major life crises will almost always have some effect on your work, whether you like it or not. The best thing is to accept that this will happen and take it in stride. It is equally important that you not wallow in your personal difficulties and let them drag down your work and you with it. Indeed, in times of personal hardship, your work, as well as other people, may provide you with some of the comfort you need. It is a mistake to completely stop yourself from thinking about personal tragedies and difficulties. Yet it is equally a mistake to allow yourself to be consumed by them.

15. *Distractibility.* There are many people who are very intelligent people yet never seem to be able to concentrate on any one thing for very long. They are highly distractible, and tend to have short attention spans. As a result, they tend not to get much done. To some extent, distractibility is an attentional variable that we cannot completely control. If you tend not to be distractible and you have good concentration, then it is not something you have to worry about particularly. If you tend to be distractible, however, and to have difficulty concentrating, then you should do your best to arrange your working environment so as to minimize distractions. Do whatever you need to do: Turn off the television or radio; unplug your phone; shut down your e-mail program; tell people not to knock on your door – whatever it takes. In

effect, you have to create an environment in which you can achieve your goals. If you do not, you will have difficulty in reaching them.

16. *Being spread too thin or too thick.* People who spread themselves too thin are people who commit to too many different projects, and therefore cannot spend enough time on each one. People with the tendency to spread themselves too thin need to recognize this tendency within themselves and to work against it as necessary. People who spread themselves too thin sometimes find that they can get nothing done. This isn't because they don't work hard enough. It is, rather, because they are making only little degrees of progress on each of the large number of projects they are pursuing. If you undertake multiple projects, it is important to stagger or otherwise arrange them so that you have a reasonable probability of finishing each of them in an acceptable amount of time.

Other people find themselves unable to undertake more than one or at most two things at a given time. This approach is fine, so long as they can progress through these projects in a reasonable amount of time and not miss opportunities that may present themselves. But undertaking too little at one time can result in missed opportunities and reduced levels of accomplishment. The important thing is to find the right distribution of activities for yourself, and then to maximize your performance within that distribution. Avoid undertaking either more or less than you can handle at a single time.

17. *Inability to delay gratification.* Mentioned earlier are the people who always seem to be doing little things at the expense of big things. Some of these are people who simply procrastinate on big things, of course. But others are people who are unable to delay gratification. They reward themselves for finishing the little things, but they end up losing the larger rewards that they could receive from doing bigger things. Any number of scientists and other scholars fail to undertake the really big projects that could make the critical difference in their careers. For example, they may repeatedly write short articles instead of books because of their inability to delay the gratification that would come from the completion of a longer but more substantial project. Serious intellectual work occasionally requires one to delay gratification, sometimes for relatively long periods of time. The inability to delay gratification is harmful through all aspects of life. One of us had a good friend who dated someone who decided that she needed a two-week vacation to Portugal. She didn't have the money for such a trip, however. Instead of delaying gratification and figuring out how to afford this vacation, she simply booked the tickets and figured it would work out in the end. Our friend didn't stick around to find out how she would end up paying for it.

18. *Inability or unwillingness to see the forest for the trees.* We have worked with several students who have been perfectly smart but who have been relatively unsuccessful as students because of their inability to see the forest for the trees. They obsess over small details and are unwilling or unable to see the larger picture in the projects they undertake. They become so absorbed with the microstructure of any project that they ignore or pay only the most minimal attention to the macrostructure. There are times and places where minutiae can become important. In designing computers or spacecraft or cars, for example, even the most minor slips can become major

when the product doesn't work. But in many aspects of life, it is necessary to concentrate on the big picture, or at least never to lose sight of it. It is very easy for students to become so bogged down in the day-to-day details of student life that they lose sight of the big picture. If this is happening to you, deliberately set aside time for thinking about large issues. Decide that during those times you will think about the meaning of what you are doing and where you wish it to lead. Without such time, you may find yourself not only losing track of what your goals originally were but losing track as well of how what you are doing will help you reach those goals.

19. *Lack of balance between critical, analytic thinking and creative, synthetic thinking.* There are times in life when we need to be critical and analytic; there are other times when we should be creative and synthetic. It is important to know which times are which. Some students seem to often make the wrong judgments. They complain bitterly that their teachers fail to recognize their creativity on objective, multiple-choice tests. Or else they complain that their teachers do not give them credit for how well organized, if uninspired, their papers are. Although these students may have good analytic and synthetic abilities, they don't know when to apply which ones. It is important to learn what kind of thinking is expected of you in different kinds of situations, and then to try to do the kind of thinking that is appropriate for the given situations. For example, a standard multiple-choice midterm does not usually provide good opportunities in which to demonstrate creativity. Research projects, by contrast, are excellent opportunities to show your creativity. The point is that it is important not only to have both analytic and synthetic abilities but also to know when to use them.

20. *Too little or too much self-confidence.* Everyone needs a lot of self-confidence to get through life. There can be so many blows to our self-esteem that without self-confidence, we are at the mercy of every minor and major setback that we face. Lack of self-confidence seems to gnaw away at some people's ability to get things done well because they actually seem to realize in their work their own self-doubt. These self-doubts become self-fulfilling prophecies. Self-confidence is often essential for success. After all, if you do not have confidence in yourself, how can you expect others to?

At the same time, it is important not to have too much or misplaced self-confidence. As many students fail through too much self-confidence as through too little. Individuals with too much self-confidence do not know when to admit they are wrong or in need of self-improvement. They may not study enough for an exam, thinking that they already know the material. As a result, they rarely improve as quickly as they could.

Too little or too much self-confidence can be especially damaging in job interviews. Applicants with too little self-confidence fail to inspire people to believe in them. Their lack of self-confidence transfers to the potential employer, who also ends up not having confidence in them. Too much self-confidence can put people off, and lead to resentment and the desire to strike back – to tell the individual in some way that he or she is not so great as he or she thinks. Unfortunately, this striking back can occur in the form of a decision not to hire that person. It is important, here as elsewhere, to strike just the right balance between too little or too much of a good thing.

SUMMING UP

This chapter has described twenty potential stumbling blocks to the fulfillment of your intellectual potential. The material in this chapter may seem only vaguely related to the topic of the book – understanding and increasing your intelligence – or may even seem moralistic. We gave serious thought as to whether to include such a chapter, but we decided to do so because we have seen so many people be unable to fully display their intellectual abilities. They have failed fully to adapt to, shape, or select their environments because of self-imposed obstacles that got in their way. It is easy, indeed, for those who wish to understand and develop the intellect to become "buried in thought." We must never lose sight of the fact that what really matters in the world is not the level of our intelligence but what we achieve with this intelligence. Our ultimate goal in understanding and increasing our intelligence should be the full realization in our lives of the intellectual potential we each have within us.

REFERENCES

Aljughaiman, A., & Mowrer-Reynolds, E. (2005). Teachers' conceptions of creativity and creative students. *Journal of Creative Behavior, 39*, 17–34.

Amabile, T. M. (1996). *Creativity in context*. Boulder, CO: Westview.

Baer, J., & Kaufman, J. C. (2005). Bridging generality and specificity: The Amusement Park Theoretical (APT) Model of creativity. *Roeper Review, 27*, 158–163.

Barnett, S. M., & Ceci, S. J. (2005). The role of transferable knowledge in intelligence. In R. J. Sternberg & J. E. Pretz (Eds.), *Cognition & intelligence: Identifying the mechanisms of the mind* (pp. 208–224). New York: Cambridge University Press.

Beck, A. T. (1976). *Cognitive therapy and the emotional disorders*. New York: International Universities Press.

Beck, A. T., Rush, A. J., Shaw, B. F., & Emery, G. (1979). *Cognitive therapy of depression*. New York: Guilford.

Beghetto, R. A. (2006). Creative self-efficacy: Correlates in middle and secondary students. *Creativity Research Journal, 18*, 447–457.

Beghetto, R. A., & Kaufman, J. C. (2007). Toward a broader conception of creativity: A case for "mini-c" creativity. *Psychology of Aesthetics, Creativity, and the Arts, 1*, 73–79.

Berg, C. A., & Sternberg, R. J. (1985). Response to novelty: Continuity versus discontinuity in the developmental course of intelligence. In H. Reese (Ed.), *Advances in child development and behavior* (Vol. 19, pp. 2–47). New York: Academic Press.

Binet, A., & Simon, T. (1973). *Classics in psychology: The development of intelligence in children*. New York: Arno Press.

Boring, E. G. (1923). Intelligence as the tests test it. *New Republic*, June 6, pp. 35–37.

Brand, C. (1996). *The g factor: General intelligence and its implications*. Chichester, UK: Wiley.

Brunvand, J. H. (1993). *The baby train*. New York: Norton.

Burt, C. (1940). *The factors of the mind*. London: University of London Press.

Butterfield, E. C., & Belmont, J. M. (1977). Assessing and improving the cognition of mentally retarded people. In I. Bialer & M. Sternlicht (Eds.), *Psychology of mental retardation: Issues and approaches*. New York: Psychological Dimensions.

Carroll, J. B. (1993). *Human cognitive abilities: A survey of factor-analytic studies*. New York: Cambridge University Press.

Caryl, P. G. (1994). Early event-related potentials correlate with inspection time and intelligence. *Intelligence, 18*, 15–46.

Cattell, J. M. (1890). Mental tests and measurements. *Mind, 15*, 373–380.

Cattell, R. B. (1971). *Abilities: Their structure, growth and action*. Boston: Houghton Mifflin.

Chase, W. G., & Simon, H. A. (1973). The mind's eye in chess. In W. G. Chase (Ed.), *Visual information processing* (pp. 215–281). New York: Academic Press.

Chen, C., Kasof, J., Himsel, A., Dmitrieva, J., Dong, Q., & Xue, G. (2005). Effects of explicit instruction to "be creative" across domains and cultures. *Journal of Creative Behavior*. 39, 89–110.

Chi, M. T. H. (1978). Knowledge structure and memory development. In R. S. Siegler (Ed.), *Children's thinking: What develops?* (pp. 73–96). Mahwah, NJ: Erlbaum.

Chi, M. T. H., Glaser, R., & Rees, E. (1982). Expertise in problem solving. In R. J. Sternberg (Ed.), *Advances in the psychology of human intelligence* (Vol. 1, pp. 7–75). Mahwah, NJ: Erlbaum.

Church, M. A., Elliot, A. J., & Gable, S. L. (2001). Perceptions of classroom environment, achievement goals, and achievement outcomes. *Journal of Educational Psychology, 93*, 43–54.

Cianciolo, A. T., & Sternberg, R. J. (2004). *A brief history of intelligence*. Malden, MA: Blackwell.

Cialdini, R. B. (1998). *Influence: The psychology of persuasion* (rev. ed.). New York: Perennial.

Cole, M., Gay, J., Glick, J., & Sharp, D. W. (1971). *The cultural context of learning and thinking*. New York: Basic Books.

Cohen, L. M. (1989). A continuum of adaptive creative behaviors. *Creativity Research Journal, 2*, 169–183.

Connell, M. W., Sheridan, K., Gardner, H. (2003). On abilities and domains. In R. J. Sternberg & E. L. Grigorenko (Eds.), *The psychology of abilities, competencies, and expertise* (pp. 126–156). New York: Cambridge University Press.

Copi, I. M. (1978). *Informal logic*. New York: Macmillan.

Cronbach, L. (2001). *Stanford Aptitude Seminar: Remaking the concept of aptitude: Extending the legacy of Richard E. Snow*. Mahwah, NJ: Lawrence Erlbaum Associates.

Cropley, A. (2006). Dimensions of creativity: A social approach. *Roeper Review, 28*, 125–130.

Csikszentmihalyi, M. (1988). Society, culture, and person: A systems view of creativity. In R. J. Sternberg (Ed.), *The nature of creativity* (pp. 325–339). New York: Cambridge University Press.

Csikszentmihalyi, M. (1999). Implications of a systems perspective for the study of creativity. In R. J. Sternberg (Ed.), *Handbook of human creativity* (pp. 313–338). New York: Cambridge University Press.

Daneman, M., & Carpenter, P. A. (1983). Individual differences in integrating information between and within sentences. *Journal of Experimental Psychology: Learning, Memory, and Cognition, 9*, 561–583.

Darwin, C. (1859). *The origin of species*. London: Murray.

Das, J. P., Naglieri, J. A., & Kirby, J. R. (1994). *Assessment of cognitive processes: The PASS theory of intelligence*. Boston, MA: Allyn & Bacon.

Davidson, J. E. (1995). The suddenness of insight. In R. J. Sternberg & J. E. Davidson (Eds.), *The nature of insight*. Cambridge, MA: MIT Press.

Davidson, J. E., & Sternberg, R. J. (1984). The role of insight in intellectual giftedness. *Gifted Child Quarterly, 28*, 58–64.

Deary, I. J. (2000a). *Looking down on human intelligence: From psychometrics to the brain*. New York: Oxford University Press

Deary, I. J. (2000b). Simple information processing. In R. J. Sternberg (Ed.), *Handbook of intelligence* (pp. 267–284). New York: Cambridge University Press.

Deary, I. J., & Stough, C. (1996). Intelligence and inspection time: Achievements, prospects, and problems. *American Psychologist, 51*, 599–608.

Dewey, J. (1933). *How we think*. Boston: Heath.

Dweck, C. S. (1999). *Self-theories: Their role in motivation, personality, and development*. Philadelphia: Psychology Press.

Edgerton, R. (1967). *The cloak of competence*. Berkeley, CA: University of California Press.

Elster, C. H., & Elliot, J. (1994). *Tooth and nail: A novel approach to the new SAT*. New York: Harvest Books.

Engle, R. W. (1994). Memory. In R. J. Sternberg (Ed.), *Encyclopedia of intelligence* (Vol. 2, pp. 700–704). New York: Macmillan.

Engle, R. W., Carullo, J. J., & Collins, K. W. (1992). Individual differences in working memory for comprehension and following directions. *Journal of Educational Research, 84*, 253–262.

Ericsson, K. A. (Ed.). (1996). *The road to excellence*. Mahwah, NJ: Lawrence Erlbaum Associates.

Ericsson, K. A., & Smith, J. (1991). Prospects and limits in the empirical study of expertise: An introduction. In K. A. Ericsson & J. Smith (Eds.), *Toward a general theory of expertise: Prospects and limits* (pp. 19–38). New York: Cambridge University Press.

Estes, W. K. (1982). Learning, memory, and intelligence. In R. J. Sternberg (Ed.), *Handbook of human intelligence*. New York: Cambridge University Press.

Feldman, R. D. (1982). *Whatever happened to the quiz kids? Perils and profits of growing up gifted*. Chicago: Chicago Review Press.

Ferguson, G. A. (1956). On transfer and the abilities of man. *Canadian Journal of Psychology, 10*, 121–131.

Feuerstein, R. (1980). *Instrumental enrichment: An intervention program for cognitive modifiability*. Baltimore, MD: University Park Press.

Fiedler, F. E., & Link, T. G. (1994). Leader intelligence, interpersonal stress, and task performance. In R. J. Sternberg & R. K. Wagner (Eds.), *Mind in context: Interactionist perspectives on human intelligence* (pp. 152–167). New York: Cambridge University Press.

Flanagan, D. P., & Kaufman, A. S. (2004). *Essentials of WISC-IV assessment*. New York: Wiley.

Flanagan, D. P., McGrew, K. S., & Ortiz, S. (2000). *The Wechsler Intelligence Scales and Gf-Gc Theory: A contemporary approach to interpretation*. Boston: Allyn & Bacon.

Flanagan, D. P., & Ortiz, S. O. (2001). *Essentials of cross-battery assessment*. New York: Wiley.

Frensch, P. A., & Sternberg, R. J. (1989). Expertise and intelligent thinking: When is it worse to know better? In R. J. Sternberg (Ed.), *Advances in the psychology of human intelligence* (Vol. 5, pp. 157–158). Mahwah, NJ: Erlbaum.

Gallagher, A. M., & Kaufman, J. C. (Eds.). (2005). *Gender differences in mathematics*. New York: Cambridge University Press.

Galton, F. (1883). *Inquiry into human faculty and its development*. London: Macmillan.

Garcia, J., & Koelling, R. A. (1966). The relation of cue to consequence in avoidance learning. *Psychonomic Science, 4*, 123–124.

Gardner, H. (1983). *Frames of mind: The theory of multiple intelligences*. New York: Basic Books.

Gardner, H. (1993). *Creating minds*. New York: Basic Books.

Gardner, H. (1999). *Intelligence reframed: Multiple intelligences for the 21st century*. New York: Basic Books.

Gardner, H. (2006). *Multiple intelligences: New horizons in theory and practice*. New York: Perseus.

Gelman, S. A., & Gottfried, G. M. (2006). Creativity in young children's thought. In J. C. Kaufman & J. Baer (Eds.), *Creativity and reason in cognitive development* (pp. 221–243). New York: Cambridge University Press.

Gigerenzer, G. (2004). Dread risk, September 11, and fatal traffic accidents. *Psychological Science, 15*, 286–287.

Gigerenzer, G., Todd, P. M., & the ABC Research Group. (1999). *Simple heuristics that make us smart*. New York: Oxford University Press.

Gillham, N. W. (2001). *A life of Sir Francis Galton*. Oxford: Oxford University Press.

Gilovich, T. (1991). *How we know what isn't so: The fallibility of human reason in everyday life*. New York: The Free Press.

Goldin, S. E. (1980). Facial stereotypes as cognitive categories. *Dissertation Abstracts International, 40*, 3995.

Goldin, S. E., & Hayes-Roth, B. (1981). Individual differences in planning processes. *Catalog of Selected Documents in Psychology, 11*, 34.

Grabner, R. H., Neubauer, A. C., & Stern, E. (2006). Superior performance and neural efficiency: The impact of intelligence and expertise. *Brain Research Bulletin, 69*, 422–439.

Grabner, R. H., Stern, E., & Neubauer, A. C. (2007). Individual differences in chess expertise: A psychometric investigation. *Acta Psychologica. 124*, 398–420.

Gray, J. R., & Thomson, P. M. (2004). Neurobiology of intelligence: Science and ethics. *Nature Reviews Neuroscience, 5*, 471–482.

Griggs, R. A., & Cox, J. R. (1982). The elusive thematic-materials effect in Wason's selection task. *British Journal of Psychology, 73*, 407–420.

Grigorenko, E. L., Geissler, P. W., Prince, R., Okatcha, F., Nokes, C., Kenny, D. A., Bundy, D. A., & Sternberg, R. J. (2001). The organization of Luo conceptions of intelligence: A study of implicit theories in a Kenyan village. *International Journal of Behavioral Development, 25*, 367–378.

Grigorenko, E. L., Meier, E., Lipka, J., Mohatt, G., Yanez, E., & Sternberg, R. J. (2004). Academic and practical intelligence: A case study of the Yup'ik in Alaska. *Learning and Individual Differences, 14*, 183–207.

Gruber, H. E., & Davis, S. N. (1988). Inching our way up Mount Olympus: The evolving-systems approach to creative thinking. In R. J. Sternberg (Ed.), *The nature of creativity* (pp. 243–270). New York: Cambridge University Press.

Guilford, J. P. (1967). *The nature of human intelligence*. New York: McGraw-Hill.

Guthrie, E. R. (1935). *The psychology of learning*. New York: Harper & Row.

Haier, R. J., Siegel, B., Tang, C., Abel, L., & Buchsbaum, M. S. (1992). Intelligence and changes in regional cerebral glucose metabolic rate following learning. *Intelligence, 16*, 415–426.

Halpern, D. (1996). *Thought and knowledge* (3rd ed.). Mahwah, NJ: Lawrence Erlbaum.

Hambrick, D. Z., Kane, M. J., & Engle, R. W. (2005). The role of working memory in higher-level cognition: Domain-specific versus domain-general perspectives. In R. J. Sternberg & J. E. Pretz (Eds). (2005). *Cognition and intelligence: Identifying the mechanisms of the mind*. (pp. 104–121). New York: Cambridge University Press.

Hayes-Roth, B., & Goldin, S. E. (1980). *Individual Differences in Planning Processes*. Santa Monica, CA: The Rand Corporation.

Hayes, J. R., & Simon, H. A. (1976). The understanding process: Problem isomorphs. *Cognitive Psychology, 8*, 165–190.

Heath, S. B. (1983). *Ways with words*. New York: Cambridge University Press.

Horn, J. L. (1979). Trends in the measurement of intelligence. *Intelligence, 3*, 229–239.

Horn, J. L. (1985). Remodeling old models of intelligence. In B. B. Wolman (Ed.), *Handbook of intelligence: Theories, measurements, and applications* (pp. 267–300). New York: Wiley.

Horn, J. L. (1994). Theory of fluid and crystallized intelligence. In R. J. Sternberg (Ed.), *The encyclopedia of human intelligence* (Vol. 1, pp. 443–451). New York: Macmillan.

Horn, J. L., & Cattell, R. B. (1966). Refinement and test of the theory of fluid and crystallized intelligence. *Journal of Educational Psychology, 57*, 253–270.

Horn, J. L., & Hofer, S. M. (1992). Major abilities and development in the adult period. In R. J. Sternberg & C. A. Berg (Eds.), *Intellectual development* (pp. 44–99). Boston, MA: Cambridge University Press.

Horn, J. L., & Noll, J. (1997). Human cognitive capabilities: Gf-Gc theory. In D. P. Flanagan, J. L. Genshaft, & P. L. Harrison (Eds.), *Beyond traditional intellectual assessment: Contemporary and emerging theories, tests, and issues* (pp. 53–91). New York: Guilford.

Hunt, E. B. (1978). Mechanics of verbal ability. *Psychological Review, 85*, 109–130.

Hunt, E. B. (1980). Intelligence as an information-processing concept. *British Journal of Psychology, 71*, 449–474.

Hunt, E. B. (2005). Information processing and intelligence: Where we are and where we are going. In R. J. Sternberg & J. E. Pretz (Eds.). *Cognition & intelligence: Identifying the mechanisms of the mind* (pp. 1–25). New York: Cambridge University Press.

Hunt, E. B., & Lansman, M. (1982). Individual differences in attention. In R. J. Sternberg (Ed.), *Advances in the psychology of human intelligence* (Vol. 1). Mahwah, NJ: Erlbaum.

Hunt, E. B., Lunneborg, C., & Lewis, J. (1975). What does it mean to be high verbal? *Cognitive Psychology, 7*, 194–227.

Ivcevic, Z., & Mayer, J. D. (2007). Creative types and personality. *Imagination, Cognition, and Personality, 26*, 65–86.

"Intelligence and its measurement": A symposium (1921). *Journal of Educational Psychology, 12*, 123–147, 195–216, 271–275.

Isaksen, S. G., & Gaulin, J. P. (2005). A reexamination of brainstorming research: Implications for research and practice. *Gifted Child Quarterly, 49*, 315–329.

Jensen, A. R. (1969). How much can we boost IQ and scholastic achievement? *Harvard Educational Review. 39*, 1–123.

Jensen, A. R. (1982). Reaction time and psychometric g. In H. J. Eysenck (Ed.), *A model for intelligence*. Heidelberg: Springer-Verlag.

Jensen, A. R. (1997). The puzzle of nongenetic variance. In R. J. Sternberg & E. L. Grigorenko (Eds.), *Intelligence, heredity, and environment* (pp. 42–88). New York: Cambridge University Press.

Jensen, A. R. (1998). *The g factor: The science of mental ability*. Westport, CT: Praeger/Greenwood.

Jensen, A. R. (2005). Mental chronometry and the unification of differential psychology. In R. J. Sternberg & J. E. Pretz (Eds.), *Cognition and intelligence: Identifying the mechanisms of the mind* (pp. 26–50). New York: Cambridge University Press.

Jensen, A. R. (2006). *Clocking the mind: Mental chronometry and individual differences*. New York: Elsevier.

Jerison, H. J. (2000). The evolution of intelligence. In R. J. Sternberg (Ed.), *Handbook of intelligence* (pp. 216–244). New York: Cambridge University Press.

Johnson-Laird, P. N., & Wason, P. C. (1970). A theoretical analysis of insight into a reasoning task. *Cognitive Psychology, 1*, 134–148.

Kaufman, A. S. (1994). *Intelligent testing with the WISC-III*. New York: Wiley.

Kaufman, A. S. (2000). Tests of intelligence. In R. J. Sternberg (Ed.), *Handbook of intelligence* (pp. 445–476). New York: Cambridge University Press.

Kaufman, A. S., & Kaufman, N. L. (2004). *Kaufman Assessment Battery for Children – Second Edition (KABC-II)*. Circle Pines, MN: American Guidance Service.

Kaufman, J. C., & Sternberg, R. J. (2007). Resource review: Creativity. *Change*, 39, 55–58.

Koehler, J. J., & Conley, C. A. (2003). The "hot hand" myth in professional basketball. *Journal of Sport and Exercise Psychology, 25*, 253–259.

Kyllonen, P. C. (2002). *g*: Knowledge, speed, strategies, or working-memory capacity? A systems perspective. In R. J. Sternberg & E. L. Grigorenko (Eds.), *The general factor of intelligence: How general is it?* (pp. 415–446). Mahwah, NJ: Erlbaum.

Kyllonen, P. C., & Christal, R. E. (1990). Reasoning ability is (little more than) working-memory capacity?! *Intelligence, 14*, 389–433.

Langer, E. (1989). *Mindfulness*. Reading, MA: Addison-Wesley.

Langley, P., & Jones, R. (1988). A computational model of scientific insight. In R. J. Sternberg (Ed.), *The nature of creativity. Contemporary psychological perspectives* (pp. 177–201). Cambridge: Cambridge University Press

Lashley, K. S. (1950). In search of the engram. *Symposia of the Society for Experimental Biology, 4*, 454–482.

Linville, P. W. (1982). The complexity-extremity effect and age-based stereotyping. *Journal of Personality & Social Psychology, 42*, 193–211.

Lederer, R. (1989). *Anguished English*. New York: Laurel.

Lohman, D. F. (2000). Complex information processing and intelligence. In R. J. Sternberg (Ed.), *Handbook of intelligence* (pp. 285–340). New York: Cambridge University Press.

Lohman, D. F. (2005). Reasoning abilities. In R. J. Sternberg, & J. E. Pretz (Eds.), *Cognition & intelligence: Identifying the mechanisms of the mind* (pp. 225–250). New York: Cambridge University Press.

MacLeod, C. M., Hunt, E. B., & Mathews, N. N. (1978). Individual differences in the verification of sentence-picture relationships. *Journal of Verbal Learning & Verbal Behavior, 17*, 493–507.

Markman, E. M. (1979). Realizing that you don't understand: Elementary school children's awareness of inconsistencies. *Child Development, 50*, 643–655.

Matarazzo, J. D. (1992). Biological and physiological correlates of intelligence. *Intelligence, 16*, 257–258.

Mayer, R. E. (2000). Intelligence and education. In R. J. Sternberg (Ed.), *Handbook of intelligence*, (pp. 519–533). New York: Cambridge University Press.

Mikkelson, B., & Mikkelson, D. P. (2002). Halloween poisonings. *Snopes*. Retrieved February 22, 2005, from http://www.snopes.com/horrors/poison/hallowee.htm.

Miller, G. A., Galanter, E. H., & Pribram, K. H. (1960). *Plans and the structure of behavior*. New York: Holt, Rinehart & Winston.

Mintzker, Y., Feuerstein, R., & Feuerstein, R. (2006). *Mediated learning experience guidelines for parents*. Oakland, CA: ICELP.

Mitchell, M. L., & Jolley, J. M. (2004). *Research design explained*. Belmont, CA: Wadsworth.

Moran, S., & John-Steiner, V. (2003). Creativity in the making: Vygotsky's contemporary contribution to the dialectic of development and creativity. In R. K. Sawyer, V. John-Steiner, S. Moran, R. J. Sternberg, D. H. Feldman, J. Nakamura, & M. Csikszentmihalyi. *Creativity and development*. (pp. 61–90). New York: Oxford University Press.

Naglieri, J. A., & Das, J. P. (1997). *Das Naglieri Cognitive Assessment System*. Chicago: Riverside.

Neubauer, A. C., & Fink, A. (2005). Basic information processing and the psychophysiology of intelligence. In R. J. Sternberg & J. E. Pretz (Eds.), *Cognition & intelligence: Identifying the mechanisms of the mind* (pp. 68–87). New York: Cambridge University Press.

Newell, A., Shaw, J. C., & Simon, H. A. (1958). Elements of a theory of human problem solving. *Psychological Review, 65*, 151–166.

Newman, S. D., & Just, M. A. (2005). The neural bases of intelligence: A perspective based on functional neuroimaging. In R. J. Sternberg & J. E. Pretz (Eds.), *Cognition & intelligence: Identifying the mechanisms of the mind* (pp. 88–103). New York: Cambridge University Press.

Okagaki, L., & Sternberg, R. J. (1993). Parental beliefs and children's school performance. *Child Development, 64*, 36–56.

Perkins, D. N. (1981). *The mind's best work*. Cambridge, MA: Harvard University Press.

Piaget, J. (1972). *The psychology of intelligence*. Totowa, NJ: Littlefield Adams.

Plucker, J. A., Beghetto, R. A., & Dow, G. T. (2004). Why isn't creativity more important to educational psychologists? Potentials, pitfalls, and future directions in creativity research. *Educational Psychologist, 39*, 83–96.

Posner, M. I., & Mitchell, R. F. (1967). Chronometric analysis of classification. *Psychological Review, 74*, 392–409.

Pretz, J. E., & Sternberg, R. J. (2005). Unifying the field: Cognition and intelligence. In R. J. Sternberg & J. E. Pretz (Eds.), *Cognition & intelligence: Identifying the mechanisms of the mind* (pp. 306–318). New York: Cambridge University Press.

Raaheim, K. (1974). *Problem solving and intelligence*. Oslo: Universitetsforlaget.

Robinson, R. (1950). *Definition*. Oxford: Oxford University Press.

Roid, G. H. (2003). *Stanford Binet Intelligence Scales – Fifth Edition*. Itasca, IL: Riverside Publishing.

Roid, G. H., & Barram, R. A. (2004). *Essentials of Stanford-Binet Intelligence Scales (SB5) Assessment*. New York: Wiley.

Rostan, S. M., Pariser, D., & Gruber, H. E. (2002). A cross-cultural study of the development of artistic talent, creativity, and giftedness. *High Ability Studies, 13*, 125–156.

Runco, M. A. (2004). Creativity. *Annual Review of Psychology, 55*, 657–687.

Samuels, S. J. (1999). Developing reading fluency in learning-disabled students. In R. J. Sternberg & L. Spear-Swerling (Eds.), *Perspectives on learning disabilities: Biological, cognitive, contextual* (pp. 176–189). Boulder, CO: Westview Press.

Schank, R. C. (1988). Creativity as a mechanical process. In R. J. Sternberg (Ed.), *The nature of creativity* (pp. 220–238). New York: Cambridge University Press.

Schneider, W., (1982). *Automatic/control processing concepts and their implications for the training of skills* (Final report HARL-ONR-8101). Champaign: University of Illinois, Department of Psychology.

Schneider, W., & Shiffrin, R. M. (1977). Controlled and automatic human information processing: I. Detection, search, and attention. *Psychological Review, 84*, 1–66.

Selby, E. C., Shaw, E. J., & Houtz, J. C. (2005). The creative personality. *Gifted Child Quarterly, 49*, 300–314.

Serpell, R. (2000). Intelligence and culture. In R. J. Sternberg (Ed.), *Handbook of intelligence* (pp. 549–580). New York: Cambridge University Press.

Simon, H. (1957). *Administrative behavior: A study of decision-making processes in administrative organization* (2nd ed.). New York: Macmillan.

Simon, H. A., & Reed, S. K. (1976). Modeling strategy shifts in a problem-solving task. *Cognitive Psychology, 8*, 86–97.

Simonton, D. K. (2000). Creative development as acquired expertise: Theoretical issues and an empirical test. *Developmental Review, 20*, 283–318.

Sjoberg, L. (2000). Factors in risk perception. *Risk Analysis, 20*, 1–11.

Sloane, P. (1992). *Lateral thinking puzzlers*. New York: Sterling.

Snow, R. E. (1979). Theory and method for research on aptitude processes. In R. J. Sternberg & D. K. Detterman (Eds.), *Human intelligence: Perspectives on its theory and measurement* (pp. 105–137). Norwood, NJ: Ablex.

Spearman, C. (1923). *The nature of "intelligence" and the principles of cognition* (2nd ed.). London: Macmillan. (1923 edition reprinted in 1973 by Arno Press, New York)

Spearman, C. (1927). *The abilities of man*. London: Macmillan.

Stenhouse, D. (1973). *The evolution of intelligence: A general theory and some of its implications*. New York: Harper & Row.

Sternberg, R. J. (1977). *Intelligence, information processing, and analogical reasoning: The componential analysis of human abilities*. Mahwah, NJ: Lawrence Erlbaum Associates.

Sternberg, R. J. (1980). The development of linear syllogistic reasoning. *Journal of Experimental Child Psychology, 29*, 340–356.

Sternberg, R. J. (1981). Reasoning with determinate and indeterminate linear syllogisms. *British Journal of Psychology, 72*, 407–420.

Sternberg, R. J. (Ed.). (1982). *Advances in the psychology of human intelligence* (Vol. 1). Mahwah, NJ: Lawrence Erlbaum Associates.

Sternberg, R. J. (Ed.). (1984). *Mechanisms of cognitive development*. San Francisco: Freeman.

Sternberg, R. J. (1985). *Beyond IQ: A triarchic theory of human intelligence*. New York: Cambridge University Press.

Sternberg, R. J. (1987). Most vocabulary is learned from context. In M. G. McKeown & M. E. Curtis (Eds.), *The nature of vocabulary acquisition* (pp. 89–105). Mahwah, NJ: Lawrence Erlbaum Associates.

Sternberg, R. J. (1990). *Metaphors of mind: Conceptions of the nature of intelligence*. New York: Cambridge University Press.

Sternberg, R. J. (Ed.). (1994). *Encyclopedia of human intelligence*. New York: Macmillan.

Sternberg, R. J. (1997). *Thinking styles*. New York: Oxford University Press.

Sternberg, R. J. (1999a). A propulsion model of types of creative contributions. *Review of General Psychology, 3*, 83–100.

Sternberg, R. J. (1999b). The theory of successful intelligence. *Review of General Psychology, 3*, 292–316.

Sternberg, R. J. (Ed.). (2000). *Handbook of intelligence*. New York: Cambridge University Press.

Sternberg, R. J. (Ed.). (2002). *Why smart people can be so stupid*. New Haven, CT: Yale University Press.

Sternberg, R. J. (2003). *Wisdom, intelligence, and creativity synthesized*. New York: Cambridge University Press.

Sternberg, R. J. (2004a). Culture and intelligence. *American Psychologist, 59*, 325–338.

Sternberg, R. J. (Ed.). (2004b). *International handbook of intelligence*. New York: Cambridge University Press.

Sternberg, R. J. (2006). The scientific basis for the theory of successful intelligence. In R. F. Subotnik & H. J. Walberg (Eds.) *The scientific basis of educational productivity* (pp. 161–184). Greenwich, CT: Information Age Publishing Co.

Sternberg, R. J. (2007a). Culture, instruction, and assessment. *Comparative Education, 43*, 5–22.

Sternberg, R. J. (2007b). Finding students who are wise, practical, and creative. *The Chronicle Review*, July 6, B11–B12.

Sternberg, R. J., Conway, B. E., Ketron, J. L., & Bernstein, M. (1981). People's conceptions of intelligence. *Journal of Personality and Social Psychology, 41*, 37–55.

Sternberg, R. J., & Davidson, J. E. (1982). Componential analysis and componential theory. *Behavioral and Brain Sciences, 53,* 352–353.

Sternberg, R. J., & Davidson, J. E. (Eds.). (1995). *The nature of insight*. Cambridge, MA: MIT Press.

Sternberg, R. J., Forsythe, G. B., Hedlund, J., Horvath, J., Snook, S., Williams, W. M., Wagner, R. K., & Grigorenko, E. L. (2000). *Practical intelligence in everyday life*. New York: Cambridge University Press.

Sternberg, R. J., & Grigorenko E. L. (Eds.). (2002). *The general factor of intelligence: Fact or fiction*. Mahwah, NJ: Lawrence Erlbaum Associates.

Sternberg, R. J., & Grigorenko, E. L. (2004). Cultural explorations of the nature of intelligence. In A. F. Healey (Ed.), *Experimental cognitive psychology and its applications* (pp. 225–235). Washington, DC: American Psychological Association.

Sternberg, R. J., & Kaufman J. C. (1998). Human abilities. *Annual Review of Psychology, 49,* 479–502.

Sternberg, R. J., Kaufman, J. C., & Pretz, J. E. (2002). *The creativity conundrum: A propulsion model of kinds of creative contributions*. New York: Psychology Press.

Sternberg, R. J., Kaufman, J. C., & Pretz, J. E. (2003). A propulsion model of creative leadership. *Leadership Quarterly, 14,* 455–473.

Sternberg, R. J., Lautrey, J., & Lubart, T. I. (Eds.). (2003). *Models of intelligence: International perspectives* (pp. 3–25). Washington, DC: American Psychological Association.

Sternberg, R. J., & Lubart, T. I. (1995a). *Defying the crowd: Cultivating creativity in a culture of conformity*. New York: Free Press.

Sternberg, R. J., & Lubart, T. I. (1995b). Ten keys to creative innovation. *R & D Innovator, 4,* 8–11.

Sternberg, R. J., Lubart, T. I., Kaufman, J. C., & Pretz, J. E. (2005). Creativity. In K. J. Holyoak & R. G. Morrison (Eds.), *Cambridge handbook of thinking and reasoning* (pp. 351–370). New York: Cambridge University Press.

Sternberg, R. J., Nokes, K., Geissler, P. W., Prince, R., Okatcha, F., Bundy, D. A., & Grigorenko, E. L. (2001). The relationship between academic and practical intelligence: A case study in Kenya. *Intelligence, 29,* 401–418.

Sternberg, R. J., & O'Hara, L. (1999). Creativity and intelligence. In R. J. Sternberg (Ed.), *Handbook of creativity* (pp. 251–272). New York: Cambridge University Press.

Sternberg, R. J., & Powell, J. S. (1983). Comprehending verbal comprehension. *American Psychologist, 38,* 878–893.

Sternberg, R. J., & Pretz, J. E. (Eds.). (2004). *Cognition & intelligence*. New York: Cambridge University Press.

Sternberg, R. J., & The Rainbow Project Collaborators (2006). The Rainbow Project: Enhancing the SAT through assessments of analytical, practical and creative skills. *Intelligence, 34,* 321–350.

Sternberg, R. J., & Rifkin, B. (1979). The development of analogical reasoning processes. *Journal of Experimental Child Psychology, 27,* 195–232.

Sternberg, R. J., & Smith, C. (1985). Social intelligence and decoding skills in nonverbal communication. *Social Cognition, 2,* 168–192.

Sternberg, R. J., & Wagner, R. K. (1982). Automatization failure in learning disabilities. *Topics in learning and learning disabilities, 2,* 1–11.

Sternberg, R. J., & Weil, E. M. (1980). An aptitude–strategy interaction in linear syllogistic reasoning. *Journal of Educational Psychology, 72,* 226–234.

Sternberg, R. J., & Williams, W. M. (1996). *How to develop student creativity*. Alexandria, VA: Association for Supervision and Curriculum Development.

Suzuki, L. A., & Valencia. R. R. (1997). Race-ethnicity and measured intelligence: Educational implications. *American Psychologist, 52*, 1103–1114.

Thurstone, L. L. (1924). *The nature of intelligence*. New York: Harcourt Brace.

Thurstone, L. L. (1938). *Primary mental abilities*. Chicago: University of Chicago Press.

Tilson, W. (2000). The danger of investor overconfidence. *The Motley Fool*. Retrieved January 27, 2005, from http://www.fool.com/boringport/2000/boringport000522.htm.

Tversky, A., & Kahneman, D. (1971). Belief in the law of small numbers. *Psychological Bulletin, 76*, 105–110.

Tversky, A., & Kahneman, D. (1974). Judgment under uncertainty: Heuristics and biases. *Science, 185*, 1124–1131.

Vernon, P. A., & Mori, M. (1992). Intelligence, reaction times, and peripheral nerve conduction velocity. *Intelligence, 16*, 273–288.

Vernon, P. A., Wickett, J. C., Bazana, P. G., & Stelmack, R. M. (2000). The neuropsychology and psycholophysiology of human intelligence. In R. J. Sternberg (Ed.), *Handbook of intelligence* (pp. 245–264). New York: Cambridge University Press.

Vernon, P. E. (1971). *The structure of human abilities*. London: Methuen.

Vos Savant, M. (1995). *The power of logical thinking*. New York: St. Martin's Press.

Wallace, A., Wallechinsky, D., & Wallace, I. (1983). *The book of lists #3*. New York: Bantam.

Watson, J. B. (1930). *Behaviorism* (rev. ed.). New York: Norton.

Wechsler, D. (1958). *The measurement and appraisal of adult intelligence* (5th ed.). Baltimore, MD: Williams & Wilkins.

Wechsler, D. (1997). *Manual for the Wechsler Adult Intelligence Scales (WAIS-III)*. San Antonio, TX: Psychological Corporation.

Wechsler, D. (2003). *Manual for the Wechsler Intelligence Scale for Children –Fourth Edition*. San Antonio, TX: The Psychological Corporation.

Weisberg, R. W. (1995). Prolegomena to theories of insight in problem solving: A taxonomy of problems. In R. J. Sternberg & J. E. Davidson (Eds.), *The nature of insight* (pp. 157–196). Cambridge, MA: MIT Press.

Weisberg, R. W. (2006). *Creativity: Understanding innovation in problem solving, science, invention, and the arts*. New York: Wiley.

Wissler, C. (1901). The correlation of mental and physical tests. *Psychological Review, Monograph Supplement 3*.

Woodcock, R. W., McGrew, K. S., & Mather, N. (2001). *Woodcock-Johnson III Tests of Cognitive Abilities*. Itasca, IL: Riverside Publishing.

Yang, S., & Sternberg, R. J. (1997). Taiwanese Chinese people's conceptions of intelligence. *Intelligence, 25*, 21–36.

Zajonc, R. B. (2001). Mere exposure: A gateway to the subliminal. *Current Directions in Psychological Science, 10*, 224–228.

AUTHOR INDEX

SUBJECT INDEX